ATLAS OF EASTERN EUROPE IN THE TWENTIETH CENTURY

ATLAS OF EASTERN EUROPE IN THE TWENTIETH CENTURY

RICHARD AND BEN CRAMPTON

London and New York

First published 1996
by Routledge
11 New Fetter Lane, London EC4P 4EE

Simultaneously published in the USA and Canada
by Routledge
29 West 35th Street, New York, NY 10001

Typeset in Garamond by Solidus (Bristol) Limited

Printed and bound in Great Britain by
Butler & Tanner Ltd., London and Frome

British Library of Cataloguing in Publication Data
A catalogue record for this book is available from the British Library

Library of Congress Cataloguing in Publication Data
A catalogue record for this book has been requested

ISBN 0–415–06689–1

To June and Fred,
with love,
as ever

CONTENTS

ABBREVIATIONS

A	Austria
ADP	Agrarian Democratic Party (Romania)
AFD	Alliance of Free Democrats (Hungary)
AFF	Agriculture, Forestry and Fishing
Ag	Agriculture
Agl Prod	Agricultural Production
Agrn	Agrarian(s) or Agrarian Party(ies)
AK	Armia Krajowa (Home Army, main resistance force in Poland, 1942–4, and active sporadically against the communists for some years after 1944)
AL	Associated List (Slovenia)
ASW	Association of Slovak Workers
Av	Average
B	Belgium
bn	billion
BANU	Bulgarian Agrarian National Union
BBWR	Non-Party Bloc for the Support of the Government (Poland, 1926–39)
BCP	Bulgarian Communist Party
BEA	British Empire in Asia
BG	Bulgaria
BLP	Beer Lovers' Party (Poland)
BRn	Belorussian
BSP	Bulgarian Socialist Party (ex communists)
C/B	Commerce and Banking
CC	Common Choice (Slovak left-wing coalition, 1994)
CCA	Centre Citizens' Alliance (Poland)
CD	Christian Democracy (Poland)
CDM	Christian Democratic Movement (Slovakia)
CDP	Christian Democratic Party

	(Lithuania and elsewhere) or Civic Democratic Party (Czechoslovakia)
CDPP	Christian Democratic People's Party (Hungary)
CDU	Croatian Democratic Union and Christian Democratic Union (Latvia)
CEA	Catholic Electoral Action (Poland)
CF	Civic Forum (Czechoslovakia)
CH	Switzerland
Chmcls	Chemicals
CIP	Confederation for an Independent Poland
CL	Concord for Latvia
ClBc	Constitutional Bloc (political grouping, Bulgaria)
Cmctns	Communications
CMEA	Council for Mutual Economic Assistance (Comecon)
Cmst	Communist
CNP	Croatian National Party
Cnstctn	Construction
Com	Commerce
Constan	Constantinescu (candidate in Romanian presidential election, 1992)
CPCS	Communist Party of Czechoslovakia
CPP	Croatian Peasant Party or Croatian People's Party
CPPP	Croat People's Peasant Party
CPR	Croatian Party of Rights
CPSU	Communist Party of the Soviet Union
CPY	Communist Party of Yugoslavia
CS	Czechoslovakia
CSCE	Conference for Security and Cooperation in Europe
CSDP	Czech Social Democratic Party

CSPP	Czechoslovak People's Party	EPC	Environmental Protection Club (Latvia)
CSRP	Czechoslovak Republican Party		
CSSDP	Czechoslovak Social Democratic Party	EPF	Estonian Popular Front
		ER	Equal Rights (Latvia)
C/T	Communications and Transport	EU	European Union
Ct	Croat	Extrmst	Extreme Nationalists (Ukraine)
Cz	Czech	F	France
D	Germany	FDSz	League of Young Democrats (Hungary)
Dab	Dabcevic (Candidate in Croatian Presidential election, 1992)	FFF	For the Fatherland and Freedom (Latvia)
DAP	Democratic Agrarian Party (Romania)	FG	Fatherland Group (*Isamaa*, Estonia)
Dbt	Debt or Debt Servicing	FIDSz	See FDSz
DCP	Democratic Centre Party (Latvia)	Fish	Fisheries
DCR	Democratic Convention of Romania	For	Forestry
		FU	Farmers' Union (Latvia)
DCVM	Democratic Community of Vojvodina Magyars	Fyp	Five-year plan
		FYROM	Former Yugoslav Republic of Macedonia
Def	Defence		
Dems	Democrats	GB	Great Britain
DK	Denmark	GDP	Gross Domestic Product
DLA	Democratic Left Alliance (Poland)	GDR	German Democratic Republic
DLP	Democratic Labour Party (Lithuania)	Ger	German
		Gm	German
DmCon	Democratic Concord (inter-war political grouping, Bulgaria)	GNP	Gross National Product
		GP	Government Party
Dmst	Domestic Service	GR	Greece
DNSF	Democratic National Salvation Front (Romania)	Gr	Greens
		GRP	Greater Romania Party
DP	Democratic Party (in Yugoslavia the party of the *Prečani* Serbs)	H	Hungary
		HDF	Hungarian Democratic Forum
Dps	Serbian Democratic Movement Coalition (*Depos*)	Hlth	Health
		HMC	Hungarian Minority Coalition (Slovakia; also known as 'Coexistence' or, in Hungarian, *Egyutteles*)
DPSM	Democratic Party of Socialists in Montenegro		
DS	Democratic Party (Slovenia)		
DU	Democratic Union (Poland and Slovakia)	HRU	Human Rights Union (Albania)
		Hsng	Housing
DUR	Hungarian Democratic Union of Romania	HSP	Hungarian Socialist Party
		HSPP	Hlinka Slovak People's Party
Dzg	Danzig	HSWP	Hungarian Socialist Workers' Party
E/C	Education and Culture		
EC	European Community	I	Italy
Econ	Economy; or Economic Subsidies in Budgets	IDP	Independent Democratic Party (Yugoslav: split from DP)
ECz	Estonian Citizens	IMRO	Internal Macedonian Revolutionary Organisation
Edn	Education		
EG	Egypt	Ind	Industry
Ent	Entrepreneurs' Party (Estonia)	Indep	Independents

IndSH	Independent Smallholders (Hungary)	n/a	Not available
		Nats	Nationalists
IndSR	Independent Social Revolutionaries (Estonia)	NDP	National Democratic Party (Albania, Bohemia, Czechoslovakia, Macedonia and Moravia)
IR	Independent Royalists		
It	Italian	NIM	National Independence Movement (Latvia)
JNA	Yugoslav National Army		
Jwsh	Jewish	NIP	National Independence Party (Estonia)
KOR	Komitet Obrony Robotników (Committee for Workers' Defence, Poland)	NL	Netherlands
		NLP	National Liberal Party (Romania)
KSS	Komitet Samoobrony Społecznej (Committee for Social Self-Defence, Poland)	NMP	Net Material Product
		NPB	Non-Party Bloc for the Support of the Government (Poland, 1990s)
L/Ind	Light Industry	NPP	Christian Democratic National Peasants' Party (Romania)
LAT	Latvia		
Lat	Latvian	NRP	National Radical Party (Serbian and Yugoslav)
LB	Left Bloc (Czechoslovakia)		
LBYA	Libya	NSF	National Salvation Front (Romania)
LCMYU	League of Communists – Movement for Yugoslavia	NVC	National Veterans' Committee (Albania)
LCY	League of Communists of Yugoslavia	OldB	Old Believers
LDC	Liberal Democratic Congress (Poland)	Om	Omonia (Greek minority organisation in Albania)
LDS	Liberal Democratic Party (Slovenia)	Orth	Orthodox
Libs	Liberals	Oth	Other
LITH	Lithuania	PA	Peasant Accord (Poland)
Lith	Lithuanian	PASOK	Panhellion Sosialistikon Kinema (Panhellenic Socialist Movement)
LSU	Liberal Social Union (Czechoslovakia)	PAV	Public Against Violence (Slovakia)
LU	Labour Union (Poland)	P/B	Professional and Civil Service
Luth	Lutheran	Pbl	Civil and Military Service
LW	Latvia's Way	PCD	Party of Christian Democrats (Poland)
m	million		
M/Ind	Mining and Industry	PDC	Party of Democratic Change (Croatia, ex communists)
Mch/Mtl	Machinery and Metallurgy		
MDS	Movement for a Democratic Slovakia	PDL	Party of the Democratic Left (Slovakia)
Mg	Magyar		
Mil	Military; Military Service in Budget Expenditure	PDP	Party for Democratic Prosperity (Albanian party in Macedonia)
Min	Mining	PL	Poland
Mins	Minority Groups	Pl	Polish
Mm	Muslim	PLA	Party of Labour in Albania (communist)
Mod	Moderates (Estonia)		
MRF	Movement for Rights and Freedom (Bulgaria)	Pol	Polish
		PP	People's Party (Yugoslavia)
MSD-SMS	Movement for Self-Governing Democracy – Society for Moravia and Silesia	Pplst	Populist
		PPP	Polish Peasant Party–Programmatic Alliance

PR	Proportional Representation	Sjds	*Sajudis* ('Movement', Lithuania)
PRC	People's Republic of China	Sk	Slovak
Prim	Primary	SKD	Christian Democratic Party (Slovenia)
Prof	Professional		
Prot	Protestant	SkNP	Slovak National Party
PU	Peasant Union (Yugoslav)	SLP	Social Liberal Party (Croatia)
PUWP	Polish United Workers Party	SLS	Slovene People's Party
PWU	Polish Western Union (Labour minority)	Sn	Slovene
		SNP	Serbian National Party (Croatia)
R	Romania	SNS	Slovene National Party
RC	Roman Catholic	SPA	Socialist Party of Albania (ex communists)
RCP	Romanian Communist Party		
REM	Romanian Ecological Movement	SPL	Socialist Party of Labour (Romania)
REP	Romanian Ecological Party	SPM	Socialist Party of Montenegro
Rgn	Regionalists (Croatia)	SPP	Slovene People's Party
Rh	Ruthene	SPS	Socialist Party of Serbia
Rm	Romanian	SRP	Serbian Radical Party
RNUP	Romanian National Unity Party	SU	Soviet Union
RP	Republican Party	Subs	Subsidies
RUA	Romanian Unity Alliance	Tert	Tertiary
Rus	Russian	TR	Turkey
S	Sweden	Trspt	Transport
SAP	Serbian Agrarian Party (includes Slovene Agrarian Party)	UDF	Union of Democratic Forces (Bulgaria)
		Ukn	Ukrainian
Sb	Serbian	UN	United Nations
ScDm	Social Democrats	Univ	University or Universities
ScFed	Socialist Federation (inter-war political grouping, Bulgaria)	USA	United States of America
		USSR	Union of Soviet Socialist Republics
ScSc	Social Services	Wrkrs	Workers' Party (Estonia)
SdP	Sudetendeutsch Partei	WTO	Warsaw Treaty Organisation (Warsaw Pact)
SDP	Social Democratic Party		
SDSS	Social Democratic Party of Slovenia	XtDP	Christian Democratic Party (Lithuania)
Sdy	Solidarity		
Sec	Secondary	XtSP	Christian Social Party (Hungary)
SED	Socialist Unity Party of Germany (GDR)	YMO	Yugoslav Muslim Organisation
		yr	year or years
SF	Finland	YU	Yugoslavia
SH	Safe Home (*Kindel Kogu*, Estonia)	ZS	Green Party (Slovenia)
SHP	Smallholders' Party (Hungary)		

INTRODUCTION

All definitions of 'the twentieth century' or of 'Eastern Europe' are subjective and transitory. The area covered in this volume is the same as that dealt with in R.J. Crampton's *Eastern Europe in the Twentieth Century* (Routledge 1994). In that book the twentieth century is characterised as that period in recent history in which mass ideologies, operating through a powerful political party, have sought, frequently successfully, to seize power in the state and then to establish one-party or totalitarian rule. A convenient starting point for the twentieth century is 1918 when mass ideologies, either of the open or the closed variety, were coming to power; its end may be set with the collapse of Communist Party rule in Eastern Europe in the period 1989–91.

The area covered varies with time. From the First World War to the Second World War it is essentially made up of the lands between Germany and Russia/the Soviet Union. After 1945 the Baltic states are excluded because of their incorporation into the USSR, but East Germany is included because it was so obviously a part of the Soviet sphere of influence. Greece, Finland and Austria are not included. Greece is obviously a Balkan country but it is much less obviously an East European one than Romania, Bulgaria or Albania. Its long coast line, its large and widely spread diaspora and, later, its political links with the states of Western Europe make it more a part of the West than of the East European world. Finland has long historic ties with Russia but its immunity to authoritarian rule and its neutrality after the Second World War divorce it from Eastern Europe. Austria did not enjoy such immunity from totalitarianism before 1939 but, after 1955, it has been a neutral state with a social and economic system of the West rather than of the East European variety.

The present Atlas is divided into seven parts. The first deals with what is, by our definition, the pre-twentieth century. In addition to providing basic background information on the physical structure of the region it also shows the ethnic and religious groups and the political extent of the three dominant empires. After 1900 the Balkan peninsula became increasingly an area of instability and eventually war. Maps showing the issues at stake in these disputes are included in this section. The Balkan crisis of 1914 spilled over into the rest of Europe and eventually affected all of civilisation.

Most West Europeans and Americans think of the First World War in terms of the conflict in the trenches of Flanders and France, but there were also mighty battles in Eastern Europe. These, together with the peace settlement which followed the war, constitute Part 2 of the Atlas.

Part 3 deals with the inter-war years. There are a number of maps on general themes such as international alignments and disputes, these maps being followed by a study of each of the constituent states of inter-war Eastern Europe: Albania, Bulgaria, Czechoslovakia, Estonia, Hungary, Latvia, Lithuania, Poland, Romania, and Yugoslavia. To some degree the nature of each state and its society determines what the maps and diagrams for that state illustrate; thus, for example, only Albania has a map showing tribal divisions. Wherever possible, however, graphs showing budget expenditure in two defined years, population by economic sector, ethnic and/or religious composition, and the distribution of landholdings are included. So too are diagrams on the distribution of trade. In drawing up these diagrams the total value of exports and imports was calculated and the top ten trading partners included in the graph. In the diagrams on land distribution the bar graph illustrates the proportion of the total number of holdings in a series of defined categories, whilst the line graph shows the percentage of the total farmed land which holdings in those same categories comprised. In the case of Hungary a series of such diagrams is included because of the importance in the inter-war history of that country of land-holding and of the attempts at land redistribution. Full coverage is also given of the parliamentary history of each country, though naturally in some instances there is less of such history to record than in others; no diagrams, for instance, are given for Albania whose elected assemblies were either too short-lived or too unrepresentative to be included. In other cases, the absence or unreliability of data has led to the exclusion of diagrams.

The relatively short Part 4 covers the years of the Second World War, starting with the territorial changes brought about in 1938. The maps deal with the attempted extermination of the Jews and with population shifts, as well as with the movement of armies and the shifting of frontiers.

In the middle of the Atlas the four maps show the way in which East European boundaries differed in 1900, 1923, 1945 and 1994.

The years of Communist Party rule form Part 5. This section serves three functions. First, it shows the growth of communist rule and with it the imposition of Soviet practices such as the collectivisation of agriculture and forced growth in the heavy industrial sector. Second, it points to the mechanisms by which Soviet domination was maintained, including both the integration of most of Eastern Europe into the military structures of the Warsaw Pact, and the economic ties imposed through trading patterns and energy supplies. Third, it illustrates the attempts to dilute or even to shed Soviet and communist domination.

The communists boasted that they would bring modernisation and improved social well-being to the countries they ruled. This claim is examined in Part 6 which also begins with a very serious questioning of one legacy of communist power: pollution. Each country is then treated individually with maps showing population density at the end of the 1980s, the spread of industry and the use made of the land. Diagrams are given, wherever possible, showing birth rates, infant mortality rates and population growth, followed by others which deal with the number of university students and the percentage of women amongst them, the number of inhabitants per medical practitioner, average annual economic growth in five year periods from 1951 to 1980, indebtedness, and net material product by economic sector. In most cases the only figures available are those provided by the communists themselves, and at times these do not always provide as much detail as one might require; how precisely a university student or a medical practitioner is defined can clearly have a major impact on the figures. In some instances convenient statistics were not available, as, for example, for the number of university students in the German Democratic Republic; the small number of diagrams for contemporary Macedonia is due to the fact that very little reliable data on that country was to hand when the text of the Atlas was finished.

The final section, Part 7, deals with the period after the fall of the communists. The results of whatever parliamentary or presidential elections have taken place are given. In addition to information showing the number of seats won, graphs are provided, where possible, showing the percentage of the seats and of the votes gained by competing parties; in most cases there is a commendable correlation between the distribution of votes and the final distribution of seats. There are also economic diagrams which do not, in the main, give such an encouraging picture. The figures for inflation and the changes in gross domestic or net material product show clearly the impact of the attempted switch from the planned to the market economy. In the tables of data for each country the figures are taken, where possible, from *Encyclopaedia Britannica, Book of the Year 1994, Events of the Year 1993*; when listing major cities the first four are recorded but only if their population is over 75,000.

The glossary of names, without making any claims to completeness, attempts to give the various names of the main towns, cities and rivers of the area. For ease of reference each name is given its own entry, and thus Breslau/Wrocław can be found under both 'B' and 'W'. Some cities changed their names for a short period in the Stalinist years of the late 1940s and early 1950s, the Bulgarian city of Varna, for example, being named Stalin. These short-lived names have not been included but longer-term changes, for example Chemnitz/Karl-Marx-Stadt and Zlin/Gottwaldow, have been.

A number of works have proved invaluable in the preparation of this Atlas. Included in them are: the *Encyclopaedia Britannica*, cited above; *Atlas of Eastern Europe*, published by the US Central Intelligence Agency in August 1990; Martin Gilbert, *The Dent Atlas of Russian History*, first edition, London 1972 (a second edition appeared in 1993); Nicolas Spulber, *The Economics of Communist Eastern Europe*, New York and London 1957; the relevant country reports published by The Economist Intelligence Unit, London; Michael Kaser (ed.), *The Economic History of Eastern Europe, 1919–75*, vols1–3, Oxford 1985–6; and the numerous statistical volumes produced by the countries of Eastern Europe. For a bibliography of works on East European history during the twentieth century, see R.J. Crampton, *Eastern Europe in the Twentieth Century*, cited above.

People as well as books have made an enormous contribution to our work and our welfare. They are too numerous to mention individually but it would be invidious to omit a number of them. Jayne Lewin not only drew the maps with great skill but has also exhibited endless patience and tolerance towards us. So too did the staff of Routledge, especially Claire L'Enfant, Heather McCallum and Patrick Proctor. Mike Bufford of St Briavals in the Forest of Dean provided invaluable help through the loan of his 1942 school atlas. Alan Fidler, Stevan K. Pavlowitch, and Professor Gale Stokes read the typescript with wondrously sharp eyes. All three made hugely helpful observations and for this we are greatly indebted to them. Above all, however, there is our unpayable debt to the one who has played her role as wife and mother respectively with boundless dedication, patience and good humour.

Ascott-under-Wychwood
Oxfordshire
October 1994

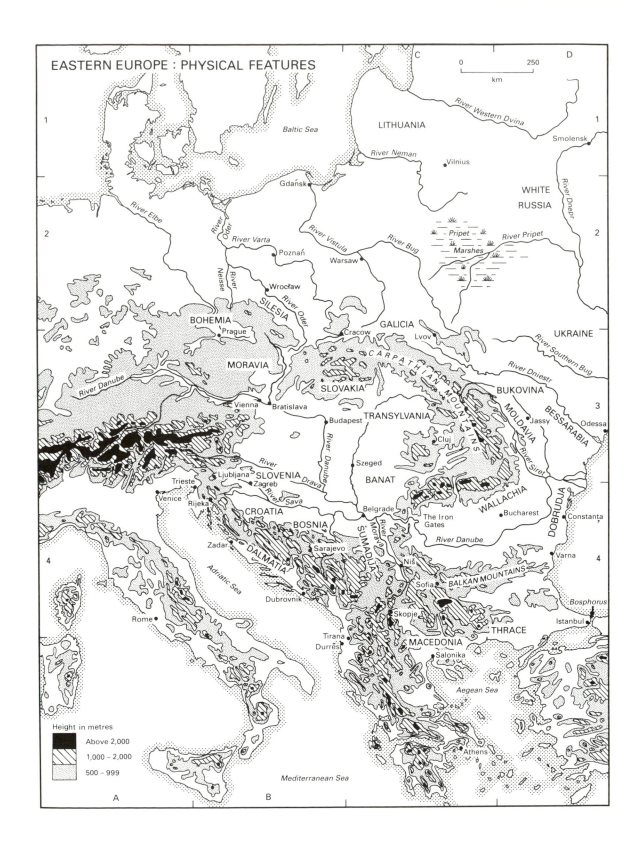

EASTERN EUROPE : PHYSICAL FEATURES

0   250
km

Height in metres

- Above 2,000
- 1,000 – 2,000
- 500 – 999

LITHUANIA
Baltic Sea
River Western Dvina
Smolensk
River Neman
Vilnius
Gdańsk
WHITE
RUSSIA
River Dnepr
River Elbe
River Oder
River Varta
River Vistula
River Bug
River Pripet
Pripet
Marshes
Poznań
Warsaw
Wrocław
UKRAINE
BOHEMIA
SILESIA
GALICIA
Prague
Cracow
Lvov
River Southern Bug
MORAVIA
CARPATHIAN MOUNTAINS
River Dniestr
BUKOVINA
BESSARABIA
SLOVAKIA
MOLDAVIA
Jassy
Odessa
River Danube
Vienna
Bratislava
TRANSYLVANIA
Budapest
Cluj
River Siret
SLOVENIA
BANAT
Szeged
Trieste
Ljubljana
Zagreb
River Sava
WALLACHIA
Bucharest
Venice
Rijeka
CROATIA
River Drava
River Morava
Belgrade
The Iron
Gates
DOBRUDJA
Constanţa
Zadar
BOSNIA
DALMATIA
Sarajevo
ŠUMADIJA
River Danube
Varna
Adriatic Sea
Dubrovnik
Niš
Sofia
BALKAN MOUNTAINS
Bosphorus
Rome
Skopje
Istanbul
Tirana
Durrës
MACEDONIA
THRACE
Salonika
Aegean Sea
Athens
Mediterranean Sea

1 BEFORE THE FIRST WORLD WAR

Eastern Europe: physical features

Of all the great river systems found in Eastern Europe only one, the Elbe, drains into an open sea: the North Sea. The remainder, for the most part, find their way into the Danube and thence to the Black Sea.

The lack of an open sea was not necessarily an impediment to economic development. The Hanseatic ports along the southern shores of the Baltic encouraged the production of export crops in the North European Plain, thus reinforcing the economic and political power of the landowner in Poland and what were to become the Baltic states. Before the First World War Romania was also to find no great handicap in having access only to a closed sea; her export trade, particularly in grain, flourished. Yet the fact that, with the exception of the Elbe, the rivers drained away from Western Europe became one of the factors which helped to isolate much of Eastern Europe from the great economic advances and social changes emanating from the spine of Europe which ran from the Lowlands of Scotland through England and the Rhine valley to northern Italy. The corollary of this is the fact that Bohemia, astride the Elbe, was one of the most economically advanced regions of the Habsburg empire.

Eastern Europe is cut in half by the Carpathian mountains and their extension into the uplands of Moravia and Bohemia. To the north the eastward extension of the North European Plain has provided invaders from both directions with easy passage, save for the vast Pripet Marshes. Another relatively easy invasion route was found between the Carpathians and the Black Sea, particularly when Byzantium offered rich

rewards to the marauder. Escape from the lower Danube valley, however, was more difficult, though it was achieved by the Magyars in the ninth century who spread westward into the upper Danube and, when repulsed, colonised the rich middle area of the valley.

In the Balkans the main ridge of the Balkan mountains stretching westward from Sofia almost to the sea cuts the peninsula in two along an east–west axis, whilst the Dinaric Alps run the length of the Adriatic coast from Trieste into Greece forming a north–south barrier which has meant that Dalmatia was for centuries linked more with the maritime states to the west than with Croatia and Bosnia. Albania remained mostly cut off from the rest of Europe from the fifteenth century until the twentieth, and it is only in the last year or so that serious plans have been concocted for an east–west route across the Balkans linking Durrës, Skopje, Sofia and Istanbul; it will follow, in part, the Via Ignatia built by the Romans.

The mountains of the Balkans offered safe refuge for the politically oppressed or the simple brigand. It was from the hills of the Šumadija that the Serbian state emerged in the early nineteenth century, and in times of upheaval Albanian, Bulgarian and Greek activists made full use of the mountains.

In the north similar refuge could be found in the forests near the Baltic coast, particularly east of the river Neman, and in the Pripet Marshes. In the latter, even in the early 1990s, there were many communities who had no wider sense of ethnic affiliation than to describe themselves as 'tutujesi', the people who live here.

Eastern Europe: main ethnic groups, 1900

Ethnicity is not determined solely by linguistic affiliation but the latter is probably the best general guide to the distribution of Eastern Europe's main ethnic groups.

The ethnic–linguistic map of Eastern Europe is dominated by the Slavs who are sub-divided into the western, eastern and southern groups. The western Slavs include the Poles, Czechs, Slovaks and Sorbs. The eastern Slavs comprise the Ruthenes, Belorussians, Ukrainians and Russians. The south Slavs are to be found in the Balkans, their main component elements being the Slovenes, Croats, Serbs, Macedonians and Bulgarians.

The southern Slavs are separated from the western Slavs by two non-Slavic peoples, the Romanians and the Magyars. The Romanians speak a Latin language whilst the Magyars, or Hungarians, who arrived in the region in the ninth century, belong to the Finno-Ugric linguistic group rather than the Indo-European which includes the Slavic, Teutonic, Baltic and Romance languages. The only other major Finno-Ugric language in the area covered by this atlas is Estonian. Turkish, which is spoken in some parts of the Balkans, is also non-Indo-European.

Both Greek and Albanian are Indo-European, as are Lithuanian and Latvian which form the separate, Baltic, branch of the Indo-European family.

Linguistic divisions, however, cannot be easily drawn. As the map illustrates, in many areas two main linguistic groups are mixed, and in some areas there are many more than two elements. Furthermore, speakers of any one language are seldom confined to one area. The Hungarians are to be found not only in what is now Hungary but in present-day Romania, Slovakia, Slovenia and Serbia. The Germans moved into many areas of Eastern Europe from the twelfth century onwards. Most of them were to be found in towns but there were also agrarian communities which survived into the second half of the twentieth century in Romania and other areas. Nor can any large-scale map show the widely dispersed ethnic groups which were so prominent a feature of East European life, particularly in the towns. The most obvious example is that of the Jews who were to be found throughout the area. They played a dominant role in commerce in Polish areas where they had been resident for centuries. In the north of Europe, if they had not acculturated to one of the resident linguistic groups, the Jews usually spoke Yiddish. In the Balkans, however, they spoke Ladino, a language akin to Spanish, their ancestors having been driven from Spain in the fifteenth century. Also in the Balkans, performing much the same commercial and financial functions as the Jews, were the Armenians and the Greeks living outside the Greek state. Most of these communities were forcibly expelled, or worse, at one point or another during the twentieth century. Another important dispersed group, the Gypsies, were also persecuted but have survived in greater numbers, many of them still speaking their own Romany dialects.

Perhaps the most interesting feature of Eastern Europe's ethnic composition, however, is the small groups whose numbers and extent were or are too limited to enable them to appear on a large-scale map. In Poland, for example, there are still small numbers of Tartars whose forebears had been prisoners of war captured in the wars of the sixteenth and seventeenth centuries; the Balkans still have communities of nomadic or semi-nomadic peoples such as the Vlachs whose language is Romance and near to Romanian.

This diversity and mixture of languages and peoples has done much to condition the history of the area.

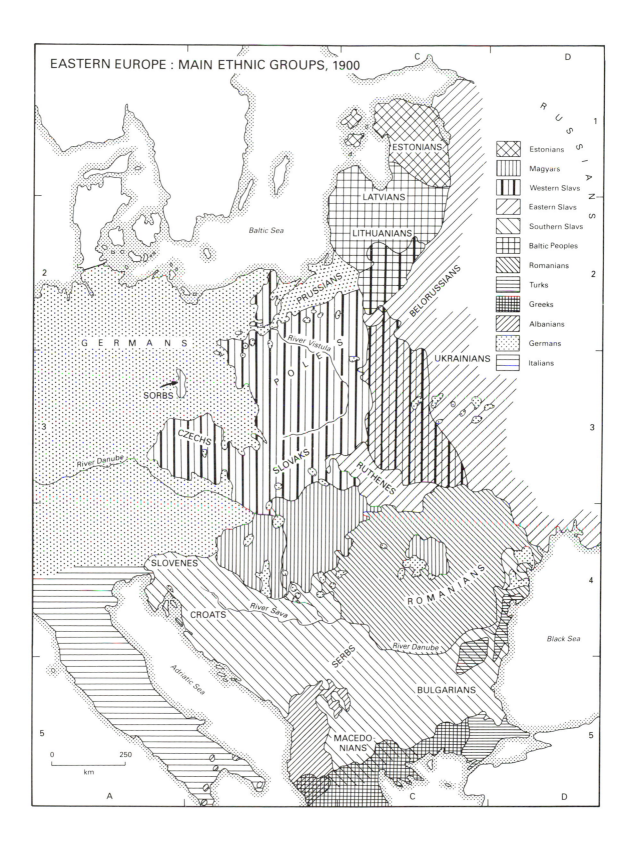

EASTERN EUROPE : MAIN ETHNIC GROUPS, 1900

Estonians
Magyars
Western Slavs
Eastern Slavs
Southern Slavs
Baltic Peoples
Romanians
Turks
Greeks
Albanians
Germans
Italians

R U S S I A N S

ESTONIANS

LATVIANS

LITHUANIANS

Baltic Sea

BELORUSSIANS

PRUSSIANS

River Vistula

P O L E S

UKRAINIANS

G E R M A N S

SORBS

CZECHS

River Danube

SLOVAKS

RUTHENES

SLOVENES

R O M A N I A N S

CROATS

River Sava

Black Sea

SERBS

River Danube

Adriatic Sea

BULGARIANS

MACEDO-
NIANS

0   250

km

3

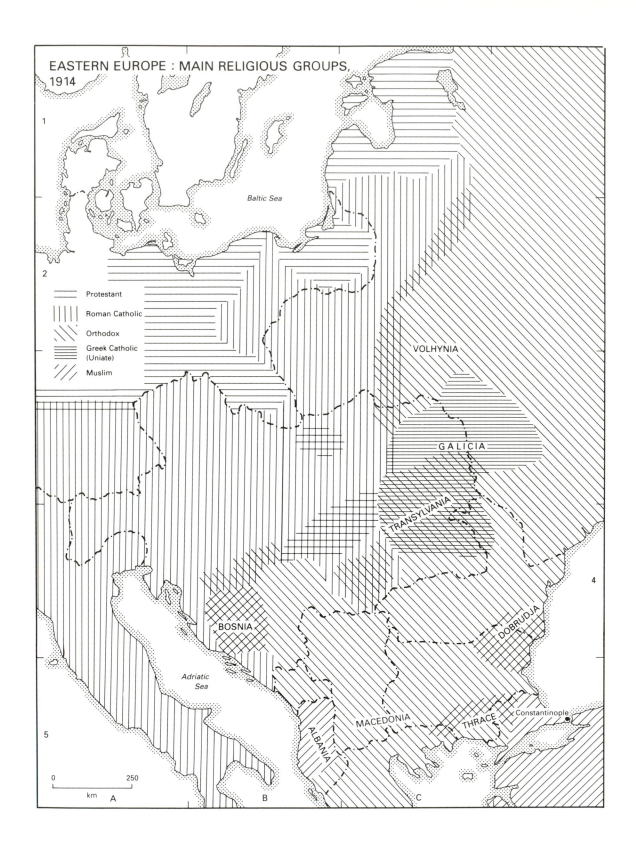

EASTERN EUROPE : MAIN RELIGIOUS GROUPS, 1914

1

Baltic Sea

2

Protestant

Roman Catholic

Orthodox

Greek Catholic
(Uniate)

Muslim

VOLHYNIA

GALICIA

TRANSYLVANIA

4

BOSNIA

DOBRUDJA

Adriatic
Sea

Constantinople

5

MACEDONIA

THRACE

ALBANIA

0   250

km   A   B   C

Eastern Europe: main religious groups, 1914

No large-scale map can portray the mixtures of religions found in some regions, for example Transylvania, nor show every small and isolated religious minority, such as the Greek Catholics of Bulgaria or the Protestants of Macedonia. Protestantism had, however, established a strong hold in eastern Hungary and Transylvania in the Reformation and it survived the Counter Reformation when those areas, particularly the latter, were relatively free from excessive intolerance.

Changes in boundaries and subsequent population movements, particularly after the Second World War, often meant changes in religious affiliation, as in East Prussia which was predominantly Protestant until 1945, whereafter it was overwhelmingly Roman Catholic and orthodox.

Many of the religious minorities were or are thinly dispersed and therefore cannot be adequately illustrated in a general map. This is primarily the case with the Jews, but it also applies to those professing the Armenian and Georgian branches of Christianity, many of whom were found in the Balkans. It also applies to minority sects such as the Old Believers. These Russian Orthodox Christians had refused to accept the modernising reforms of Peter the Great and many of them left central Russia to settle in what became Lithuania, Poland or Romania. Frequently, members of minority sects established predominance in or monopoly over specific trades or professions; in the southern Balkans at the beginning of the twentieth century, for example, most guards on the Oriental Railway Company's trains were Armenians. Times of economic privation tended to promote extreme sects, and in the 1930s in Hungary there were many isolated and some not altogether wholesome religious minorities on the great plains; in Bulgaria in the inter-war period the Dûnovists commanded great interest, perhaps because they were said to indulge in sun worship and free love.

Islam's presence in Eastern Europe was primarily the result of the Ottoman invasions of the fourteenth century. The invaders did not frequently indulge in forcible conversion but the legal system did discriminate in favour of Muslims. This in part was the reason for conversions in Bosnia and Albania where local landlords became Muslims partly to retain their land. In Bosnia conversion also took place because many Bosnians were already outside the two main Christian churches and felt persecuted by both of them. In Thrace and southern Bulgaria some local Bulgarians accepted Islam, and were subsequently known as 'Pomaks', and a number of Muslim landowners established large estates in these areas, partly because of their proximity to the Ottoman capital, Constantinople. In the early years of the empire they were required to provide fighting troops in return for their land which was technically owned by the Sultan. Some of the Muslims of the Dobrudja and northeastern Bulgaria, on the other hand, were much more recent arrivals. Many of them were Tartars or Circassians displaced by Russian territorial advances around the Black Sea in the nineteenth century and then deliberately planted by the Ottomans in order to strengthen the northern boundaries of the empire.

The Greek Catholic (Uniate) Church had its origins in the late sixteenth century. It practised Orthodox rite but recognised the Pope as the head of the Church. Originally this had been a device to secure diplomatic protection from the Habsburg empire which was recognised as the defender of all Catholics. This was useful for those threatened by the Ottoman advance or, in later years, by attempts from St Petersburg to suppress non-Russian cultural characteristics; the Uniates had been suppressed in Russian Volhynia in the 1830s but they remained strong in both Austrian and Russian Galicia.

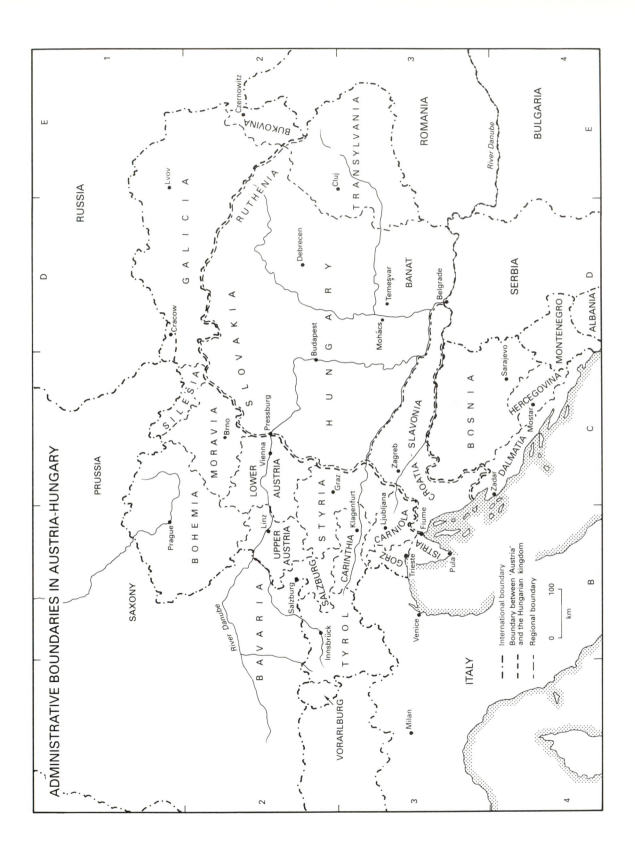

ADMINISTRATIVE BOUNDARIES IN AUSTRIA-HUNGARY

International boundary
Boundary between 'Austria' and the Hungarian kingdom
Regional boundary

Austria-Hungary

The Austro-Hungarian empire was, in legal terms, the lands owing allegiance to the Habsburg dynasty. Its heart was the upper and middle Danube basin. The boundaries of the empire did, however, cross the watershed of the Danube to include Bohemia, Galicia, the Bukovina, southern Tyrol, Dalmatia and the Adriatic coast down to the Montenegrin border.

These lands had been acquired through the centuries by war, diplomacy and, according to an old adage, felicitous marriages. The most important acquisition had come with the union of the Austrian and Hungarian crowns as a result of the death of the Hungarian king in the battle of Mohács against the Ottoman armies in August 1526. Even if most of the Hungarian lands were lost to the Turks for over a century the Habsburgs had now uncontested claim to the Hungarian kingdom and the lands of the crown of Bohemia, which had been united with that of Hungary.

During the years 1815 to 1848 there was growing tension between Vienna and Budapest where the Magyars wished to see restored the constitutional rights of the Hungarian kingdom, most of which had been lost during a centralisation drive in the 1790s. In the April laws of 1848 the Magyars achieved their objective, only to be deprived of it after the defeat of the revolutionary Hungarian forces by Russian armies at Világos in 1849.

In 1866 Prussia defeated Austria in the contest for supremacy in Germany as a result of which Austria lost Venetia. The defeat of Austria was exploited by the Hungarians who secured their famous 'compromise' (*Ausgleich*) in 1867. Under this fundamental restructuring of the monarchy the Hungarian kingdom became self-governing in everything but foreign affairs and defence. The Hungarian kingdom had achieved great power in what had now become the Dual Monarchy. Relations between Vienna and Budapest became less of a problem although there was a fierce confrontation between them at the turn of the century over military questions.

The Hungarian kingdom included Croatia, which had become attached to the Hungarian crown in the early twelfth century, Ruthenia, Slovakia, the Banat of Temeșvar, and Transylvania. Unlike Austria the Hungarian kingdom was highly centralised, and of these constituent territories only Transylvania and Croatia had any degree of local autonomy. Transylvania had enjoyed virtual self-rule during the Ottoman period but little of this survived. The Croats, however, were given their own version of the *Ausgleich*, the *Nagodba*, which theoretically allowed them extensive rights of self-government. These were soon rendered formal and Croatia, like the remainder of the Hungarian kingdom, was subjected to fierce policies of Magyarisation, especially after the draconian Hungarian language laws of 1907.

The Czechs, the largest minority in the Austrian section of the monarchy, aspired to their own version of the *Ausgleich* but they were not as well-organised as the Magyars and, unlike the latter, they had to try and wrest control of the local bureaucracy from the hands of the Germans. They never entirely succeeded in this in Bohemia though more progress was made in Moravia.

By the Treaty of Berlin (1878) Austria-Hungary was given the right to administer Bosnia-Hercegovina. In 1908 these areas were annexed to the empire. Neither the Austrians nor the Hungarians wanted this backward, Slav and partly Muslim territory included in their part of the monarchy, but both were equally determined that the other should not grow larger by acquiring it. Bosnia-Hercegovina was therefore placed in the hands of the small government department which controlled the finances of the few joint Austro-Hungarian administrative institutions.

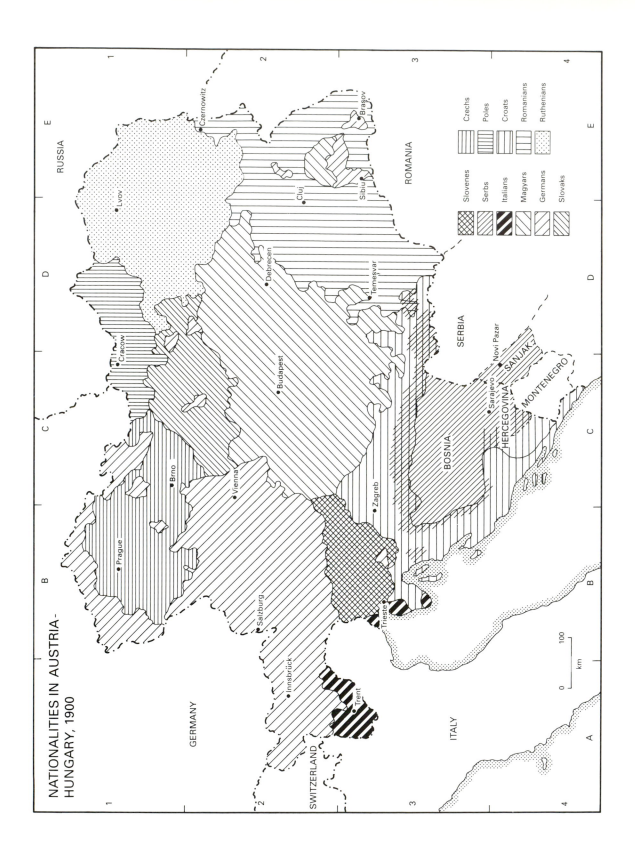

NATIONALITIES IN AUSTRIA-HUNGARY, 1900

Czechs
Poles
Croats
Romanians
Ruthenians

Slovenes
Serbs
Italians
Magyars
Germans
Slovaks

RUSSIA

Czernowitz

Brasov

Lvov

Cluj

Sibiu

ROMANIA

Debrecen

Temesvar

Cracow

SERBIA

Budapest

Novi Pazar

SANJAK

Brno

Sarajevo

BOSNIA

HERCEGOVINA

Vienna

Zagreb

MONTENEGRO

Prague

Salzburg

Trieste

Innsbrück

Trent

GERMANY

SWITZERLAND

ITALY

0   100

km

8

Nationalities in Austria-Hungary, 1900

According to the census of 1910 the total population of the Habsburg Monarchy was 51.39 million, of whom 28.572 million (55.6 per cent) lived in the Austrian section, 20.886 million (40.64 per cent) in the Hungarian Kingdom, and 1.932 million (3.76 per cent) in Bosnia-Hercegovina.

The Austrian and the Hungarian censuses both used mother-tongue as the defining element in assessing ethnicity. Most Hungarian Jews spoke Magyar whilst those in the Austrian section, whether they spoke German or Yiddish, were counted as German-speakers. According to returns for religious affiliation the Jewish population numbered 1.343 million (4.7 per cent) in Austria and 0.94 million (4.5 per cent) in the Hungarian Kingdom; there were 11,500 Jews (0.6 per cent) in Bosnia-Hercegovina.

There was considerable conflict in the Austrian part of the Monarchy between Czechs and Germans over jobs in the bureaucracy in Czech-speaking areas. Figure 3 shows the number of members of an ethnic group per thousand of the population alongside the number of officials of that group per thousand bureaucrats. The disparity amongst the Germans is striking but explicable by their long historical domination of the administrative machine. Of the other groups, only the Italians have a higher proportion of bureaucrats than their proportion of the total population.

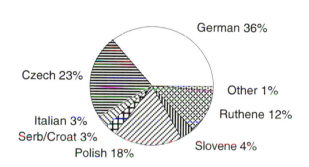

Figure 1 Austria, 1910

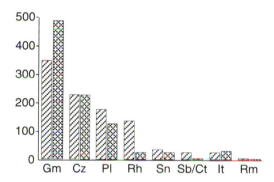

Figure 3 Population and office holders, Austria 1910

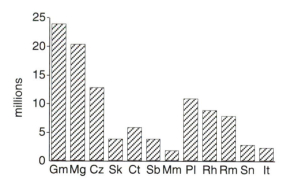

Figure 2 Population: all Monarchy, 1910

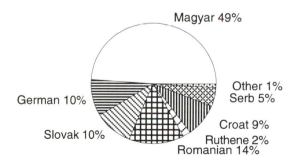

Figure 4 Hungarian kingdom, 1910

9

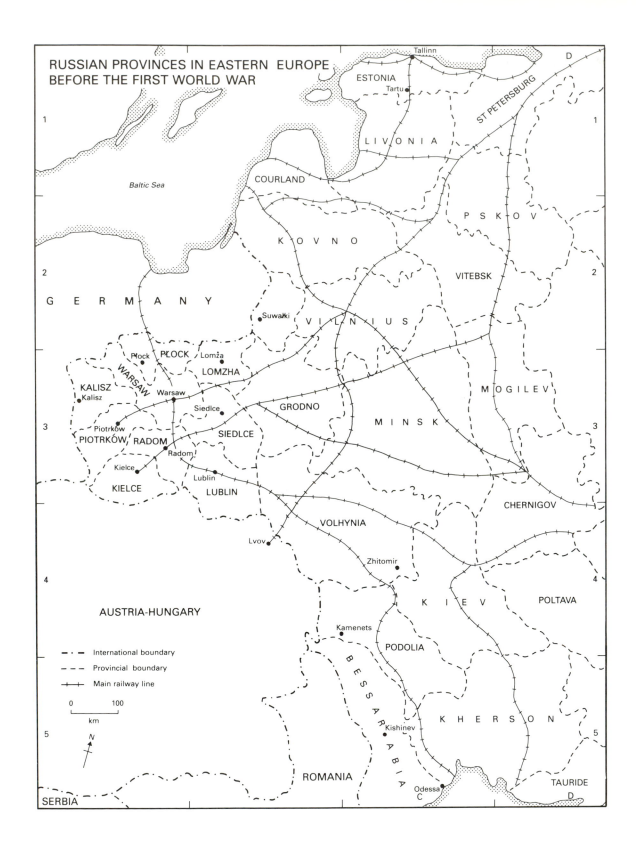

RUSSIAN PROVINCES IN EASTERN EUROPE
BEFORE THE FIRST WORLD WAR

Baltic Sea

GERMANY

ESTONIA

Tallinn

Tartu

LIVONIA

ST PETERSBURG

COURLAND

PSKOV

KOVNO

VITEBSK

Suwałki

VILNIUS

Płock PŁOCK Lomża

Plock WARSAW LOMZHA

KALISZ Warsaw

Kalisz Siedlce GRODNO

MOGILEV

MINSK

Piotrków RADOM

PIOTRKÓW SIEDLCE

Kielce Radom

KIELCE LUBLIN

Lublin

CHERNIGOV

VOLHYNIA

Lvov

Zhitomir

KIEV POLTAVA

AUSTRIA-HUNGARY

Kamenets

PODOLIA

BESSARABIA

KHERSON

— · — · International boundary
— — — Provincial boundary
—+—+— Main railway line

0   100
        km

N

Kishinev

ROMANIA

Odessa

TAURIDE

SERBIA

10

Russian provinces in Eastern Europe

Russia had been expanding into Eastern Europe since the end of the seventeenth century. In the first half of the eighteenth century it acquired the Baltic provinces of Estonia and Livonia and made some advances into Ukraine. The partitions of Poland brought what became the provinces of Vitebsk and Mogilev by the first partition in 1773; Minsk, Podolia and much of Volhynia were acquired by the second partition in 1793; Courland, Kovno, Vilnius, Grodno and western Volhynia came with the third partition two years later. After the Napoleonic wars Russia was given the congress kingdom included in which were Suwałki, Lomzha (Polish: Lomża), Płock, Siedlce, Kalisz, Piotrków, Kielce, Radom and Lublin. It was also given Bessarabia but this it lost in 1856 after its defeat in the Crimean War, only to reclaim it in the Treaty of Berlin in 1878.

From 1815 to 1830 the congress kingdom of Poland enjoyed some local freedoms and had its own constitution, though the king of Poland, who was the tsar of Russia, retained executive power and appointed all senior officers of state.

In 1830 Polish nationalists rebelled. They were soon crushed and the kingdom was subjected to fierce centralisation and control from St Petersburg. After a second Polish uprising, in 1863, even fiercer retribution was exacted and there were efforts to stamp out Polish culture. The tsarist authorities insisted on the use of Russian in public affairs, including law courts, and there were severe limitations on the teaching of Polish and even on teaching in Polish. After 1863 a number of Polish landowners who had been implicated in the rising were dispossessed, their property being transferred to Russian owners. The Russians did all they could to encourage the suspicion, which some Polish peasants entertained, that nationalism was a gentry notion whose real purpose was to perpetuate noble power over the land and those who worked on it.

St Petersburg was suspicious of all nationalists, not merely Polish ones. In 1839 the Greek Catholic (Uniate) Church had been dissolved in Volhynia and Podolia; there were fears that the Uniates would see the Pope in Rome or the Habsburg emperor in Vienna rather than the tsar of all the Russias as their true leader. In the Baltic provinces the long-established German landowners posed no political threat to tsardom, and indeed many of the tsars' most able servants, especially in diplomacy, came from these families. But despite this the great German university at Dorpat (Tartu), a seventeenth-century foundation, was russified in the 1880s.

Railway development in European Russia began in the 1840s and received considerable stimulus in the 1880s and 1890s when Russia needed to export grain through the Baltic and Black Sea ports in order to service its mounting foreign debt obligations. Much of the money invested in Russia came from France, more particularly after the conclusion of the Dual Alliance in 1894. In the decade before the First World War the French encouraged the building of strategic railways in the west of the empire.

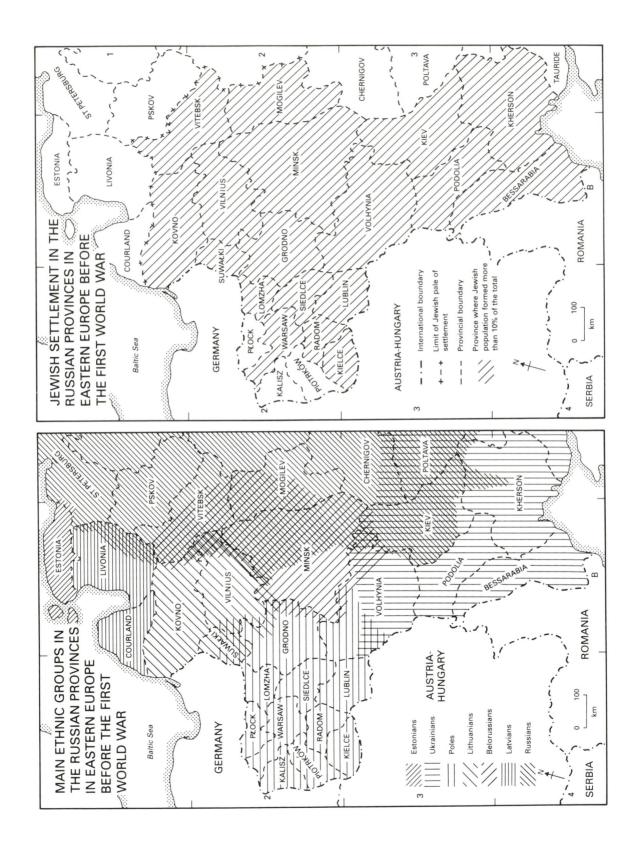

JEWISH SETTLEMENT IN THE RUSSIAN PROVINCES IN EASTERN EUROPE BEFORE THE FIRST WORLD WAR

International boundary
Limit of Jewish pale of settlement
Provincial boundary
Province where Jewish population formed more than 10% of the total

MAIN ETHNIC GROUPS IN THE RUSSIAN PROVINCES IN EASTERN EUROPE BEFORE THE FIRST WORLD WAR

Estonians
Ukrainians
Poles
Lithuanians
Belorussians
Latvians
Russians

Main ethnic groups in the Russian provinces in Eastern Europe before the First World War

Using the 1897 census an approximation for the population of the whole of European Russia from Kalisz to the Urals gives the ethnic distribution shown in Table 1.

Local ethnic patterns were frequently extremely complex. Natural movement of populations had brought many groups together in areas where they mingled, but these complications had been compounded by government policies and the social traditions of Russia. From the sixteenth century onwards foreign communities, usually from western Europe, had been imported into all parts of European Russia. Many were settled in the regions into which the Russian state was expanding; thus in the southern parts of Russia and Ukraine were to be found a bewildering mixture of peoples, many of them not numerous enough to be recorded in any but the most detailed tables of statistics; one nineteenth-century British traveller discovered a settlement entitled *Shotlandskoe Celo* (Scottish village) whose inhabitants wore kilts and retained the eighteenth-century English their forebears had brought from the Highlands.

Some generalisations, however, may be attempted. Although some Germans entered Russia as small-scale farmers, most were urban dwellers, particularly in Russian Poland where industrial expansion in the late nineteenth century brought sizeable German immigration; in the Baltic provinces many large landowners were of German descent. Greeks and Armenians were also town-dwellers, usually in the southern provinces.

Table 1 Ethnic distribution in Russia (1897 census)

Nationality	Total number	Percentage age of total
Russian	48,825,881	51.17
Ukrainian	20,750,203	21.75
Belorussian	5,852,730	6.13
Polish	7,865,437	8.24
Lithuanian	1,650,482	1.73
Latvian	1,427,085	1.50
Romanian	1,126,892	1.18
German	1,719,435	1.80
Jewish	4,982,189	5.22
Estonian	994,255	1.04
Others	228,697	0.24
Total	95,423,286	100.00

The Jews were in theory limited to the provinces in the so-called Pale of Settlement, although wealthier families could purchase or procure exemption from such regulations. Within the Pale the vast majority of Jews lived in towns and cities where they were subject to occasional mistreatment, more especially in the late nineteenth and early twentieth centuries when anti-Jewish pogroms were encouraged by the government as an means of deflecting popular discontent at declining economic and social conditions.

In many areas Jews alone were allowed to keep inns or small shops because the Christians were tied to the land as a cheap source of labour for landlords who wished to export grain through the Baltic to central and western Europe.

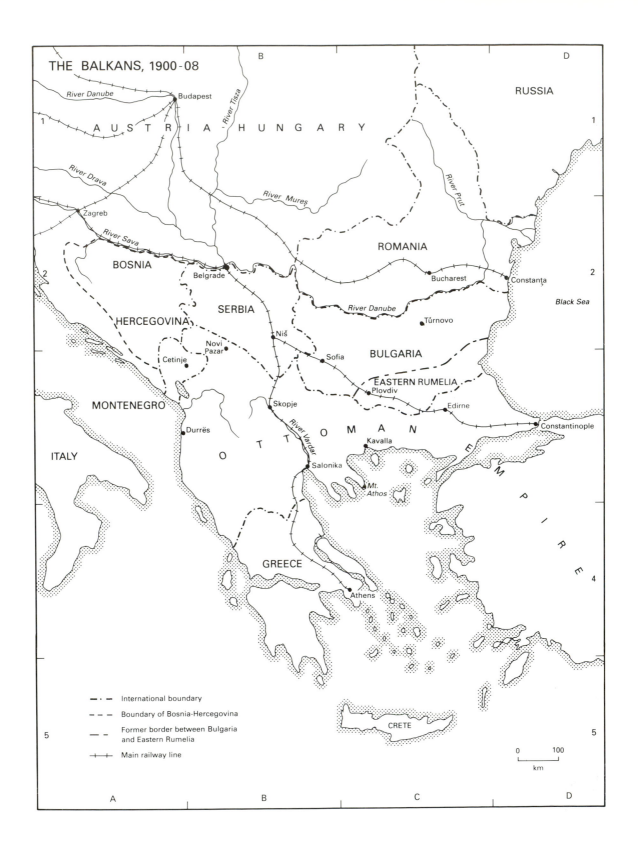

THE BALKANS, 1900-08

River Danube
Budapest

A U S T R I A - H U N G A R Y

River Drava

River Tisza

RUSSIA

River Mureş

River Prut

Zagreb

River Sava

BOSNIA

ROMANIA

Belgrade

Bucharest

Constanţa

SERBIA

Black Sea

HERCEGOVINA

River Danube

Niš

Tŭrnovo

Novi
Pazar

Cetinje

Sofia

BULGARIA

Skopje

EASTERN RUMELIA

Plovdiv

MONTENEGRO

Edirne

Durrës

O   T   T

River Vardar

Constantinople

O   T   T   O   M   A   N

Kavalla

E
M
P
I
R
E

ITALY

Salonika

Mt. Athos

GREECE

Athens

Athens

CRETE

- · - · - International boundary
- - - - Boundary of Bosnia-Hercegovina
- - - - Former border between Bulgaria
            and Eastern Rumelia
-+-+- Main railway line

0   100

km

14

The Balkans, 1900–08

A major redefinition of political boundaries in the Balkans had been enacted by the Treaty of Berlin in 1878. This had given full independence to Romania, Serbia and Montenegro, and had created both the principality of Bulgaria, and the autonomous Ottoman province of Eastern Rumelia to the south of it. In 1881 Greece was extended northwards; in 1885 Eastern Rumelia declared for union with Bulgaria. In 1897 reports of massacres of Christians in Crete so inflamed Greek opinion that the country went to war with the Ottoman empire. Despite a crushing defeat the Greeks were not required to cede territory and the second son of the Greek king was made governor-general of an autonomous Crete. The peninsula of Athos enjoyed a special status as the heads of its monasteries owed nominal allegiance to the Orthodox Patriarch in Constantinople.

The Balkan states were all monarchies and all, except Montenegro, were representative democracies. All these democracies, except Romania, had almost universal male suffrage. For the most part, however, the political systems were heavily influenced by local traditions of clientism and corruption. In Serbia the constitution was modified in the direction of authoritarianism by the Obrenović kings in 1869 and 1889 but this did not prevent the rise of the Serbian National Radical Party (NRP) which borrowed many ideas from the Russian Narodniks and from the Greek constitutionalists. After the overthrow of the Obrenović dynasty in 1903 the NRP became the dominant party in Serbia.

Bulgaria's constitution, devised by an assembly in Tûrnovo in 1879, was extremely liberal but from 1881 to 1883 Prince Alexander Battenberg attempted to rule without it. He was overthrown in 1886 and his successor, Ferdinand of Saxe-Coburg-Gotha, retained the constitution but used influence and patronage in such a way that it was effectively by-passed.

Romanian politics were dominated by the Liberal and the Conservative parties, neither of which had much in common with its British namesake. Both were basically cliques of the owners of large estates who dominated the country, but the Liberals, despite their name, wished to use the state to create the mechanisms of a modern economy and were pro-French in their foreign policy orientation. The Conservatives were more suspicious of industrialisation and were pro-German.

In Romania the most important event in the period 1900–14 was the great peasant rising of 1907 when peasants, hard-pressed by their landlords and bailiffs, burnt manor houses, manorial records, and some bailiffs. The restoration of order required massive military force and is thought to have cost as many as ten thousand lives.

Bulgaria too experienced rural unrest, though on nothing like the same scale. An attempt to substitute tithes in kind for cash payments in the late 1890s ignited long-smouldering unrest and led to the formation of the Bulgarian Agrarian National Union (BANU), perhaps the most important and original political phenomenon produced in the Balkans before the First World War.

Throughout the years between 1900 and 1914, however, Balkan politics were dominated by the question of the future of Turkey-in-Europe (see p. 17).

In 1908 a military revolt brought a new government to power in Istanbul (Constantinople). The so-called Young Turks convoked a new parliament which was to include deputies from all lands technically within the Ottoman empire, including Bosnia-Hercegovina and Eastern Rumelia (southern Bulgaria). This was too much for the Austro-Hungarian and Bulgarian governments; the first therefore annexed Bosnia-Hercegovina and the second declared full independence. These were *de jure* rather than *de facto* changes but Russia considered it had been duped by Austria-Hungary and provoked a European diplomatic crisis which lasted until blunt German threats forced the Russians to climb down.

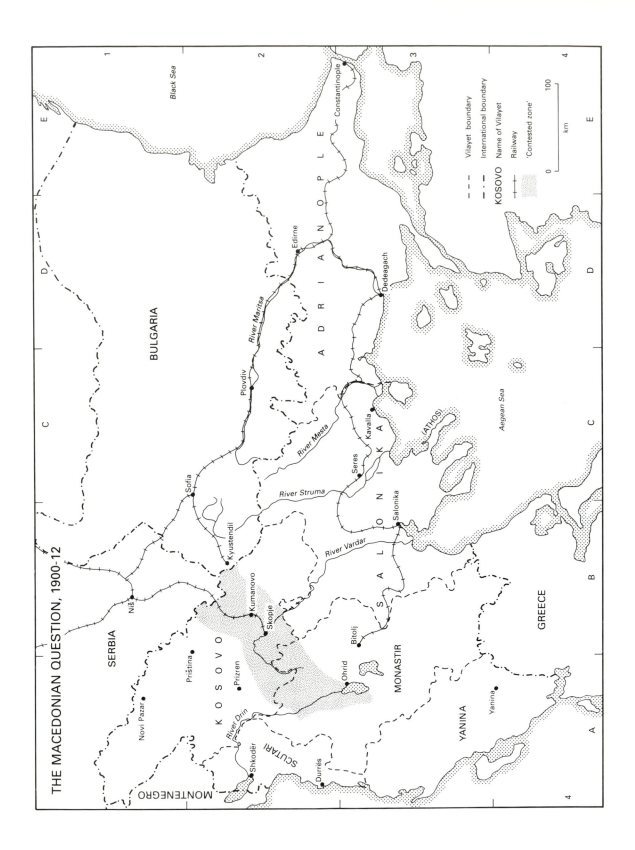

THE MACEDONIAN QUESTION, 1900-12

Vilayet boundary
International boundary
KOSOVO Name of Vilayet
Railway
'Contested zone'

km
0   100

Black Sea

BULGARIA

ADRIANOPLE

Constantinople

Edirne

River Maritsa

Dedeagach

Plovdiv

River Mesta

Kavalla

SALONIKA

(ATHOS)

Aegean Sea

Seres

River Struma

Sofia

Kyustendil

River Vardar

Salonika

Niš

Kumanovo

Skopje

SERBIA

Novi Pazar

Priština

Prizren

KOSOVO

Bitolj

Ohrid

MONASTIR

River Drin

YANINA

Yanina

GREECE

SCUTARI

Shkodër

Durrës

MONTENEGRO

16

The Macedonian question, 1900–12

The Ottoman empire was divided administratively into *vilayets* which were subdivided into *sanjaks*. One *sanjak*, that centred upon Novi Pazar, became famous because Austria-Hungary insisted that it must remain Ottoman to prevent the union of Serbia and Montenegro. The three *vilayets* of Kosovo, Salonika and Monastir (Bitolj) were generally regarded as comprising 'Macedonia'. The ethnic composition of Ottoman Europe, and especially of the Macedonian *vilayets*, was so complex that it cannot be defined cartographically, nor do any reliable statistics for it exist; each interested party so exaggerated their own population that none can be trusted.

The Sultan had been required by the Treaty of Berlin (1878) to reform the administration of his empire and this he had failed to do. The states surrounding the Ottoman empire in Europe – Bulgaria, Greece, Montenegro and Serbia – began to cast covetous glances at it. Initially the contest for the allegiance of the local Christian population was a cultural, and more particularly an ecclesiastical one; the Ottoman rulers divided their subjects not into ethnic but into religious categories and thus a 'Greek' meant not an ethnic Greek but an adherent of the Greek Orthodox Church. By the 1890s, however, military action was also being taken, first by supporters of the Bulgarian cause. In 1893 the situation was complicated by the establishment of the Internal Macedonian Revolutionary Organisation (IMRO) which advocated the creation of a separate Macedonia within a Balkan federation.

The Bulgarians went to considerable lengths to neutralise IMRO and by 1903 had infiltrated its leadership. In August 1903 IMRO staged a large-scale revolt in the Macedonia and Edirne (Adrianople) *vilayets*.

The 'Ilinden' rising, named, in the local Slav languages, after St Elijah on whose name-day it began, was soon crushed and thereafter the great powers stepped in to enforce administrative reforms and to impose European supervision of the local police force.

After the Young Turk revolution of 1908 there were hopes that Macedonia would settle happily into the new system. It did not. Nor did the previously largely untroubled Albanian regions in the *vilayets* of Scutari (Shkodër), northern Yanina and western Kosovo. The Albanians had previously been loyal to Constantinople (Istanbul) because they had been left untroubled by such modern plagues as conscription and taxation. The Young Turks changed this and in retaliation the Albanians revolted every summer from 1909 to 1912. In the latter year their revolt spread into the centre of Macedonia and actually toppled the Young Turk administration.

The Balkan states now became nervous. The Albanians seemed about to establish their own administrative unit, or the great powers might intervene to shore up the Ottoman regime. In either case Bulgaria, Greece, Montenegro and Serbia would be unable to partition the area. In the face of these dangers the Balkan states buried their myriad hatchets and signed a series of alliances, the first and most important being that signed by Bulgaria and Serbia in February/March 1912. There was an attempt to divide territory but because full agreement was impossible a 'contested zone' was defined, the ultimate fate of which was to be determined by the Russian emperor who had sponsored the treaty. In the Bulgarian–Greek treaty of 29 May there was no attempt at all to divide any spoils which might be gained. In the summer, with disorder in Turkey-in-Europe mounting rapidly, Montenegro agreed verbally to join the alliance.

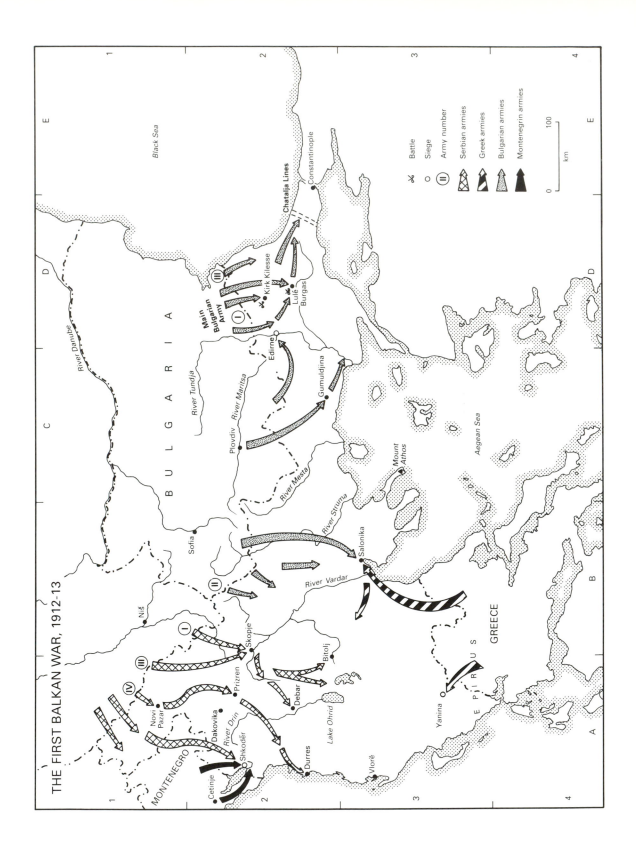

THE FIRST BALKAN WAR, 1912-13

Black Sea

River Danube

D

E

C

B U L G A R I A

Sofia

Niš

River Tundja

Plovdiv

River Maritsa

Edirne

Main
Bulgarian
Army

Kirk Kilesse

Lulé

Burgas

Chatalja Lines

Constantinople

Gumuljina

River Mesta

River Struma

Salonika

River Vardar

Mount
Athos

Aegean Sea

Skopje

Bitolj

Debar

Lake Ohrid

Prizren

Djakovika

Novi
Pazar

River Drin

Shkodër

Cetinje

MONTENEGRO

Durres

Vlorë

Yanina

E P I R U S

GREECE

Battle
Siege
Army number
Serbian armies
Greek armies
Bulgarian armies
Montenegrin armies

0   100

km

The first Balkan war, 1912–13

Despite frenzied diplomatic action by the European powers war broke out in the Balkans when Montenegrin troops moved across the border into the Ottoman empire on 8 October 1912. The other members of the Balkan alliance (Bulgaria, Greece and Serbia) joined the war a few days later.

Serbian forces crossed into the Sanjak of Novi Pazar and then divided, some making for Shkodër (Scutari), towards which the Montenegrins were also advancing, others driving for Durrës and the Adriatic coast, whilst units of the First and Third armies entered Macedonia and made for Skopje before bifurcating and heading towards Debar in Kosovo and Bitolj in central Macedonia. They met little resistance.

The Greek army had two main objectives: the fortress of Yanina, which commanded the whole of Epirus and southern Albania; and Salonika, the natural port of Macedonia and a prize of enormous economic and strategic importance.

Its value was also appreciated by the Bulgarians. Units of their Second Army also raced for the city. And because Salonika had such a large Jewish population – some sources say up to 80 per cent of its inhabitants were Jewish at this time – the Bulgarians placed as many Jewish officers as they could in the van of their advancing troops. The Bulgarians were beaten to the city by the Greeks by a few hours.

The main Bulgarian effort, however, was in its direct advance towards the Ottoman capital. The First and Third Bulgarian armies crossed into Ottoman territory and, to the astonishment of the rest of Europe, administered two crushing defeats upon the Sultan's forces in the battles of Kirk Kilesse on 22–3 October and Lulé Burgas between 28 and 31 October. By then the great Ottoman fortress at Edirne (Adrianople) had been invested by the Bulgarians. It was said that King Ferdinand of Bulgaria was dreaming of entering Istanbul (Constantinople) in triumph and had ordered sumptuous regalia appropriate to the occasion. He was to be thwarted. The Turks took up defensive positions along the strongly fortified Chatalja lines and cholera broke out amongst the Bulgarian troops. An ill-judged attempt to force the Chatalja lines marked the furthest point of the Bulgarian advance.

By the end of 1912 the only Ottoman possessions left in Europe outside the Chatalja lines were the besieged fortresses of Edirne (Adrianople) and Yanina, and the town of Shkodër. Before it fell to the Bulgarians early in 1913 Edirne was to be the first town on which bombs were dropped from an aeroplane. Yanina too fell early in 1913 and on 23 April Shkodër was virtually sold to the besieging Montenegrins and Serbs by its Albanian commander.

This produced a major European crisis. The great powers had agreed at the end of 1912 that a new Albanian state would be created and Austria-Hungary was adamant that Shkodër should be included in it; the Russians backed the Slav demand that it should be Montenegrin. In the end the king of Montenegro agreed to place the fate of the city in the hands of the powers who awarded it to Albania.

TERRITORIAL CHANGES AFTER THE BALKAN WARS

ROMANIA

Belgrade

Bucharest

River Danube

DOBRUDJA

SERBIA

Black Sea

BULGARIA

Novi Pazar

MONTENEGRO

Sofia

River Maritsa

Shkodër

Skopje

River Vardar

River Struma

Edirne

Kiyikoy

Adriatic Sea

THRACE

Constantinople

Kavalla

Alexandropolis

Enez

Salonika

Samothrakei

ALBANIA

Gokceada

Mt. Athos

EPIRUS

Limnos

Yanina

Lesvos

GREECE

Aegean Sea

Athens

DODECANESE

- · - 1911 boundaries

Acquired by Montenegro from Ottoman Empire

Acquired by Bulgaria from Ottoman Empire during first Balkan war but lost again in second Balkan war

Southern Dodecanese, occupied by Italy

Acquired by Romania from Bulgaria

Acquired by Bulgaria from Ottoman Empire

Acquired by Greece from Ottoman Empire

Acquired by Serbia from Ottoman Empire

0   100
km

20

Territorial changes after the Balkan wars

After the destruction of the Ottoman empire in Europe by the Balkan allies in 1912–13 the great powers (Austria-Hungary, France, Germany, Great Britain, Italy, and Russia) insisted that an independent Albania was to be created with borders to be defined by the powers, that the Ottoman empire should retain the area to the south and east of a line drawn from Enos (Enez) on the Aegean to Midia (Kiyikoy) on the Black Sea, and that Mount Athos should continue to enjoy its particular autonomous privileges. With these restrictions, the belligerents were left free to divide the spoils.

The Bulgarians considered that they had made the greatest military efforts and had suffered the highest casualties, and that they should therefore be awarded the lion's share of those spoils. The complication was that the original treaty between Serbia and Bulgaria had been nullified by the creation of an independent Albania; the Serbs, who had already partitioned the Sanjak of Novi Pazar with Montenegro, insisted that they should receive territory in Macedonia, including all of the former 'contested zone', to compensate for the lands they had lost by the creation of an independent Albania.

The Greeks, who had gained large areas of Epirus, southern Macedonia and western Thrace, were concerned to defend these areas against any Bulgarian expansion, and therefore backed the Serbs. This common interest against Bulgaria led the Serbs and Greeks to conclude an alliance in May by which they agreed to divide Macedonia west of the Vardar between themselves, and to allow Macedonia east of the river to be determined on the principle of effective possession. The Bulgarians soon knew of the supposedly secret treaty and tension rose rapidly. On 29 June 1913 Bulgarian forces attacked those of their former allies in what was probably meant to be a gesture to force the Serbs and Greeks to the negotiating table.

If that had been the plan it went disastrously wrong. Greek forces marched into the Struma valley whilst the Serbs attacked eastward across the Vardar. Much more devastating for the Bulgarians was the fact that the Turks resumed hostilities, driving the depleted Bulgarian army back up the Maritsa valley beyond Edirne (Adrianople). The city and much of eastern Thrace reverted to Ottoman rule. Not only did the Turks attack in the south-east but the Romanians crossed into the undefended north-east of Bulgaria. There was nothing to stop them marching to Sofia and the Bulgarians therefore sued for peace. In the Treaty of Bucharest, 10 August 1913, Bulgaria was forced to accept the loss of eastern Thrace and of southern Dobrudja, the richest and most advanced agricultural area in Bulgaria. Serbian and Greek gains in Macedonia were also confirmed and of its conquests in 1913 Bulgaria was left only with parts of western Thrace, a poor region with a population which included large numbers of Turks and Bulgarian Muslims. She did, however, have access to the Mediterranean and to the port of Dedeagach (Alexandropoulis).

During the first Balkan war Greece also occupied a number of islands in the northern Dodecanese. Despite these sizeable gains the Greeks were still discontented primarily because they had claims in northern Epirus which they feared would be handed to Albania. There were attempts before the First World War to engineer a deal whereby Greece sacrificed some of its claims in Epirus in return for islands in the southern Dodecanese which had been taken by Italy in its war with the Ottoman empire in 1911–12, but the negotiations were still in progress when the outbreak of the First World War ended all hopes of any such deal.

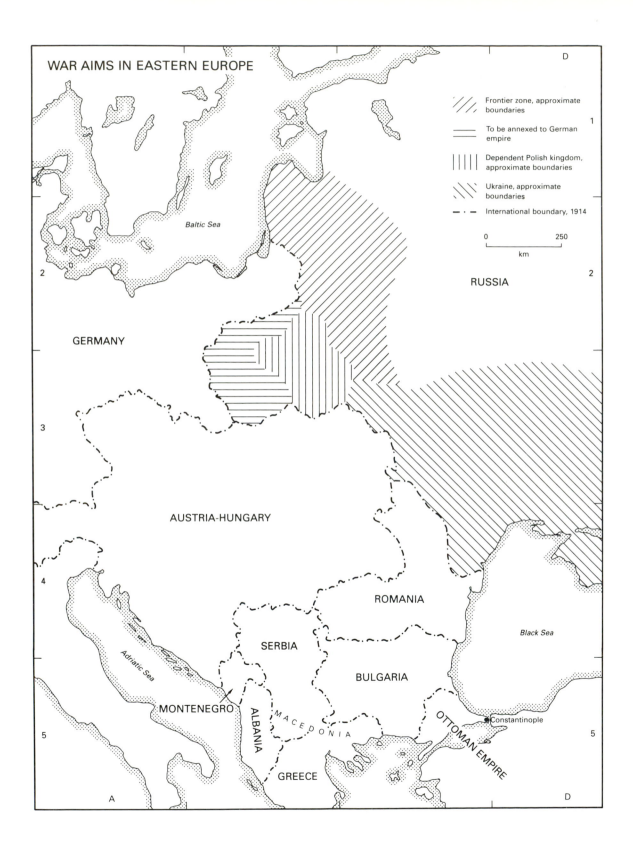

WAR AIMS IN EASTERN EUROPE

Frontier zone, approximate boundaries

To be annexed to German empire

Dependent Polish kingdom, approximate boundaries

Ukraine, approximate boundaries

International boundary, 1914

0   250
         km

RUSSIA

Baltic Sea

GERMANY

AUSTRIA-HUNGARY

ROMANIA

Black Sea

SERBIA

BULGARIA

Adriatic Sea

MONTENEGRO

ALBANIA

MACEDONIA

Constantinople

OTTOMAN EMPIRE

GREECE

2 THE FIRST WORLD WAR AND THE VERSAILLES PEACE SETTLEMENT

War aims in Eastern Europe

Wars are much easier to begin than to end, a realisation that usually only comes with war. In the summer of 1914 the expectation was of a short war; in August in Britain it was said that 'The Boys will be Home by Christmas', whilst in Berlin Kaiser Wilhelm II told his troops they would be home before the leaves fell from the trees.

That the war was to last for four long, devastating years was in part due to the fact that technological advances, particularly in the weight of fire power, had been more rapid than those in mobility, and therefore war, especially in the west, became a slogging match between artillery interrupted with occasional and usually suicidal bursts of infantry action in which the hapless foot soldiers were slaughtered by machine gunners. There is also little doubt that most military thinking in the First World War was based on the notion of knocking out the enemy, which usually meant trying to eliminate his strongest point rather than exploiting his weakest; it meant reliance on attack rather than on defence in which all sides were stronger. A further tragedy was that the Germans, because they were in occupation of Belgium and parts of France, considered they were in a winning position even when the allied blockade was sapping the strength of the population in Germany itself.

In the end it was the slow attrition of social decay as much as events on the battlefield which decided the issue. In the west the naval blockade of Germany reduced its population to dangerous levels of deprivation, whilst in the east the enormous sufferings on the Russian home front were in the end too much for the population to bear.

In 1914 few statesmen, let alone soldiers, had any real idea of what they were fighting for. War aims were more a product than a cause of the war. The French wanted the return of Alsace-Lorraine, the British to preserve the balance of power and their own mastery of the seas. German scholars and publicists had toyed with notions such as a German-dominated 'Mitteleuropa', a fanciful European version of the British dream of an Africa red from the Cape to Cairo. When the initial months of the fighting brought Germany territorial gains these vague notions were pummelled into actual policy demands. In eastern Europe those aims extended to annexing more Polish territory, establishing a frontier zone under military occupation, and, if necessary, creating a dependent Polish state and also a Ukraine which would be technically independent but dependent in reality on Germany.

Russia too had war aims. Its Western allies, in order to keep it in the war, were prepared to allow it to realise the age-old Orthodox dream of taking Constantinople. To secure Italian support the Western allies promised Italy territory on the eastern side of the Adriatic, territory to which Italy had no claim if ethnicity were a consideration. The likelihood of an Italian presence on the eastern Adriatic intensified Serbian determination not to give up one square metre of its

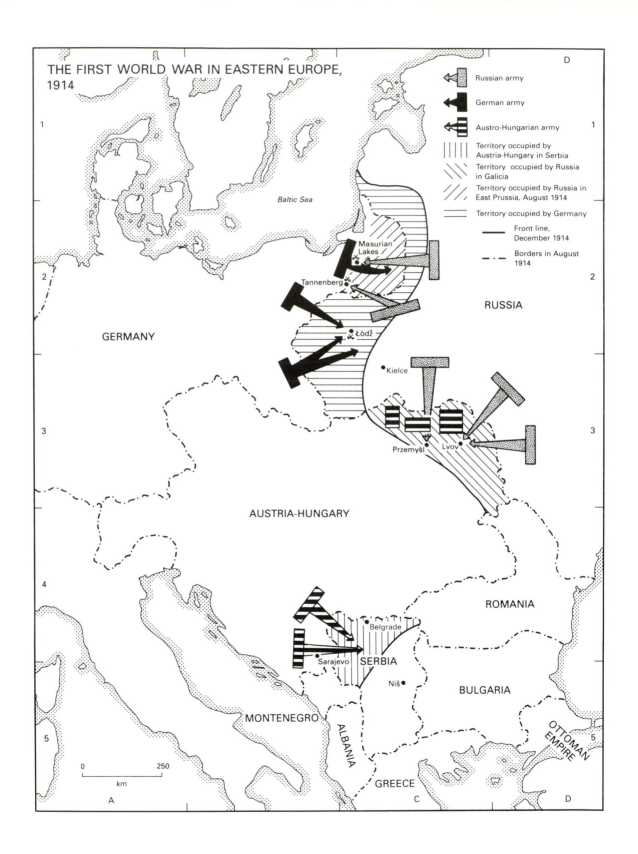

THE FIRST WORLD WAR IN EASTERN EUROPE, 1914

Russian army

German army

Austro-Hungarian army

Territory occupied by Austria-Hungary in Serbia

Territory occupied by Russia in Galicia

Territory occupied by Russia in East Prussia, August 1914

Territory occupied by Germany

Front line, December 1914

Borders in August 1914

Baltic Sea

GERMANY

RUSSIA

Masurian Lakes

Tannenberg

Łódź

Kielce

Przemyśl

Lvov

AUSTRIA-HUNGARY

ROMANIA

Belgrade

Sarajevo

SERBIA

Niš

BULGARIA

MONTENEGRO

ALBANIA

OTTOMAN EMPIRE

GREECE

0   250
km

recent gains in Macedonia (see p. 17). The Serbs needed precious little encouragement towards obduracy, but their insistence on retaining all their previous possessions in Macedonia meant that the Western allies had little chance of winning Bulgaria to their side because Macedonia was a central part of Bulgaria's war aims when it joined the war, also in 1915.

By the middle of 1915 war aims had become yet another factor prolonging the fighting.

The First World War in Eastern Europe, 1914

The Archduke Franz Ferdinand of Austria-Hungary was assassinated in Sarajevo on 28 June 1914. Austria-Hungary held the Serbian government partially responsible for the killing and demanded that the Serbs make promises of good behaviour and allow Austria-Hungary some hand in the supervision of the Serbian police. The Serbs accepted all Austria's terms except the latter. As a result Austria-Hungary declared war on Serbia on 28 July. The intervening month had been needed not only for negotiations with the Serbs but also with Germany and Italy, Austria-Hungary's diplomatic partners.

Russia mobilised in support of Serbia and when the tsar refused to demobilise Germany declared war on Russia on 1 August. Two days later Germany declared war on France; the iron law of the alliances was in force, and the Balkan conflict had become a European war. Austria-Hungary declared war on Russia on 6 August. Britain entered the conflict against Germany on 4 August and against Austria-Hungary on 12 August. The Ottoman empire made a secret undertaking to join the central powers, Germany and Austria-Hungary, and implemented this promise in November. Despite its alliance with Austria-Hungary Romania remained neutral, as did Italy. Bulgaria and Greece had no commitments and also remained out of the fray.

Germany had calculated on a slow Russian mobilisation which would give the German armies time to neutralise France before turning eastwards. In fact, the Russian forces mobilised and moved much more rapidly than the Germans had expected and two Russian armies moved into lightly defended East Prussia. After the initial shock the Germans recovered their composure and, exploiting a gap between the two Russian armies, inflicted severe defeats at the battles of Tannenberg (26–29 August), where the Germans took 90,000 prisoners, and at the Masurian Lakes (10–14 September). The Russians renewed their attack on East Prussia in November but by then the Germans were already driving into Russian Poland where they secured an important victory in the battle of Łódż (11–24 November).

Interestingly, 1914 was the only time in its history when Russia had entered a major European conflict by moving forwards rather than backwards. Russian troops also advanced into Austria-Hungary. Here they had more success, at least until the Habsburg armies were strengthened by the arrival of German troops and commanders. Nevertheless, the Russians had moved into Galicia and had taken the important rail junction at Lvov and the strategic fortress of Przemyśl which guarded the approach to the Carpathian passes. The Russians were not able to advance any further and as winter set in lines of trenches were dug along the foothills of the mountains.

A minor feature of the early fighting in the East was action by the Polish Military Organisation under the command of Józef Piłsudski. His forces captured and for a few days held the city of Kielce. Such independent action was not altogether to the taste of the Austro-Hungarian and German high commands but it showed that the Poles were a factor to be reckoned with and that Piłsudski was a leader of imagination and determination.

There had also been fighting in the Balkans. The conflict had begun as a result of Austria-Hungary's anger with Serbia, and the Dual Monarchy's armies advanced into that country.

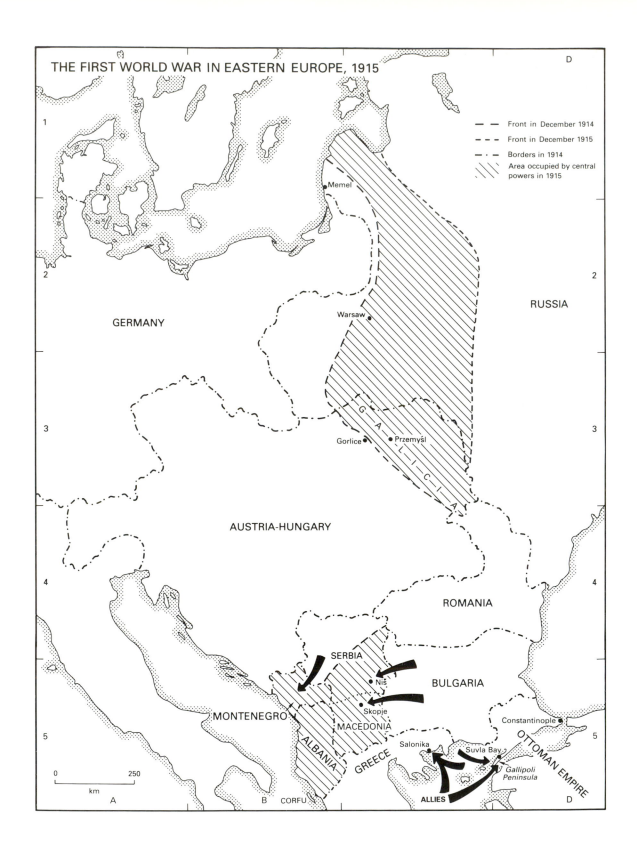

THE FIRST WORLD WAR IN EASTERN EUROPE, 1915

Front in December 1914
Front in December 1915
Borders in 1914
Area occupied by central powers in 1915

Memel

RUSSIA

GERMANY

Warsaw

G - A - L - I - C - I - A

Gorlice   Przemýsl

AUSTRIA-HUNGARY

ROMANIA

SERBIA

Niš   BULGARIA

Skopje

Constantinople

MONTENEGRO

MACEDONIA

Salonika   Suvla Bay

ALBANIA

GREECE   Gallipoli Peninsula

OTTOMAN EMPIRE

0   250
km
A

CORFU   ALLIES   D

They were soon repulsed and the Serbs entered southern Hungary. They could not maintain their positions for long in the face of renewed Austro-Hungarian drives on Belgrade, but it was not until December that Habsburg troops entered the Serbian capital and they were not able to progress much beyond it. The Serbian government moved to Niš.

The First World War in Eastern Europe, 1915

Early in 1915 Russian forces made some advances and in March took Memel (Klaipeda).

These attacks confirmed the German high command in its growing suspicion that the war in the west would never be won until all German forces could be concentrated there, and this could be done only if Russia were forced out of the conflict altogether. To that end, on 2 May a massive attack was launched on a wide front centred on Gorlice. The Russian line broke. On 4 June the Austro-German armies retook Przemyśl which gave them a free passage across Galicia. By the end of the year the Russians had fallen back over three hundred miles, ceding territory greater in area than the whole of France. They had also lost valuable industrial potential in Warsaw and other areas of Russian Poland as well as 750,000 prisoners of war and uncounted thousands of dead and wounded.

The Russian disaster had many causes. The army was not well led. The professional soldiers who dominated the officer corps at the beginning of the war had been greatly reduced in number and in some units virtually eliminated. Their replacements were less well-trained and less committed. The conscript masses were also pitifully ill-prepared, both in training and equipment, some soldiers having no weapons other than those they could seize from their fallen comrades.

The desire to ensure supplies of military equipment to Russia was in part the motivation for the allied landings in Gallipoli. The grand strategic purpose was to force a way through to Istanbul (Constantinople) and thus eliminate the Ottoman empire from the war. The success of the operation would also, it was assumed, persuade the Bulgarians to join the allied side; if they did so the Romanians were likely to follow suit and pressure on Serbia would be relieved. Above all, however, the Gallipoli landings were intended to break out of the stalemate on the western front.

Naval forces passed the mouth of the Dardanelles on 18 March only to return after encountering uncharted mines. Had they but known, Turkish ammunition was almost exhausted and the ships could easily have carried on as far as Istanbul, the allies' ultimate objective. Troops were landed in the Gallipoli Peninsula on 25 April and again the way to the Ottoman capital would have been open if better intelligence and more assertive leadership had been to hand. They were not and the allied troops were pinned on their beaches, as were those landed on 6 August in Suvla Bay. The troops were eventually withdrawn in December 1915 and January 1916.

Before then there had been decisive fighting in the Balkans. The Gallipoli emergency had shown both how dependent the Turks were on supplies of ammunition from Germany and how much Serbia impeded that essential traffic. Serbia, it was decided, would be eliminated, and on 7 October large Austro-German forces attacked the Serbs who, after a heroic trek across the Albanian mountains, established their new headquarters in Corfu. Bulgaria had been won over to the central powers with the promise of Macedonia and on 11 October the Bulgarian army attacked on two fronts, one towards Niš and the other towards Skopje. Anglo-French forces which had landed in Salonika on 5 October failed in their attempt to prevent the Bulgarian advance into Macedonia. By the end of the year Austria-Hungary had occupied Montenegro and Albania.

In May 1915 Italy joined the war on the allied side after being promised territorial gains on the eastern shore of the Adriatic.

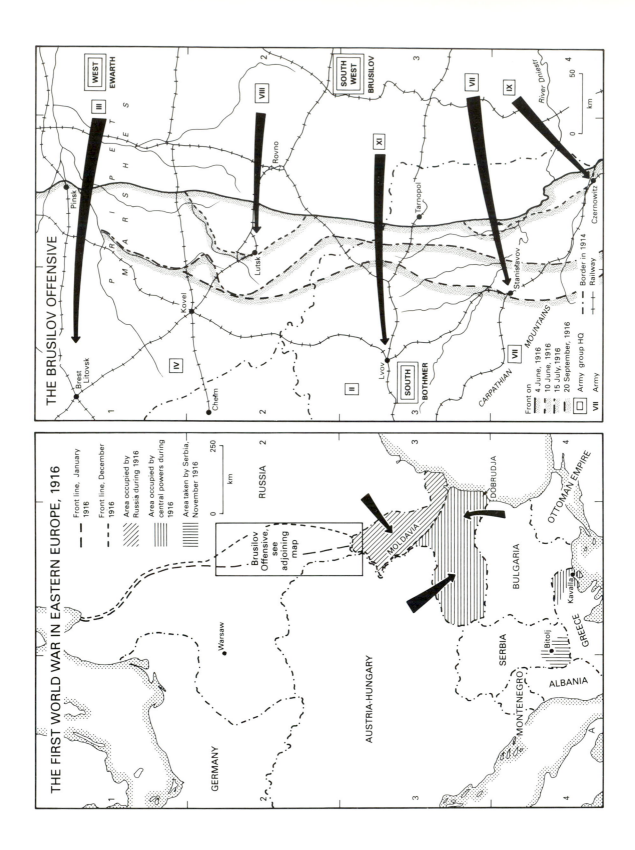

THE BRUSILOV OFFENSIVE

WEST EWARTH

SOUTH WEST BRUSILOV

III

VIII

XI

VII

IX

SOUTH BOTHMER

II

IV

Pinsk

Brest Litovsk

Chełm

Kovel

Lutsk

Rovno

Tarnopol

Lvov

Stanisłavov

Czernowitz

River Dniestr

P R I P E T   M A R S H E S

CARPATHIAN MOUNTAINS

Front on   4 June, 1916
            10 June, 1916
            15 July, 1916
            20 September, 1916

VII Army group HQ

VII Army

Border in 1914
Railway

50 km

THE FIRST WORLD WAR IN EASTERN EUROPE, 1916

Front line, January 1916
Front line, December 1916
Area occupied by Russia during 1916
Area occupied by central powers during 1916
Area taken by Serbia, November 1916

250 km

GERMANY

AUSTRIA-HUNGARY

RUSSIA

Warsaw

Brusilov Offensive, see adjoining map

MOLDAVIA

DOBRUDJA

BULGARIA

SERBIA

MONTENEGRO

ALBANIA

GREECE

OTTOMAN EMPIRE

Bitolj

Kavalla

The First World War in Eastern Europe, 1916

In February 1916 the French and German armies joined hideous battle around Verdun. In an effort to relieve pressure on the besieged French fortress plans were drawn up for a two-pronged Russian attack, one in the north towards East Prussia and one in the centre directed towards the recapture of Warsaw. Both attacks failed utterly.

In the summer of 1916 the allied offensive on the Somme and Italian difficulties in the Tyrol again raised the need for Russian relief. This time it was left to the south-western command under General Alexis Brusilov. He decided to attack towards Lvov and Stanisłavov. He had little time to prepare but this also meant that there was not enough time for the enemy to be fully forewarned and when the attack was launched on 4 June the Austro-Hungarian forces were unprepared. They collapsed and within three weeks Brusilov had taken 350,000 prisoners and had advanced, in some places, fifty miles.

The Germans rushed to the aid of their ally. Seven divisions earmarked for Verdun were diverted to the south-eastern front and these eventually held the Russian advance. Brusilov's forces were by then in need of reinforcement. There were no reserves available in the south-western area and replacements of men and *matériel* could not easily be moved from the other army groups because the railways, already under enormous strain, ran mainly east–west rather than north–south. By the end of the year the Russians had been pushed back and had lost over a million men.

The Brusilov offensive was in many ways a turning point in the history of Eastern Europe. It broke the spirit of the Austro-Hungarian army which, though it did not dissolve, never again enjoyed the same cohesion; henceforth, it had to be stiffened with German units and Germany took real control of the Habsburg war effort from this point. When Franz Josef died in November 1916 an era seemed to end; he had come to the throne in 1848. Austria-Hungary was now a satrapy of Germany; non-German ethnic groups which had tolerated life under Franz Josef had no taste for becoming virtual vassals of Kaiser Wilhelm.

The Brusilov offensive cost Austria-Hungary dear but it was no less costly to Russia. Massive casualty rates and increasing shortages of food and other commodities were causing great social tension which found expression in strikes, demonstrations and political agitation amongst soldier and civilian alike.

The initial success of the Brusilov offensive convinced the Romanians that the allies were about to win the war. On 27 August they declared war on the central powers, and initially they met with some military success against German and Austrian forces under the command of General von Mackensen. It did not last. The Bulgarian Third Army, strengthened with Turkish units, moved into the Dobrudja and then crossed the Danube into Romania proper. This was a feint to draw the Romanian army southwards before the Germans and Austrians, now commanded by General Falkenhayn, launched a massive attack. The Romanians could not withstand such power and capitulated. The Russians meanwhile occupied eastern Moldavia to prevent it falling into German-Austrian hands.

There was also some fighting in the southern Balkans. The Bulgarians were allowed by the Germans to cross the Greek border and took a number of towns in western Thrace, including the valuable port of Kavalla. Towards the end of the year, however, the tide seemed to turn further west when the Serbs reconquered a portion of Macedonia, including Bitolj.

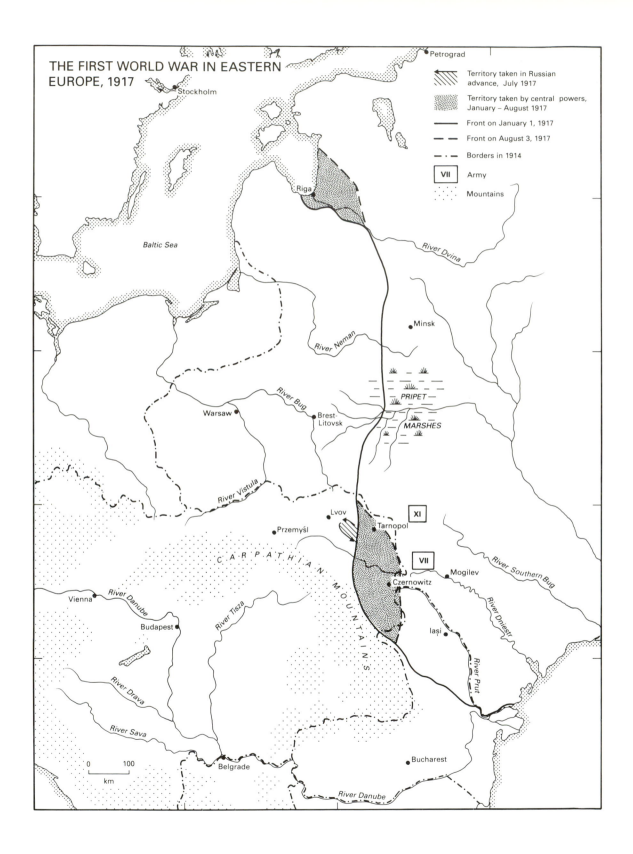

THE FIRST WORLD WAR IN EASTERN
EUROPE, 1917

Territory taken in Russian
advance, July 1917

Territory taken by central powers,
January – August 1917

Front on January 1, 1917

Front on August 3, 1917

Borders in 1914

VII Army

Mountains

Petrograd

Stockholm

Baltic Sea

Riga

River Dvina

River Neman

Minsk

River Bug

Warsaw

Brest-
Litovsk

PRIPET

MARSHES

River Vistula

Lvov

XI

Przemyśl

Tarnopol

VII

C A R P A T H I A N   M O U N T A I N S

Mogilev

River Southern Bug

Vienna

River Danube

Czernowitz

River Dniestr

Budapest

River Tisza

Iaşi

River Prut

River Drava

River Sava

0   100

km

Belgrade

Bucharest

River Danube

30

The First World War in Eastern Europe, 1917

The year 1917 began on the eastern front with a retreat by Russian armies in Romania but soon thereafter it was political rather than military events which demanded most attention.

Privation and shortages were experienced by all belligerent nations but nowhere more so than in Russia. An incompetent administration, casualty rates which seemed to speak of callousness as well as inefficiency, and a shortage of essentials, especially food and fuel, reduced the population to despair. In February 1917 breaking point was reached. The population of Petrograd, as St Petersburg had been called since the summer of 1914, took to the streets and after a few days the local garrison refused to restore order; the soldiers were desperate not to be sent to the front.

By March a new, liberal government had been installed and it remained loyal to the Western allies. In July it launched an offensive to the west of Tarnopol but this petered out after a few days. The army was broken in spirit and could do little to resist the counter-attack which the Germans launched soon after. The Germans also advanced in the north and on 1 September took Riga, usually accounted the last obstacle on the road to Petrograd.

In Russia the socialist leader, Kerensky, suggested a negotiated peace but the allies, who since April had counted the United States amongst their number, refused. Nor did they give any encouragement to a socialist-inspired peace conference in Stockholm. The Russian army began to disintegrate. In November the radical Bolsheviks, using the slogan 'Peace, Bread and Land', seized and then held power in the major cities. They began negotiations with the Germans and on 15 December 1917 an armistice was signed. The front line at that point was not much different from that of a year before except for the advance beyond Riga in the north and into Romania in the south.

In the remainder of Eastern Europe there had been little change in the disposition of the armies. The Anglo-French forces in Salonika had not moved forward, nor had the Serbs been able to expand greatly on their successes at the end of 1916. Italy, however, had declared a protectorate over Albania.

If the military picture was relatively static the political one showed more change. The central powers had wanted to raise troops from amongst the Poles, to which nationalist Poles had responded by saying that without a national administration there could be no conscription. In November 1916, therefore, an Interim Council of State had been established in Warsaw but in 1917, with the fall of tsardom, the Poles' appetite for real independence was whetted; it seemed that mighty empires could be toppled and subject peoples could free themselves – the Ukrainians had declared independence on 29 June. To counter the new Polish threat the Germans and Austrians imprisoned a number of Polish leaders, including Piłsudski; as a sop to Polish nationalism the central powers also created a Polish kingdom with an interim regency council at its head.

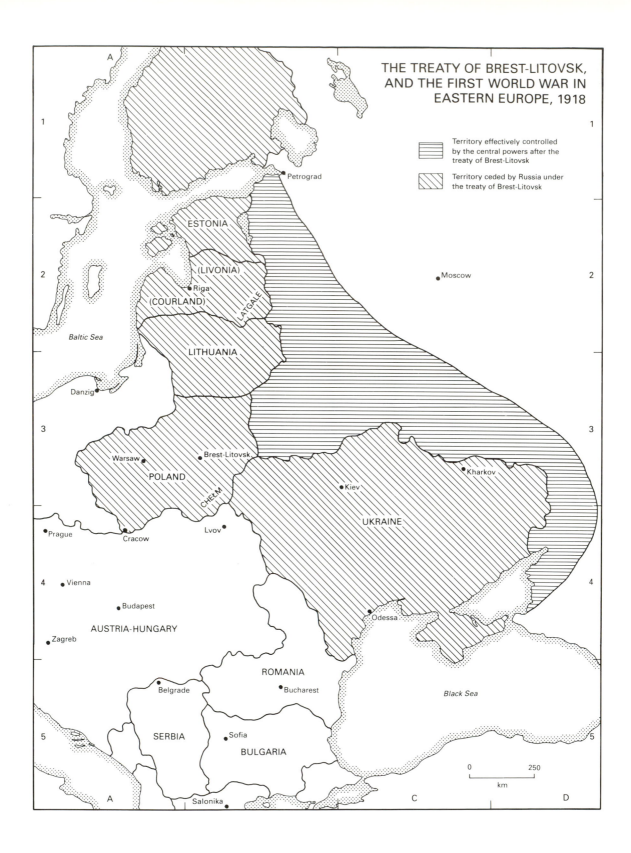

THE TREATY OF BREST-LITOVSK,
AND THE FIRST WORLD WAR IN
EASTERN EUROPE, 1918

Territory effectively controlled
by the central powers after the
treaty of Brest-Litovsk

Territory ceded by Russia under
the treaty of Brest-Litovsk

Petrograd

Moscow

ESTONIA

(LIVONIA)

Riga

(COURLAND)

LATGALE

Baltic Sea

LITHUANIA

Danzig

Warsaw

Brest-Litovsk

Kharkov

POLAND

CHELM

Kiev

Prague

Cracow

Lvov

UKRAINE

Vienna

Budapest

Odessa

Zagreb

AUSTRIA-HUNGARY

ROMANIA

Belgrade

Bucharest

Black Sea

SERBIA

Sofia

BULGARIA

0   250

km

Salonika

The Treaty of Brest-Litovsk and the First World War in Eastern Europe, 1918

The negotiations which had led to the armistice of 15 December 1917 between Germany and Russia were continued in 1918 and led to the signing of the Treaty of Brest-Litovsk on 3 March 1918. It was a device, the Bolsheviks admitted, to trade space for time, the time which they needed to consolidate their revolutionary rule in the territory they held and to defeat anti-Bolshevik forces, some of them bolstered by allied landings, in areas outside their control. Yet the space they yielded was enormous. The Treaty gave the Germans and Austrians domination over the vast food-producing areas as well as the rich mining regions and industrial zones in the south-west of now technically independent Ukraine.

In the west the Russians ceded Estonia, which had declared independence on 24 February. Latvian representatives from Livonia, Courland and Latgale established a provisional government even before the Germans took Riga in September 1917, but the Latvians had been deeply divided and it was not until November 1918 that a unified Latvian People's Council was set up in Riga. The Lithuanians had had to act with even greater caution because their country had been under German occupation since 1915; in June 1917 a Lithuanian council was established and in March 1918 the German emperor accepted the notion of an independent Lithuanian state. But in all three Baltic states the political and military situations remained fluid and not until the spring of 1920 was there stability enough for real national independence.

Meanwhile the Poles, furious at having been left out of the Brest-Litovsk negotiations, especially after the area around Chełm had been allocated to Ukraine, threw off German domination and established an independent state in November 1918, though its borders were yet to be defined.

As Russia dissolved the Romanians were left defenceless against further German pressure and in May 1918 concluded the Treaty of Bucharest by which they virtually passed control of their country to the Germans. The Russian collapse also persuaded Czech prisoners of war in the country to organise themselves into a legion which promised to present itself to the allies as a fighting force for use on the western front. This helped the Czechs enormously to win allied recognition in June 1918.

In the last year of the war the civilian population throughout Eastern Europe was brought to despair. There were strikes and demonstrations even in Prague and Budapest but it was in the south-east that civilian discontent first translated into military capitulation. In September allied forces broke out of Salonika and drove the Bulgarians back into the Struma valley. Desperately short of ammunition and demoralised by the knowledge of excruciating food shortages at home, the Bulgarian forces sued for peace, signing an armistice in Salonika on 28 September. The Bulgarians had been the last of the central powers to join that group and had now become the first to leave it.

The Bulgarian surrender wrecked the central powers which were already debilitated by growing national discontent, undisciplined prisoners returning from Russia, and a despairing civilian population. On 28 October Czech nationalists in Prague seized power in the name of the Czechoslovak nation. At much the same time moderate revolutionaries under the leadership of Mihály Károlyi took control in Budapest, and in Zagreb local south-Slav enthusiasts threw in their lot with the Serbs of Serbia. On 9 November Romania rejected central powers domination and joined the war on the allied side.

Eastern Europe had ceased to be the domain of the great multi-national empires.

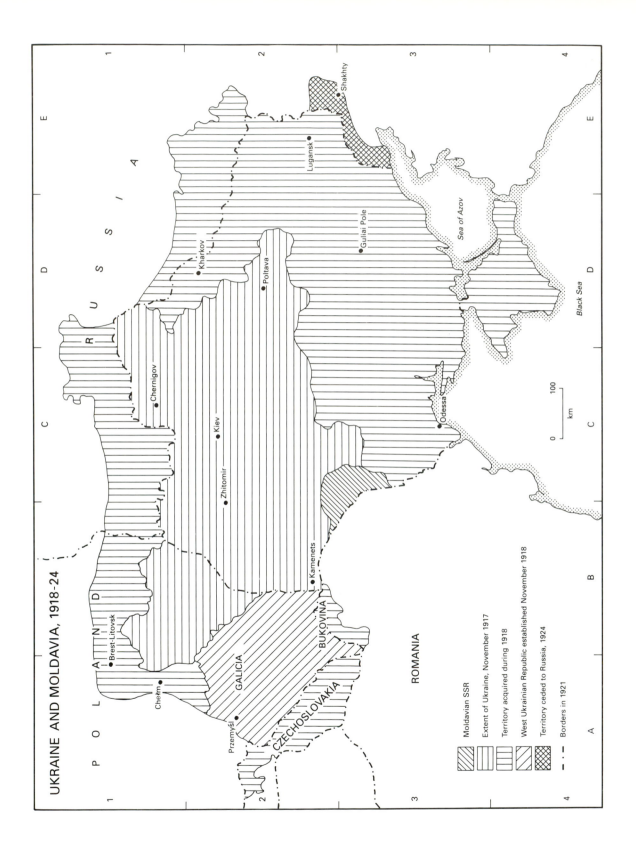

UKRAINE AND MOLDAVIA, 1918-24

POLAND

RUSSIA

Brest-Litovsk

Chełm

Przemyśl

GALICIA

CZECHOSLOVAKIA

BUKOVINA

Kamenets

Zhitomir

Kiev

Chernigov

Poltava

Kharkov

Lugansk

Guliai Pole

Shakhty

Odessa

Sea of Azov

Black Sea

ROMANIA

Moldavian SSR

Extent of Ukraine, November 1917

Territory acquired during 1918

West Ukrainian Republic established November 1918

Territory ceded to Russia, 1924

Borders in 1921

100

km

0

Ukraine and Moldavia, 1918–24

The name 'Ukraine' derives from a Slav word meaning border or boundary. The area was settled during tsarist times by many cossacks – that is, those who were given the right to hold and use land in return for defending that land against invaders and, later, performing whatever military or police duties the authorities might require of them.

Oppressive centralism and in particular a desire on the part of the rulers in St Petersburg to suppress any manifestation of Ukrainian separatism had created a discontented Ukrainian intelligentsia. The peasantry too had much reason for complaint; it was in the rich agricultural areas of Ukraine that financial pressure on the peasantry was at its greatest.

In 1917 with the collapse of the tsarist regime, Ukrainian intellectuals immediately established a national council or *Rada*. In Ukraine the Bolsheviks won much peasant approval by granting them possession of the land, but the Bolsheviks had competitors for peasant loyalty in the strong anarchist movement which emerged in 1917 led by Nestor Makhno; unlike the Bolsheviks the anarchists were not associated with Russia.

In 1918 the central powers forced the Bolsheviks to recognise an independent Ukraine with its capital in Kiev and including parts of Galicia, the Bukovina, and the Chełm region. In return the *Rada* was required to provide Austria and Germany with grain. This proved difficult because the peasants resented grain requisitioning by an independent Ukraine just as much as by tsarist landowners or officials; and the population at large also resented the presence of large numbers of German troops in what was supposedly an independent state. The inability of the *Rada* to obtain the grain demanded by the Germans led the latter to replace it by an administration under Hetman Skoropadski.

Ukraine in fact was never really subjected to proper central control from Kiev. In the west the largely Uniate population of western Galicia were not attracted to living in a predominantly Orthodox or Bolshevik state and in November 1918 declared for a separate Ukrainian republic in Galicia. In the autumn of 1918 Skoropadski was overthrown by Simon Petliura, a romantic socialist nationalist, who joined with the Poles to conquer Ukraine. By the mid-summer of 1919 Petliura and the Poles had taken Kiev but could not establish permanent control.

Ukraine was beset by warring factions. In addition to the Poles and Petliura there were Bolshevik armies, White Russian armies under General Denikin, and the anarchists under Makhno who had his headquarters at Guliai Pole.

That the Bolsheviks emerged as the strongest factor was due in part to the withdrawal of Western support from the Whites, in part to the disorganisation of the anarchists, but mostly to the Bolsheviks' firm commitment to giving the land to the peasants. By the spring of 1920 the Poles and Petliura had been pushed out of the Ukraine and when the war between the Poles and the Bolsheviks was concluded by the Treaty of Riga in March 1921 the Poles agreed that Ukraine should be part of the Bolshevik imperium. Ukraine became a constituent element of the USSR when it was formed in 1924. When the boundaries of 1924 were drawn Ukraine lost the rich mining area around Shakhty to Russia.

To the south-west of Ukraine, between the southern Bug and the Dniestr, was an area with a large Romanian population. Russian workers in its industrial areas and Romanian peasants on its estates had joined the revolution in 1917, and to prevent any Romanian intrusion this area was incorporated into the USSR in 1924 to become the Moldavian Soviet Socialist Republic.

THE PEACE SETTLEMENT, 1919-23

FINLAND

Helsinki
Leningrad

Stockholm

ESTONIA

Tallinn

DENMARK

Copenhagen

Riga

LATVIA

Hamburg

Memel

LITHUANIA

Vilnius

Minsk

Berlin

EAST
PRUSSIA

Danzig

GERMAN REPUBLIC

Leipzig

P   O   L   A   N   D

Warsaw

Breslau

Kiev

UPPER
SILESIA

Prague

CZECHOSLOVAKIA

Cracow

TESCHEN

GALICIA

BUKOVINA

Czernowitz

Munich

RUTHENIA

BESSARABIA

Vienna

AUSTRIA

Sopron

Budapest

HUNGARY

R   O   M   A   N   I   A

Innsbrück

CARINTHIA

SOUTH
TYROL

SLOVENIA

TRANSYLVANIA

Milan

Fiume

CROATIA

Y   U   G   O   S   L   A   V   I   A

VOJVODINA

Belgrade

Bucharest

DOBRUDJA

Black Sea

ITALY

Zadar

BOSNIA

HERCE-
GOVINA

Varna

Sofia

Rome

MONTENEGRO

Naples

ALBANIA

MACEDONIA

TURKEY

Constantinople

GREECE

Smyrna

Athens

U
S
S
R

Legend

	Territory lost by Russia
	Territory lost by Germany
	Territory lost by Austria-Hungary
	Territory lost by Bulgaria
	Territory lost by Turkey (until 1923)
---	Old border
-·-	New border

0   250
km

The peace settlement, 1919–23

The process of drawing up and applying a definitive peace settlement after the First World War was protracted, frustrating for those involved, and not always effective. And not until 1924 was there full agreement on Memel (Klaipeda) or on the fate of Fiume (Rijeka).

The peace settlement was contained in the treaties of Versailles with Germany (28 June 1919), St Germain with Austria (10 September 1919), Neuilly-sur-Seine with Bulgaria (27 November 1919), Trianon with Hungary (4 June 1920), and Sèvres with the Ottoman empire (10 August 1920). From these treaties emerged the new states of Poland, Czechoslovakia, and Yugoslavia; Lithuania, Latvia, and Estonia appeared from other agreements. Serbia and Montenegro were merged into the new Yugoslavia, Romania was greatly enlarged, and Bulgaria shorn of most of its acquisitions since 1912. The treaties themselves were only general agreements. Details were frequently left for later settlement by whatever means might be thought appropriate. It was not the peacemakers in Paris but conferences of ambassadors, for example, which decided the fate of Teschen and the line of the Italo-Yugoslav border.

The application of the agreements, general or specific, could cause difficulties. In some areas the allies had armed forces to hand which could enforce the settlement, as in Hungary, in Germany itself, or to some degree in the Baltic states where the British navy helped contain local pro-Bolshevik elements. In other instances there were no allied armies, and local forces were left free to decide both the general principle and the detailed application of a settlement. This was most notably the case on Poland's eastern border which, after the Russo-Polish war of 1919–21, was drawn far to the east of the line the allies had envisaged. It was also force which gave the Lithuanians effective possession of Memel.

One of the great underlying principles of the peace settlement was that of national self-determination. The plebiscite was seen as a means of measuring popular feeling and it was used in a number of disputed areas including East Prussia, Carinthia, Upper Silesia and Sopron (Oedenburg). People did not always vote for ethnic reasons, however, and the system was open to abuse, but it did cut a number of Gordian knots in Eastern Europe.

The principle of national self-determination could not always be adhered to and in some cases it was openly abandoned. The Czechs argued that they should have what became known as the Sudetenland, not on ethnic grounds but because without these areas Czechoslovakia, the linchpin of the post-war settlement in Central Europe, was indefensible. Similar strategic arguments were employed to justify Czechoslovak rule in Ruthenia and Yugoslav possession of the Bačka, a part of the Vojvodina to the north of Belgrade.

With hindsight it is easy to decry and belittle what was achieved in the settlement of 1919–23, but it did leave far fewer Central and East Europeans under foreign, alien rule than had been the case in 1914. Furthermore, the peacemakers of 1919–23 knew that they were dealing with areas of enormous racial complexity and that clear lines of division between ethnic groups could not be drawn. It was for that reason that they insisted that all states in the area must sign treaties guaranteeing the individual rights of members of minority communities, even going to the length of stipulating in the case of Poland that no general elections could be held on Saturdays, the Jewish sabbath.

The great defect of the settlement, however, was that it divided Europe between, on the one hand, the victorious, allied powers, and on the other hand the defeated 'revisionist' states who wished to redefine the treaties.

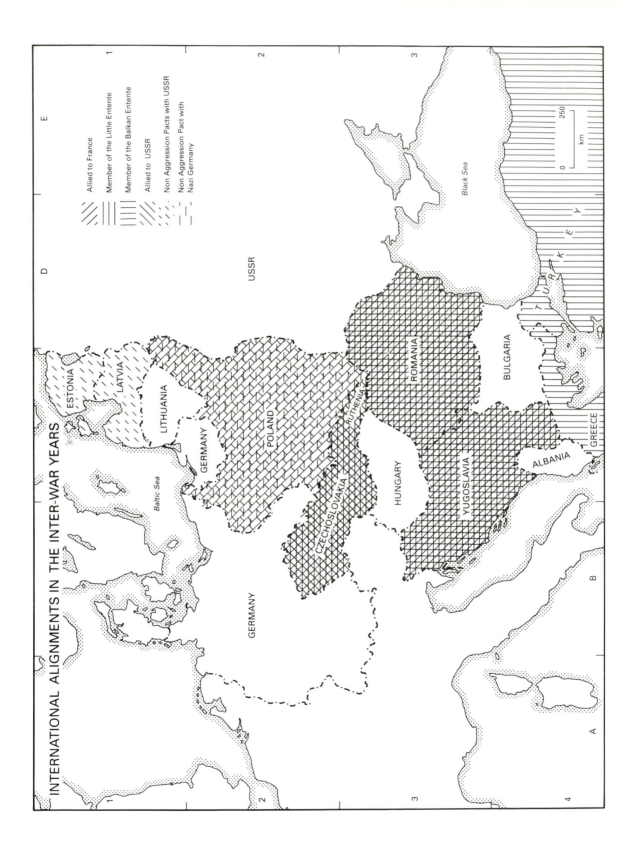

INTERNATIONAL ALIGNMENTS IN THE INTER-WAR YEARS

Allied to France
Member of the Little Entente
Member of the Balkan Entente
Allied to USSR
Non Aggression Pacts with USSR
Non Aggression Pact with Nazi Germany

0   250
km

ESTONIA
LATVIA
LITHUANIA
GERMANY
POLAND
USSR
CZECHOSLOVAKIA
RUTHENIA
HUNGARY
ROMANIA
YUGOSLAVIA
BULGARIA
ALBANIA
GREECE
TURKEY
Black Sea
Baltic Sea
GERMANY

3 THE INTER-WAR YEARS

International alignments in the inter-war years

Whilst the boundaries of the new Eastern Europe were being settled there were moves to ensure that the frontiers, once drawn, would remain secure. The hope was that the mechanisms of the League of Nations would prevent the outbreak of war, and there were also measures aimed at preventing tensions reaching such danger levels; the discontented states were not to be allowed to challenge the 1919–20 settlement. With Britain preoccupied with imperial obligations and the United States withdrawing into isolation, it fell to France to be the main guarantor of the new European system. She therefore concluded alliances with Poland, Czechoslovakia, Romania, and Yugoslavia. The three latter states came together in 1921 to form their own grouping, which rapidly became known as the 'little entente'.

The primary function of the little entente was to contain Hungarian revisionism. The little entente also made Czechoslovak possession of Ruthenia much more important in that this territory made the three allies contiguous. Nevertheless, the little entente never progressed much beyond the initial anti-revisionist alliance, failing to develop any really effective consultative bodies or to do much to foster trade between the allies.

The little entente depended greatly upon France but doubts over that power's commitment to its East European allies were felt even in the 1920s, especially after the Locarno pact of 1925 had guaranteed the Franco-German frontier. A German–Soviet friendship pact signed in

April 1926 also caused considerable alarm in Eastern Europe. As yet, however, the USSR showed no aggressive intent and the adoption of the first five-year plan and the drive to construct Soviet society and the Soviet economy forced Stalin to seek reassurances on his western borders. By 1932 he had signed non-aggression pacts with Estonia, Latvia and Poland, and had a trading agreement with Lithuania.

The advent of Hitler revolutionised diplomacy in Eastern Europe; revisionism seemed now to be a real possibility. The Polish government, losing faith in a France which was increasingly entrenched in its Maginot mentality, concluded a ten-year non-aggression pact with Nazi Germany in January 1934. In the same year Romania, Yugoslavia, Turkey and Greece signed the Balkan entente which was intended to guard the peninsula against encroachment by any great power. Plans for the incorporation of Bulgaria into the alliance, which the Yugoslav government in particular was keen to achieve, were stymied by Bulgaria's reluctance to recognise existing boundaries as permanent, the condition which the Romanians and Greeks stipulated for admitting her. In 1938 Bulgaria and Yugoslavia concluded a treaty of friendship.

In the meantime the USSR had been brought more into the Central and East European system with the Soviet–Czechoslovak alliance of May 1935. If Czechoslovakia were attacked, the treaty stipulated, the USSR would come to its aid as long as France also did so.

Hitler made much propaganda use of the

INTER-WAR INTERNATIONAL INCIDENTS AND DISPUTES

ESTONIA
Valga
LATVIA
Memel
LITHUANIA
Vilnius
USSR
Danzig
EAST PRUSSIA (GERMANY)
THE POLISH CORRIDOR
GERMANY
POLAND
SUDETENLAND
SILESIA
Teschen
CZECHOSLOVAKIA
SOUTHERN SLOVAKIA RUTHENIA
BESSARABIA
AUSTRIA
TRANSYLVANIA
HUNGARY
ROMANIA
ITALY
ISTRIA
Fiume
CROATIA
YUGOSLAVIA
DOBRUDJA
BULGARIA
ALBANIA
MACEDONIA
Petrich
TURKEY
EPIRUS
CORFU
GREECE
C

0   250
km

Soviet–Czechoslovak treaty and it did not deter him when he set out to dismember Czechoslovakia during 1938–9 (see p. 67). In destroying Czechoslovakia Hitler also wrecked the little entente. Britain and France made desperate efforts to build new alliances in Eastern Europe to fend off Nazi aggression, hoping that the USSR would be a partner in this enterprise. In August 1939 the Western powers were astounded when Hitler himself forged the infamous Nazi–Soviet pact. Its purpose was to deter Britain and France from coming to the aid of Poland and thus precipitating another European war. If it failed in this purpose the pact could serve as the instrument for the German–Soviet partition of Eastern Europe.

Inter-war international incidents and disputes

Despite the many problems created by the peace treaties in Eastern Europe, from 1921 to 1938 no East European state went to war with another. War, when it broke out, came, as in 1914, because the great European powers used East European issues to pursue their own policy goals.

Germany was inevitably involved in East European affairs both because of the large German minorities in the area, and because one part of Germany, East Prussia, was physically isolated from the remainder of the country. The 'Polish Corridor' was to become a subject of bitter dispute in the second half of the 1930s. At the same time Berlin began to campaign actively for the interests of the *Volksdeutscher*, those of German stock who lived outside the confines of the German state. Nowhere was this more important than in Czechoslovakia with its large concentration of Germans in the Sudetenland.

There was also a large German presence in Memel but this area had been seized by Lithuania in 1923 and there was relatively little German pressure on this question until 1939 when it was incorporated into Hitler's Reich. Pressure on another great German Baltic port, Danzig, had begun somewhat earlier. The peace settlement had placed this area under League of Nations administration with the Poles having rights to use the wharves and port facilities of the city. In Silesia the German minority made constant complaint at the alleged discrimination they suffered at the hands of the Poles.

The Poles and the Czechs could never mend their differences over Teschen. The Czechs had seized the area in 1919, but the allies had intervened and eventually decided that the Poles should have most of the city and the Czechs the surrounding area with its mineral reserves and vital rail link between the Czech lands and Slovakia.

There was no compromise on the dispute between the Poles and the Lithuanians over the Vilnius area, seized by the former in 1920. It remained a serious bone of contention between the two states throughout the inter-war period.

Of the defeated states Hungary maintained a constant vigil for its lost territories, an attitude which prevented any really close relations between Hungary and Romania because of Transylvania, between Hungary and Yugoslavia because of Croatia, and between Hungary and Czechoslovakia because of southern Slovakia and Ruthenia.

The peninsula of Istria, in particular the port of Fiume (Rijeka), was disputed by Yugoslavia and Italy, whilst Yugoslavia also had to face the threat of Bulgarian subversion in Macedonia. Greece, too, was threatened over this issue and the Internal Macedonian Revolutionary Organisation (IMRO) operated until 1934–35 virtually unhindered from its base at Petrich in Bulgaria.

The Bulgarian state was restrained in its pursuit of its Macedonian interests but was more assertive in its demands for the return of the Dobrudja, and even more clamorous for the implementation of article 48 of the Treaty of Neuilly which promised it economic access to the Aegean Sea. This claim was never granted.

Albania feared Yugoslav encroachment and, with more reason, Greek claims upon southern Albania or northern Epirus.

There were, however, successful efforts at the containment of these disputes. In 1925 the Greeks retaliated against yet another incursion from Petrich by sending troops into southern Bulgaria. The League of Nations intervened to arrange a withdrawal and compensation for Bulgaria. In the north, the League of Nations had enjoyed one of its very early successes when Estonia and Latvia agreed to the virtual partition of the disputed town of Valga (Valka).

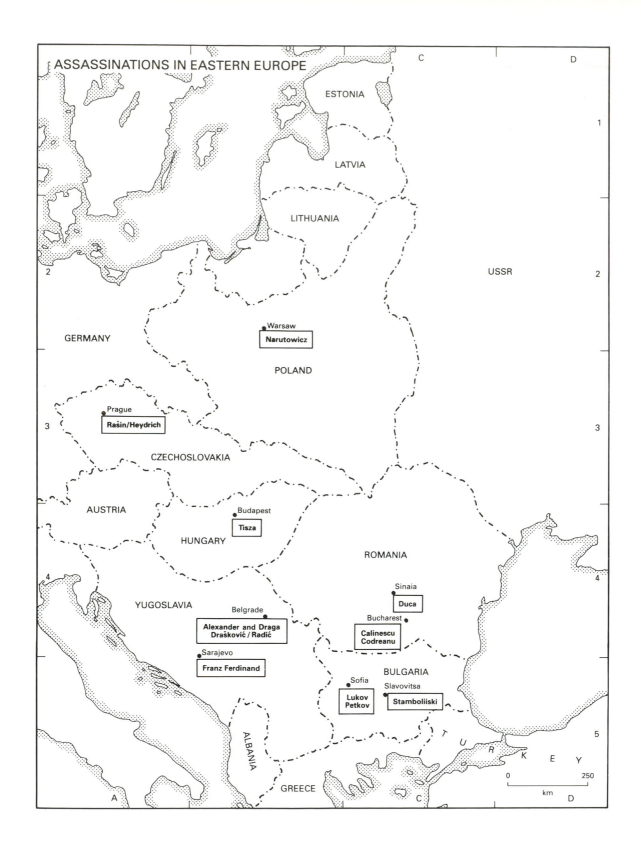

ASSASSINATIONS IN EASTERN EUROPE

ESTONIA

LATVIA

LITHUANIA

USSR

GERMANY

• Warsaw
Narutowicz

POLAND

• Prague
Rašin/Heydrich

CZECHOSLOVAKIA

AUSTRIA

• Budapest
Tisza

HUNGARY

ROMANIA

YUGOSLAVIA

• Sinaia
Duca

Belgrade •
**Alexander and Draga
Drašković / Radić**

Bucharest •
**Calinescu
Codreanu**

• Sarajevo
Franz Ferdinand

BULGARIA

• Sofia
**Lukov
Petkov**

Slavovitsa
Stamboliiski

ALBANIA

T
U
R
K
E
Y

GREECE

0   250
km

Assassinations in Eastern Europe

Alexander and Draga, King and Queen of Serbia. In June 1903 a military coup toppled the king and queen of Serbia in particularly brutal fashion. The Obrenović dynasty had traditionally followed a pro-Habsburg foreign policy. Their rivals, the Karadjcordjevićes, who now came to the throne, were more inclined towards Russia.

Petkov, Petko: prime minister of Bulgaria from summer 1906, murdered Sofia 27 February/11 March 1907 in an act of personal revenge.

Franz Ferdinand: Archduke and heir to the Habsburg throne. An advocate, at least for a time, of the administrative reconstruction of the empire on lines which would have given greater influence to Slavs. Murdered in Sarajevo by Bosnian extremists for south Slav union on 28 June 1914. The diplomatic crisis which followed culminated in the First World War.

Tisza, István: leader of Liberal Party which he renamed the Party of Work; prime minister of Hungary 1904–05, 1913–17; assassinated in his Budapest flat by soldiers on 31 October 1918.

Drašković, Milorad: Yugoslav minister of the interior after the First World War. In July 1921 he was assassinated by a communist. The murder was used to justify the suppression of the communists and the restriction of left-wing propaganda and activity.

Narutowicz, Gabriel: a scientist who became foreign minister of Poland in June 1922. In November 1922 he was elected president of Poland. However, extreme nationalists resented the fact that his nomination had been carried by the votes of non-Polish deputies. On 16 December 1922 he was assassinated by an extreme nationalist.

Rašin, Alois: Czechoslovak minister of finance who kept inflation at bay after the First World War; he was murdered in Prague in January 1923 by a communist student. He was the only prominent Czechoslovak politician to die at the hands of an assassin before the Second World War.

Stamboliiski, Aleksandûr: prime minister of Bulgaria from 1919, murdered June 1923 after a violent coup against his radical agrarian government. Stamboliiski's friendly attitude towards Yugoslavia had incurred the wrath of the Macedonian faction in Bulgaria, and other political groups feared he was about to impose one-party agrarian rule.

Radić, Stjepan: leader of the Croat People's Peasant Party and the dominant figure in Croat politics in post-First World War Yugoslavia. For the most part he refused any compromise with Belgrade. On 20 June 1928 he was shot in parliament by a Montenegrin deputy; he died seven weeks later.

Duca, Ion: leader of the Romanian Liberal Party appointed prime minister 14 November 1933. Assassinated by an Iron Guardist student, 30 December 1933. His removal strengthened the extreme right and the king.

Alexander, King of Yugoslavia was assassinated at Marseilles when on a visit to France on 9 October 1934. He had attempted to build a new Yugoslavia by down-playing all ethnic affiliations, and in 1929 imposed a centralised, authoritarian regime. The conspirators who murdered him had connections with both Croatian and Macedonian dissidents.

Codreanu, Zelea: leader of the Romanian fascist Iron Guards. He was arrested in April 1938 and garrotted on 29–30 November 1938; officially he died 'whilst attempting to escape'.

Calinescu, Armand: a close adviser to the king of Romania whom the Iron Guard held responsible for the death of their leader, Codreanu. Calinescu was killed in Bucharest by Guardists at the outbreak of European war in September 1939.

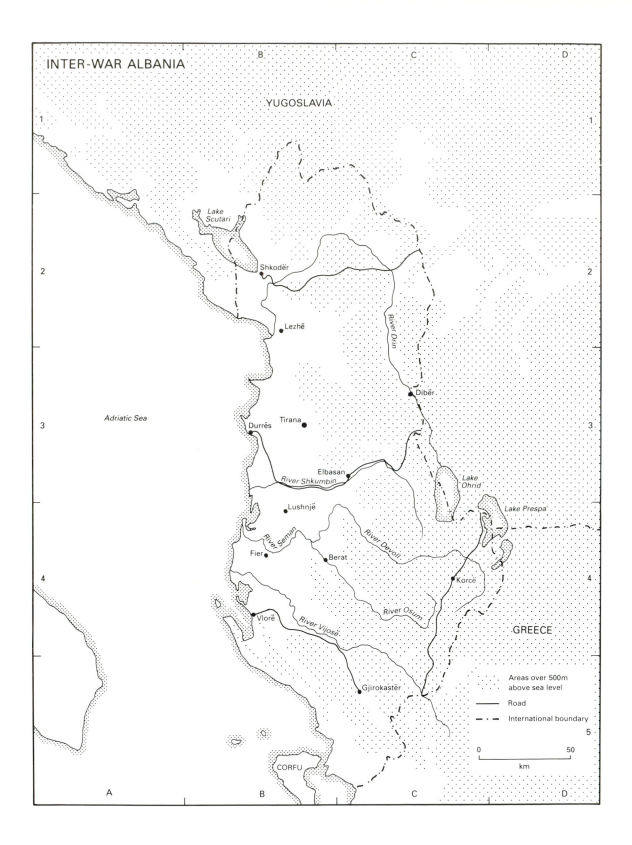

INTER-WAR ALBANIA

YUGOSLAVIA

Lake Scutari

Shkodër

Lezhë

Adriatic Sea

River Drin

Dibër

Durrës Tirana

Elbasan

River Shkumbin

Lake Ohrid

Lushnjë

Lake Prespa

River Seman

Fier Berat

River Devoll

Korcë

River Osum

Vlorë

River Vijosë

GREECE

Gjirokastër

Areas over 500m above sea level

Road

International boundary

CORFU

0   50
km

44

Heydrich, Reinhard: SS Obergruppenführer, appointed acting Protector of Bohemia and Moravia, September 1941, he presided over a tightening of Nazi controls in the Czech lands. On 27 May 1942 he was attacked by agents parachuted in from Britain; he died on 4 June. A personal favourite of Hitler, he was the highest-ranking Nazi to be killed by resistance forces in occupied Europe. The Nazis exacted a high price in vengeance, part of which was the systematic destruction of the village of Lidice and its inhabitants.

Lukov, General Ivan: Bulgarian minister of war, 1935 to 1938, and leader of a right-wing group. Assassinated in Sofia by left-wing extremists, February 1943.

Inter-war Albania

At the end of the First World War Albania was the least-developed country in Europe; the only working motorised vehicles in the country were three dilapidated Ford trucks left behind by allied troops, and four-fifths of the population were illiterate.

Albania was almost entirely cut off from the rest of the Balkans by the mountains which cover a large proportion of the country. Although some oil was extracted from the Berat region there had been little, if any, foreign investment; communications depended on roads which in many cases were no more than mule tracks over the mountains and which followed the rivers and therefore ran east–west rather than north–south, the direction which would have been far more beneficial to the evolution of political and economic unity and progress. Although both Durrës and Vlorë had potential as major ports there was little trade for them to carry. Tirana became the capital only after political stability had been established.

The first steps towards establishing that security came after the Lushnjë congress of February 1920 at which the Albanians secured the withdrawal of foreign forces and elaborated a scheme for Albania's future political structure. Real stability was not to be secured until the second half of the 1920s under the internal domination of Ahmed Zogu (after 1928, King Zog) and the growing external patronage of Italy. Zog attempted to modernise his kingdom and made some progress, particularly in the gradual replacement of tribal law by a unified, centrally determined national penal code.

A land act of 1930 was meant to limit individual holdings to forty hectares of arable land with additional amounts for the fifth and every subsequent member of the family, but the reform was ineffective and by the end of the 1930s little more than a thousand hectares had been redistributed, most of it to refugees from Kosovo.

Any attempt to meddle with the traditional tribal way of life met with resistance, and Zog also had to cope with the tensions created by the great economic depression, tensions which led to a serious rebellion in Fier in August 1935.

In 1936 Zog signed a financial agreement with Italy which greatly increased the latter's influence in Albania. Zog's marriage to a Hungarian countess in April 1938 produced a son and heir, but the founding of a dynasty was not enough to save Zog and his country from Mussolini's expansionist ambitions. In March 1939 Mussolini demanded the incorporation of Albania into Italy. The Albanians refused and on 7 April (Good Friday) 1939 Italian forces landed to enforce the Duce's will.

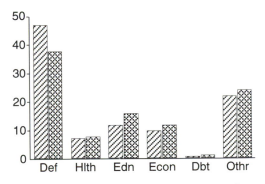

Figure 5 Budget expenditure, 1928/9, 1935/6 (%)

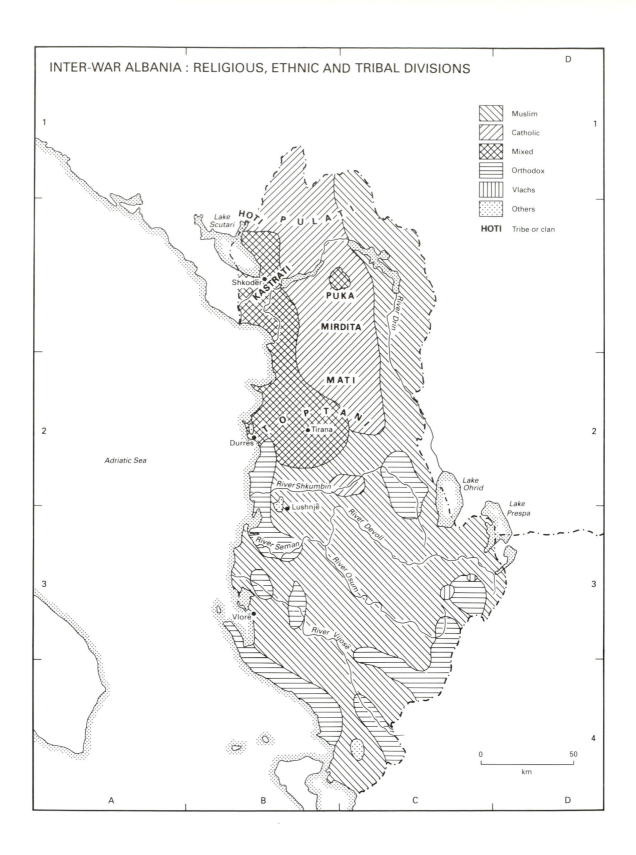

INTER-WAR ALBANIA : RELIGIOUS, ETHNIC AND TRIBAL DIVISIONS

Muslim

Catholic

Mixed

Orthodox

Vlachs

Others

HOTI Tribe or clan

Lake
Scutari

HOTI P U L A T I

Shkodër

KASTRATI

PUKA

MIRDITA

MATI

T O P T A N I

Durrës

Tirana

River Drin

Adriatic Sea

River Shkumbin

Lake
Ohrid

Lushnjë

River Devoll

Lake
Prespa

River Seman

River Osum

Vlorë

River Vijosë

0   50

km

Inter-war Albania: religious, ethnic and tribal divisions

Definitive and reliable ethnic statistics for inter-war Albania do not exist, not least because many Albanians did not understand the modern concept of ethnicity. Following the Ottoman pattern of classification they saw themselves as members of religious rather than ethnic groups and, following Albanian traditions, in the north they identified themselves primarily as members of a clan or a tribe. The map is based on a French military map drawn up in 1915; it drastically under-represents the Greek minority in the south of Albania. It must be assumed, though no accurate data are to hand, that many of those south of the rivers Seman and Osum who are depicted as 'Orthodox' were ethnic Greeks.

Religion was not something which weighed heavily upon Albanians. Many travellers describe the fondness of Muslim Albanians for swearing by Christian saints and for alcohol. There were few serious tensions between Muslims and Christians and Catholic–Orthodox clashes were few except where Catholic and Orthodox met near the Montenegrin border. The north had remained part of the Roman Church although the south aligned with Byzantium. In the fourteenth and fifteenth centuries the country was conquered by the Ottomans, following which many Albanian landowners, particularly in the relatively fertile central coastal plain, converted to Islam, primarily to retain their property; their tenants were also required to convert.

In the mountains of the north the social structure was dominated by the clans and tribes. A prominent feature of life in these areas was the blood feud. It, like many other aspects of clan and tribal custom, was regulated by the laws of Dukajin which dated back to the fourteenth century. Tribal rivalries had bedevilled any attempt to create a unified political entity, and did much to wreck the fragile hold on power 'enjoyed' by Albania's first modern ruler, Prince Wilhelm zu Wied, nominated by the great powers in 1913. Wied arrived in the spring of 1914 but was expelled soon after the outbreak of the First World War. His main opponent had been Esad Pasha, a prominent member of the Toptani tribe. The power of tribal custom was not broken by the First World War, which brought with it the occupation of much of the country by foreign troops. In February 1920 the Lushnjë congress met to secure the withdrawal of those troops and to draw up plans for Albania's future political system, but before the congress could convene there had to be a general *besa*, or suspension of all blood feuds.

Tribal loyalties remained important in the inter-war period even though King Zog, himself a member of the Mati tribe, did his best to weaken such traditionalism. After the Second World War the new rulers took much tougher measures, but many Albanian customs outlasted even the communists, and in 1990 there were reports of blood feuds in some northern areas.

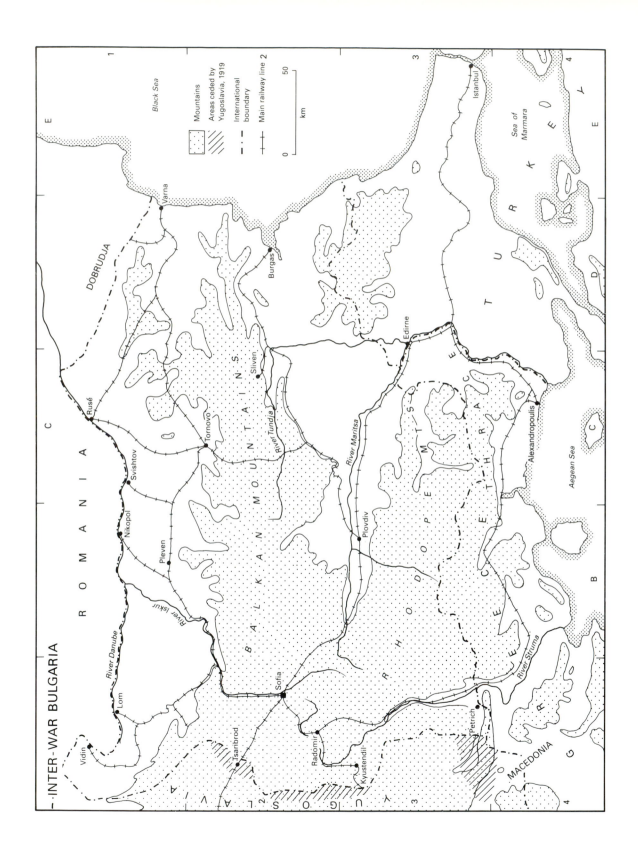

INTER-WAR BULGARIA

Mountains
Areas ceded by
Yugoslavia, 1919
International
boundary
Main railway line

0   50
km

Black Sea

DOBRUDJA

Varna

Burgas

E

Sliven

River Tundja

BALKAN MOUNTAINS

Rusé

Tornovo

Svishtov

Nikopol

Pleven

River Iskŭr

ROMANIA

River Danube

Lom

Vidin

C

Y U G O S L A V I A

Tsaribrod

Radomir

Kyustendil

Sofia

River Maritsa

Plovdiv

R H O D O P E M T S

W E S T E R N T H R A C E

Edirne

Istanbul

Sea of
Marmara

T U R K E Y

Alexandropoulis

Aegean Sea

Petrich

River Struma

G R E E C E

MACEDONIA

48

Inter-war Bulgaria

Shortly after the Salonika armistice of 28 September 1918 (see p. 33) a military rebellion at Radomir forced King Ferdinand to abdicate. He was replaced by his son, King Boris III.

Despite the change of monarch, Bulgaria retained the 1879 constitution. Until the mid-1930s, however, there was a constant threat of destabilisation because of the activities of Macedonian extremists who had established a virtual state within the state in the Petrich area. From here activists of the Internal Macedonian Revolutionary Organisation launched raids into Yugoslav and Greek Macedonia. Bulgaria had a long-standing interest in Macedonia, whose Slav population was regarded by most Bulgarians as part of the Bulgarian race. Before the First World War it had been hoped to build a railway to link Bulgaria with Macedonia but the Ottoman authorities had never granted the necessary permission; the line built to Kyustendil had been extended to the frontier but had never been able to cross it.

Immediately after the First World War Bulgaria saw a contest for power between the communists and the peasant party, the Bulgarian Agrarian National Union (BANU) led by Aleksandûr Stamboliiski. The latter emerged victorious in 1919–20 but after a spate of energetic reforms his government, which was showing increasing signs of moving towards a one-party state, was overthrown in an exceedingly violent coup in June 1923. More violence followed with a ham-fisted communist revolt in September 1923 and the blowing up of the Sveta Nedelya cathedral in Sofia by the communists in April 1925. Both these acts were used by the government to justify massive measures of repression against the left. After 1925, with the exception of a strong showing in the Sofia municipal elections in 1932 and of a strike amongst the traditionally militant tobacco workers in Plovdiv in 1935, little was heard of the left.

A coup in 1934 brought to power an authoritarian regime which was soon pushed aside by the king. By 1936 Boris III was in full control of the country. His internal rule has been described as 'controlled democracy'; it was never totalitarian but it included as much control as democracy. Boris did, however, seek to establish a new constitution, although his main preoccupation was with foreign affairs.

Until the mid-1930s the chief objective of Bulgarian foreign policy had been to secure the implementation of article 48 of the Treaty of Neuilly (see p. 37). Failure in this regard meant that Bulgaria's external trade was forced to rely on the Black Sea ports of Varna and Burgas, and on the rail lines to the Danubian harbours of Vidin, Lom, Svishtov and Rusé, as well as the international trunk line northwards to Niš, Belgrade and the centre of Europe. By the time he seized complete control of affairs Boris had become convinced that the major issue was now avoiding involvement in the war which would inevitably descend upon Europe.

When it did so he maintained Bulgarian neutrality, even refusing an offer of territorial aggrandisement in return for helping the Italians in their attack on Greece. But when Germany decided to attack Greece Boris could no longer withstand Berlin's pressure. He decided that the only way to preserve some of Bulgaria's independence was to join Hitler's tripartite pact and to sanction the use of Bulgarian territory for the German attack on Greece. In March 1941 Bulgaria joined the Axis powers.

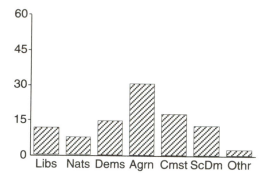

Figure 6 National Assembly 1919 (% votes)

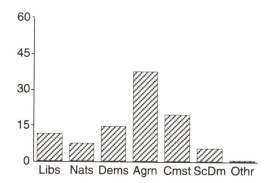

Figure 7 National Assembly 1920 (% votes)

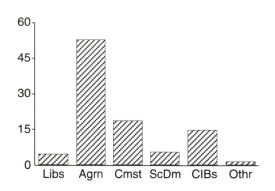

Figure 8 National Assembly, April 1923 (% votes)

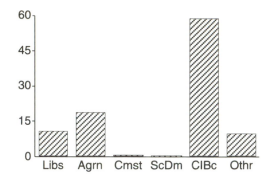

Figure 9 National Assembly, Nov. 1923 (% votes)

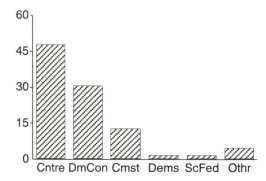

Figure 10 National Assembly 1931 (% votes)

Note Voting percentages given in Figures 6–10 for Liberals, Nationalists and Democrats refer to groups of parties

Inter-war Bulgaria: political

The elections of 1919 and 1920 in Bulgaria were in effect three-cornered fights between the pre-war, or established, political groups, the agrarians and the socialist left. The agrarians of the Bulgarian Agrarian National Union (BANU) had been growing in strength since 1908, and the socialists, particularly the leftists, were greatly encouraged by the victory of Bolshevism in Russia.

The established parties were largely blamed for the sufferings brought about by the First World War. A further problem for them was that few were national or mass parties but largely Sofia-based intelligentsia groups. Nor were they united. The liberal factions differed greatly, frequently on personal issues, and there was considerable tension between the National Liberals and, for example, the Progressive Liberals. The largest of the liberal groups was the Progressive Liberals who took 5.66 per cent of the vote in 1919 and 5.08 per cent in 1920; the National Liberals took 4.22 per cent and 4.32 percent. Before the First World War, of the established groups, the Democratic Party had been the most consistently critical of ruling administrations and for this reason it survived the war slightly better than the other parties.

The established parties were driven together after 1920 by increasing fears that Stamboliiski would overthrow the constitution and establish a one-party, agrarian dictatorship, one sign of which was the abolition of proportional representation and the reintroduction of single-member constituencies. With the exception of some Liberal factions the established parties formed the Constitutional Bloc (ClBc) to fight the election of April 1923.

At the end of the First World War it had seemed that political power would lie with either the agrarians or the socialists. The latter had split in 1903, the leftist faction forming itself into the Bulgarian Communist Party (BCP) in 1919, and the moderates constituting the Social Democratic Party (SDP). The communists had spurned an alliance with the agrarians from 1918–19 and the two groups fought a bitter battle, particularly when prime minister Stamboliiski used tough methods to suppress a general strike fomented by the communists late in 1919. In the 1920 elections Stamboliiski had been disappointed not to secure an absolute majority and therefore declared the returns of a number of opposition deputies invalid, their removal giving the agrarians control of the assembly. After three years of hectic reform, and considerable corruption, a combination of the army, the Macedonian extremists, and the established parties brought about a coup in June 1923 in which Stamboliiski and many of his adherents were murdered. The agrarians never recovered their unity or their strength of purpose.

The BCP's share of the vote before November 1923 remained steady at 18–20 per cent, but after the spectacularly unsuccessful uprising of September 1923 it was compromised and after the bomb outrage in Sveta Nedelya cathedral in 1925 (see p. 49) it was banned. It reappeared as the Bulgarian Workers' Party and did surprisingly well in municipal elections in 1932.

The Democratic Concord (DmCon) formed after the violence of 1923 and 1925 imposed tough controls on political life. These were relaxed somewhat during the early 1930s and the election of 1931 was a rare opportunity for Bulgarians to vote freely. The Centrist alliance which emerged as the strongest group consisted of some agrarians together with three of the established parties: the Democrats, the National Liberals, and the Radicals. Some Democrats broke away and fought the election alone. The Socialist Federation (ScFed) was a weak combination of various factions lacking in organisation, policy or leadership. It was massively overshadowed by the communists.

The coup of May 1934 put an end to real parliamentary life in Bulgaria in effect until 1990.

Table 2 Population by ethnicity, 1920 and 1934

	1920		1934	
Bulgarian	4,041,276	83.4	5,274,854	86.8
Turkish	542,904	11.2	618,268	10.2
Greeks	46,759	1.0	9,601	0.1
Gypsy	61,555	1.3	80,532	1.3
Jewish	41,927	0.8	28,026	0.5
Russians	9,247	0.2	11,928	0.2
Others	103,303	2.1	54,730	0.9
Total	4,846,971	100.0	6,077,939	100.0

Table 3 Population by religion, 1920 and 1934

	1920		1934	
Orthodox	4,061,829	83.8	5,128,890	84.4
Muslim	690,734	14.3	821,298	13.5
Rom. Catholic	34,072	0.7	45,704	0.8
Protestant	5,617	0.1	8,371	0.1
Jewish	43,232	0.9	48,398	0.8
Armenian-Gregorian	10,848	0.2	23,476	0.4
Others	639	0.0	1,802	0.0
Total	4,846,971	100.0	6,077,939	100.0

Inter-war Bulgaria: ethnic and religious composition

Bulgaria remained overwhelmingly a Bulgarian and an Orthodox state during the inter-war period. Its largest minority was the Turkish. When Bulgaria had declared its full independence from the Ottoman Sultan in 1908 a number of legal problems had been created with regard to the status of Muslims and of Muslim property, particularly of the *vakufs*, or Muslim cultural and charitable institutions financed by land or monies left in wills. The Balkan and First World Wars delayed action to simplify the situation and clarification did not come until legislation was passed in 1919. This gave wide-ranging rights to the Muslims to educate their children in Turkish and in the 1920s, when Turkey itself was ruled by the reforming and modernising Kemal Atatürk, this was welcomed – especially by the more conservative practitioners of Islam. After the coup of 1934 there was more pressure on Turks to adopt Bulgarian names and to use the Bulgarian language; of the 2,091 changes in topographical names in Bulgaria between 1920 and 1935 more than nine out of ten occurred in 1934. These pressures, together with a series of minor outrages such as the desecration of a Muslim cemetery, encouraged a certain amount of emigration from Bulgaria to Turkey and the total number of Turks therefore declined in the second half of the 1930s. In 1940, however, when Bulgaria acquired the southern Dobrudja from Romania 130,000 more Turks were brought within the Bulgarian state, together with a number of Tartars.

The Greeks declined in numbers following population exchange treaties in the early 1920s; the Greeks had previously lived mainly in and near Plovdiv and along the Black Sea coast. Until the early twentieth century relations between Bulgaria and Greece had generally been good but the excitements caused by national rivalry over Macedonia and concerning jurisdiction over a number of churches in Bulgaria itself had led to a series of attacks on Greek religious institutions and communities in 1906. The war years, 1912–18, exacerbated many of these tensions as a result of which the Greek and Bulgarian governments signed a Convention Respecting Mutual Emigration in November 1919. In the 1920s nearly 50,000 Greeks left Bulgaria under the terms of the convention.

The number of Russians in Bulgaria increased after 1920 as a consequence of the settlement in the country of refugees from the Russian civil war, a large portion of them arriving with General Wrangel's defeated army. The decline in those registering as Jewish was the result of a change in census definition from 'mother tongue' to 'language of usual discourse'. The number of Muslims is larger than that of ethnic Turks because many Gypsies were Muslim, but the difference also reveals the existence of the 'Pomaks' or Bulgarian-speaking Muslims.

In general, official Bulgarian policies towards the non-Bulgarian minorities were moderate. The exception was the regime brought to power by the coup of May 1934, but even here the assimilationist policies which were adopted owed less to a sense of racial or ethnic superiority than to a desire for rationalisation and centralisation.

The official statistics do not reveal any information as to the number of Macedonians. Bulgarian governments did not recognise Macedonian as a separate language or the Macedonians as a different ethnic group. Most of the thousands of refugees who entered Bulgaria from Greek and Yugoslav Macedonia shared this view, but there were some who did not, and their belief that they were ethnic Macedonians rather than Bulgarians was shared by an unknown proportion of the inhabitants of south-western Bulgaria.

Inter-war Bulgaria: economic and social

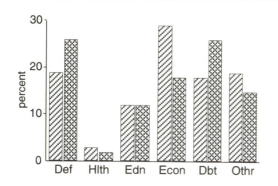

Figure 11 Budget expenditure, 1924, 1938

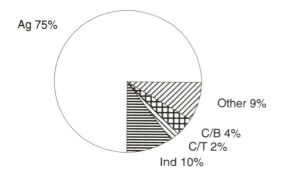

Figure 12 Population by economic sector, 1934

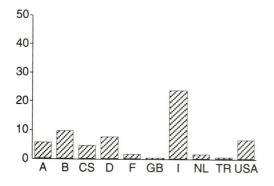

Figure 13 Distribution of trade, 1920 (% value)

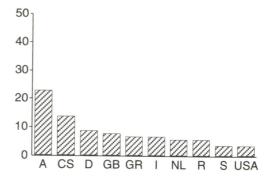

Figure 14 Distribution of trade, 1925 (% value)

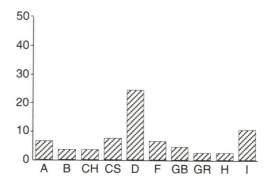

Figure 15 Distribution of trade, 1930 (% value)

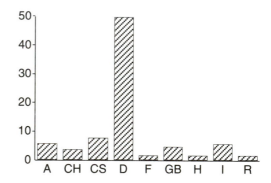

Figure 16 Distribution of trade, 1935 (% value)

Inter-war Bulgaria: landholdings

Bulgaria was the quintessential small peasant proprietor society. The average size of holdings was low even by East European standards, though it was often depressed by the parcellisation of landholdings into dispersed strips; some of these, acquired by marriage, might be in villages different from that in which the property-holder lived. The area of land owned by individual proprietors was not the same, therefore, as the size of holding. Nevertheless, parcellisation was a problem which was tackled by attempts at commassation, or bringing scattered strips together into compact holdings. As in other countries, the larger holdings constituted a larger proportion of the land than they represented as a total number of the holdings; but in Bulgaria this difference was much less marked in the larger holdings than it was in other countries. This was primarily because there were very few holdings above 30 hectares, and this in turn was in part the result of the loss of the southern Dobrudja in 1913.

In the inter-war years the Bulgarian budget was increasingly strained by debt obligations most of

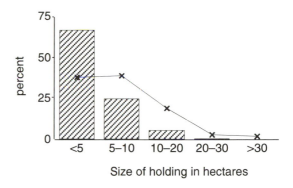

Figure 17 Landholdings: size and area

which arose from loans concluded before 1914. The country remained overwhelmingly agricultural and the 75 per cent figure for 1934 (see Figure 12, p. 54) is an underestimate in that many of those classified as employed in industry also worked small plots of land. In trade Germany had, by the beginning of the 1930s, already established a preponderance which was to be consolidated as the decade progressed.

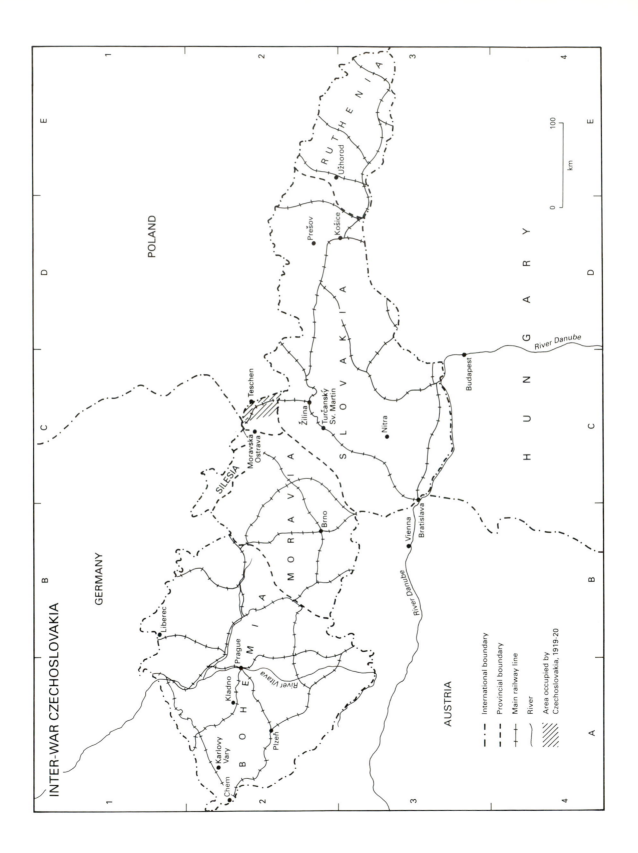

INTER-WAR CZECHOSLOVAKIA

GERMANY

POLAND

AUSTRIA

HUNGARY

B O H E M I A

M O R A V I A

SILESIA

S L O V A K I A

R U T H E N I A

Chem

Karlovy
Vary

Plzeň

Kladno

Prague

River Vltava

Liberec

Brno

Moravská
Ostrava

Teschen

Žilina

Turčanský
Sv. Martin

Nitra

Vienna

Bratislava

River Danube

River Danube

Budapest

Prešov

Košice

Užhorod

River Danube

International boundary

Provincial boundary

Main railway line

River

Area occupied by
Czechoslovakia, 1919-20

100

km

0

Inter-war Czechoslovakia

The new state of Czechoslovakia had four main constituent elements. The dominant one was that formed by the former Austrian provinces of Bohemia and Moravia/Silesia where the Czechs had evolved sophisticated and competent economic and political cadres.

The Slovaks spoke a language very near but clearly distinct from Czech and the Slovak counties had been part of the Hungarian crown for nine centuries. Slovak social, political and economic experience had therefore been very different from that of the Czechs. Education in Slovak, outside private, mostly Protestant, schools, was minimal; there were few officials competent in Slovak and industrial development depended on subsidies from Budapest. In Slovakia the strongest social, cultural and political force was the Roman Catholic Church to which all but 17 per cent of Slovaks belonged. Its chief Slovak centre was at Nitra. The Slovaks in 1918 had little choice but to unite with the Czechs and those of their leaders who were in Slovakia agreed to do this at a meeting in Turčanský Sväty Martin in May 1918. Emigres in Pittsburgh confirmed that decision shortly afterwards.

Ruthenia was even more backward than Slovakia. Here the predominant force was again ecclesiastical, but this time the Greek Catholic (Uniate) Church.

The fourth and smallest element in the new state was the area near Teschen. Claimed by both Czechoslovakia and Poland, it had particular importance for the former because the one major railway linking Bohemia-Moravia to Slovakia ran through it. The Czechs seized the whole area in 1919 during the Russo-Polish war; the great powers awarded most of the city to Poland, and the surrounding territory (with the railway line) to Czechoslovakia.

Teschen was not the only area where the new state found its authority contested. In the spring of 1919 there were attempts by radical Hungarians to repossess Slovakia and Ruthenia; under their tutelage a short-lived soviet republic was established in Prešov.

The years 1919–20 saw social unrest throughout the new republic. The economic consequences of the territorial changes in Europe were profound. Bohemian industry no longer had access to markets and sources of raw materials in the same state; Slovak industry lost its subsidies; the railway systems were focused more on Vienna and Budapest than on Prague and Bratislava, and there were the problems of demobilisation and the return to peacetime production. The worst of the unrest was in the Kladno coalfield in late 1920 when thirteen miners were killed.

Czechoslovakia was saved from revolution by land reform which gave the peasants what they wanted; by a split in the socialist party which weakened the extremists who formed the Czechoslovak Communist Party; and by the announcement of the remaining politicians that, in the face of the social crisis, 'We have agreed that we shall agree.'

This was the beginning of the consensus which lasted in Czechoslovakia until the mid-1930s. It was based upon the political parties' willingness to compromise and accommodate one another in coalitions; upon strong discipline and control by all parties over their members; and upon the unofficial consultations between political leaders which became a regular feature of Czechoslovak affairs.

In the 1920s the habits of consensus spread to include ethnic as well as political cooperation. Immediately after the end of the war the Germans who lived along the northern and western borders of Bohemia (the Sudetenland) refused to participate in the political life of the state, but by 1925 attitudes had softened and in that year two German parties agreed to enter a new coalition then being established.

This happy state of affairs could not survive the great depression and the rise of militant German nationalism in the 1930s.

Table 4 Parliamentary elections, April 1920

Party	Chamber of Deputies		Senate	
	Votes (%)	Seats	Votes (%)	Seats
Czech National Democrat	6.2	19	6.8	10
Czech Small Trader	2.0	6	2.1	3
Czech and Slovak People's	11.3	33	11.9	18
Czech Agrarian	9.7	28	10.1	14
Slovak Agrarian	3.9	12	3.5	6
Czech National Socialist	8.1	24	7.1	10
Czech Progressive Socialist	0.9	3	0.1	0
Czechoslovak Social Democrat	25.7	74	28.1	41
German National Socialist	5.3	15	5.7	8
German Democrat	1.7	5	2.3	3
German Christian Social	3.5	10	2.7	4
German Agrarian	3.9	11	4.0	6
German Social Democrat	11.1	31	11.4	16
Magyar Christian Social	2.2	5	1.9	2
Magyar Agrarian	0.4	1	0.8	1
Magyar Social Democrat	1.8	4	0	0
Jewish List	1.3	0	1.1	0
Others	1.0	0	0.4	0
Total	100.0	281*	100.0	142

Note: *The Czechoslovak Legions from Siberia elected four deputies: two Czech National Socialist, one Czech Social Democrat and one Czech Agrarian.

The elections to the Chamber of Deputies were held on 18 April and those to the Senate on 25 April.

Table 5 Parliamentary elections, November 1925

Party	Chamber of Deputies		Senate	
	Votes (%)	Seats	Votes (%)	Seats
Czech National Democrat	4.0	13	4.2	7
Czech Small Trader	4.0	13	4.2	6
Czech People's	9.7	31	10.1	16
Slovak People's	6.9	23	6.9	12
Czechoslovak Agrarian	13.7	45	13.8	23
Czech National Socialist	8.6	28	8.5	14
Czechoslovak Social Democrat	8.9	29	8.8	14
German Nationalist	3.4	10	3.5	5
German National Socialist	2.4	7	2.3	3
German Christian Social	4.4	13	4.7	7
German and Magyar Agrarian	8.0	24	8.3	12
German Social Democrat	5.8	17	6.0	9
Magyar Christian Social	1.4	4	1.4	2
Polish List	0.4	1	0.4	0
Jewish List	1.6	0	0.9	0
Communist	13.2	41	12.7	20
Ruthene Autonomist	0.5	1	0.5	0
Others	3.1	0	2.8	0
Total	100.0	300	100.0	150

Note: Both elections were held on 15 November 1925.

Inter-war Czechoslovakia: political

Under the Czechoslovak constitution drafted in 1918 and given full confirmation ten years later, the head of state was a president elected every seven years. The office was held by Tomás Masaryk from 1918 to 1935 and by Eduard Beneš from 1935 to 1938.

The legislature consisted of a Senate of 150 members and a Chamber of Deputies twice that size. All adults were to have the vote which was to be direct, secret and compulsory. There was to be proportional representation and this was so contrived that votes could be redistributed on ethnic as well as on party political lines.

The party machines were the most powerful political factor in inter-war Czechoslovakia. The large parties were strong because they were the employers of their parliamentary representatives and because they dispensed patronage in the form of jobs; government departments tended to be allotted to particular parties in coalitions and thus in the railways, for example, most employees were members or supporters of the Czechoslovak Social Democratic Party.

The main parties were the Czechoslovak Social Democratic Party (CSSDP) which had been formed from the Czech and Slovak parties in 1919 but had split the following year, the extremists forming the Communist Party of Czechoslovakia (CPCS). Because, until 1935, the international communist movement favoured decentralisation or even the dismemberment of multi-national states the CPCS's main support came from Slovakia and Ruthenia.

The split meant that the CSSDP was no longer the largest party, that position being taken in 1922 by the Czechoslovak Agrarian Party, formed in that year from a merger of the Czech and Slovak peasant parties. The National Democratic Party (NDP) had been the main representative of Czech interests in the Austrian parliament before 1918 and had assumed power in November of that year but it declined in importance thereafter. The Czechoslovak National Socialists bore no resemblance to their later German namesake. The Czech People's Party represented Catholic interests in Bohemia and Moravia. The Slovak People's Party (after 1925 named after its leader, the Hlinka Slovak People's Party, HSPP) was the largest party in Slovakia and led the increasingly strong campaign for greater autonomy in that area. There were also nationally based agrarian parties for the Germans and Hungarians, as well as the German Christian Socials and the German National Socialists. Smaller parties represented the fringes; such as the fascists, or sectional interests, for example the Tradesmen's Party; or specific lobbies, such as the demand for the abolition of fixed-lists in the electoral process.

From 1922 to 1926 the ruling coalition was a 'red–green' alliance of agrarians and social democrats but this fell apart because of disagreement over the question of agricultural tariffs. In the elections of 1925 the HSPP's strong showing reflected Slovak discontent with the previous government's attitude to the Catholic Church. The coalition constructed in 1926 included the HSPP as well as two German parties; it was the only one in inter-war Czechoslovakia from which the CSSDP was absent. The presence of the HSPP brought about local government reform and an agreement with the Catholic Church but by 1929 there were severe tensions, primarily because of extremist activity in Slovakia.

In the 1929 elections the HSPP vote declined and thereafter they left the cabinet never to return. The new government was politically broader but ethnically narrower than its predecessor, being Czech–Czechoslovak–German rather than Czech–Czechoslovak–Slovak–German. Its efforts were concentrated on dealing with the effects of the great depression.

In 1935 the elections showed little change in the Czech and Slovak votes but seismic shifts in the German. The consequences of this were to dominate the remaining years of Czechoslovakia's First Republic.

Table 6 Parliamentary elections, October 1929

Party	Chamber of Deputies		Senate	
	Votes (%)	Seats	Votes (%)	Seats
Czech National Democrat	4.9	15	5.0	8
Czech Small Trader	3.9	12	4.3	6
Czech People's	8.4	25	8.7	13
Slovak People's	5.7	19	5.9	9
Czechoslovak Agrarian	15.0	46	15.2	24
Czech National Socialist	10.4	32	10.3	16
Czechoslovak Social Democrat	13.0	39	13.0	20
Anti-Fixed List Voting	1.0	3	0.8	1
German Nationalist	2.5	7	2.6	0
German National Socialist	2.8	8	2.6	4
German Christian Social	4.7	14	4.9	8
German and Magyar Agrarian	5.4	16	5.6	9
German Social Democrat	6.9	21	6.9	11
Magyar Christian Social	3.5	9	3.6	6
Polish and Jewish Lists	1.4	4	0.4	0
Communist	10.2	30	10.0	15
Ruthene Autonomist	0	0	0	0
Others	0.3	0	0.2	0
Total	100.0	300	100.0	150

Note: Both elections were held on 27 October 1929.

Table 7 Parliamentary elections, May 1935

Party	Chamber of Deputies		Senate	
	Votes (%)	Seats	Votes (%)	Seats
Czech National Democrat and Fascist	5.6	17	5.6	9
Czech Small Trader	5.4	17	5.4	8
Czech People's	7.5	22	7.7	11
Slovak People's Alliance*	6.9	22	6.8	11
Czechoslovak Agrarian	14.3	45	14.3	23
Czech National Socialist	9.2	28	9.3	14
Czechoslovak Social Democrat	12.6	38	12.5	20
Czech Fascist (Gajda)	2.0	6	2.0	0
Sudetendeutsch Partei	15.2	44	15.0	23
German Christian Social	2.0	6	2.1	3
German Agrarian	1.7	5	1.8	0
German Social Democrat	3.6	11	3.7	6
Magyar Christian Social	3.5	9	3.6	6
Communist	10.3	30	10.2	16
Others	0.2	0	0	0
Total	100.0	300	100.0	150

Note: *An alliance of Slovak People's Party, Slovak Nationalists, Ruthene Autonomists and Polish Parties.
Both elections were held on 19 May 1935.

Inter-war Czechoslovakia: ethnic composition

Table 8 Population by ethnicity

Nationality	1921		1930	
	Total number	*%*	*Total number*	*%*
Czechoslovak	8,760,937	65.51	9,688,770	66.91
Ruthene	461,849	3.45	549,169	3.79
German	3,123,568	23.36	3,231,688	22.32
Magyar	745,431	5.57	691,923	4.78
Polish	75,853	0.57	81,737	0.57
Jewish	180,855	1.35	186,642	1.29
Other	25,871	0.19	49,636	0.34
Total	13,374,364	100.00	14,479,565	100.00

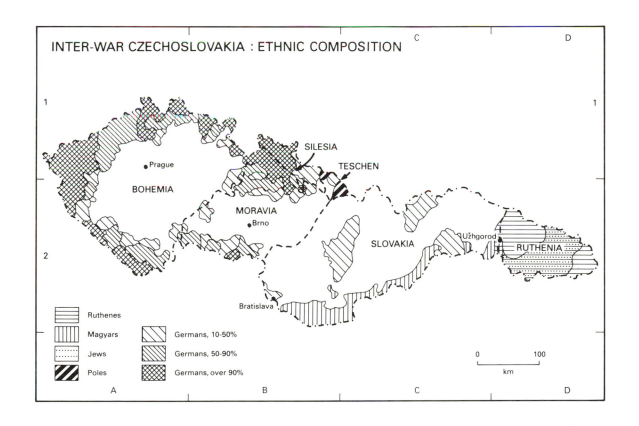

61

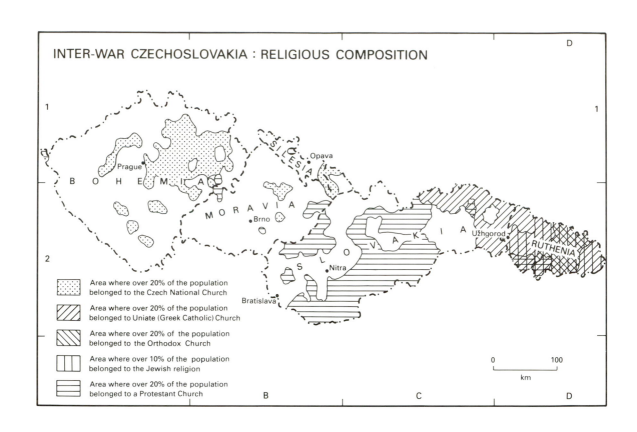

INTER-WAR CZECHOSLOVAKIA : RELIGIOUS COMPOSITION

Area where over 20% of the population belonged to the Czech National Church

Area where over 20% of the population belonged to Uniate (Greek Catholic) Church

Area where over 20% of the population belonged to the Orthodox Church

Area where over 10% of the population belonged to the Jewish religion

Area where over 20% of the population belonged to a Protestant Church

Table 9 Inter-war Czechoslovakia, population by religion

Denomination	1921		1930	
	Total number	*Percentage*	*Total number*	*Percentage*
Roman Catholic	10,384,833	76.29	10,831,696	73.54
Uniate	535,543	3.93	585,041	3.97
Bohemian Brethren	233,868	1.72	297,977	2.02
Lutheran	535,382	3.93	586,775	3.99
Calvinist	207,906	1.53	219,108	1.49
Other Protestant	13,163	0.09	25,898	0.18
Orthodox	73,097	0.54	145,598	0.99
Czech National	525,333	3.86	793,385	5.39
Old Catholic	20,255	0.15	22,712	0.15
Jewish	354,342	2.60	356,830	2.42
Others	2,824	0.02	8,252	0.05
No religion	724,507	5.32	854,638	5.80
Unknown	2,119	0.02	1,626	0.01
Total	13,613,172	100.00	14,729,536	100.00

Inter-war Czechoslovakia: religious composition

In almost all areas of the country, except Ruthenia, where the Uniates predominated, the majority of the population were Roman Catholic.

The National Church had been founded in 1919 because many Czechs considered the Roman Catholic Church had been too closely associated with the Habsburgs. Of the Protestants the Bohemian Brethren were mostly Czech, the Lutherans were Slovak and German, and the Calvinists Magyar. A notable feature of the Czechoslovak religious situation was that the second largest category was that of non-believer.

Many of the 17 per cent of the Slovaks who were Protestant were from the German minority and many had been enthusiastic advocates of a close relationship with the Czechs. There were, however, Catholics who, initially at least, adopted a similar line, including Andrej Hlinka whose political influence in Slovakia was so great that after 1925 the large Slovak People's Party was generally known as Hlinka's Slovak People's Party (HSPP).

Religious issues could play an important part in Czechoslovak political life. The Slovaks were generally suspicious of anti-clericalism in Prague, and in 1925 there was particular anger at plans to make Jan Hus's day of martyrdom a national holiday; Hus represented the great Czech humanist and reforming traditions which culminated in the Reformation, but he had been burnt at the stake in 1415 as a heretic and Slovak Catholics had little inclination to honour one so condemned by their church. In the coalition of 1926–29 a number of concessions were made to Catholic opinion, including the signing of an agreement between the government in Prague and the Vatican.

In the 1930s the central authorities needlessly offended Hlinka by excluding him from the celebrations held in August 1933 to mark the 1,100th anniversary of the founding of the Christian church in Slovakia. Hlinka gate-crashed and in doing so increased yet further his popularity in Slovakia. Hlinka died in 1938 but he was not the last cleric to lead the Slovaks. The head of the Slovak independent state established in 1939 was Mgr Jozef Tiso who proclaimed that the new state had been established on the principle of 'Christian Solidarism'.

The anniversary celebrations in 1933 had been held in Nitra which was the senior Slovak bishopric. Until 1935, however, all Slovak bishoprics were subject to the ecclesiastical jurisdiction of an archbishop whose seat was at Esztergom in Hungary.

Inter-war Czechoslovakia: size of landholdings

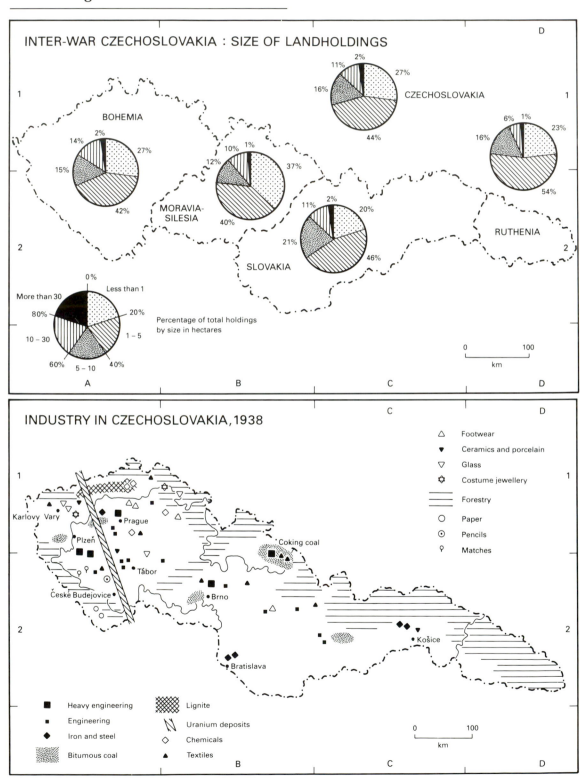

INTER-WAR CZECHOSLOVAKIA : SIZE OF LANDHOLDINGS

CZECHOSLOVAKIA

2%
11%
16%
27%
44%

BOHEMIA

2%
14%
15%
27%
42%

MORAVIA-SILESIA

10% 1%
12%
37%
40%

6% 1%
16%
23%
54%

RUTHENIA

SLOVAKIA

11% 2%
21%
20%
46%

0%
More than 30   Less than 1
80%   20%
10 – 30   1 – 5
60%   5 – 10   40%

Percentage of total holdings
by size in hectares

0   100
km

A   B   C   D

INDUSTRY IN CZECHOSLOVAKIA, 1938

△ Footwear
▼ Ceramics and porcelain
▽ Glass
✿ Costume jewellery
▬ Forestry
○ Paper
⊙ Pencils
⚲ Matches

Karlovy Vary
Prague
Plzeň
Coking coal
Tábor
České Budějovice
Brno
Košice
Bratislava

■ Heavy engineering   Lignite
▪ Engineering   ⩘ Uranium deposits
◆ Iron and steel   ◇ Chemicals
   Bitumous coal   ▲ Textiles

0   100
km

B   C   D

64

Inter-war Czechoslovakia: economic

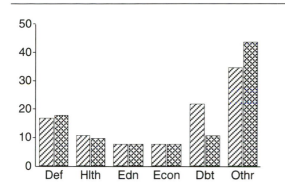

Figure 18 Budget expenditure, 1924, 1934 (%)

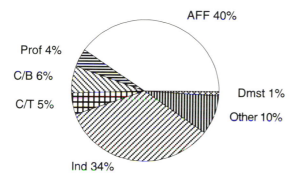

Figure 19 Population by economic sector, 1921

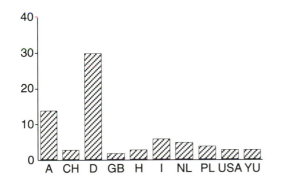

Figure 20 Distribution of trade, 1923 (% value)

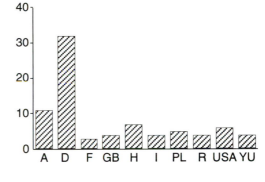

Figure 21 Distribution of trade, 1927 (% value)

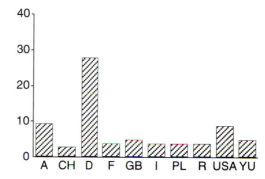

Figure 22 Distribution of trade, 1932 (% value)

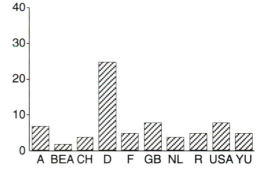

Figure 23 Distribution of trade, 1936 (% value)

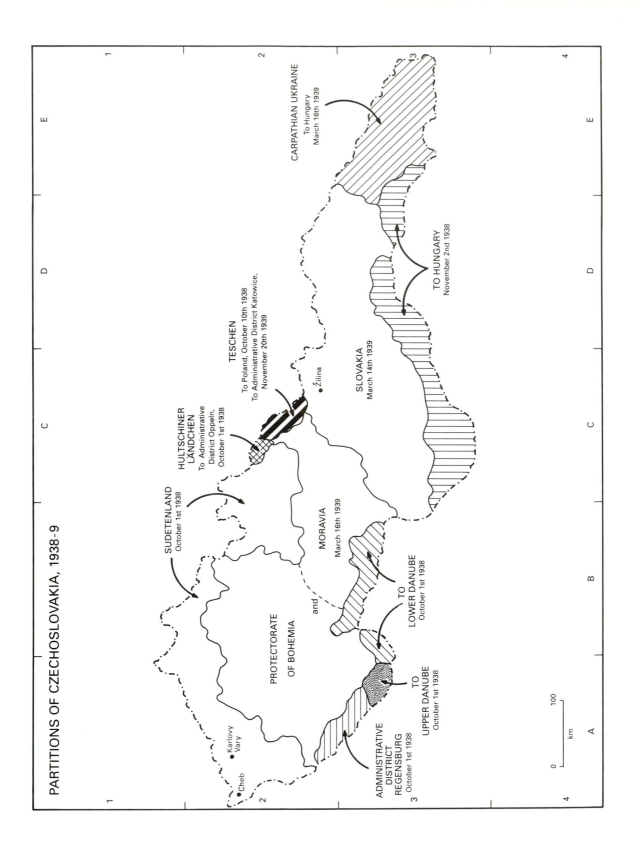

PARTITIONS OF CZECHOSLOVAKIA, 1938-9

SUDETENLAND
October 1st 1938

HULTSCHINER
LÄNDCHEN
To Administrative
District Oppeln,
October 1st 1938

TESCHEN
To Poland, October 10th 1938
To Administrative District Katowice,
November 20th 1939

• Žilina

CARPATHIAN UKRAINE
To Hungary
March 16th 1939

SLOVAKIA
March 14th 1939

TO HUNGARY
November 2nd 1938

PROTECTORATE
OF BOHEMIA

and

MORAVIA
March 16th 1939

TO
LOWER DANUBE
October 1st 1938

TO
UPPER DANUBE
October 1st 1938

ADMINISTRATIVE
DISTRICT
REGENSBURG
October 1st 1938

• Karlovy
Vary

• Cheb

0   100
km

The partition of Czechoslovakia, 1938–9

Slovak demands for autonomy had been growing since the late 1920s. They reached their apogee in the so-called Whitsun programme which formed the basis of the third Slovak autonomy bill presented to the Chamber of Deputies in Prague in August 1938. On 22 September President Beneš agreed to recognise the Slovaks as a separate nation, though even now he attempted to dilute the Slovak victory by suggesting that there be three distinct nations, Czech, Slovak, and Czechoslovak.

Beneš had been forced to give way because he was also faced with an equally, if not more, strident campaign from extremists within the German community. Although many Germans in Czechoslovakia, particularly the German social democrats, remained loyal to Prague, others distanced themselves more and more from the Czech government. The Sudetendeutsch Partei (SdP), led by Konrad Henlein, orchestrated the movement.

After his success in the 1935 elections (see Table 7, p. 60) Henlein declared loyalty to Masaryk, but in a speech at Cheb (Eger) on 12 June 1936 the SdP leader declared that existing minority legislation was inadequate because it offered protection to individuals not to groups, and at the same time he nominated three Sudeten German deputies to the Reichstag in Berlin. On 27 April 1937, in the Chamber of Deputies, he went on to demand that members of the different racial groups should be enrolled in national organizations which would constitute separate legal entities and would direct all the internal affairs of that nation. This was corporatism on a national basis and could have destroyed the Czechoslovak state had it been accepted.

Until 1938 Henlein had not advocated the incorporation of the Sudetenland into Germany, not least because to have done so would have been illegal. But in 1938 it became obvious that this was the direction in which he was travelling or in which he was being pulled. In February Hitler announced that he was the defender of all *Volksdeutsche* (Germans living outside the German state), and in March he annexed Austria. This meant that Bohemia and Moravia were virtually surrounded by Germany, and the southern border was almost without defence. In April, at its conference in Karlovy Vary (Karlsbad), the SdP put forward eight demands which amounted in effect to the federalisation of Czechoslovakia.

Beneš accepted the so-called Karlsbad demands in September, but by then it was too late. After provoking disorder in the Sudentenland Hitler demanded its incorporation into Germany. Czechoslovakia's British and French allies acquiesced. On 1 October 1938 the Sudetenland was absorbed into the adjoining German *Gaue* or administrative districts.

On 10 October the Poles took advantage of Czechoslovakia's tribulation to seize Teschen. The Hungarians did not wish to be left out of the partition and on 2 November the 'First Vienna Award' gave them southern Slovakia and southern Ruthenia.

Inside what was left of Czechoslovakia the political system was redesigned. On 6 October members of all Slovak parties, the communists excepted, met at Žilina and decided to declare Slovak autonomy; the Hlinka Slovak People's Party soon established a one-party system. Ruthenia declared autonomy shortly afterwards. In Bohemia and Moravia political parties were merged into two new groups: the Party of National Unity for right and centre-right factions, and the Party of National Labour for those on the left. Real power, however, lay in Berlin.

In March 1939 Czech police and troops were moved into Slovakia to curb anti-Czech excesses there. Hitler seized the opportunity to liquidate Czechoslovakia. Bohemia and Moravia became a Protectorate of the German Reich, Slovakia declared itself an independent state and the remains of Ruthenia were taken by Hungary.

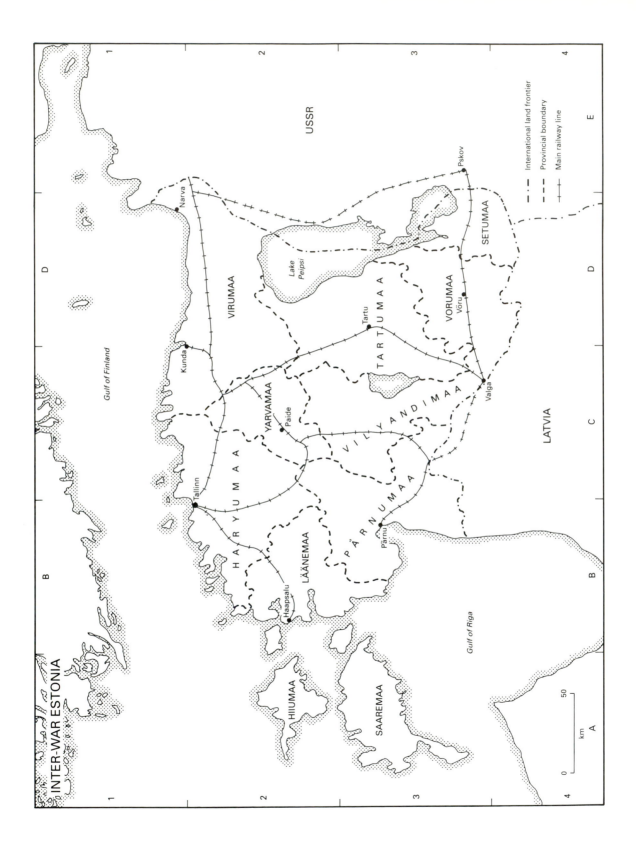

INTER-WAR ESTONIA

Gulf of Finland

Narva

VIRUMAA

Lake Peipsi

Kunda

YARVAMAA

Paide

TARTUMAA

Tartu

USSR

Pskov

SETUMAA

VORUMAA

Võru

Valga

HARYUMAA

Tallinn

LÄÄNEMAA

Haapsalu

VILYANDIMAA

PÄRNUMAA

Pärnu

LATVIA

Gulf of Riga

HIIUMAA

SAAREMAA

International land frontier
Provincial boundary
Main railway line

km

50

0

68

Inter-war Estonia

From the early eighteenth century to the end of the First World War the Finno-Ugric, Lutheran Estonians had been socially dominated by German and/or Russian landlords and politically subjected to Russian state power.

Political and social liberation came with the end of the First World War and the local conflicts which followed it in the Baltic region. When peace was concluded with the Bolsheviks in the Treaty of Tartu, 2 February 1920, Estonia was at last secure enough to enjoy the independent statehood it had claimed since 1918.

Estonia adopted an extremely liberal constitution in 1920 with a unicameral legislature with a wide franchise based on universal, equal, secret and proportional voting. The most powerful political body was the parliament, the *Riigikogu*; the head of the cabinet was for a number of years the head of state.

The open franchise, proportional representation, and a paucity of restrictions on the formation of political associations led to a multiplicity of parties and this, together with the vast powers vested in parliament, caused instability in government. Between 1919 and 1934 Estonia had twenty-one different administrations, the average life of a cabinet being eight months and twenty days. The agrarians, under the leadership of Konstantin Päts, were the strongest party and led ten of those cabinets. Amongst the other parties, national liberal groups held the centre ground and the non-Marxist socialists commanded the left; in 1925 the social democrats and the independent socialists joined to form the Socialist Workers' Party. The Communist Party, which had some support amongst the dockers of Tallinn and the Russian minority in Narva and other border areas, was banned in January 1924 but nevertheless attempted a coup in December of the same year.

In January 1934 a new constitution was drawn up, creating the office of president. Presidential, parliamentary, and local elections then made Päts president but also produced significant gains for the extreme right which now had control of the three most important towns: Tallinn, Tartu, and Narva. On 12 March 1934 Päts, fearing a fascist takeover, ordered the army to restore order. The extreme rightist military organizations were disbanded and parliament prorogued, and in February 1935 existing political parties were dissolved. Constitutional amendments to align political procedures with authoritarian principles were introduced, and in February 1936 Päts staged a plebiscite to confirm the changes and his own assumption of power. Further constitutional reform in 1938 introduced a bicameral parliament but there was little dilution of the tough regime which Päts and the army had established in their pre-emptive coup.

Estonia, like the other Baltic states, had an advanced system of social welfare – Estonia had one university student for every 332 inhabitants, the highest ratio in the world – but it also had concerns for its national security. Hopes for a Baltic–Scandinavian bloc did not survive the early 1920s because the Scandinavian states did not wish to compromise their neutrality, whilst the Polish–Lithuanian dispute over Vilnius (see p. 93) meant that Estonia and Latvia were reluctant to be drawn too close to Lithuania for fear of offending Poland. Through British and League of Nations mediation Estonia reached an easy agreement with Latvia over the disputed town of Valga, but relations were not always good, particularly in the 1930s.

The real danger came, however, from the great powers. Commercial treaties had been agreed with the Soviet Union in 1927 and 1929 and a non-aggression pact was signed in July 1932. Commercial ties with Germany developed rapidly in the 1930s; after 1935 up to half of the output of Estonia's developing oil-shale fields was bought for the German navy.

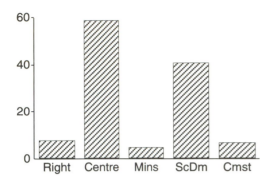

Figure 24 Composition of Assembly, 1919–20 (seats won)

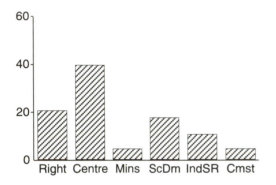

Figure 25 Composition of Assembly, 1920–3 (seats won)

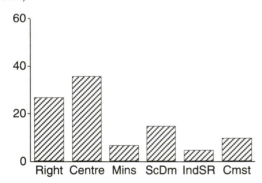

Figure 26 Composition of Assembly, 1923–6 (seats won)

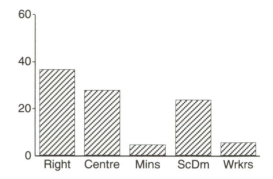

Figure 27 Composition of Assembly, 1926–9 (seats won)

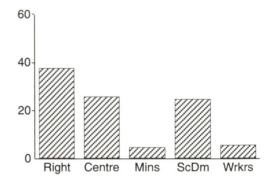

Figure 28 Composition of Assembly, 1929–32 (seats won)

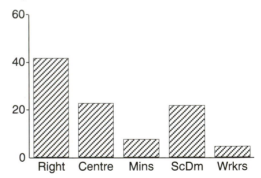

Figure 29 Composition of Assembly, 1933–4 (seats won)

Inter-war Estonia: political

If Estonian political groupings are divided into the right, centre, minority and left categories, not one of those categories achieved an absolute majority in any of the elections held in inter-war Estonia.

Generally speaking it was the centre which made the strongest showing. In 1919 it returned 59 deputies to the *Riigikogu*, but thereafter its representation declined with 40 seats in 1920, 36 in 1923, 28 in 1926, and 26 in 1929. The centre consisted of: the House Owners' Party, a fringe faction which returned between 1 and 3 deputies in the elections of 1920, 1923, 1926 and 1929; the Christian Democratic Party which had representatives in all the assemblies between 1919 and 1929, their numbers being 4 (1919), 7 (1920), 8 (1923), 5 (1926) and 4 (1929); the populists or Estonian Nationalist Party also returned deputies to each *Riigikogu*, the numbers being 25 (1919), 10 (1920), 8 (1923 and 1926), and 9 (1929); the Labour Party, which formed the backbone of the centre group, again returned deputies at all elections before 1933, with 30 seats in 1919, 22 in 1920, 12 in 1923, 13 in 1926 and 10 in 1929; of the other groups three were successful in the 1923 election – the National Liberal Party returning 4 deputies, and the Ex-Servicemen's Party and the Smallholders' Party one each.

On the right there were two groups. The Agrarian Party secured 8 seats in 1919, 21 in 1920, 23 in 1923 and 1926, and 24 in 1929. The Settlers' or New Farmers' Party had 4 deputies in 1923 and 14 in both 1926 and 1929.

The left was dominated by the Social Democrat Party which far outnumbered any other faction in that broad grouping. In the constituent assembly elected in 1919 they were the largest party of all with 41 deputies; they were third largest in 1920 (18 seats to 22 for the Labour Party and 21 for the agrarians); in 1923 they were second with 15 seats to the agrarians' 23; in 1926 and 1929 they again were the strongest party with 24 and 25 seats respectively. The Independent Socialist, or Social Revolutionary Party, returned 7 deputies in 1919, 11 in 1920 and 5 in 1923, after which the appeal of revolutionary rural radicalism wilted in the face of massive land redistribution, cooperatives and widespread credit for the small farmer. The Communist Party had some support amongst the Russian minority and amongst the radicalised dockers of Tallinn, and they won 5 seats in 1920 and double that number in 1923. After the party was made illegal in January 1924 it regrouped around the Workers' Party which returned 6 deputies in 1926 and 1929.

By 1933 Estonia was moving towards a more authoritarian structure. The two main agrarian factions had come together to form the United Agrarian Party, which won 42 seats in the elections of 1933; the centre parties had likewise joined to create the National Centre Party which won 23 seats in 1933; the Social Democrat Party remained separate and still managed to return 22 deputies, whilst on the extreme left the Workers' Party had 5 seats.

Three minority communities were represented in the *Riigikogu*: the Russian, the German and the Swedish. The Russians had 1 deputy in the assemblies of 1919 and 1920, 4 in 1923, 3 in 1926, 2 in 1929, and 5 in 1933. The Germans returned 3 deputies in 1919, 4 in 1920, 3 in 1923, and 2 in 1926 and 1929; the Swedes, who lived mainly in the off-shore islands, returned one deputy in 1919 and one in 1929. In 1933 the Germans and the Swedes combined to send 3 representatives to the assembly.

Estonia between the wars: ethnic and religious composition

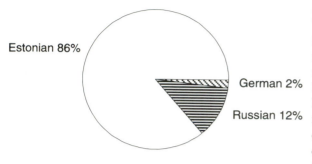

Figure 30 Ethnic composition, 1934

The constitution of 1920 allowed the minorities generous rights and a law of 1925 gave them virtual autonomy in cultural affairs. The Germans took immediate advantage of the new law and the Jewish community followed suit in 1926. With the 1925 legislation it seemed that the Estonian government had found an exemplary solution to the problem of the minorities. The fact that the minorities did not form a large parliamentary presence in the pre-coup years may suggest that they did not feel any great threat to their established way of life. On the other hand, the docility of the Germans may have indicated more resignation than contentment for they did have some cause for complaint. In 1927 the Estonian government in effect nationalised the German cathedral in Tallinn and in the 1930s the pressures grew appreciably, despite, or perhaps because of, the rise of strident nationalism in Germany. English replaced German as the first foreign language in Estonian schools, German names could no longer be used for streets, and legislation in 1935 requiring the use of Estonian for the transaction of government business made it much more difficult for Estonian Germans to follow careers in the civil service or the army. Despite these restrictions, however, Estonia's record in the treatment of minorities is generally regarded as one of the best in Eastern Europe in the inter-war period.

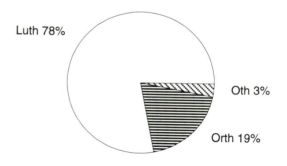

Figure 31 Population by religion, 1934

Inter-war Estonia: landholdings

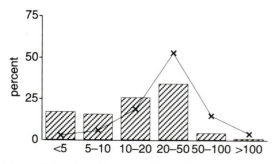

Figure 32 Landholdings: number and area

The first major legislation enacted by the Estonian parliament was a far-reaching programme of land redistribution. By the expropriation law of 10 October 1919 over a thousand estates, 96.6 per cent of the total number, were broken up and the land redistributed to small farmers or the landless agricultural labourers. The social and political power of the former German and Russian landlords, who before 1914 had owned 56 per cent of all landed property, was broken. Compensation of about 3 per cent of the value of confiscated estates was eventually agreed in 1926 but it was to be paid in government bonds rather than cash and there was to be no payment for expropriated forest land. Thereafter the small farmer dominated Estonian agriculture and if many holdings were too small to be viable on their own the cooperative system was well-developed and enabled most farmers to survive. Yet, as is seen in Figure 32, where the blocked columns represent the number of holdings in one category as a percentage of the total number of holdings, and the line represents the area covered by holdings in the same category as a percentage of the total area of land, in all smaller holdings – that is, those under 20 hectares – the share of those holdings as a percentage of the total number of holdings is greater than the percentage of the total area covered by those holdings. In holdings over 20 hectares the reverse is the case and a smaller number of holdings cover a greater proportion of the total area.

Inter-war Estonia: economic

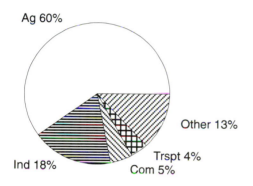

Figure 33 Population by economic sector, 1934

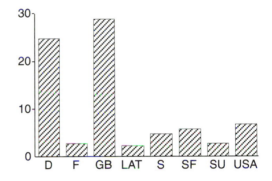

Figure 35 Distribution of trade, 1935 (% value)

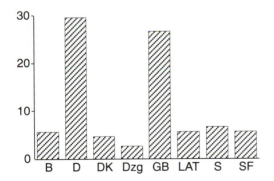

Figure 34 Distribution of trade, 1923 (% value)

73

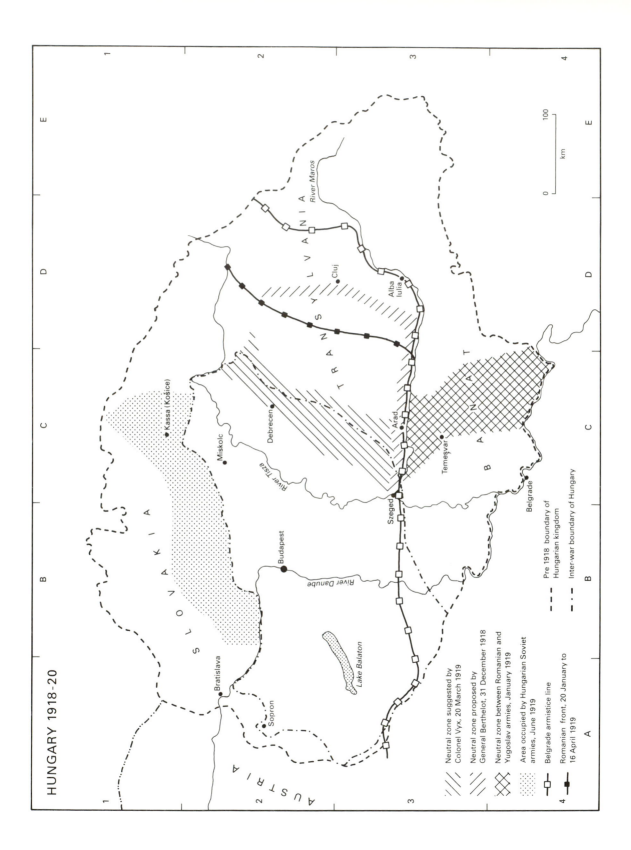

HUNGARY 1918-20

Neutral zone suggested by
Colonel Vyx, 20 March 1919

Neutral zone proposed by
General Berthelot, 31 December 1918

Neutral zone between Romanian and
Yugoslav armies, January 1919

Area occupied by Hungarian Soviet
armies, June 1919

Belgrade armistice line

Romanian front, 20 January to
16 April 1919

Pre 1918 boundary of
Hungarian kingdom

Inter-war boundary of Hungary

SLOVAKIA

AUSTRIA

TRANSYLVANIA

BANAT

River Maros

River Tisza

River Danube

Lake Balaton

Bratislava

Sopron

Budapest

Miskolc

Kassa (Košice)

Debrecen

Szeged

Arad

Temesvar

Belgrade

Cluj

Alba
Iulia

km

0

100

Hungary, 1918–20

In October 1918 leading Hungarians admitted that the war was lost. Delegates were dispatched to the allied headquarters at Belgrade where an armistice was signed in the middle of November. Hungarian forces were left in control of Transylvania up to the line of the river Maros (Mureş), although the Banat was divided into three with a neutral zone interposed between areas occupied by Yugoslav and by Romanian forces.

In Transylvania the line did not hold for long. On 1 December an assembly of Romanian nationalists at Alba Iulia declared for union with Romania, whereupon the Romanian army advanced, occupied Cluj, and established a front at which it was to remain until April. At the same time Czechoslovak troops had moved into Slovakia, half of which was occupied by them by the end of December 1918.

The government established in Budapest after the end of the war was led by Count Mihály Károlyi. He had always been pro-French and it was hoped that his pro-Western record would save Hungary from dismemberment. This illusion was shattered on 20 March when the allied Colonel Vyx ordered the Hungarians to withdraw not only from Transylvania but far into Hungary itself. A neutral zone was to be set up between the Hungarians and the Romanians but in it were to be included towns such as Debrecen and Szeged which many regarded as being in the heartland of Hungary.

Károlyi could not survive such a blow and was replaced by an extreme left-wing, Soviet-style regime under Béla Kun.

The advent of such a regime terrified the allies who now placed no obstacle in the path of Hungary's enemies. On 16 April Romanian troops moved forward from the line established in January and on 26 April the Czechoslovak army again assumed the offensive and moved as far into Hungary as Miskolc. This rallied all Hungarians, socialist and non-socialist. On 30 May, Kun's army went onto the attack. Miskolc was retaken and by mid-June Hungarian forces were advancing deep into Slovakia.

In July they assumed the offensive against the Romanians, crossing the river Tisza on 20 July. Here they met with less success and nine days later it was the Romanians who were crossing the river. Kun could not survive such humiliation. His extreme radical policies had already created great resentment, not least amongst the peasantry who were angered that the great estates were not subdivided but rather nationalised; the bourgeoisie, meanwhile, were totally alienated from a regime which not only confiscated almost all forms of their wealth but also forced them to open their bathrooms to the proletariat on Saturdays. And no one enjoyed the prohibition which Kun enforced.

On 2 August Kun fled Hungary. His armies were already in a state of collapse and there was nothing to hinder the Romanians' advance. On 4 August they entered Budapest and within a few days most of the rest of the country was under their occupation. This occupation lasted until the middle of November when, with allied mediation, forces at Szeged loyal to Admiral Miklós Horthy moved into Budapest.

Once installed in power the Szeged forces repealed all legislation stemming from the revolutionary regimes, reinstated landlords and restored the monarchy. They did not, however, restore the monarch, not least because that would have alarmed the allies; instead Horthy was declared regent and the crown remained as a symbol of that unified Hungary which was then so much under threat from the impending peace treaty.

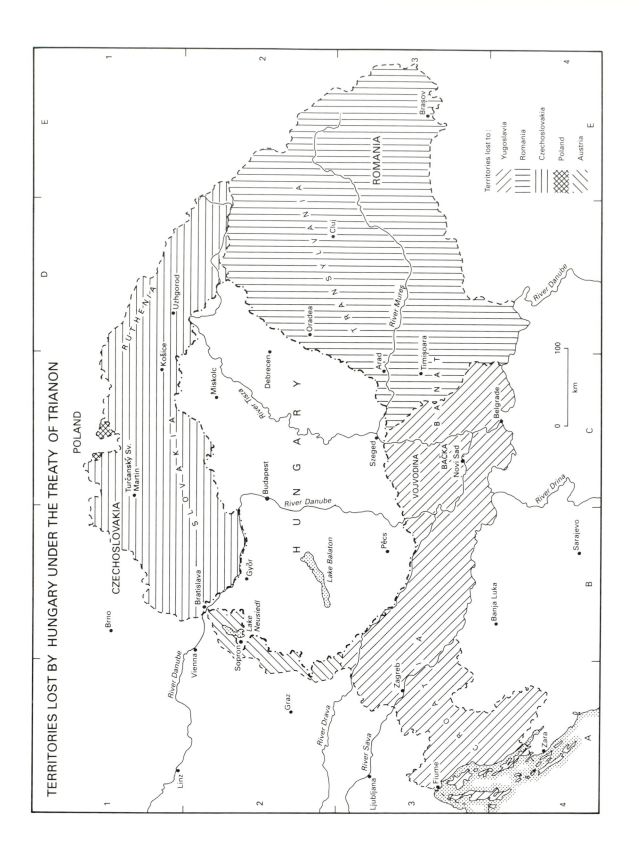

TERRITORIES LOST BY HUNGARY UNDER THE TREATY OF TRIANON

Territories lost to:

Yugoslavia

Romania

Czechoslovakia

Poland

Austria

POLAND

CZECHOSLOVAKIA

Turčanský Sv.
Martin

R U T H E N I A

S L O V A K I A

Brno

Vienna

Bratislava

Sopron

Lake
Neusiedl

Győr

Graz

Linz

River Danube

River Danube

Budapest

River Danube

H U N G A R Y

Lake Balaton

Pécs

Ljubljana

River Drava

River Sava

Zagreb

C R O A T I A

Fiume

Zara

Sarajevo

Banja Luka

River Drina

Belgrade

VOJVODINA

BAČKA

Novi Sad

Szeged

B A N A T

Timișoara

Arad

Debrecen

River Tisza

Miskolc

Košice

Uzhgorod

T R A N S Y L V A N I A

Oradea

River Mureş

Cluj

ROMANIA

Braşov

River Danube

km

100

0

The Treaty of Trianon

The Treaty of Trianon was signed on 4 June 1920. It deprived the pre-war Hungarian kingdom of 67.4 per cent of its territory. To Romania were lost most of the Banat and all Transylvania, regarded by many Magyars as the cultural cradle of their nation; most of Slovakia and Ruthenia were included in Czechoslovakia, though small enclaves went to Poland; the remainder of the Banat, the Vojvodina, the Bačka, and Croatia were allocated to Yugoslavia; and in the only transfer of territory to a defeated power, part of western Hungary became Austrian.

The Treaty shattered the economy of the Hungarian kingdom. Industry lost large portions of both its raw materials and its markets; the great grain mills of Budapest, for example, had relied heavily on grain from the Vojvodina and Slovakia. The new boundaries cut Hungary off from the sea. They also deprived the railway system of its former rationale which had been to bind the kingdom together; now its main lines led into foreign countries, and 58 per cent of its track lay outside Hungary. So too did 60 per cent of the former road network, 84 per cent of the kingdom's timber resources, 43 per cent of the arable land, 28 per cent of its coal reserves and 83 per cent of its iron ore deposits. The new borders even broke up twenty-three flood control agencies on rivers such as the Danube and the Tisza.

Other clauses of the treaty limited the Hungarian army to 30,000 men, and forbad the Hungarians an airforce, tanks, heavy artillery, or a general staff; and there was also a prohibition on conscription. That the new Hungary was very much a nation-state, with almost 90 per cent of its population being Magyar, was little compensation for the fact that a third of all Magyars now lived outside the Hungarian state.

The bitterness felt by Hungarians was increased because plebiscites, which had been held in some disputed areas, were not allowed in Ruthenia, southern Slovakia, Transylvania or the Banat; in that allowed in Sopron in western Hungary the city had voted to remain in Hungary whilst the surrounding countryside opted for Austria.

The reason for the severity of the Treaty was partly that Hungary was being punished for what were considered its past sins with regard to its minority groups, and for its flirtation with Bolshevism under Béla Kun. Furthermore, the peace treaties were compiled in such a way that although there were separate committees to oversee Czechoslovak, Yugoslav, and Polish affairs, there was not one for defeated Hungary, and the overall, detailed impact of the changes was not therefore appreciated. It is doubtful, however, whether the terms of the Treaty would have been any less harsh had such a Hungarian committee existed. By the time consideration of Hungary began seriously the peacemakers, and more importantly their armies of civil servants, were tired and frustrated; the future Lord Beveridge told Károlyi that the allies had 'more important things to do than worry about the fate of ten million Hungarian people in Hungary'.

For those Hungarians in Hungary there were constant reminders of their losses. Budapest had a memorial garden laid out as a map of the old kingdom, and all national flags were flown at half-mast until some of the lost territory was regained in the period 1938–9. Inevitably, Hungary became an inveterately revisionist state, and, more importantly, because it had been the democracies which handed down the Treaty, democracy was discredited in Hungary.

With the left eliminated after the Kun episode, and democracy discredited by the Treaty of Trianon, Hungarian politics in the inter-war period were therefore dominated by a struggle between the conservative and the radical right.

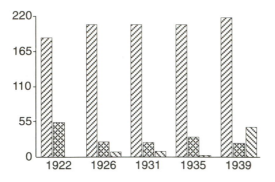

Figure 36 Composition of parliament, 1922–39 (seats won)

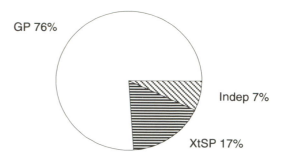

Figure 39 Composition of government bloc, 1931

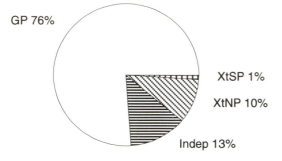

Figure 37 Composition of government bloc, 1922

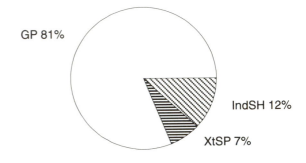

Figure 40 Composition of government bloc, 1935

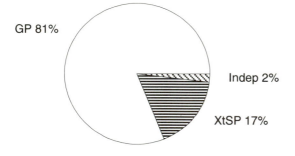

Figure 38 Composition of government bloc, 1926

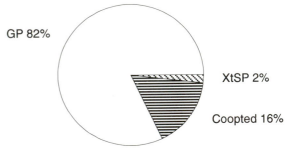

Figure 41 Composition of government bloc, 1939

Inter-war Hungary: political

After the upheavals of 1918–20 Hungarian parliamentary life achieved a stability which was based upon the domination of the government faction. The government bloc varied somewhat in composition but its mainstay was always the 'Government Party'. This was dedicated to the 'Szeged Idea' which was, in effect, the preservation of the social and political domination of the magnates, gradual industrial expansion, a foreign policy dedicated to the reclamation of the lost territories, the containment of left-wing subversion or agitation, and the avoidance of embarrassing excesses of rightist radicalism, be it in the form of overt anti-Semitism or a thoroughgoing redistribution of landed property. The Government Party was skilled in electoral and in coalition management and therefore easily controlled the other and much smaller groups which made up the ruling coalition.

The inter-war system was primarily the work of Count István Bethlen, a Calvinist magnate from Transylvania who was appointed prime minister in April 1921. His skilful management neutralised the pro land-reform Smallholders' Party which had emerged as the largest group in the 1920 elections. Other parties were small, fluid in composition, and lacking national organisational infrastructures. The elections of 1920 had been the first held in Hungary under a secret ballot and this mistake Bethlen did not repeat. Open voting was reintroduced into rural constituencies in 1922 and remained in force until the elections of 1939. Control of the bureaucracy and of the lord-lieutenants of the counties gave the Government Party a firm hold on both central and local government, and guaranteed its dominance of parliament. (See Figure 36 in which the first column shows the government bloc, the second the conservative, centre and left opposition, and the third the radical right opposition for the years 1922–39.)

Of the non-government parties the centre-left consisted mainly of the anti-government Independent Party, whose numbers were 31 in 1922, 12 in 1926, 11 in 1931, and 12 in 1935 (they were unrepresented in 1939), and the Socialist Party which had 25 deputies in 1922, 14 in both 1926 and 1931, 11 in 1935 and 5 in 1939. The socialists were tolerated because in 1921 they had agreed to cut all links with the communists and the more extreme of the leftists who had gone into exile in 1920.

The extreme right was the main opposition force because the extreme left had been discredited by the Kun uprising and the democratic centre-left compromised by its association with the powers responsible for Trianon. Careful electoral management and a handful of mostly hollow concessions contained the extreme right until the early 1930s when the depression and the rise of Nazism forced the Hungarian political establishment into compromise with its right–radical critics. It was to placate them that one of their most prominent leaders, Gyula Gömbös, was made prime minister in October 1932, a position he held until his death in 1936. The fact that Gömbös was prime minister in 1935 accounted for the decline of extreme right opposition.

The return to Hungary of southern Slovakia and Ruthenia during 1938–9 meant that the number of deputies in parliament rose from 245 to 296. Of the 51 new members 36 were coopted by and were supporters of the government. But the newly acquired areas also increased the strength of the extreme right; Magyars living in Czechoslovakia had experienced land reform and found the right–radical calls for the redistribution of property attractive. The success of Hitlerite Germany further strengthened the fascists in Hungary and helped to increase their representation in parliament; in 1939 the Arrow Cross had 31 deputies compared to 2 in 1935, and there were another 18 MPs from other extreme rightist factions, none of which had previously been represented.

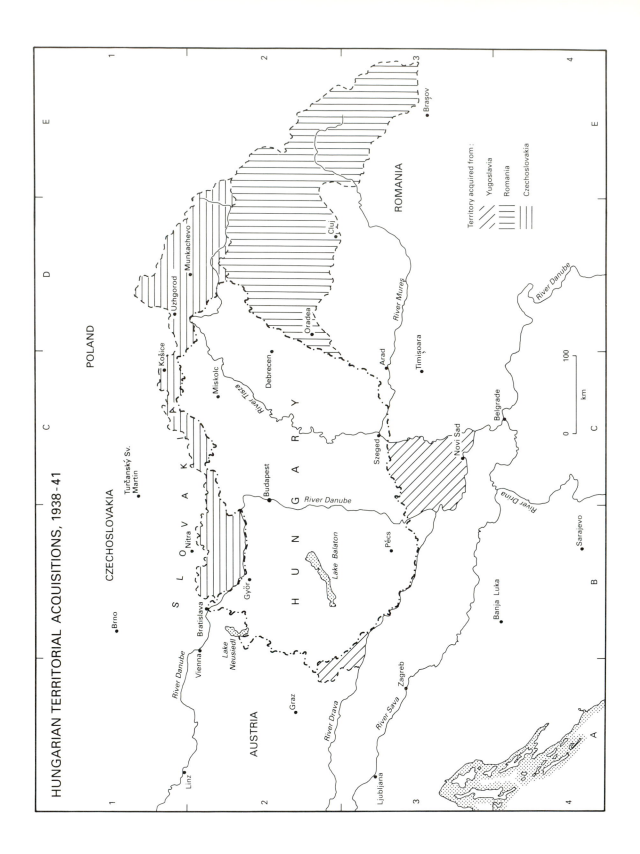

HUNGARIAN TERRITORIAL ACQUISITIONS, 1938-41

POLAND

CZECHOSLOVAKIA

Brno

Turčanský Sv. Martin

Košice

Uzhgorod

Munkachevo

S L O V A K I A

Nitra

Miskolc

Debrecen

Oradea

Cluj

Brașov

ROMANIA

River Mureș

Arad

Timișoara

River Tisza

H U N G A R Y

Budapest

River Danube

Szeged

Novi Sad

Belgrade

River Danube

Bratislava

Győr

Lake Balaton

Pécs

River Drina

Vienna

Lake Neusiedl

Linz

River Danube

AUSTRIA

Graz

River Drava

Zagreb

River Sava

Ljubljana

Banja Luka

Sarajevo

Territory acquired from:

Yugoslavia

Romania

Czechoslovakia

0   100

km

80

Hungarian territorial acquisitions, 1938–41

For Admiral Horthy and most Hungarian magnates the success of Hitler posed a serious dilemma. They found him and his movement vulgar and distasteful, and they feared the effect his radicalism could have upon property ownership in their own country. On the other hand, Hitler and the Nazis had shown that the post-First World War settlement could be changed. By 1938 it was obvious that if Hungary were to achieve any of its revisionist aims this could only be done in cooperation with Germany and, to a lesser degree, Italy.

The first gains came with the Munich crisis of 1938. The Western allies in effect abandoned Czechoslovakia and after the German Reich had taken possession of the Sudeten areas other powers submitted their claims. German and Italian arbitration resulted in what was to become known as the first Vienna award, under which Hungary was allowed to repossess southern Slovakia including Košice (Kassa) but excluding Bratislava (Pozsony) and Nitra. Hungary also repossessed a large proportion of Ruthenia, including Uzhgorod and Munkachevo. The remainder of Ruthenia was taken on 14 March 1939 when Slovakia's declaration of independence destroyed what had remained of the post-Munich Czecho-Slovak state.

The fall of France in the summer of 1940 brought about large-scale territorial readjustments in Eastern Europe. Stalin insisted that promises made secretly by the Germans in 1939 now be fulfilled and as a result the Soviet Union took possession of Bessarabia and northern Bukovina. Hungary used this as the opportunity to press for the return of Transylvania. Negotiations with Romania made no headway and Hitler, fearing that instability in the Balkans might interrupt the flow of Romanian oil to Germany, rapidly organised a second Germano-Italian arbitration in Vienna. The second Vienna award, signed on 30 August 1940, gave Hungary northern Transylvania – in all about 40 per cent of that region but including the counties with the largest proportion of Magyars.

In November 1940 Hungary joined the German-sponsored tripartite pact and in December signed a treaty of eternal friendship with Yugoslavia. In March 1941, however, the Germans demanded right of passage for their troops who were then attacking Hungary's new ally. The Hungarian prime minister considered compliance with the German request dishonourable and committed suicide when overruled by his cabinet colleagues and the regent. On 11 April Hungary joined in the assault on Yugoslavia and in the partition of that country, taking the area between the Danube and the Tisza.

Between November 1938 and April 1941 Hungary regained 52.9 per cent of the territory lost at Trianon. In so doing Hungary had become an associate of Nazi Germany and, as such, in June 1941 joined Germany in the war against the Soviet Union.

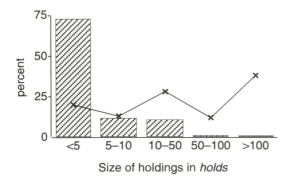

Figure 42 Landholdings: size and area, 1921

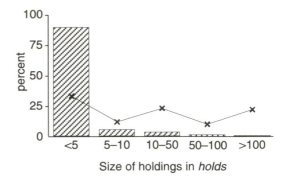

Figure 45 Landholdings: size and area, 1935

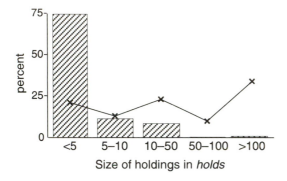

Figure 43 Landholdings: size and area, 1925

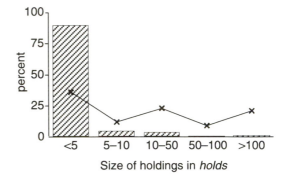

Figure 46 Landholdings: size and area, 1940

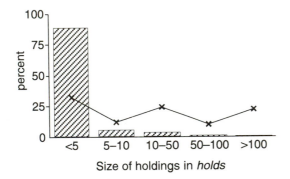

Figure 44 Landholdings: size and area, 1931

Inter-war Hungary: landholdings

In inter-war Hungary the magnates retained more property and influence than in any other East European state.

Figures 42–6 illustrate the distribution of land. Total landed property is divided into five categories according to extent; category 1 is under 5 *holds* (a *hold* was 1.4 hectares); category 2 from 5 to 10 *holds*; category 3 from 10 to 50 *holds*; category 4 from 50 to 100 *holds*; and category 5 for over 100 *holds*. In each diagram the column shows what percentage of the total number of properties holdings in that category formed, whilst the line indicates the percentage of the total area of land covered by holdings in the same category.

In 1921 properties under 5 *holds* were 73 per cent of the total number of holdings but covered only 20 per cent of the total area. At the other end of the scale estates over 100 *holds* accounted for only 1 per cent of total holdings but 38 per cent of the land. Only in the second category, from 5 to 10 *holds*, did the two proportions approximate, being 13 per cent and 12 per cent.

A land reform act in 1922 promised to redistribute about 1.25 million *holds*. This had some effect on the overall pattern of land distribution, though much of the redistributed land was of poor quality. In 1925 holdings under 5 *holds* comprised 77 per cent of the total and accounted for 21 per cent of the area, thereafter the number remained at or near 90 per cent of the total but the area covered rose to 32 per cent in 1931, to 33 per cent in 1935, and to 36 per cent in 1940 after the incorporation of southern Slovakia and Ruthenia, though in these areas nobles were soon restored to lands they had lost by Czechoslovak land reforms.

Holdings between 5 and 10 *holds* were 13 per cent of the total in 1925 and accounted for 12 per cent of the land, but thereafter the percentage of holdings in this category declined to around 5 per cent of the total, though its share of the total area remained stable at 12 per cent.

This meant that after 1925 there was not one category in which the two proportions were similar.

Holdings between 10 and 50 *holds* declined steadily from 11 per cent in 1921 to 9 per cent in 1925, and 4 per cent thereafter. Their share of the land, which stood at 28 per cent in 1921, declined somewhat in the next few years and settled at or near 23 per cent.

Properties of 50 to 100 *holds* were always about 1 per cent of the total number whilst their share of the total land ranged from 9 to 12 per cent.

Estates over 100 *holds* hardly changed as a percentage of the total number of holdings between 1921 and 1940, but their share of the total land fell from 38 to 20 per cent. It was always much in excess of their share of the total number.

In absolute numbers holdings in the smallest category grew from 7,831 in 1921 to 25,534 in 1940; in the same years the number of properties over 100 *holds* fell from 108 to 79.

The dependence of the mass of the peasantry on the large landowners was even greater than the figures indicate. Many of those who held property in the smallest category did not have enough land to function as independent farmers. They were therefore dependent on the landlord for employment if they were to survive.

The architect of Hungary's political system in the 1920s, Count István Bethlen, argued that if post-Trianon Hungary were to re-industrialise and to become of sufficient power to achieve its national aims it must have an agricultural system which was sufficiently strong to generate capital. This, as well as personal interests, made him a resolute opponent of further land reform but in 1939 right–radical pressure did force the regime to pass a second land reform bill which promised to redistribute a further 1.2 million *holds*, but the involvement of Hungary in the Second World War prevented any systematic application of this Act.

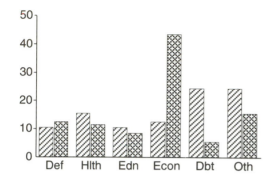

Figure 47 Budget expenditure, 1924/5, 1936/7 (%)

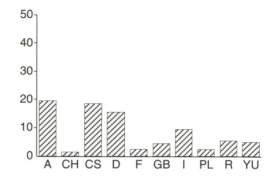

Figure 50 Distribution of trade, 1930 (% value)

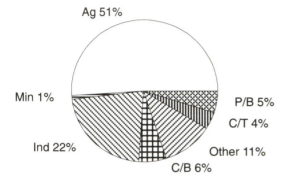

Figure 48 Population by economic sector, 1930

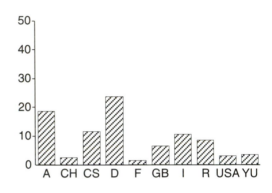

Figure 51 Distribution of trade, 1935 (% value)

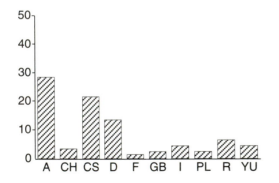

Figure 49 Distribution of trade, 1925 (% value)

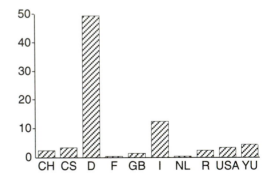

Figure 52 Distribution of trade, 1940 (% value)

Inter-war Hungary: economic

In the middle of the inter-war period Hungary was still predominantly an agricultural society with 51 per cent of its population engaged in agriculture in 1930. This proportion did decline somewhat to 49 per cent in 1941 whilst those engaged in industry rose by just under 5 per cent in the same years.

In government expenditure subsidies to Hungarian industry and other economic sectors showed that pre-war attitudes prevailed, and they were strengthened by the knowledge that Hungary had to have a strong industrial base if it were to have any chance of retrieving the territories lost under Trianon.

The direction of Hungarian trade changed significantly after the First World War in that the former Habsburg lands which before 1914 had accounted for 70 per cent of Hungary's external trade took a much less dominant part. In 1920, in a period of extreme uncertainty, the old ties had continued with Austria providing 51 per cent of imports and buying 61 per cent of exports, but by 1930 the figures were 12 per cent and 28 per cent respectively. Political ties with Italy helped the growth of exports to that country. In 1920 they had measured 3 per cent of the total and in 1925 had risen by 2 per cent. After a political agreement concluded in 1927 there was significant change and exports to Italy were 13, 14 and 16 per cent of the total in 1930, 1935 and 1940 respectively. A trade war with Czechoslovakia after 1930 brought about a sharp fall in imports from a country which previously had supplied between a fifth and a quarter of the total (19 per cent in 1920, 24 per cent in 1925 and 21 per cent in 1930); in 1935 they had fallen to only 5 per cent.

The position of Germany calls for especial comment in Hungary as elsewhere. As a source of imports Germany accounted for 15 per cent in 1925, 21 per cent in 1930, 23 per cent in 1935 and 53 per cent in 1940. As a destination for Hungarian exports the figures were 13 per cent for 1925, 10 per cent for 1930, 24 per cent for 1935 and 49 per cent for 1940. The dramatic rise from 1935 to 1940 in both imports and exports is in part the result of the incorporation of Austria into Germany; Germany and Austria combined supplied 37 per cent of imports in 1925, 33 per cent in 1930, and 42 per cent in 1935; in exports they bought 48 per cent in 1925, 38 per cent in 1930, and 43 per cent in 1935. Trade with Germany rose not only because of the *Anschluss* but also because of the blocked currency system introduced into Germany just before the Nazis took power. Under these arrangements German purchasers of Hungarian exports paid for them by depositing German currency in accounts in Berlin, this money then being available to pay for imports from Germany. In this way Hungarians at last found buyers for their primary produce whilst the Germans were assured easy export markets.

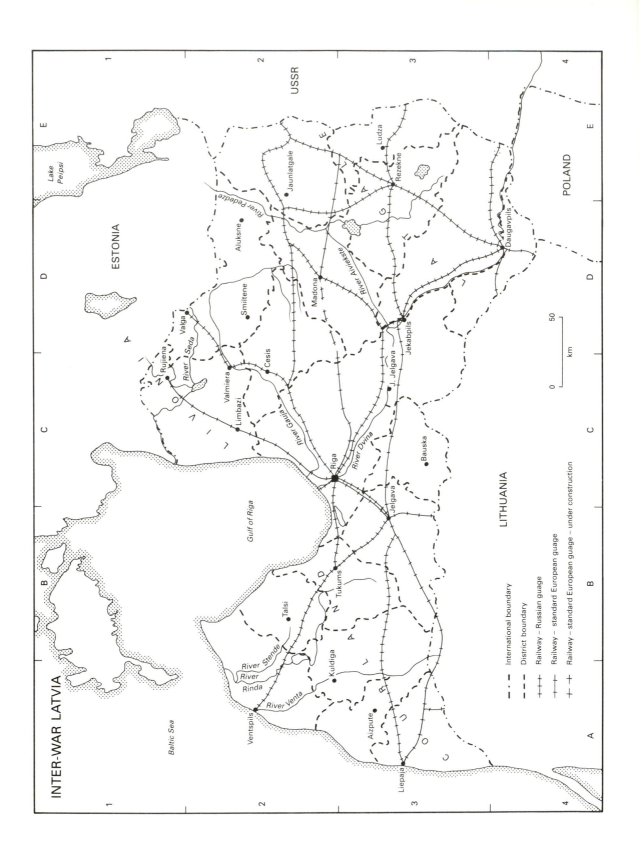

INTER-WAR LATVIA

ESTONIA

USSR

POLAND

LITHUANIA

Lake Peipsi

Baltic Sea

Gulf of Riga

Jaunlatgale

Ludza

Rezekne

Daugavpils

Aluksne

River Pededze

Smiltene

Madona

River Aiviekste

Valga

Rujiena

River Seda

Valmiera

Cesis

River Gauja

Jekabpils

J. Jelgava

Limbazi

River Dvina

Riga

Bauska

Jelgava

Talsi

Tukums

River Stende

River
Rinda

Kuldiga

Ventspils

River Venta

Aizpute

Liepaja

50

km

0

International boundary
District boundary
Railway – Russian guage
Railway – standard European guage
Railway – standard European guage – under construction

86

Inter-war Latvia

The Latvians speak a Baltic language and for the most part belong to the Lutheran Church, though in Latgale in the south they are predominantly Catholic; in 1935 the Catholics of Latgale constituted just under a quarter of the total population (24.5 percent).

In March 1917 a Latvian provisional council representing southern Livonia, Courland, and Latgale was established. It declared Latvian independence when the Germans took Riga in September 1917. Great confusion reigned then and until the final defeat of the Bolsheviks in 1920. Latvia's political situation was complicated. The administrative history of the three main constituent elements was different, and there was a sizeable Russian minority whose working-class members showed strong sympathy for the Bolsheviks. In addition to this, there were large numbers of German troops in the area, many of whom joined the *Freikorps* or irregular units formed to fight against Bolshevism and for the protection of German interests. Not until the middle of 1920 was stability achieved, partly through the intervention of British warships.

The Latvian constitution of 1920 gave wide-ranging freedoms. Its legislature was unicameral and was elected by universal suffrage and proportional representation. A striking feature of Latvian political life in the 1920s was the number of political parties; there was in fact one political party for every forty-five thousand persons in the population, this proliferation of political groupings being much helped by the regulation that only one hundred signatures were needed for a political party to be registered and therefore entitled to some government financial support. Between 1919 and 1934 thirty-nine different parties were represented at one time or another in the all-powerful *Saeima*, or parliament. The most powerful, even if it was not the most numerous, party in the 1920s was the agrarian and essentially conservative Peasants' League; the three most important centre parties came together in 1922 to form the Democratic Centre, whilst on the left the Social Democratic Party retained its Marxist ideology without adopting Leninist, totalitarian methods.

In political terms there was considerable instability, Latvia having eighteen separate governments between 1920 and 1935. Cabinet instability increased pressure from the right for more stable and more authoritarian government. The main representative body of the extreme right was the Thunder Cross which by the early 1930s had adopted overt Nazi methods and policies. In October 1933 the agrarians proposed a series of constitutional reforms which were intended to strengthen the executive. In May 1934 came a *coup d'état* by President Karlis Ulmanis, one of the founding fathers of the modern Latvian state. He banned both the Communist Party and the Thunder Cross before proscribing all parties, including his own. Thereafter Ulmanis ruled through the bureaucracy, the army, and the para-military *Aizsargi* (defence league).

For Latvia foreign affairs presented few complications; it had no 'lost territory' nor were there significant Latvian communities outside the state. The one exception was the border town of Valka (Valga) which had been settled by arbitration early in the 1920s. Latvia signed a joint non-aggression pact with Finland, Poland and Estonia in 1922, and although this proved moribund by 1925 Latvia continued to participate in Baltic and Scandinavian diplomatic combinations such as the Baltic entente of 1934. It also signed trade agreements with the Soviet Union in 1927 and a non-aggression pact with the same power in 1932. Estonian and Latvian plans for a customs union were abandoned because of an Estonian–Finnish trade treaty in 1937, and plans for a joint academy of sciences were dropped after a furious row between Riga and Tallinn over an Estonian professor's publications on Latvian folklore.

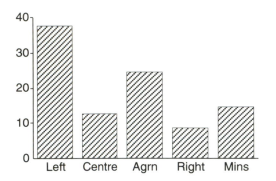

Figure 53 Composition of Assembly, 1922–5 (% seats)

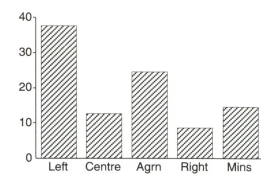

Figure 55 Composition of Assembly, 1928–31 (% seats)

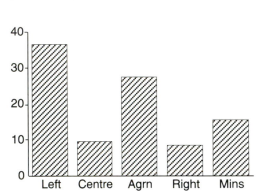

Figure 54 Composition of Assembly, 1925–8 (% seats)

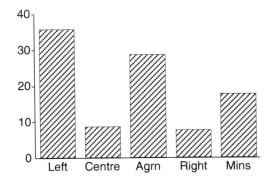

Figure 56 Composition of Assembly, 1931–4 (% seats)

Inter-war Latvia: political

Inter-war Latvia had a plethora of political parties. This was in part a result of regional loyalties and the ethnic divisions of the country. Latgale, for example, with its predominantly Catholic, rather than Protestant, population had its own branch of the Social Democratic Party as well as its own Progressive Group and the 'Non-Party Latgalians' who formed part of the political centre. Amongst the agrarians there were Latgalian Christian Farmers, Latgalian Progressive Farmers and Latgalian Independent Farmers, whilst there was a Latgalian Union amongst the right-wing factions. Another regional group was the Semgalian Christian Farmers. Latvian Jews had been prominent in the pre-1914 socialist Bund of imperial Russia and after 1918 a separate Socialist Jewish Bund was maintained.

The minority groups consisted of Germans, Russians, Jews and Poles. But only the first and last of these were united. The Russians were divided into Old Believers, Orthodox Workers, 'Officials in Latvian Municipalities', a Russian Peasant Union, and the Russian National Democrats. The Jews divided mainly on religious lines into 'Agudas Israel', 'Misrachi', and 'Ceire Zion'. Amongst the national minorities the Germans always had the largest number of deputies, 6 in all assemblies except that of 1925 when there were 5; the Poles had 1 or 2, the Russians between 3 and 6, and the Jews 4 or 5.

The left was dominated by the social democrats who returned 30, 31, 25 and 20 deputies in the elections of 1922, 1925, 1928, and 1931 respectively. The other groups on the left were the Latgalian Social Democrat Party, the Jewish Bund, the Independent Social Democrat Party, the Right Social Democrats and the Peasant and Labour Group. None of these smaller groups were represented in all *Saeimas*, though the Right Social Democrats had 7 seats in 1922 and 4 in 1925. The Peasant and Labour Group had 6 in 1928 and 7 in 1931.

In the centre the Democratic Centre alone was present in all elected assemblies, the other groups only managing to scrape together a handful of deputies between them. The other groups were: the Labour Union, the Progressive Union, the Economic Union, the Radical Democrats, the Non-Party Latgalians, the Young Farmers, the Christian Labour Party, and the Latgalian Progressives.

The agrarians were powerful because of their links both with the peasantry and with the cooperative movement. The main element in the agrarian group was the Peasant Union which took 16 seats in each election, except that of 1931 when it had 14. The other agrarian parties were the Latgalian and Semgalian factions mentioned above, together with the New Farmers' and Smallholders' Party, and the bizarrely named 'Devastated Areas Party'.

None of the rightist groups was represented in all assemblies. The elements making up the right were: the Christian Union; the National Union; the Christian Nationals; the Party for Peace and Order; the Latgalian Union; the National Farmers; and the New Peasants' Union.

Inter-war Latvia: ethnic composition

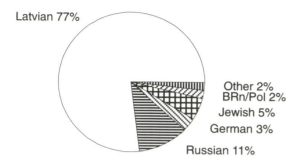

Latvian 77%

Other 2%
BRn/Pol 2%
Jewish 5%
German 3%
Russian 11%

Figure 57 Ethnic composition, 1935

The presence of a large Russian minority in Latvia was due in considerable measure to the influx of Russians to work in the factories which were established in the area in the late nineteenth century. The statistics are not entirely clear on the distinction between Belorussians and Poles.

Ethnic minorities in Latvia were allowed by the constitution of 1920 the right to control their own schools. By the late 1920s, however, there was increasing pressure from the growing right wing of the Latvian political spectrum for some restriction of minority rights. The Germans were particularly vulnerable, for since the land reforms and the departure of many German families their influence had declined considerably. A number of German and other churches were taken over by the Latvians, the German agrarian association was closed, its funds being merged into those of the Latvian chamber of agriculture, and in 1935 the guilds, many of which were of medieval origin, were closed down and their property, which included many ancient churches and historic buildings, nationalised under the so-called new year laws. These laws also made it obligatory to use Latvian names within the bureaucracy and for streets.

Inter-war Latvia: religious composition

Lutheran Protestants made up over half the Latvian population in 1930. Over half of the remainder – that is, nearly a quarter of the total – were Roman Catholics, most of whom lived in the Latgale in the south of the country. Russian Orthodox families accounted for 9 per cent of the total, in addition to which almost 5 per cent were Old Believers, a sect whose founders had rejected the modernising reforms of Peter the Great and had therefore fled beyond the confines of his empire. Of the Baltic states, Latvia had the largest proportion of Jews in its population, almost 5 per cent. They were to be found in Riga and the other main urban centres.

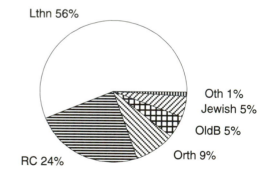

Lthn 56%

Oth 1%
Jewish 5%
OldB 5%
Orth 9%
RC 24%

Figure 58 Population by religion, 1930

Inter-war Latvia: landholdings

One of the first items of legislation in the new republic was a land reform act. In Latvia the former landowners were allowed to retain up to fifty hectares of land but, by a parliamentary decision of 1924, they were not to be given compensation. Some thirteen hundred estates were broken up and redistributed with a total of 1.7 million hectares changing hands, to create approximately a quarter of a million new holdings, none of which was larger than twenty-five hectares. Veterans of the wars for national libera-

tion were given priority in the allocation of redistributed land. The cooperatives were essential to the survival of many of the smallholdings created by the land reform, not least in the dairy industry. In 1939 Latvia had 225 consumer cooperatives and 244 for dairy farmers.

Inter-war Latvia: a note on trade statistics

In the diagrams on the distribution of trade the figures for Estonia and Lithuania were included with 'Others' for 1927; after 1923 the figures for Danzig were included in those for Poland.

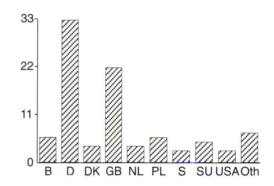

Figure 61 Distribution of trade, 1927 (% value)

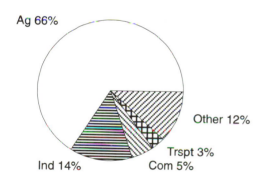

Figure 59 Population by economic sector, 1930

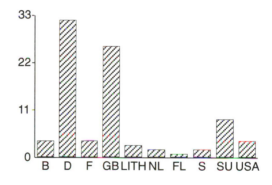

Figure 62 Distribution of trade, 1932 (% value)

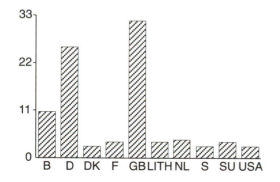

Figure 60 Distribution of trade, 1923 (% value)

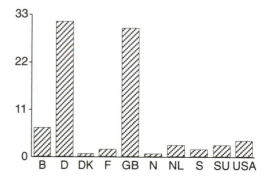

Figure 63 Distribution of trade, 1937 (% value)

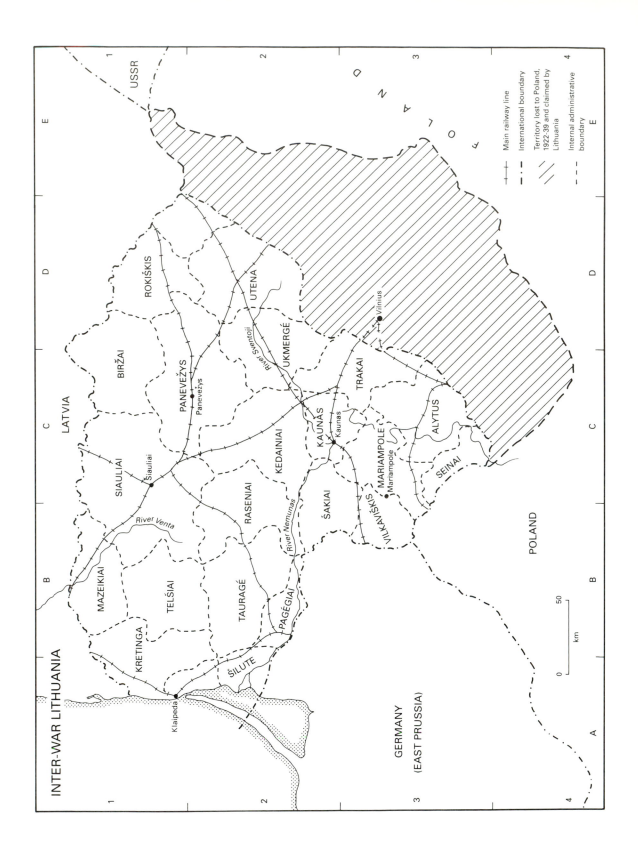

INTER-WAR LITHUANIA

USSR

POLAND

LATVIA

ROKIŠKIS

UTENA

BIRŽAI

PANEVĖŽYS

River Šventoji

UKMERGĖ

Panevėžys

SIAULIAI

KĖDAINIAI

TRAKAI

Šiauliai

KAUNAS

Kaunas

Vilnius

ALYTUS

RASENIAI

MARIAMPOLE

River Venta

ŠAKIAI

Mariampole

SEINAI

River Nemunas

VILKAVIŠKIS

MAZEIKIAI

TELŠIAI

TAURAGĖ

PAGĖGIAI

POLAND

KRETINGA

ŠILUTE

GERMANY
(EAST PRUSSIA)

Klaipeda

50

km

0

Main railway line

International boundary

Territory lost to Poland,
1922-39 and claimed by
Lithuania

Internal administrative
boundary

Inter-war Lithuania

Lithuania differed from the other Baltic states in that the majority of its population were Roman Catholic rather than Protestant, and because its landowning elite had been Polish or Russian rather than German; also in Lithuania serfdom was not abolished until 1861 rather than in the decade after the Napoleonic wars.

The Germans occupied what was to become Lithuania in 1915. In September 1917 a Lithuanian Provisional Council, or *Taryba*, was established and chose as its leader Antanas Smetona. In November 1918 the *Taryba* declared itself to be a constituent assembly, drew up an extremely liberal constitution, and nominated Augustinas Voldermaras, a professor from Perm, as president. Voldermaras and Smetona were to dominate Lithuania in the inter-war period.

The country was not free of foreign troops until the spring of 1920. In July of that year a treaty with the Bolsheviks recognised Lithuania's independence and territorial integrity. However, that integrity could not be guaranteed. In October 1920 Polish forces incorporated Vilnius and the surrounding area into Poland. The city had been the Lithuanian capital, a status which was now given 'temporarily' to Kaunas. The Vilnius issue dominated inter-war Lithuanian politics, producing serious tension in 1927 and an ultimatum from Poland in 1938.

In January 1923, when the French occupied the Ruhr, the Lithuanians occupied Klaipeda (Memel) which until then had been under joint allied administration. Klaipeda was of vital importance as one of the few ice-free ports in the eastern Baltic. Lithuanian sovereignty over the area was recognised in May 1924.

In the early 1920s the Lithuanian parliament, or *Seimas*, was dominated by the Christian Democrat Party, which was the political wing of the agrarian Peasants' League and closely associated with the Catholic Church. The main group on the left was the Social Democratic Party, whilst the populist People's Socialist Party was the chief centre party. Lithuania did not, however, enjoy ministerial stability, there being eleven cabinets between November 1918 and December 1926. In 1925 a concordat between Poland and the Catholic Church included a clause in which the latter recognised Polish sovereignty over Vilnius. The Lithuanian Christian Democrats were severely damaged and in the following year lost their parliamentary majority. A left-of-centre administration was formed which in September established diplomatic relations with the Soviet Union. The extreme right and the army reacted by staging a coup in December 1926, installing Smetona as president and Voldemaras as prime minister. Thereafter Lithuania drifted to authoritarianism. A new constitution in 1928 increased the powers of the president, but greater executive power did not ensure stability. The left fretted at growing authoritarianism whilst tension grew between Voldemaras and Smetona. In September 1929 Smetona sacked Voldemaras and instituted personal rule.

Relations between the two figures deteriorated even further in 1933 when Smetona enacted more constitutional reforms to bolster his own authority; in 1934 he jailed a number of opponents, including Voldemaras, and in the following year banned all political parties except his own, the Nationalist Party. He also introduced yet another new constitution, Lithuania's fifth since 1920, and put more pressure on the national minorities.

Smetona's image as the defender of Lithuanian nationalism was destroyed by external forces. After a frontier incident in March 1938 the Poles issued an ultimatum demanding Lithuania end the state of war it had declared in 1920, establish diplomatic relations with Poland and open the frontier. Lithuania was too weak to resist. A year later Hitler demanded the cession of Klaipeda and once again Smetona had to accede.

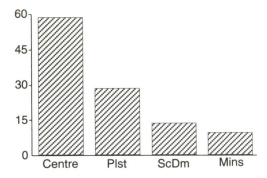

Figure 64 Composition of Assembly, 1920–2 (seats won)

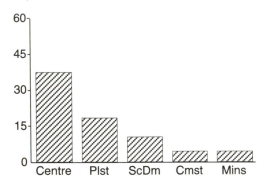

Figure 65 Composition of Assembly, 1922–3 (seats won)

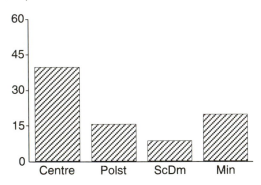

Figure 66 Composition of Assembly, 1923–6 (seats won)

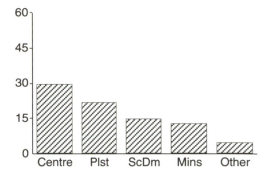

Figure 67 Composition of Assembly, 1926–7 (seats won)

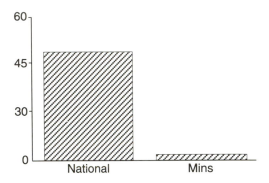

Figure 68 Composition of Assembly, 1936–40 (seats won)

Inter-war Lithuania: political

When the constituent assembly met in 1920 it was dominated by the old coalition which had fought the main political battles for national independence. After the constituent assembly this essentially centrist alliance split with the Christian Democrat Party emerging as the dominant group. In subsequent elections it secured 15 seats in 1922, and 14 in both 1923 and 1926. The other constituent elements of the centre grouping were the Peasant Union which took 12 seats in 1922, 14 in 1923 and 11 in 1926, and the Federation of Labour which took 11 seats in 1922, 12 in 1923 and 5 in 1926.

The Populists (Plst) were to the right of centre, whilst the main group on the left was the Social Democrat Party. The minorities' representation varied somewhat; the Jews had 6 seats in 1920 and 1923, and 3 in 1922 and 1926; the Poles had 3 in 1920, 2 in 1922, 4 in 1926, and a surprisingly high 11 in 1923; the Germans had a single deputy in 1920, 2 in 1923 and 6 in 1926; and the Russians had a single representative who was elected in 1923. The communists were represented only once, in 1922, when they had 5 seats in the assembly. The Farmers' Union was also represented only once, having 2 deputies in the *Seimas* of 1926.

The political situation was transformed by the coup of December 1926 and constitutional changes in 1928, 1929 and 1934. The elections of 1926 had seen the first deputies returned to the *Seimas* by the National Party and after the rise in authoritarianism they became the only tolerated party amongst the Lithuanians. It was also reflective of the times that the Germans were the only national minority which had deputies in the ineffective assembly elected in 1936.

Inter-war Lithuania: ethnic composition

A distinct feature of the Lithuanian political scene in the early 1920s was that there were always ministers who took special responsibility for the Russian and the Jewish minorities. This changed after the coup of 1926. Thereafter the state authorities encouraged Christians in a number of ways; whereas in 1926, for example, Christian-owned shops had been rare in Lithuania, a decade later they were commonplace.

A comparison of the figures for ethnic composition and religious affiliation reveals the close correlation between the ethnic and religious divisions in Lithuania. Paradoxically, where the religious division did not apply – that is, between Lithuanians and Poles – the ethnic tensions were

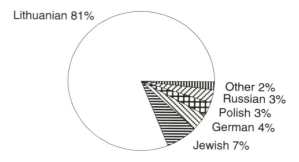

Figure 69 Ethnic composition, 1923

at their worst. This was, of course, because the Polish state had seized Vilnius and its surrounding area.

Inter-war Lithuania: religious composition

Lithuania forms part of the eastern rim of Roman Catholicism which stretches up from Croatia through Slovenia, Slovakia and Poland. Over four-fifths of Lithuanians in 1923 were affiliated to the Roman Catholic Church. The only other denomination of any size was the Lutheran, almost 9 per cent. Jews formed 7 per cent and there were sizeable Jewish communities in towns such as Kaunas.

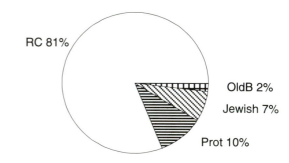

Figure 70 Religious composition, 1923

Inter-war Lithuania: landholdings

Primarily because of the influence of the Catholic Church land reform legislation in Lithuania was moderate. The maximum holding allowed under the 1922 law was 150 hectares, rather than the 80 contained in the original proposal, and some compensation was to be paid, though not to Russian landowners. The land reform also broke up the village commune system which had been imported by the Russians.

The relative moderation of the law gave larger farms a presence they did not have in many

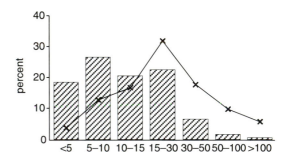

Figure 71 Landholdings: number and area

other European states. Data from the late 1930s (see Figure 71) show that holdings over 15 hectares covered a greater proportion of the area than they formed a proportion of the whole number, whilst farms over 50 hectares covered 16.01 per cent of the total area; 6.33 per cent of the area was accounted for by farms of over 100 hectares.

A relatively large number of bigger holdings, the cooperative movement, and government assistance helped to make Lithuanian agriculture by the late 1930s one of the most efficient in Eastern Europe; Lithuania produced 10 per cent more food than it needed; Denmark's excess was only 6 per cent.

The obverse of this coin was that a number of smaller farmers migrated to the cities or left the country altogether.

Inter-war Lithuania: economic

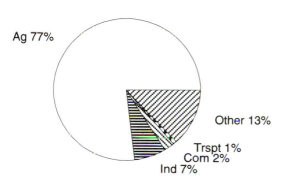

Figure 72 Population by economic sector, 1936

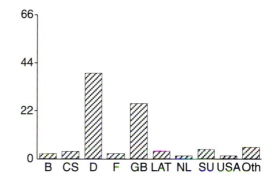

Figure 74 Distribution of trade, 1932 (% value)

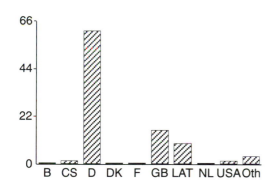

Figure 73 Distribution of trade, 1923 (% value)

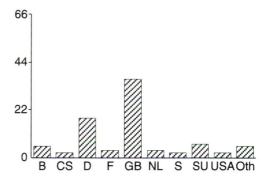

Figure 75 Distribution of trade, 1937 (% value)

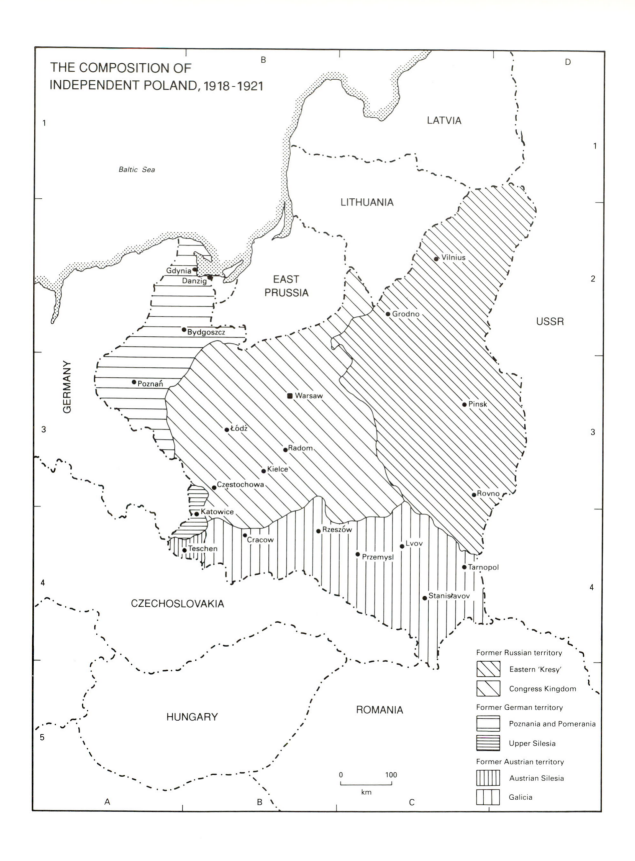

THE COMPOSITION OF
INDEPENDENT POLAND, 1918-1921

LATVIA

Baltic Sea

LITHUANIA

EAST
PRUSSIA

GERMANY

Gdynia
Danzig

Bydgoszcz

Poznań

Warsaw

Łódź

Radom

Kielce

Czestochowa

Katowice

Teschen

Cracow

Rzeszów

Przemysl

Lvov

Tarnopol

Stanisłavov

Vilnius

Grodno

Pinsk

Rovno

USSR

CZECHOSLOVAKIA

HUNGARY

ROMANIA

Former Russian territory

Eastern 'Kresy'

Congress Kingdom

Former German territory

Poznania and Pomerania

Upper Silesia

Former Austrian territory

Austrian Silesia

Galicia

0   100

km

The composition of independent Poland, 1918–21

The Polish republic of 1918–39 was created from territory formerly belonging to the German, the Austro-Hungarian and the Russian empires. In the west Poznania, Pomerania (Pomorze) and Silesia were formally under German administration. Galicia and Austrian Silesia, including Teschen, were former Habsburg lands, and the remainder were once part of the Russian empire. The former Russian territories consisted of two parts, the congress kingdom and the 'kresy'. The kingdom of Poland, created at the Congress of Vienna in 1815, had had its own constitution and political life under its king, who was also the emperor of Russia. The constitution was abolished after the Polish revolt of 1830 but some differences between the kingdom and the rest of the Russian empire, especially in landholding and tenurial systems, remained. Those parts of Poland which had formerly been in Russia but which had not been part of the congress kingdom were known as the 'kresy', or borderlands. Here there were extremely antiquated tenurial relationships. East Prussia voted in a plebiscite, undertaken at the time of the Red Army's advance westwards in the summer of 1920, to remain within Germany.

In the west, Danzig was separated from its hinterland and made a free city. Poland was to have access to wharves and other port facilities and it was to control the foreign policy of Danzig, but the city was explicitly not part of the Polish state.

There had been great difficulties over Silesia, a region rich in minerals and developed industries. The Germans were extremely reluctant to relinquish the area and by March 1921, when a plebiscite organised by the Western allies was held, there had already been two uprisings by local Poles. The voting was not purely on national lines; Jews, terrified of alleged Polish anti-Semitism, voted for inclusion in Germany, as did some Poles who feared that the area and its inhabitants would wither economically if cut off from the rest of Germany and the generous social welfare benefits imperial Germany had provided. The result of the plebiscite was that 700,000 voted for inclusion in Germany and 450,000 for Poland. To make matters worse many of the pro-Polish supporters were found in the areas abutting Germany and many of the pro-Germans in those adjacent to Poland. The allies saw partition as the only solution; Upper Silesia, centred upon Katowice, went to Poland and Lower Silesia to Germany; one million Silesian Germans were left in Poland and two million Poles remained in Germany.

There were further disputes over Austrian Silesia, and more specifically over Teschen which was claimed by both Poland and Czechoslovakia. The Czechoslovaks seized their opportunity to occupy the area in 1919 during the Russo-Polish war. The Western allies feared that Poland might be about to fall under Bolshevik domination and therefore did not contest the Czechoslovak action. Instead, Teschen, like German Silesia, was partitioned. Poland retained most of the city and its immediate surroundings, but Czechoslovakia kept the area across the river Olza with its valuable mineral reserves and its 140,000 Poles, most of whom were Protestant.

The need to knit together areas which included three different railway gauges, at least three military traditions, together with three educational, legal, and taxation systems imposed an enormous burden on the new Polish state but by 1939 most of the difficulties had been overcome. Furthermore, the loss of the main natural harbour, Danzig, had been to some extent remedied by the construction of a new port at Gdynia.

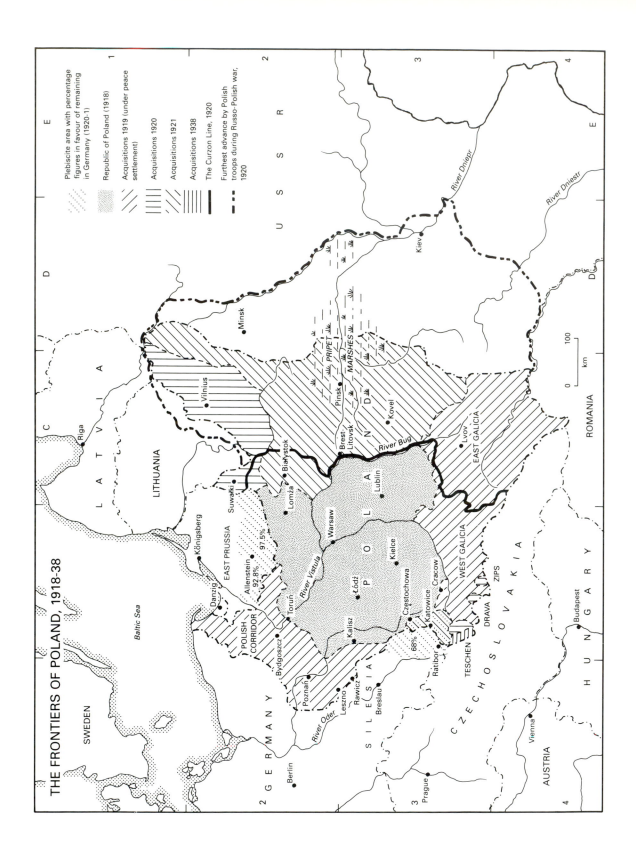

THE FRONTIERS OF POLAND, 1918-38

Legend:

- Plebiscite area with percentage figures in favour of remaining in Germany (1920-1)
- Republic of Poland (1918)
- Acquisitions 1919 (under peace settlement)
- Acquisitions 1920
- Acquisitions 1921
- Acquisitions 1938
- The Curzon Line, 1920
- Furthest advance by Polish troops during Russo-Polish war, 1920

SWEDEN

Baltic Sea

U S S R

River Dniepr

River Dniestr

River Dniestr

D

E

D

U

C

LATVIA

Riga

Minsk

LITHUANIA

Vilnius

Königsberg

EAST PRUSSIA

Danzig

Suwałki

PRIPET MARSHES

Pinsk

Brest-Litovsk

Kovel

Kiev

Allenstein
92.8%

97.5%

POLISH
CORRIDOR

Bydgoszcz

Toruń

Łomża

Białystok

River Bug

Lublin

Lvov

EAST GALICIA

ROMANIA

G E R M A N Y

Berlin

Poznań

Leszno

Rawicz

River Oder

Breslau

S I L E S I A

Kalisz

River Vistula

Łódź

Warsaw

P O L A N D

Kielce

Częstochowa

68%

Katowice

Cracow

WEST GALICIA

ZIPS

DRAVA

TESCHEN

Ratibor

C Z E C H O S L O V A K I A

Prague

AUSTRIA

Vienna

HUNGARY

Budapest

0 — 100 km

The frontiers of Poland, 1918–38

With the natural exception of the land-locked states of Hungary and Czechoslovakia, Poland had the lowest ratio of coastal-to-land frontier of any country in Europe.

At the end of the First World War the victorious allies had leverage in the western and southern areas of the new Polish state and were therefore able to stage plebiscites and make other arrangements for the determination of Poland's southern and western borders (see p. 100). It was a different question in the east where the collapse of German military power had left a vacuum. The elements likely to fill that vacuum included the new Poland, the various Ukrainian factions, and, much to the horror of the Western allies, Lenin's Bolshevik regime in Russia.

The immediate preoccupation of Poland's new rulers was with the city of Lvov which was regarded as an integral part of Polish national territory but which was threatened with occupation by the Ukrainians. After Lvov had been secured Vilnius (Wilno) was taken. This city, too, was regarded as an integral part of Poland, and the heart of the great Polish military leader, Józef Piłsudksi, was eventually to be buried here, but the Lithuanians also coveted the city which they regarded as their natural capital.

By the spring of 1919 Polish forces had clashed with those of the Bolsheviks. The Russo-Polish war of 1919–21 was to be decisive for Poland and for the rest of the continent; it stopped that westward expansion of Bolshevism which the statesmen of Europe feared so much.

The war, which was to determine Poland's eastern boundary until 1939, began fitfully but by August 1919 the Poles had advanced as far as Minsk. In 1920 Polish forces combined with dissident Ukrainians and by the early summer had taken Kiev, but the advance was soon reversed; by July Bolshevik forces were racing into Poland and threatening Warsaw itself. The Polish commander, Piłsudski, then effected a brilliant regrouping and broke the Red Army in the battle of Warsaw in August. In the autumn the Poles chased the Bolsheviks eastward through Belorussia and Ukraine until an armistice was agreed in October. The definitive peace was signed at Riga on 18 March 1921. Poland was left in possession of large areas of Belorussia and eastern Galicia, her border with Russia thus running far to the east of that originally suggested by Lord Curzon during the peace negotiations in Paris.

In October 1920, after the victory at Warsaw, Polish troops under the command of General Lucjan Żeligowski reoccupied Vilnius and the surrounding district. After March 1921 there followed a series of intrigues and minor adjustments on the eastern border before the frontiers were settled in 1922 and finally recognised by the Western powers in March 1923.

The borders of Poland were to remain as determined in 1923 until 1938 when the dismemberment of Czechoslovakia (see p. 67) afforded the Poles the opportunity to take possession of the rest of the Teschen enclave. The question of Vilnius was a source of constant friction with Lithuania and led to a Polish ultimatum to Kaunas in 1938.

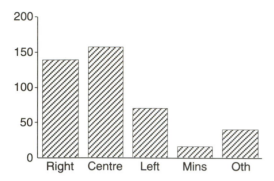

Figure 76 Constituent Assembly, 1921 (seats won)

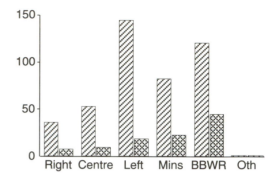

Figure 79 *Sejm* and Senate elections, 1928 (seats won)

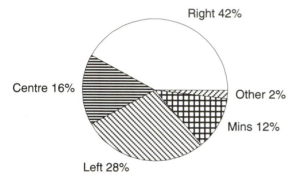

Figure 77 Share of votes, Constituent Assembly (seats won)

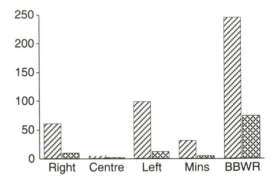

Figure 80 *Sejm* and Senate elections, 1930 (seats won)

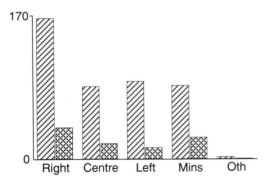

Figure 78 *Sejm* and Senate elections, 1922 (seats won)

Inter-war Poland: political

The constituent assembly was elected before the final borders of Poland had been settled and thus minorities claimed thereafter that they had been under-represented in the body which devised the constitution.

Between 1921 and 1926 the most powerful element in the political arena was the lower house of the assembly, the *Sejm*. The use of proportional representation, the relatively large number of minority parties, and the fact that each political faction – right, left, centre and agrarian – tended to have separate parties for each of the three main pre-1918 'partitions', all contributed to the fragmentation which so characterised Polish politics, at least between 1921 and 1926. By 1925 there were ninety-two registered political parties. No party could form a government alone, and parties were so small that they frequently came together in 'blocs'. Poland was in effect governed by a coalition of coalitions, few of which lasted more than a few months. The only successful cabinet was that led by Władysław Grabski from December 1923 to November 1925, and his success owed much to the fact that he was given extraordinary power by the *Sejm*.

Before Piłsudski's *coup d'état* of May 1926 there was only one general election. (The columns in Figures 78–80 show, on the left-hand side, the *Sejm* seats gained by that group of parties; the right-hand column shows Senate seats.) In that one election the parties of the right took 30 per cent of the votes, the centre 23 per cent, the left 25 per cent, and the minority groups 22 per cent. The distribution of votes in subsequent elections was much affected by the formation of the Non-Party Bloc for the Support of the Government (BBWR) which took votes mainly from the right. In the 1928 elections the BBWR had 24 per cent of the poll, the right 9 per cent, the centre 10 per cent, the minority groups 26 per cent, and the left 31 per cent. The vote reflected rising discontent with the conduct of the post-coup administration, and the left and minority groups were never again to enjoy such a high degree of support. In the 1930 elections the government decided to use more influence but it is probable that the BBWR would have emerged the strongest party in any case. Its share of the vote was 47 per cent, that of the right 13 per cent, the centre 4 per cent, the minority groups 15 per cent, the left 20 per cent, with 1 per cent going to other groups.

The year 1930 saw Poland pass through a severe crisis. In addition to the tensions of the world economic depression there was a growing terrorist campaign by Ukrainian extremists and the government was in open confrontation with an alliance of centre and left factions. The government took refuge in strong measures and locked up a number of its leading opponents in the fortress of Brześć (Brest-Litovsk). They were tried and most of them went into exile, but the needlessly humiliating and brutal treatment to which they had been subjected poisoned the atmosphere of Polish politics for years. In domestic affairs Poland was subjected to the 'rule of the colonels' – associates and friends of Piłsudski – the marshal himself taking little interest in anything outside military affairs or foreign policy.

In 1935 a new constitution was introduced by which proportional representation was abolished, the size and the powers of the *Sejm* reduced, and much greater power given to the president. The constitution had been tailored to suit Piłsudski but he died shortly after its introduction. The elections held between 1935 and 1939 were heavily manipulated by the government and cannot be taken as an accurate indication of popular opinion. In the first of the two elections in this period the opposition's call for a boycott meant that under half of the potential electorate turned out to vote; in the second election in November 1938 just under two-thirds of the electorate did so.

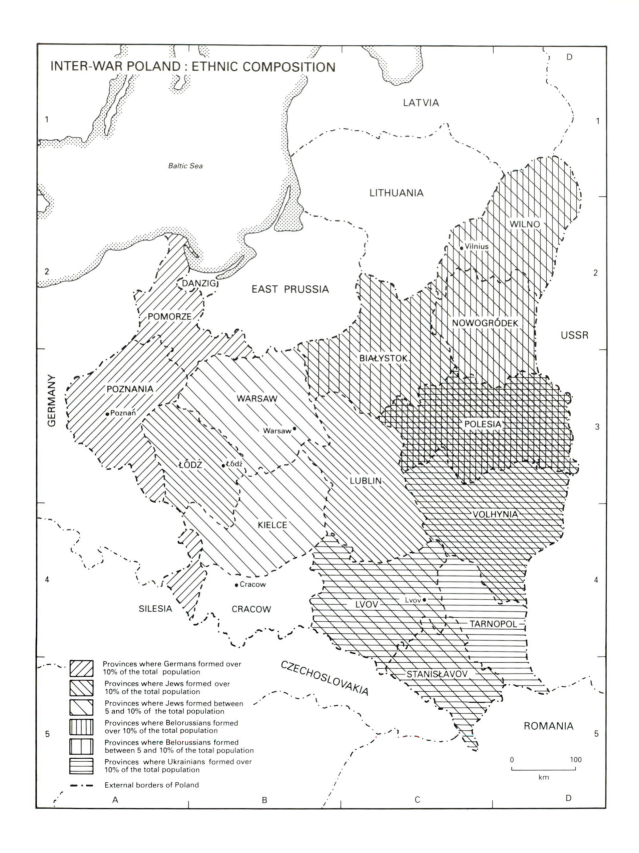

INTER-WAR POLAND : ETHNIC COMPOSITION

LATVIA

Baltic Sea

LITHUANIA

EAST PRUSSIA

DANZIG

POMORZE

WILNO

• Vilnius

NOWOGRÓDEK

USSR

BIAŁYSTOK

POZNANIA

• Poznań

WARSAW

Warsaw •

POLESIA

ŁÓDŹ

• Łódź

LUBLIN

GERMANY

KIELCE

VOLHYNIA

• Cracow

SILESIA   CRACOW

LVOV   Lvov •

TARNOPOL

CZECHOSLOVAKIA

STANISŁAVOV

ROMANIA

Provinces where Germans formed over 10% of the total population

Provinces where Jews formed over 10% of the total population

Provinces where Jews formed between 5 and 10% of the total population

Provinces where Belorussians formed over 10% of the total population

Provinces where Belorussians formed between 5 and 10% of the total population

Provinces where Ukrainians formed over 10% of the total population

—·—·— External borders of Poland

0   100
km

104

Inter-war Poland: ethnic and religious composition

Poles formed the majority in all provinces except Polesia, Volhynia, Tarnopol, and Stanisłavov. In Polesia, the most mixed of the provinces, Poles constituted 24.3 per cent of the population, Ukrainians 17.7 per cent, Jews 10.6 per cent, and Belorussians 42.6 per cent. The highest percentages of Poles were to be found in the central provinces of Cracow (93 per cent), Kielce (91.4 per cent), Warsaw (89.9 per cent), and Lublin (85.4 per cent).

Silesia had the highest proportion of Germans (28.3 per cent); Pomorze (18.8 per cent) and Poznania (16.7 per cent) came next.

Belorussians were found predominantly in the north-east, forming 25.7 per cent of the population in Vilnius (Wilno), 37.6 per cent in Nowogródek, and 42.6 per cent in Polesia.

Ukrainians were concentrated in the south-east and were the only minority group to constitute an absolute majority in any Polish province. They were 70.2 per cent of the population of Stanisłavov, 68.4 per cent in Volhynia, and 50 per cent in Tarnopol.

Jews were the most widely dispersed of the minority groups. The largest proportion of Jews was to be found in those areas of the former Russian pale now included in Poland: 12.5 per cent in Białystok, 10.9 per cent in Lublin, 10.6 per cent in Volhynia, 10.4 per cent in Polesia, 8.5 per cent in Kielce, 8.2 per cent in Vilnius (Wilno), 7 per cent in Lvov, and 6.8 per cent in both Nowogródek and Stanisłavov. The Jews lived mainly in the cities; in Warsaw province, for example, they formed 7.8 per cent of the total population, but 26.9 per cent of the total in Warsaw city.

The highest proportion of Lithuanians (4.9 per cent) was in Vilnius (Wilno).

The Polish government policy of planting Polish settlers in the east did little to strengthen the Polish element there.

Religious divisions were apparent in the economic structure. The vast majority, 98.5 per cent, of those involved in agriculture were Christians of whom only 2.6 per cent were Protestants. More than half of those engaged in commerce and insurance were Jewish, as were 21.3 per cent of those in mining and industry, and 21.5 per cent of those in education and culture.

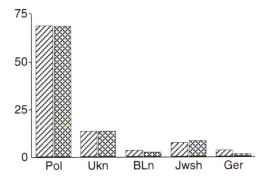

Figure 81 Ethnic groups; 1921 and 1931 (% total)

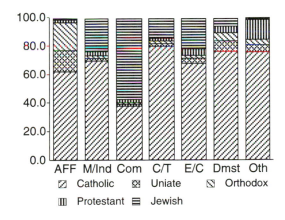

Figure 82 Economic sectors by religion, 1931

105

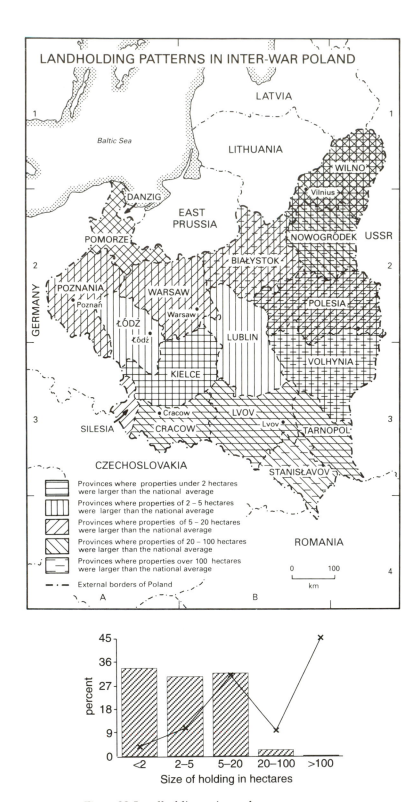

Figure 83 Landholdings: size and area

106

Inter-war Poland: landholdings

In September 1921 there were 3,262,179 separate landholdings in Poland covering a total of 30,340,659 hectares, giving an overall average size of 9.3 hectares per holding.

Holdings under 2 hectares formed 33.99 per cent of the total number but covered only 3.54 per cent of the total area; those between 2 and 5 hectares were 30.71 per cent of the total number and covered 11.31 of the total area; those from 5 to 20 hectares were 32.03 per cent of the total number and covered 30.81 per cent of the area; those from 20 to 100 hectares were 2.68 per cent of the total and covered 9.55 per cent of the total area; and the large estates of over 100 hectares, whilst only 0.59 per cent of the total number, accounted for 44.79 per cent of the total agricultural land.

The average size per holding in each category was 0.97, 3.47, 8.95, 33.06, and 708.29 hectares respectively. The map shows provinces where the average size in each category is greater than the national average. In the eastern lands holdings were clearly larger than in the centre and the west. In Vilnius (Wilno), holdings in all categories except the largest were higher than average; in Nowogródek all were larger except those between 5 and 20 hectares; Polesia had farms which were larger than the national average in all categories except that between 20 and 100 hectares. Estates of over 100 hectares were larger than the national average in Białystok, Nowogródek, Polesia, Volhynia, and Stanisłavov; those between 20 and 100 hectares were larger than the national average in Vilnius, Nowogródek, Pomorze, Cracow, Lvov, Stanisłavov, and Tarnopol.

The largest concentration of the number of estates of over 100 hectares was in Poznania (12.67 per cent of the total of those estates), Warsaw (11.96 per cent), Lvov (7.80 per cent), Pomorze (7.30 per cent), and Lublin (6.75 per cent). These estates were generally smaller than those to the east; they averaged 566.55 hectares in Poznania, 411.63 hectares in Warsaw, 573.09 hectares in Lvov, 559.57 hectares in Pomorze, and 681.59 hectares in Lublin; in Białystok, on the other hand, the provincial average in this category was 1,015.85 hectares, in Polesia 2,132.64 hectares, in Stanisłavov 1,074.53 hectares, in Volhynia 970.06 hectares, and in Nowogródek 711.68 hectares. The tendency for holdings to be larger in the east is confirmed by the fact that the provinces in which holdings over 20 hectares covered over 50 per cent of the agricultural land were: Białystok, 52.89 percent; Vilnius, 62.44 per cent; Nowogródek, 60.18 per cent; Polesia, 75.17 per cent; and Stanisłavov, 61.06 per cent. In Tarnopol 49.89 per cent and in Volhynia 49.80 per cent of land was held in units of over 20 hectares. The critical point, however, was that whereas in the west, particularly in the former German territories, the larger estates were worked as single agrarian units, often with a considerable degree of capital input, in the east the large holdings were generally split and rented out in tiny plots to local peasants.

Estates over 20 hectares also accounted for the majority of agricultural land in Poznania, 71.77 per cent; Pomorze 74.71 per cent; and Silesia 53.94 per cent. This was the heritage of the pre-First World War Prussian system. Estates over 20 hectares were exactly half the agricultural land in Warsaw. In the remainder the small farmer predominated, holdings of less than 20 hectares making up 61.77 per cent of the land in Łódż, 62.12 per cent in Kielce, 60.34 per cent in Lublin, 51.87 per cent in Lvov, and 68.17 per cent in Cracow.

In general the larger estates were more predominant in areas where there was a significant rural non-Polish minority.

After 1921 there were some measures of land reform and redistribution forced on the government by fear of Bolshevism. In 1925 further legislation enacted a maximum size of 180 hectares (300 hectares in the east) for all properties, but the pace of reform was slow and the new law was never fully applied throughout the country. The great depression from 1929 to the mid-1930s acted as a further brake on the reforming process.

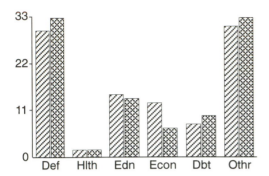

Figure 84 Budget expenditure, 1928/9, 1937/8 (%)

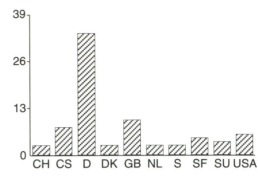

Figure 87 Distribution of trade, 1930 (% value)

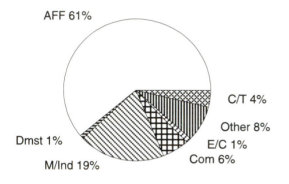

Figure 85 Population by economic sector, 1931

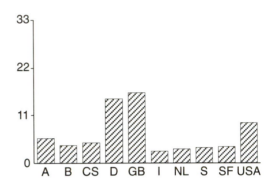

Figure 88 Distribution of trade, 1935 (% value)

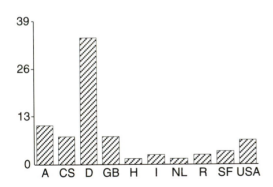

Figure 86 Distribution of trade, 1925 (% value)

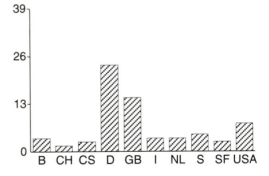

Figure 89 Distribution of trade, 1938 (% value)

Inter-war Poland: economic

By the middle of the inter-war period Poland remained a country predominantly of primary producers – agriculture, fishing and forestry accounting for 60.6 per cent of the workforce in 1931, when 19.3 per cent were involved in mining and industry, and 6.1 per cent in communications and transport.

Until the mid-1920s Central Europe had dominated Poland's foreign trade; in 1925 45.8 per cent of imports came from Austria, Czechoslovakia and Germany combined, and these three countries bought 62.8 per cent of Polish exports. By 1935 these figures had fallen to 23.27 per cent and 27.23 per cent respectively, and even in 1938 when German economic domination was being felt throughout Europe, the figures were little changed at 26.17 per cent for imports and 27.77 per cent for exports.

Whilst Central European states declined as factors in Poland's external trade, Northern and Western Europe became more important. In 1925 Denmark, Sweden, Norway and Finland had provided 8.42 per cent of Poland's imports and taken 4.73 per cent of her exports; by 1930 these figures had risen to 10.66 per cent and 13.95 per cent; thereafter they declined somewhat, ending in 1938 at 9.3 per cent and 12.89 per cent. In the same period Belgium and Holland increased their share of Polish trade from 3.6 per cent of imports and 4.9 per cent of exports in 1925, to 5.93 per cent and 5.95 per cent in 1930, and 6.9 per cent and 9.34 per cent in 1938. There were also steady rises in Poland's trade, particularly in exports, with Great Britain and the United States. A notable absentee from Poland's major trading partners was France.

Just over two-fifths of Polish exports in the late 1930s consisted of farm produce. Within this category there had been steady increases in the value of bacon and tinned ham exports, mainly to Great Britain, Germany and the United States. Cattle and dairy produce also featured as prominent export items. Taken together coal, timber and wood products accounted for about a third of exports. Timber and wood products went mainly to Britain, Germany, the Netherlands and Belgium. Coal went to Scandinavia, the Low Countries and some to France. The Poles had taken advantage of the 1926 British coal miners' strike to find lucrative markets in Scandinavia and the Baltic states, but in the 1930s British commercial agreements with the Baltic states limited the opportunities for Polish coal exporters in these areas.

Raw materials and semi-manufactured goods made up most of Poland's imports. Cotton and wool, most of the former from the United States, made up about a fifth of imports for the majority of the inter-war period; machinery, machine tools and means of transport accounted for about an eighth of the total, and scrap-iron, cinders and ores about a tenth. The latter consisted of a number of minerals which Poland did not have on her own territory, including copper, nickel, tin and silver.

THE PARTITION OF POLAND, 1939

LATVIA

Baltic Sea

LITHUANIA

Memel

Königsberg

EAST PRUSSIA

Vilnius

Suwałki

Augustow

Grodno

Lomza

Białystok

UNION

Poznań

Pinsk

Warsaw

Brest-Litovsk

Pripet

Łódź

Marshes

Radom

GERMANY

Lublin

GENERAL

GOVERNMENT

Lutsk

Sokal

Rovno

SOVIET

Cracow

Lvov

Tarnopol

Soviet/German
partition line

Annexed by Germany

Annexed by Lithuania

Annexed by the
Soviet Union

Polish border
before September
1939

Border between
General Government
and territory annexed
to Germany

Stanisławov

SLOVAKIA

0   100

km

HUNGARY

ROMANIA

110

The partition of Poland, 1939

After the conclusion of the Polish–German non-aggression pact in 1934 the Polish government maintained correct if not cordial relations with Nazi Germany. The Poles could not afford to be overtly aggressive. Hitler and the Nazis could easily stir up trouble amongst the German and the Ukrainian minorities in Poland and they could equally easily raise awkward demands over Danzig or over land access to East Prussia. On the other hand, the Poles were by no means overawed by the Nazis. Piłsudski regarded Hitler as a 'windbag', and far less of a threat to Poland than the old Prussian military aristocracy had been. It was also assumed that Hitler, as an Austrian, would be more interested in expansion to the south and the south-east rather than in the north; and it was further assumed that Poland might be of help to Hitler should he ever seek to implement that grand design outlined in *Mein Kampf* of colonising western Russia and Ukraine. In 1938, after the Munich settlement had detached the Sudeten areas from Czechoslovakia, the Poles took back Trans-Olza and the areas around Teschen which the Czechoslovaks had taken in 1919.

Soon after that, however, it became clear that Hitler's gaze was not set primarily on the south and south-east. In March 1939 the Germans retook Memel and renounced the 1934 non-aggression pact with Poland. Danzig was clearly the next target. Britain and France concluded treaties with Poland guaranteeing its independence but not its territorial integrity; these did not deter Hitler who had determined upon expansion further east, concluding the pact with the Soviet Union in August in an attempt to dissuade the Western allies from honouring their promises to Poland.

The German invasion began on 1 September 1939; on 17 September the Soviet Union advanced its forces from the east. Poland could not withstand attack from two sides. In the ensuing partition Vilnius was returned to Lithuania, whilst the Soviet Union, after 'organising' a plebiscite, absorbed the territories it had occupied. The Nazis did not bother with such niceties. They annexed Pomerania, Pomorze, Danzig, Polish Silesia, Teschen, and the Suwałki salient which had been detached from East Prussia. Even parts of the Cracow and Łódź provinces were incorporated into the German Reich. The incorporated areas covered over 90,000 square kilometres and involved over 10 million people; of these 8.9 million were Polish, 603,000 Jewish, and 600,000 German.

The Germans had originally intended to establish a dependent Polish government once the Western powers had accepted that the war was lost and had concluded peace. Such a plan was foiled both by Western obstinacy and by the refusal of any Pole of whatever political complexion, even fascist, to serve in any collaborationist administration. The rump of inter-war Poland was therefore formed into the 'General-Government' which was subdivided into four districts based on Warsaw, Lublin, Radom and its capital, Cracow. The new unit was landlocked and designed to serve as little more than a recruiting ground for slave labour by the Reich and a dumping ground for racial groups thought to be undesirable. It was ruled with great brutality by Hans Frank.

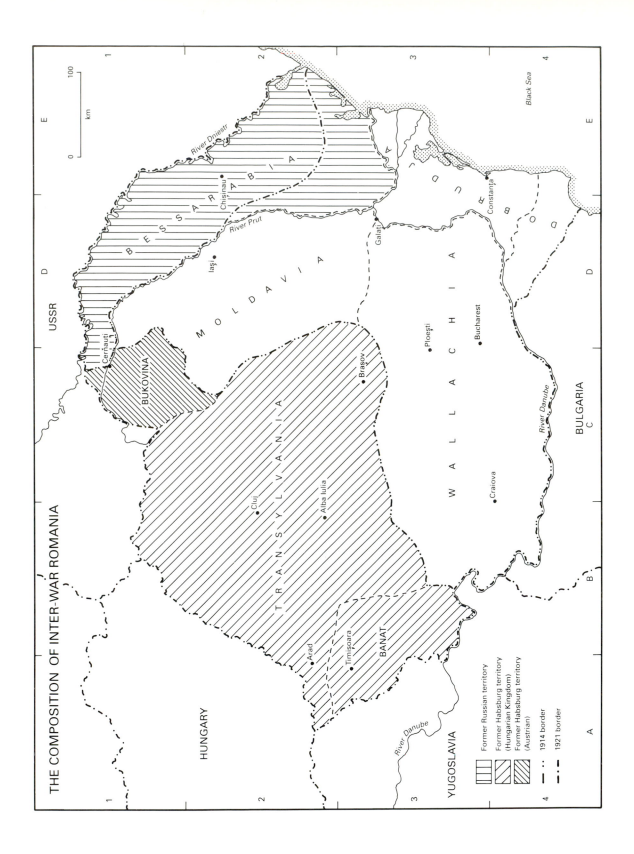

THE COMPOSITION OF INTER-WAR ROMANIA

Former Russian territory

Former Habsburg territory (Hungarian Kingdom)

Former Habsburg territory (Austrian)

1914 border

1921 border

USSR

River Dniestr

BESSARABIA

Chişinău

River Prut

Iaşi

Cernăuţi

BUKOVINA

MOLDAVIA

Galaţi

Black Sea

DOBRUDJA

Constanţa

Ploeşti

Bucharest

Braşov

Cluj

Alba Iulia

TRANSYLVANIA

WALLACHIA

Craiova

River Danube

BULGARIA

Arad

Timişoara

BANAT

River Danube

HUNGARY

YUGOSLAVIA

km

100

0

The composition of inter-war Romania

The territories acquired in 1918–20 formed 51.3 per cent of the area of the inter-war Romanian kingdom; Transylvania and the Banat accounted for 30.7 per cent of the new state, Bessarabia for 15.9 per cent and the Bukovina for 4.7 per cent. Southern Dobrudja, acquired from Bulgaria after the second Balkan war (see p. 21), was retained. The new territories were far from being all Romanian by population. Transylvania had a large Hungarian element and there were many Protestant Germans; the Banat was a bewildering mixture of peoples including Catholic Germans, Albanians, Bulgarians, Hungarians, Slovaks, Serbs, and even tiny pockets of French. In Bessarabia there were many Ukrainians, Jews, Bulgarians and Gagauze or Turkish-speaking Christians. The Bukovina had a large percentage of Ukrainians and a substantial Jewish population. The southern Dobrudja was also an area of great racial mixture. In addition to Bulgarians and Romanians there were Tartars and Turks, Gagauze and Gypsies. In the expanded Romania 28.1 per cent of the population were non-Romanian; in the old kingdom, the *Regat* as it was known, only 8 per cent of the population had belonged to national minority groups.

Such a large accretion of territory brought many problems. The newly acquired lands were at very different stages of economic and political development. Bessarabia was the most backward and had no proper rail connection with the *Regat*; not even Moldavia or its capital, Iaşi, were well served by the existing rail network, and the entire area was beset with deep social problems. Bukovina, too, was desperately poor but it had benefited from honest and relatively enlightened administration from Vienna. Transylvania had little in the way of developed or modern industries but its administration was more sophisticated than that of Bessarabia or the *Regat*. Differing levels of development were reflected in statistics such as those for literacy above seven years of age, which ranged from 67.3 per cent in Transylvania and 65.7 per cent in the Bukovina to as low as 45.5 per cent in southern Dobrudja and 38.2 per cent in Bessarabia. In the *Regat* it was 56.1 per cent and the overall average was 57.1 per cent.

That Romania was able to acquire so much territory at the end of the First World War – in the inter-war period it was second in size in Eastern Europe only to Poland – had much to do with the political instability which followed the collapse of the Austro-Hungarian and Russian empires. The victor powers feared revanchism from the right and radicalism from the left. Romania was built up as a bastion against both: it would, it was assumed, contain both Hungarian and Bulgarian revisionism and Hungarian and Russian Bolshevism. The Romanians were also helped by the fact that they had powerful supporters in figures such as Robert Seton-Watson and Henry Wickham-Steed who advised the peacemakers in Paris.

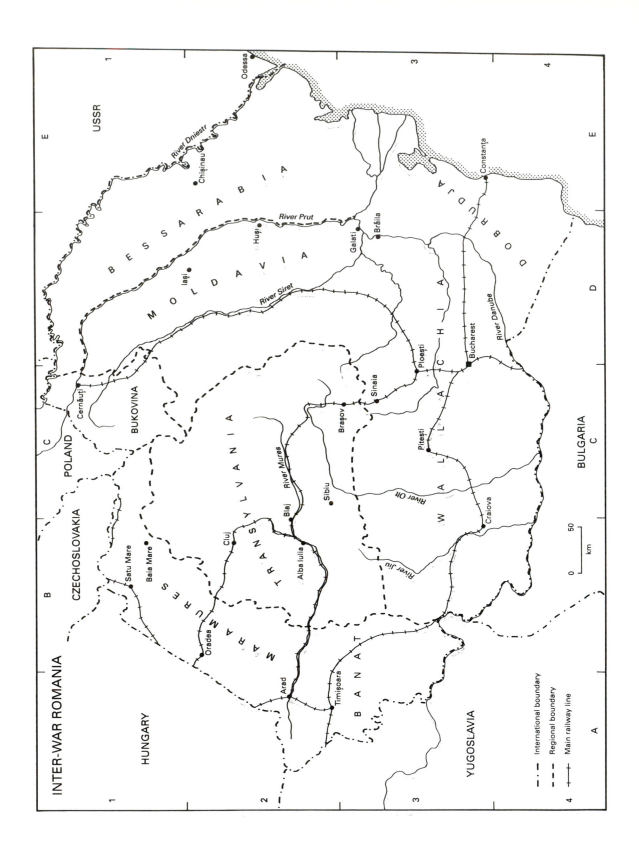

INTER-WAR ROMANIA

Inter-war Romania

The foundation stone of the expanded Romanian state which emerged from the First World War was laid in December 1918 at Alba Iulia when the Romanians of Transylvania agreed to join those of the pre-war kingdom, the *Regat*, on condition that they were granted a considerable degree of autonomy. A similar proviso had been made by the Romanians of Bessarabia a year previously when they had expressed a wish to become part of Romania. The politicians of Bucharest, however, were not anxious to forgo the patronage which the new territories offered and thus the *Regat* extended its domination over all parts of the state, creating considerable tensions between the new and the old parts of the kingdom.

From 1918 to 1922 Romania was preoccupied with the tasks of absorbing the new lands and of staving off the threat from militant Bolshevism, a threat manifested in Romania by a series of strikes. At the same time the new territories had to be bound together with each other and with the *Regat*. By 1923 a single currency had been introduced and all main railway lines converted to standard gauge, but the country still bore the marks of its varied origin. Bessarabia, for example, still had no proper rail connection with the *Regat*.

The achievement of some form of unity was also marked in 1923 by the promulgation of a new constitution. It was strongly centralist and in 1925 the country was divided into 71 *préfectures* in an attempt to break up remaining regional affiliations. But regional identity was never fully erased, not least in Transylvania whose population was politically mature and many of whose Romanians adhered to the Uniate Church with its centre in Blaj.

From 1923 to 1928 the dominant element in Romanian public life was the Liberal Party, one of the traditional, pre-war parliamentary groups.

By 1928 it was being challenged by the National Peasant Party (NPP), a combination of the Romanian Peasant Party and the (Romanian) Nationalist Party of Transylvania. In 1928 the NPP won a resounding victory in one of the very few free elections ever held in Romania. The NPP government was wrecked by the great depression and by the machinations of King Carol who, despite promises not to do so, reappeared in Romania with his mistress, Madame Lupescu.

The 1930s saw the rise of the strongest native fascist movement in Eastern Europe, the Iron Guards. It was led by Corneliu Zelia Codreanu, a native of Huşi in Moldavia who had come to political prominence and popularity by murdering the police chief of Iaşi. Codreanu was himself murdered by the police on *Walpurgisnacht* 1938, and until 1940 King Carol managed by a mixture of political sagacity and massive bribery to retain control of Romanian affairs.

The King's regime collapsed with the partition of Romania in 1940 (see map on p. 120) and after his departure in September of that year the Iron Guard came to power for a few hectic months. The Guard murdered many of its political opponents and indulged in a series of hideous outrages on Jews; in Constanţa there was 'a column of infamy' to which Jews were tied and at which some were, according to some reports, publicly castrated.

Such disorders were not to the liking of the Germans. They had long had their eyes on Romania's greatest natural asset, the oil fields around Ploeşti. Hitler, having recently decided to attack the Soviet Union, would not welcome political instability in Romania which might threaten oil supplies. The Germans therefore condoned the suppression of the Guard by General Antonescu in January 1941.

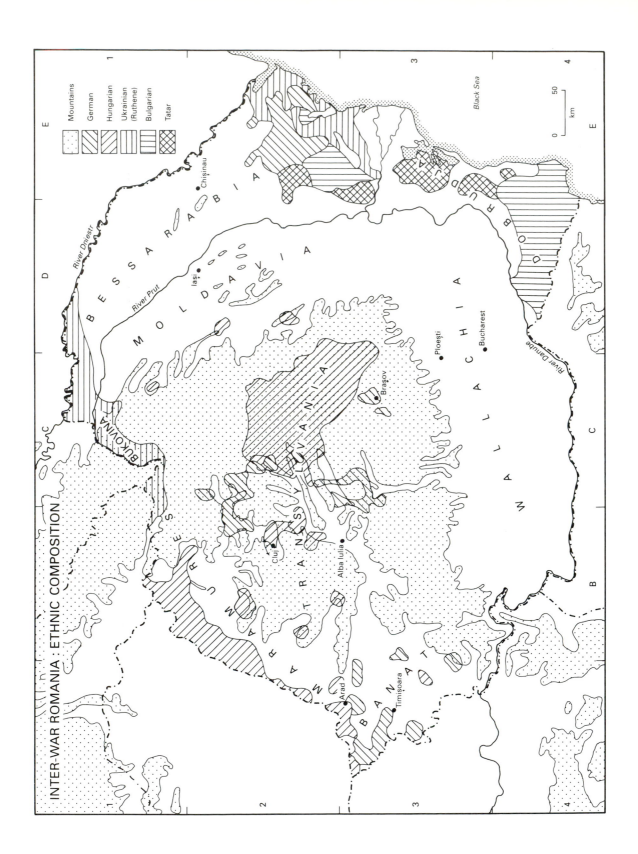

INTER-WAR ROMANIA : ETHNIC COMPOSITION

Mountains
German
Hungarian
Ukrainian
(Ruthene)
Bulgarian
Tatar

Black Sea

50
km
0

River Dniestr

BESSARABIA

Chişinău

River Prut

MOLDAVIA

Iaşi

BUKOVINA

TRANSYLVANIA

Braşov

WALLACHIA

Ploeşti

Bucharest

Cluj

Alba Iulia

River Danube

MURES

BANAT

Arad

Timişoara

DOBRUDJA

116

Inter-war Romania: ethnic composition

Most of Romania's ethnic minorities had been acquired in the post-First World War territorial resettlements. Transylvania included large numbers of Hungarian-speakers. Those in the eastern, most mountainous regions were the so-called Székelys whose dialect was regarded by many as the purest form of spoken Hungarian. The Germans of Transylvania had also been early colonists. They were first introduced in the mid-twelfth century. The majority of the Transylvanian Saxons became Lutherans but German settlers in the Banat, who were later arrivals, retained their Catholicism; they were known as 'Swabians' or 'Schwabs' rather than Saxons.

In the Dobrudja the Bulgarians dominated the southern portion, though there were also considerable numbers of Tartars and Turks. Tartars were also found in the northern Dobrudja and in some areas of southern Bessarabia where there were also a number of Bulgarians together with some Gagauze, or Turkish-speaking Christians. Ukrainians were numerous in southern Bessarabia and were also to be found along much of Romania's northern border; there were further sizeable Ukrainian communities distributed throughout Bessarabia.

Romania also included two significant dispersed minorities, the Gypsies and the Jews. These were so widely spread that they did not form the majority in any area, though the Jews had a relatively high proportion of the population in the Bukovina and in the towns of Bessarabia.

A number of minority groups were too small to be shown on any map. Some of these were exotic in origin and in life-style. The sturgeon fishers of the Danube delta, for example, were nearly all Old Believers, a Russian sect which had fled from Russia in the early eighteenth century to escape reforms of the Orthodox Church. In Bucharest most *droshky* (horse-drawn cabs) drivers were from the *skoptsy* sect, a bizarre group which insisted upon castration of husbands after the birth of two sons.

Table 10 Population by ethnicity, 1930

Ethnic group	Total number	Percentage of total
Romanian	12,981,324	71.9
Magyar	1,425,507	7.9
German	745,421	4.1
Russian	409,150	2.3
Ukrainian	582,115	3.2
Serb, Croat, and Slovene	51,062	0.3
Bulgarian	366,384	2.0
Czech and Slovak	51,842	0.3
Jewish	728,115	4.0
Turk and Tartar	176,913	1.0
Gypsy	262,501	1.5
Gagauze	105,750	0.6
Others	170,944	0.9
Total	18,057,028	100.0

Table 11 Population by religion, 1930

Religion	Total number	Percentage of total
Orthodox	13,108,227	72.6
Uniate	1,427,391	7.9
Catholic	1,234,151	6.8
Calvinist	710,706	3.9
Lutheran	398,759	2.2
Unitarian	69,257	0.4
Baptist	60,562	0.4
Jewish	756,930	4.2
Muslim	185,486	1.0
Others	105,559	0.6
Total	18,057,028	100.0

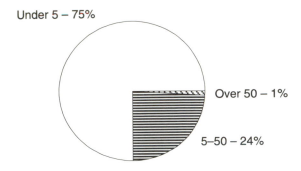

Figure 90 Size of landholdings, 1930 (ha)

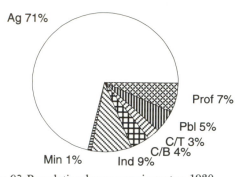

Figure 93 Population by economic sector, 1930

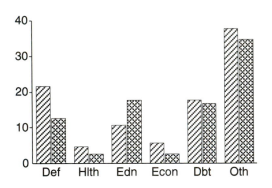

Figure 91 Size of landholdings, 1941 (ha)

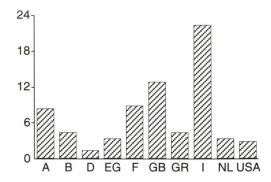

Figure 94 Distribution of trade, 1920 (% value)

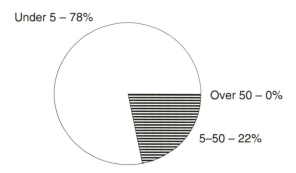

Figure 92 Budget expenditure, 1925, 1933/4 (%)

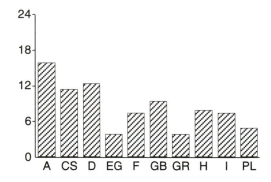

Figure 95 Distribution of trade, 1925 (% value)

118

Inter-war Romania: social and economic

Romania was fortunate amongst East European states in that it had valuable and easily accessible reserves of mineral resources in the Ploeşti oilfields. Yet despite this asset Romania's remained overwhelmingly an agrarian economy and a peasant society. Land reform had been made necessary by the threat of another 1907 (see p. 15) and was enacted immediately after the First World War. Small plots then became the

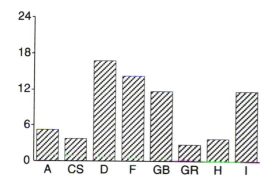

Figure 96 Distribution of trade, 1932 (% value)

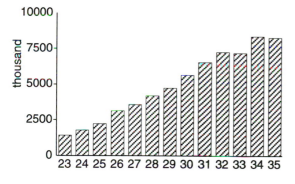

Figure 97 Petroleum production, 1923–35 (tonnes)

dominant feature of Romanian agriculture, though the vagaries of Romanian statistics make it difficult to establish regional patterns of land-holding or, in many cases, to decide how much land any individual owner held.

The distribution of population by economic sector (Figure 93), taken from the 1930 census, shows only 9 per cent of the population engaged in industry and 1 per cent in mining. The weight of the bureaucracy and the military is indicated by the fact that they were equal to half the proportion of those in mining and industry.

In the structure of Romania's exports, however, oil did show a strong presence and it formed the major component of the raw materials category which rose from 35.4 per cent of the total averaged over the years 1922–4 to a high of 61.8 per cent in 1935, whereafter it fell back to 52 per cent for 1937–8.

In Romania's trading relations the rise of Germany after 1920 is striking. Italy, Great Britain and France remained import trading partners throughout the inter-war period, and Hungary, despite the differences over Transylvania, soon re-established its significance as a market for Romanian produce after political stability had been achieved in 1920. Also notable is the prominence in 1925 of Czechoslovakia; in 1932, however, with the onset of the depression, Romania was buying less than 5 per cent of its total imports from that country whereas in 1925 the figure had been 14.28 per cent. This is one indication of the little entente's lack of value in the economic sector; so too is the fact that Yugoslavia does not feature in these figures at all.

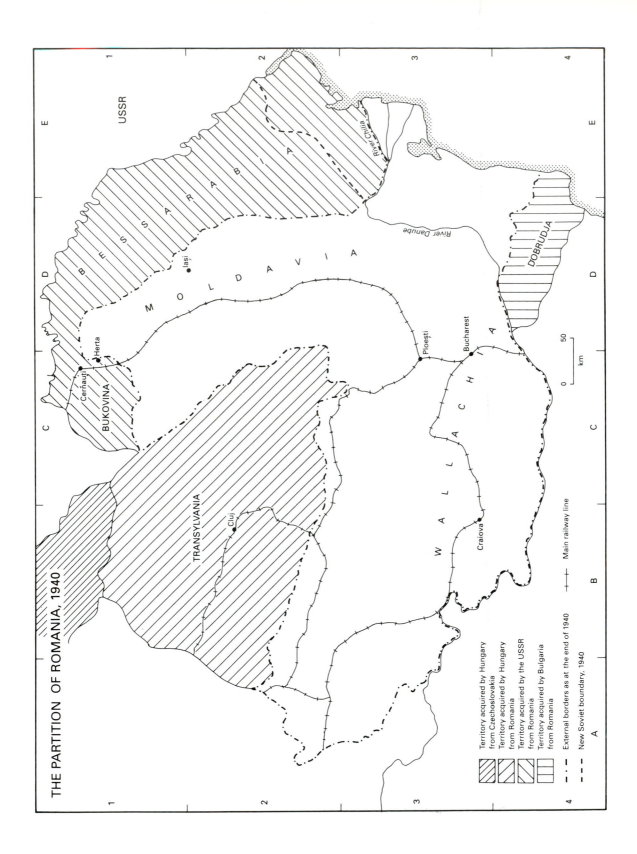

THE PARTITION OF ROMANIA, 1940

USSR

B E S S A R A B I A

M O L D A V I A

River Chilia

River Danube

DOBRUDJA

Iaşi

Herta

Cernăuţi

BUKOVINA

Ploeşti

Bucharest

TRANSYLVANIA

Cluj

W A L L A C H I A

Craiova

0 50 km

Territory acquired by Hungary
from Czechoslovakia

Territory acquired by Hungary
from Romania

Territory acquired by the USSR
from Romania

Territory acquired by Bulgaria
from Romania

External borders as at the end of 1940

New Soviet boundary, 1940

Main railway line

The partition of Romania, 1940

During the second half of the 1930s King Carol strove to save Romania from involvement in the war which was threatening the continent. His failure in this endeavour fatally compromised his rule and he left Romania in September 1940.

The undoing of Carol had been the defeat of France. In the first place this made the Iron Guard far more confident and assertive in their attacks upon the traditionally francophile Romanian political establishment. Much more importantly, the fall of France led Stalin to demand compensation for the aggrandisement of Nazi Germany, compensation which he had in effect been promised in the secret deal between Germany and the Soviet Union in August 1939. In June 1940, therefore, Stalin demanded the return of Bessarabia and also the cession of the northern Bukovina, though this had never been Russian territory. Hitler, not yet willing to cross swords with the Soviet leader, advised King Carol to give way; he did so on 28 June. In drawing up his maps the Soviet commissar for foreign affairs, Molotov, used a thick red pencil, a slip of which accidentally included the north Moldavian town of Herta and some twenty surrounding villages in the USSR. No efforts by the Romanians could remedy the mistake. The Soviets also altered their internal boundaries by transferring the southernmost counties of Bessarabia to the Ukraine thus cutting Bessarabia off from the sea.

The advance of the Soviet Union and the obvious weakening of Romania encouraged Hungarian revisionist hopes. Budapest suggested therefore that Hungary should repossess Transylvania from which it could guard the flank of any Soviet advance towards the Ploeşti oil-fields. Few believed that this was the real reason for the Hungarian claim, and Hitler was not prepared to grant that country all of Transylvania. Following Italo-German mediation the second Vienna award, signed on 30 August 1940, gave Hungary northern Transylvania, including Cluj. The terms so horrified the Romanian delegate to the 'negotiations' that he fainted at the conference table when they were pronounced.

With Hungarian and Soviet claims on Romania partially or fully met it only remained for the Bulgarians to demand territorial concessions. When they did so they received the backing of both Stalin and, less enthusiastically, Hitler. The Treaty of Craiova, 7 September 1940, ceded southern Dobrudja to Bulgaria. In so far as it had a dominant ethnic element the southern Dobrudja was Bulgarian, and it is significant that after the Second World War the area remained in Bulgarian hands.

By October German troops had moved into Romania to protect the Ploeşti oilfields. In response the Soviet Union occupied a number of islands in the river Chilia which formed the northern arm of the Danube delta and the new boundary between Soviet Bessarabia and Romania.

In a few weeks Romania had lost one-third of its territory, two-fifths of its arable area, and a third of its population; of this third, one-half (six million) were Romanians. Although these were grievous losses the oilfields had remained in Romanian hands, not least because an agreement of March 1939 had given the Germans huge influence in the Romanian economy.

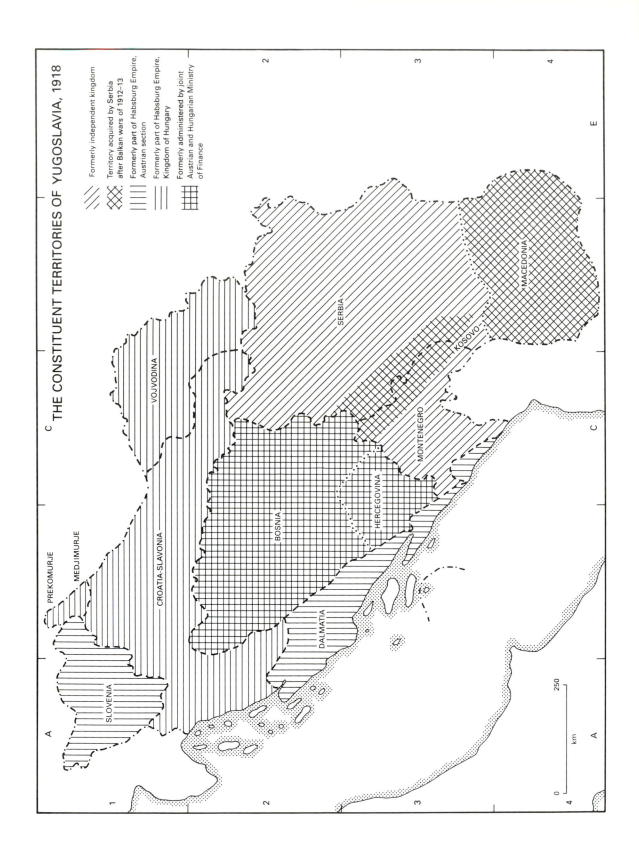

THE CONSTITUENT TERRITORIES OF YUGOSLAVIA, 1918

Formerly independent kingdom

Territory acquired by Serbia after Balkan wars of 1912–13

Formerly part of Habsburg Empire, Austrian section

Formerly part of Habsburg Empire, Kingdom of Hungary

Formerly administered by joint Austrian and Hungarian Ministry of Finance

PREKOMURJE

MEDJIMURJE

SLOVENIA

CROATIA-SLAVONIA

VOJVODINA

DALMATIA

BOSNIA

HERCEGOVINA

MONTENEGRO

SERBIA

KOSOVO

MACEDONIA

km

0   250

The formation of Yugoslavia

Of the main historic units comprising Yugoslavia, Serbia and Montenegro had before the First World War been independent kingdoms. By 1914 Serbia had incorporated into its boundaries the Macedonian areas taken during the Balkan wars. Bosnia-Hercegovina had been a part of the Habsburg empire but had been administered by a small government department which was neither part of the Austrian nor of the Hungarian section of the Dual Monarchy. In Bosnia Orthodox Serbs formed the largest section of the population but there was also a large Muslim element; Hercegovina was more Catholic, the Franciscans having a powerful influence in the region. Dalmatia, too, was predominantly Catholic. It had been included in the Austrian half of the Monarchy though its population was a mixture of Italians and Slavs. Croatia-Slavonia had been within the Hungarian kingdom since the twelfth century but within that kingdom had established, at least in theory, its own constitutional position. Slovenia, again Catholic, had been within the Austrian part of the Dual Monarchy. The Slovenes had not been the most prominent of national groups in the political life of Austria but they had, with quiet efficiency, established effective mechanisms for defending and furthering their interests. The Vojvodina, an area of great ethnic mixture, had been within the Banat of Temeşvar and therefore had been an integral part of the Hungarian kingdom; it had little in the way of indigenous political organisations.

Within Serbia itself there was a sizeable Albanian population, most of which was to be found in the Kosovo area to the south-west of the kingdom. The Serbs made few if any concessions to Albanian cultural identity, nor did they tolerate any manifestation of Macedonian sentiment in Macedonia, or, as the Serbs called it, Old Serbia.

Table 12 Population by historic units, 1921

Historic unit	Total	Percentage
Serbia and Macedonia	4,133,478	34.50
Montenegro	199,227	1.66
Bosnia and Hercegovina	1,890,440	15.77
Dalmatia	620,432	5.18
Croatia-Slavonia	2,642,996	22.05
Slovenia	962,624	8.03
Vojvodina	1,535,714	12.81
Total	11,984,911	100.00

Table 13 Ethnic composition of Yugoslavia, 1918

	Number	Percentage
Serbs	4,665,851	38.83
Croats	2,856,551	23.77
Slovenes	1,024,761	8.53
Bosnian Muslims	727,650	6.05
Macedonians/Bulgarians	585,558	4.87
Other Slavs	174,466	1.45
Germans	513,472	4.27
Hungarians	472,409	3.93
Albanians	441,740	3.68
Romanians, Vlachs, Gypsies	229,398	1.91
Turks	168,404	1.40
Jews	64,159	0.53
Italians	12,825	0.11
Others	80,079	0.67
Total	12,017,323	100.00

Source: Ivo Banac, *The National Question in Yugoslavia: Origins, History, Politics*, Ithaca and London, Cornell University Press, 1984, p. 58.

Table 14 Population by ethnicity (mother tongue), 1921 and 1931

	1921		1931	
	Number	Percentage	Number	Percentage
Serbo-Croat	8,911,509	74.36	10,730,823	77.01
Slovene	1,019,997	8.51	1,135,410	8.15
Czech and Slovak	115,532	0.96	129,320	0.93
German	505,790	4.22	499,969	3.59
Magyar	467,658	3.90	468,185	3.36
Romanian/Vlach	231,068	1.93	137,879	0.98
Albanian	439,657	3.67	505,259	3.63
Turkish	150,322	1.25	132,924	0.95
Gypsy	–	–	70,424	0.51
Others	143,378	1.20	123,845	0.89
Total	11,984,911	100.00	13,934,038	100.00

Inter-war Yugoslavia: ethnic and religious composition

In the inter-war years the Yugoslav authorities classified their peoples by language and by religion; neither provided a full picture of the ethnic composition of the country. The Croats spoke Serbo-Croat but were Catholic, as were the Slovenes and some of the smaller, non-Slav groups. It is possible, by judicious mathematics, to produce figures such as those Professor Banac provides (Table 13) for 1918, but no computation can give the full picture; many Montenegrins, for example, thought of themselves as a separate group, but were never identifiable as such because they spoke Serbo-Croat and were Orthodox. Nor do the official figures (Tables 14, 15) make it possible to calculate the number of Macedonians; they were put under the jurisdiction of the Serbian Orthodox Church and their language, said the Serbs, was a variant of Serbo-Croat.

The Serbs were to be found not only in Serbia. There were Serb settlements in the Vojvodina, southern Croatia and northern Bosnia. Serbs living outside Serbia were known as *Prečani* Serbs, or those who had 'crossed' the river Sava. The Croatian and Bosnian settlements dated from the early eighteenth century when the Habsburgs had invited the Serbs to colonise and defend the military frontier with the Ottoman empire.

Croats populated not only Croatia but also formed a sizeable proportion of the population in Hercegovina.

The origins of the Bosnian Muslims is still the subject of some controversy. The area seems to have been a refuge for Christian dissidents of various kinds in the late Middle Ages and many of the local landowners in the area converted to Islam after the Ottoman conquest in order to preserve their rights to property. The Albanians of Kosovo were also predominantly Muslim, and there were still Muslim Turkish quarters in many Macedonian towns and villages, and in the former Sanjak of Novi Pazar which Montenegro and Serbia had partitioned after the first Balkan war (see map on p. 20).

Of the smaller groups the Hungarians lived mainly in the Vojvodina, though there were also Magyar villages in Prekomurje and Medjimurje. The Germans were to be found primarily in the Vojvodina and in Slovenia, whilst the Italians had populated the Dalmatian coast. The Vojvodina was also the main area of settlement for the Romanians; the Vlachs, whose language was akin to Romanian, were mainly transhumant shepherds and had for centuries been a feature of the Macedonian ethnic landscape.

The constituent peoples of Yugoslavia had vastly differing historical experiences and levels of economic development. Macedonia, Kosovo, the Sanjak and parts of southern Serbia were little advanced beyond the last days of Ottoman feudalism, whilst Slovenia and the Vojvodina had developed a commercialised agriculture with, in the former, a well-developed cooperative system to help the small farmer.

Table 15 Population by religion, 1921 and 1931

| | 1921 | | 1931 | |
	Number	Precentage	Number	Percentage
Orthodox	5,593,057	46.67	6,785,501	48.70
Roman Catholic	4,708,657	39.29	5,217,847	37.45
Uniate	40,338	0.34	44,671	0.32
Muslim	1,345,271	11.22	1,561,166	11.20
Protestant	229,517	1.91	231,169	1.66
Jewish	64,746	0.54	68,405	0.49
Other or unknown	3,325	0.03	25,279	0.18
Total	11,984,911	100.00	13,934,038	100.00

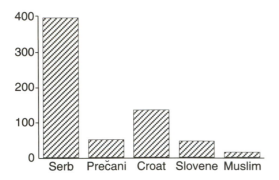

Figure 98 Ethnic composition of cabinets, 1918–41

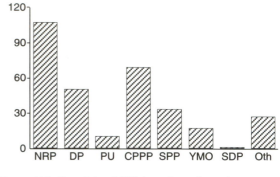

Figure 101 Skupshtina, 1923 (number of seats)

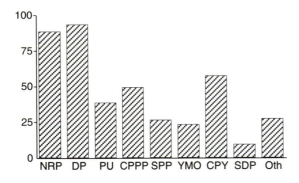

Figure 99 Ethnic composition of cabinets, 1918–41

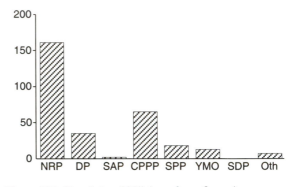

Figure 102 Skupshtina, 1925 (number of seats)

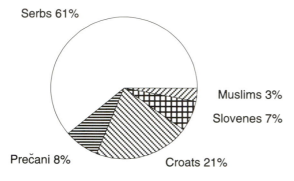

Figure 100 Constituent Assembly (number of seats)

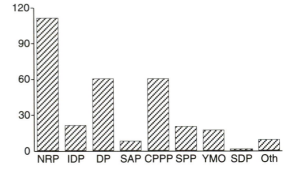

Figure 103 Skupshtina, 1927 (number of seats)

Inter-war Yugoslavia: political, 1918–29

When Yugoslavia emerged from the ruins of the Dual Monarchy there was only one force capable of defending the new state against Hungarian revanchism, Italian aggrandisement and internal subversion: the Serbian army. By November 1920 the new Yugoslav state was stable enough to hold elections to a constituent assembly which enacted a constitution on 28 June 1921, St Vitus's Day or *Vidovdan*.

Of the main parties in the assemblies between 1920 and 1929 the NRP (National Radical Party) had originally been radical in programme as well as name, but by the end of the First World War was seen chiefly as the party which had brought about Serbia's territorial enlargement; that this party should be so prominent in Yugoslavia fed fears that the new Yugoslavia was little but an expanded Serbia. The DP (Democratic Party) represented Serbs outside Serbia and had strongly centralist inclinations. The SPP (Slovene People's Party) was closely associated with the Catholic Church and had long been the main political grouping amongst the Slovenes. The CPPP (Croat People's Peasant Party), led by Stjepan Radić, campaigned for dualism – in effect wide-ranging autonomy – and enjoyed extensive support in Croatia. The PU (Peasant Union) was another centralist force and combined Serbian, Croat and Slovene agrarians. The YMO (Yugoslav Muslim Organisation) represented the interests of the Bosnian Muslims. The CPY (Communist Party of Yugoslavia) fared well in the backward regions, especially Montenegro, but was banned in 1921; despite communist international policy it was centralist.

The Vidovdan constitution enacted a unicameral legislature but, more important in the Yugoslav context, it also divided the country into thirty-three centralised departments; both federalism and dualism had been rejected, though in a concession to regional loyalties the official name of the new state was to be the Triune Kingdom of the Serbs, Croats and Slovenes.

The crucial problem in Yugoslavia was the relationship between the Serbs of Serbia and the other peoples and territories. Non-Serbs used statistics such as those in Figure 98 and 99 on the ethnic composition of inter-war cabinets to plead their case. (The first column in Figure 98 shows Serbs from Serbia and the second *Prečani* Serbs, or Serbs living outside Serbia; the number for Croats includes Croats from Croatia and also ethnic Croats from elsewhere.)

The Slovenes, whose institutions of local administration were well-developed and whose language differed considerably from Serbo-Croat, were reasonably content; the leader of the SPP, Anton Korošec, was the only non-Serb to become prime minister in inter-war Yugoslavia. The Macedonians were rigidly controlled by Belgrade, and the Bosnian Muslims – who would have liked decentralisation – feared to oppose Belgrade lest the ruling Serbs divide Bosnia and thus eliminate the one unit in Yugoslavia which had a Muslim majority.

The major problem was the Croats who hated the centralised system of administration and until 1925 refused to countenance the idea of any compromise with Belgrade. In February 1925, however, Radić agreed to enter a coalition with the Serbs. By August 1925 tension had relaxed sufficiently for King Alexander to pay his first visit to Zagreb since the foundation of the state.

Such tranquillity did not last. In August 1926 prime minister Nikola Pašić was forced to resign because of allegations of corruption on the part of his son. Chaos returned to Yugoslav political life and on 20 June 1928 it assumed violent form when a Montenegrin deputy killed two deputies in the *Skupshtina* (national assembly or parliament); he also wounded Radić who died seven weeks later.

King Alexander could see no solution emerging from the established political system which he therefore abolished on 6 January 1929. Along with the *Skupshtina* he disbanded the political parties, the trade unions and all organisations – even choral societies – having a regional basis or allegiance.

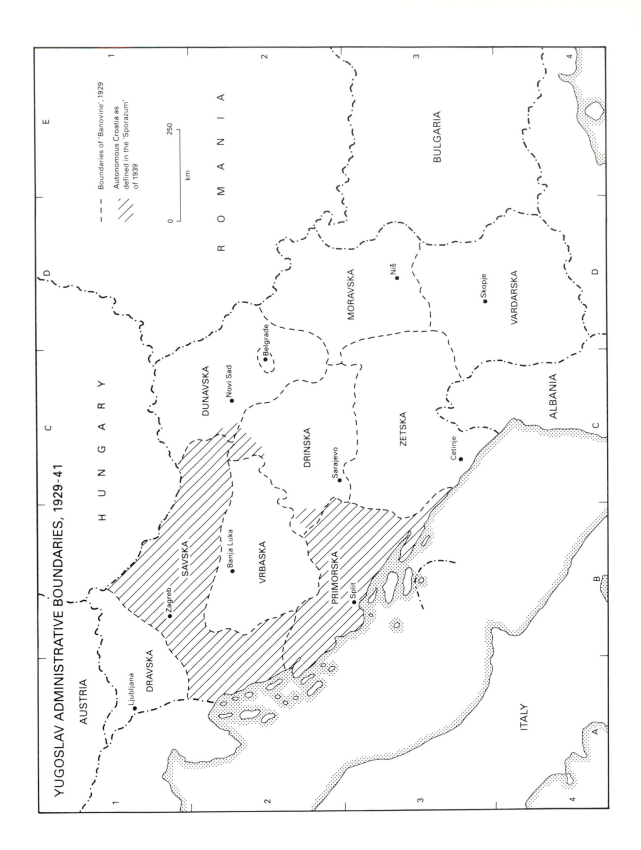

YUGOSLAV ADMINISTRATIVE BOUNDARIES, 1929-41

- - - Boundaries of 'Banovine', 1929

///// Autonomous Croatia as defined in the 'Sporazum' of 1939

0   250
km

AUSTRIA

HUNGARY

ROMANIA

BULGARIA

ITALY

ALBANIA

• Ljubljana

DRAVSKA

SAVSKA

• Zagreb

VRBASKA

• Banja Luka

DUNAVSKA

• Novi Sad

• Belgrade

MORAVSKA

• Niš

DRINSKA

• Sarajevo

PRIMORSKA

• Split

ZETSKA

• Cetinje

VARDARSKA

• Skopje

Inter-war Yugoslavia: political, 1929–41

The immediate purpose of the royal coup of 6 January 1929 was to prevent political collapse. The king became the only legitimate source of authority.

King Alexander hoped to create a new Yugoslav consciousness to replace the regional ones which, he believed, had vitiated the 1921 constitution. He therefore discarded the old title of the state which was now to be known as Yugoslavia. A new legal code, applicable throughout the country, was enacted, regional differences in taxation were reduced, and a new Yugoslav Agrarian Bank was established, the existing regional banks being regarded as centres of particularism. The coup was followed by a purge of the bureaucracy which had shed a third of its number by May 1929. In October the country's thirty-three departments were replaced by nine new administrative units, the *banovine*, with topographical rather than historic names. Each unit was to be administered by a *ban* who was to have extensive powers.

Of the new *banovine* two had Croat majorities, one was overwhelmingly Slovene, and in the remainder the Serbs were predominant. The Croats suffered most from the new arrangements for their historic units had been more mutilated than others, but the reform also angered the Muslims because in none of the new units did they constitute a majority. A new constitution was introduced in 1931 with a bicameral legislature elected by universal male suffrage in a direct but not secret ballot. The new assembly, however, had little authority and the political parties were required to reconstitute themselves on a basis which was not sectoral, regional, religious or ethnic. Few communities were happy with the new administrative arrangements and when the Slovenes, under Korošec, withdrew their original approval its supporters were nearly all Serbs. The new system seemed as Serb-dominated as the old. Alexander himself did not long survive the new constitution. On 9 October 1934 he was assassinated in Marseilles by a terrorist who had connections with both Macedonian and Croatian extremists. The heir to the throne, King Peter, was a minor, and his uncle, Prince Paul, became regent. Paul refused to undertake any major constitutional initiatives whilst the king was still not of age.

This was perhaps a blessing in that during the first half of the 1930s at least the major preoccupation of most Yugoslavs was with the effects of the great depression. Some political movement did become apparent towards the end of the decade in the latter half of the premiership of Milan Stojadinović. Stojadinović was anxious to secure domestic peace in the face of increasing external complications; Italy was a constant threat because of its claims on Dalmatia and the help it could give to Croatian and Macedonian separatists, whilst the *Anschluss* of 1938 brought the German borders down to Slovenia. Stojadinović relaxed political controls and made overtures to the Croats, even allowing them to erect a statue to Radić.

Stojadinović resigned in February 1939. In the following month the creation of an independent Slovakia made Croat and even Slovene separatists look with interest to Germany and this pushed Stojadinović's successor, Cvetković, further in the direction of compromise with the Croats. So too did the Italian occupation of Albania in April. In August 1939 the *sporazum* (agreement) between Belgrade and Zagreb allowed for the creation of a new, much enlarged and overwhelmingly Croat *banovina*. An assembly, *Sabor*, was to sit in Zagreb and have jurisdiction in all matters except defence, internal state security, foreign affairs, and external trade.

For the first time since the creation of the new state it seemed that a *modus vivendi* had been reached between the crown and the leadership of the Croat majority party. This was an illusion, but Croatian borders as defined in 1939 were remembered in 1991.

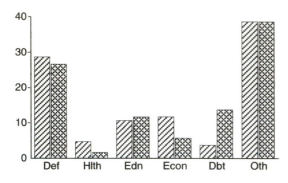

Figure 104 Budget expenditure, 1924/5, 1933/4 (%)

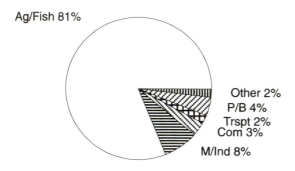

Figure 105 Population by economic sector, 1921

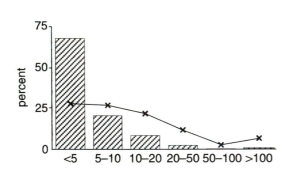

Figure 106 Landholdings: number and area

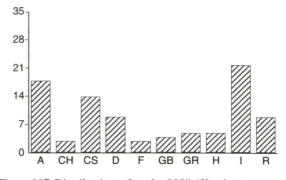

Figure 107 Distribution of trade, 1925 (% value)

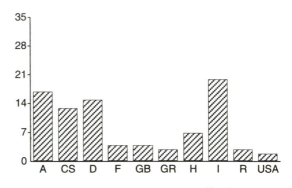

Figure 108 Distribution of trade, 1930 (% value)

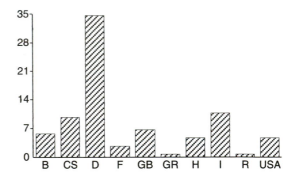

Figure 109 Distribution of trade, 1939 (% value)

Inter-war Yugoslavia: social and economic

Of the four Balkan states, Albania excluded, Yugoslavia in 1921 had the largest proportion of its population engaged in agriculture and fishing; on the other hand, the proportion employed in public services and the free professions was the lowest of the four states.

At the end of the First World War the new Kingdom of the Serbs, Croats and Slovenes was faced with huge social problems. There was a widespread demand for land reform. In Serbia itself very few large estates had existed before 1914 and most holdings were the property of and worked by a single family; but this was not the case in those south Slav lands which had been under Habsburg domination. In February 1917 the Serbian government, in an effort to win over fellow south Slavs, had promised land to south Slav volunteers from the Habsburg Monarchy; fighting men were to be given five hectares and non-combatants three hectares. When the fighting ceased there was widespread disorder in the area, especially in Croatia, and the local south Slav authorities there had issued a decree promising land to returning soldiers and to former tenants. When the new kingdom was formed the king made confirmation of this promise the subject of his first public pronouncement, in which he declared, 'In our free state there can and will be only free landowners.' On 25 February 1919 came the interim decree on the preparation of the agrarian reform which applied to all the kingdom except pre-1912 Serbia and which provided for the redistribution of estates in excess of one hundred cadastral *yokes*, though in some less favoured areas the figure was five hundred *yokes* (one *yoke* was 1.58 hectares). Priority in the redistribution was to be given to volunteers and to victims of the war; compensation was to be paid to all except the Habsburgs and members of other enemy dynasties. Over two million hectares, excluding forest land, were to be redistributed to some half a million households, over a quarter of the national total. The reform was a preliminary enactment and its implementation was frequently delayed, in some cases by as much as fifteen years, though it served its immediate purpose of containing radical passions.

In addition to this immediate and essential service the reform served other political functions. In Bosnia-Hercegovina the dispossessed landowners were predominantly Muslim and therefore the redistribution increased the relative social and political power of the Christians, whilst in Slovenia, Croatia, the Vojvodina, and Macedonia those who lost property were frequently non-Slav and those who received it were Slav. The land reform therefore benefited the Christian Slavs who dominated the new state.

For most of the inter-war period the dominant trading partners of Yugoslavia were Austria and Italy, a reflection of the fact that most trade was generated by the northern Yugoslav regions which had close historic ties with those two countries. In 1920 Austria and Italy had accounted for 63 per cent of total Yugoslav trade; this fell to 40 per cent in 1925, 37 per cent in 1930, and 26.5 per cent in 1935; in 1939 Austria no longer existed. Germany had been fifth in rank of Yugoslavia's trading partners in 1920 and was equal fifth in 1925, by 1930 it had risen to third position and by 1935 it was first. In 1939 Germany accounted for 35.6 per cent of total trade but of course this was distorted because the figures for that year combined Germany and Austria. The combined German and Austrian share of trade was 36.1 per cent in 1920, 27 per cent in 1925, 31.9 per cent in 1930, and 30.5 per cent in 1935. Czechoslovakia ranked third as a trading partner in 1920, 1925 and 1939, fourth in 1930, and second in 1935.

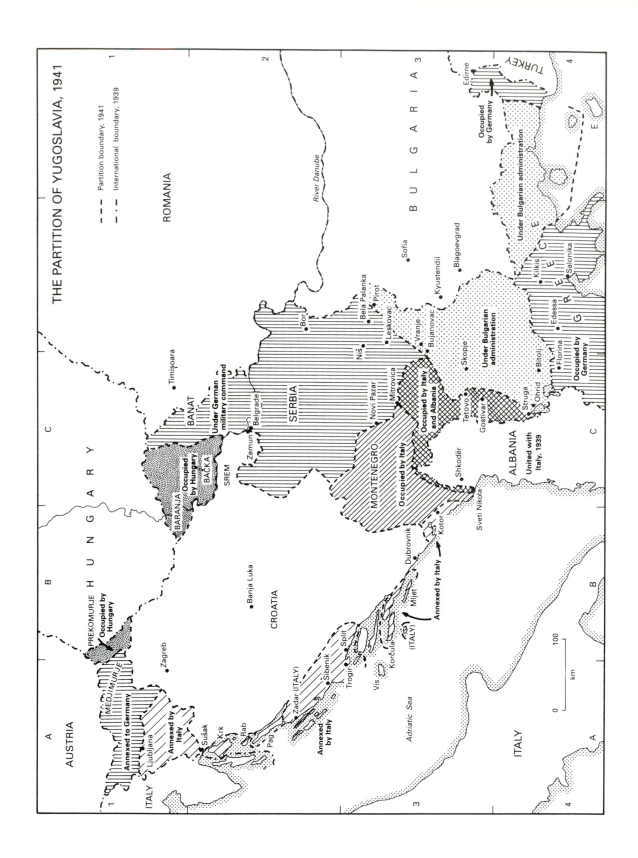

THE PARTITION OF YUGOSLAVIA, 1941

– – – Partition boundary, 1941
– · – International boundary, 1939

ROMANIA

River Danube

BULGARIA

AUSTRIA

HUNGARY

Timişoara

Sofia

Blagoevgrad

Kyustendil

BANAT

Under German
military command

Belgrade

SERBIA

Bor

Bela Palanka

Pirot

Niš

Leskovac

Vranje

Bujanovac

Skopje

Under Bulgarian
administration

Kilkis

Edessa

Salonika

GREECE

Occupied
by Germany

Edirne

TURKEY

Occupied
by Germany

Under Bulgarian administration

BARANJA Occupied
by Hungary

BAČKA

SREM

Zemun

Novi Pazar

Mitrovica

Occupied by Italy
and Albania

Tetovo

Gostivar

Struga

Ohrid

Bitolj

Florina

MONTENEGRO

Occupied by Italy

Sveti Nikola

Shkodër

ALBANIA

United with
Italy, 1939

PREKOMURJE Occupied by
Hungary

Banja Luka

CROATIA

Zagreb

MEDJIMURJE

Annexed to Germany

Annexed by
Italy

Ljubljana

Susak

Krk

Rab

Pag

Zadar (ITALY)

Šibenik

Trogir

Split

Vis

Korčula

Mljet

Kotor

Dubrovnik

Annexed by Italy

Kortula
(ITALY)

Annexed
by Italy

Adriatic Sea

ITALY

100

km

0

ITALY

132

The partition of Yugoslavia, 1941

The *sporazum* of August 1939 (see p. 129), though popular with most Croats, had its opponents. The Serbs in Serbia resented the privileges given to the Croats whilst the Serbs in Croatia felt abandoned and threatened, the more so when the authorities in Zagreb allowed back into Croatia a number of extremist exiles. The exiles themselves were far from content with the *sporazum*; for them it was the beginning of the process of separation from Belgrade, not the end.

The critical danger now for Yugoslavia, as for all European states, was international. The regent, Prince Paul, was by sentiment pro-British and pro-French, as was much of the Serbian population and political establishment. On the other hand, Britain and France were distant, ineffective and apparently unreliable, whilst Germany was now a direct neighbour as well as a close economic partner. When France fell in the summer of 1940 Yugoslavia lost a friend and a historic ally, but more importantly Mussolini's joining hands with Hitler meant Yugoslavia was threatened from the north and the west.

In 1941 Hitler turned his attention to the Balkans. He had three main reasons for doing so. The Italians had come unstuck in their attack upon Greece; he wanted to protect his southern flank in the forthcoming attack upon the Soviet Union; and a Germany established in the Balkans would be in a good position to harry British communications through the Mediterranean. For these reasons Yugoslavia came under great pressure to join the tripartite pact, the German–Italian–Japanese alliance. Such pressures intensified greatly in March 1941 when German troops began entering Bulgaria, en route to Greece. Cvetković decided in the second half of March that he could no longer resist and set off for Vienna to sign the pact.

Signature of the pact would not necessarily have committed Yugoslavia to fighting alongside the Germans, but a group of pro-British military and air-force officers in Belgrade assumed that it would. They made Cvetković's departure for Vienna the excuse for a coup which removed him and placed power in the hands of the regent. The coup was bloodless and, in Belgrade at least, immensely popular. Opposition to a pro-German orientation was not the only reason for this popularity. Many Serbs saw the coup as a chance to reassert the Serbian domination compromised in the *sporazum* whilst many Croats also welcomed the Serbian basis of the putsch, believing that it provided them with the excuse they had so long been looking for to cut all links with Belgrade and to set up a completely independent Croatian state on the Slovak model.

Hitler was greatly angered and lost all control when the new Yugoslav government signed an agreement with the Soviet Union on 6 April. On that day he unleashed a savage air assault upon Belgrade whilst German, Bulgarian, Italian and Hungarian troops entered Yugoslav territory.

Yugoslavia could not have withstood such forces even if it had had perfect internal unity. The latter was certainly absent and in Croatia and Macedonia the invaders met little resistance. Yugoslavia was rapidly dismembered. Hungary took the Prekomurje in the north-eastern corner of Croatia; Slovenia was partitioned between Germany and Italy; Macedonia fell mostly to the Bulgarians, with the Italians having the western border areas; the Italians also occupied Kosovo and Montenegro. Serbia was given a puppet government under General Nedić although the Banat was placed under the administration of local Germans. Croatia was made into an independent state, though the Italians annexed the Dalmatian coast.

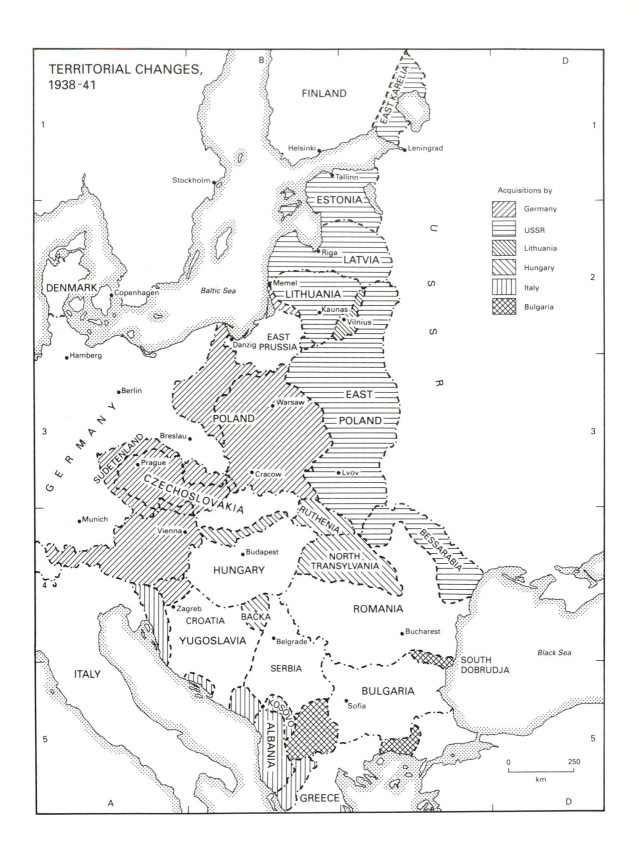

TERRITORIAL CHANGES,
1938-41

FINLAND

EAST KARELIA

Helsinki

Leningrad

Stockholm

Tallinn

ESTONIA

Acquisitions by

Germany

USSR

Lithuania

Hungary

Italy

Bulgaria

Riga

LATVIA

DENMARK

Copenhagen

Baltic Sea

Memel

LITHUANIA

Kaunas

Vilnius

Hamberg

Danzig

EAST
PRUSSIA

Berlin

EAST

POLAND

POLAND

Warsaw

G E R M A N Y

SUDETENLAND

Breslau

Prague

CZECHOSLOVAKIA

Cracow

Lvov

RUTHENIA

Munich

Vienna

BESSARABIA

Budapest

NORTH
TRANSYLVANIA

HUNGARY

Zagreb

CROATIA

BACKA

ROMANIA

YUGOSLAVIA

Belgrade

Bucharest

SERBIA

Black Sea

ITALY

BULGARIA

SOUTH
DOBRUDJA

KOSOVO

Sofia

ALBANIA

0   250

km

GREECE

U S S R

134

4 THE SECOND WORLD WAR

Territorial changes, 1938–41

The territorial changes in Eastern Europe between 1938 and 1941 were reminiscent of the eighteenth-century partitions of Poland in the speed and ruthlessness with which they redistributed territory amongst great powers, though this time there were two of the latter rather than three.

Again Poland was the chief victim. In the partition of 1939 Lithuania was allowed some former Polish territory, that around Vilnius, but in 1940 Lithuania itself, together with the other two Baltic states, disappeared from the map. The Soviet Union acquired the lands Russia had lost in the period 1918–21 and in addition took the northern Bukovina which had never belonged to it before. The new disposition had come about through the Nazi–Soviet pact of August 1939 which Hitler had signed in an attempt to dissuade Britain and France from standing by their recent guarantee to the Polish state which he wished to eliminate. The pact served Stalin well. It gave him security, he believed, against a Germany which had waged a vicious propaganda war against him since 1933. For that reason, and to prevent any change of mind on the part of Hitler, Stalin abided punctiliously by the terms of the 1939 agreement which had economic as well as territorial provisions. Soviet wheat and oil poured into Germany and were essential ingredients in the German victories in Scandinavia, the Low Countries and France in 1940 and in the Balkans in 1941. Until the actual German attack on the Soviet Union on 21–2 June 1941 Stalin refused to believe, or at least to act upon, the mounting body of intelligence information which pointed to an impending German assault.

In central and south-eastern Europe the changes of 1938–41 made the vanquished and the discontented of 1918–21 the victors. The losers were those who had benefited from the Versailles system: Poland, Czechoslovakia and Romania. The Croats were given a separate state, as were the Slovaks, though the former were forced to relinquish land to the Italians and the latter to the Hungarians. In the Balkans Bulgaria was given the southern Dobrudja in September 1940 and after participating in the partition of Yugoslavia in April 1941 it had succeeded in repossessing much of the territory it had been given in the short-lived preliminary peace of San Stefano in 1878, though it had to allow the Italians to take parts of western Macedonia.

The Italians had believed the post-First World War settlement had deprived them of their due rights east of the Adriatic and this they had made good, first by the occupation of Albania in April 1939 and then by taking Kosovo and parts of Croatia and Slovenia a year later.

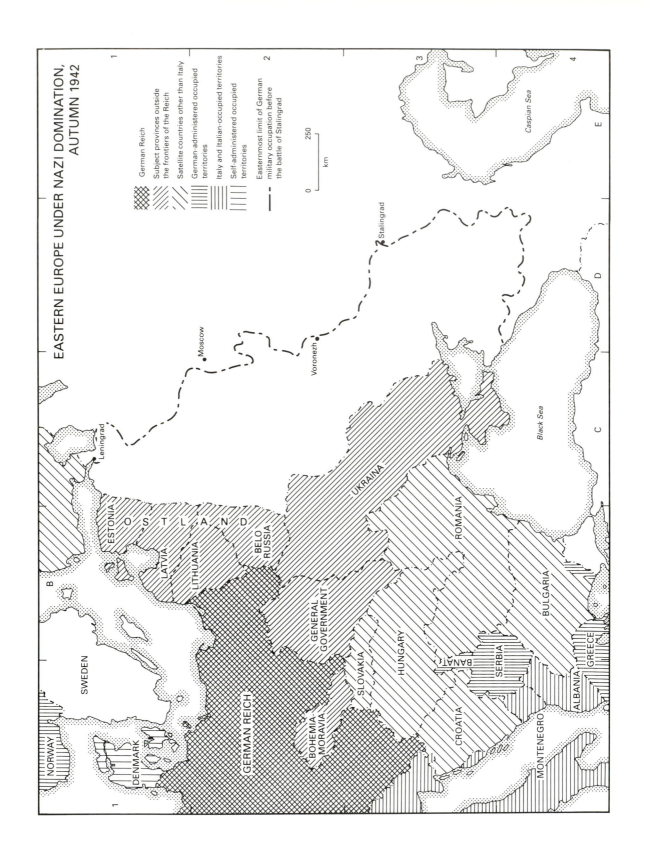

EASTERN EUROPE UNDER NAZI DOMINATION,
AUTUMN 1942

German Reich

Subject provinces outside
the frontiers of the Reich

Satellite countries other than Italy

German-administered occupied
territories

Italy and Italian-occupied territories

Self-administered occupied
territories

Easternmost limit of German
military occupation before
the battle of Stalingrad

0   250
km

NORWAY

SWEDEN

DENMARK

Leningrad

Moscow

Voronezh

Stalingrad

ESTONIA

O S T L A N D

LATVIA

LITHUANIA

BELO
RUSSIA

UKRAINA

Black Sea

Caspian Sea

GENERAL
GOVERNMENT

GERMAN REICH

BOHEMIA-
MORAVIA

SLOVAKIA

HUNGARY

ROMANIA

BULGARIA

BANAT

SERBIA

CROATIA

MONTENEGRO

ALBANIA

GREECE

136

Eastern Europe under Nazi domination

After invading the Soviet Union on 21–2 June 1941 the German armies pressed rapidly eastward, expecting after a few weeks to be in Moscow. They reached the outskirts of the city shortly before Christmas but winter and dogged resistance denied them entrance; Leningrad, too, kept the invader at bay but had to endure a horrific siege lasting over 900 days. The great turning point came in late 1942 when the German armies reached Stalingrad; by February 1943 the Sixth Army was forced to surrender and thereafter the Soviet forces began their grinding, inexorable and slow drive westwards.

As the German armies moved forward large tracts of territory were clearly still under military control but further to the rear two new administrative units, the Reichskommissariat Ostland and the Reichskommissariat Ukraina, were established. The former included the Baltic states and most of Belorussia; the remainder of Belorussia was included in the Reichskommissariat Ukraina, together with all conquered areas of Ukraine. The boundaries of the Reichskommissariat Ukraina were never fully defined because of fluctuations in Germany's military fortunes on the eastern front. The two Reichskommissariats came under the Reich ministry for the occupied eastern territories created in July 1941 and headed by the Nazi theoretical expert and Baltic German, Alfred Rosenberg.

As in the remainder of the Nazi-ruled lands the occupied territories suffered from a bewildering number of separate and usually competing administrative empires. The regular army, the Wehrmacht, frequently found itself at odds with the SS, originally the Nazi Party's military wing, whilst economic matters could be subject to the power of the Organisation Todt, Sauckel's labour recruitment forces, Speer's armaments industry, Goering's economic administration, or specialised agencies such as that for food procurement.

The armies which invaded the USSR were predominantly but not solely German. There were units of most of those East European states which were still nominally independent; the Romanians were fully engaged in and suffered horrendously in the battles around Stalingrad, whilst the best of the Hungarian armies were destroyed around Voronezh. Slovak units proved to be so disturbed and demoralised by what they saw of Nazi-inspired atrocities that they had to be stiffened with German officers and NCOs. The exception to the rule of cooperation on the eastern front was Bulgaria. King Boris refused to commit his troops, arguing that they were not equipped to fight a modern war and that they would not fight well against the Russians with whom they felt ties of race and religion. Instead, Bulgarian forces supplemented those coping with partisan insurgency in the Yugoslav lands, and were held in readiness in case of a Turkish invasion of the Balkans.

After Stalingrad the rulers of Hungary, Romania and Bulgaria attempted to escape from their ties to Germany before the Red Army arrived. It was to prevent its defection that German troops occupied Hungary in March 1944 and in October imposed a native fascist government on the country. In Romania King Michael finally deposed General Antonescu in August 1944 and switched to the allied side. Bulgaria failed to rid itself of German troops in time to prevent the entry of the Red Army in September 1944, after the USSR had declared war on Bulgaria.

The persecution of European Jewry, 1942–5

As soon as they began their conquest of Eastern Europe the Nazis began to implement their anti-Jewish policies. Jews were concentrated into designated areas, ghettos. Beginning in May 1940 the larger ghettos were sealed off and as more and more Jews were forced into them, particularly after the conquest of the western regions of the Soviet Union with their large Jewish populations, conditions deteriorated rapidly.

By the end of the summer of 1941 so great were the number of Jews falling into Nazi hands

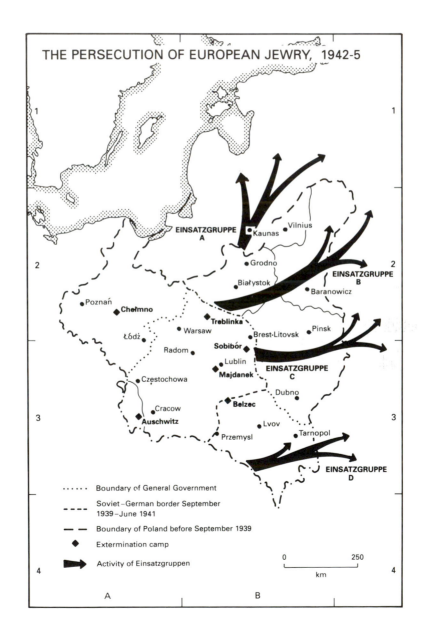

THE PERSECUTION OF EUROPEAN JEWRY, 1942-5

Vilnius
EINSATZGRUPPE A
Kaunas
EINSATZGRUPPE B
Grodno
Białystok
Baranowicz
Poznań
Chełmno
Treblinka
Pinsk
Warsaw
Brest-Litovsk
Łódź
Sobibór
Radom
Lublin
EINSATZGRUPPE C
Majdanek
Częstochowa
Dubno
Bełzec
Cracow
Lvov
Auschwitz
Tarnopol
Przemysl
EINSATZGRUPPE D

· · · · ·   Boundary of General Government
- - - -   Soviet–German border September 1939–June 1941
— · —   Boundary of Poland before September 1939
◆   Extermination camp
➤   Activity of Einsatzgruppen

0   250
km

that rather than transport them all to established ghettos many were killed immediately. The instruments of this hideous policy were the special detachments, the *Einsatzgruppen*. Four of these were formed: *Einsatzgruppe* A in the north, *Einsatzgruppe* B which operated in northern Belorussia, *Einsatzgruppe* C in southern Belorussia and northern Ukraine, and *Einsatzgruppe* D in eastern Galicia and southern Ukraine.

By the end of 1941 the Nazis determined upon their 'Final Solution' of the Jewish 'problem' – that is, the extermination of all remaining Jews. This was a task too great even for the apparently limitless brutality and blood-lust of the *Einsatzgruppen*. Death factories would be more efficient. In the following months slave labour was used to establish these at Auschwitz, Treblinka, Sobibór, Majdanek, Belzec and Chełmno in occupied Poland. There were smaller camps dotted around the Nazi empire and if these did not

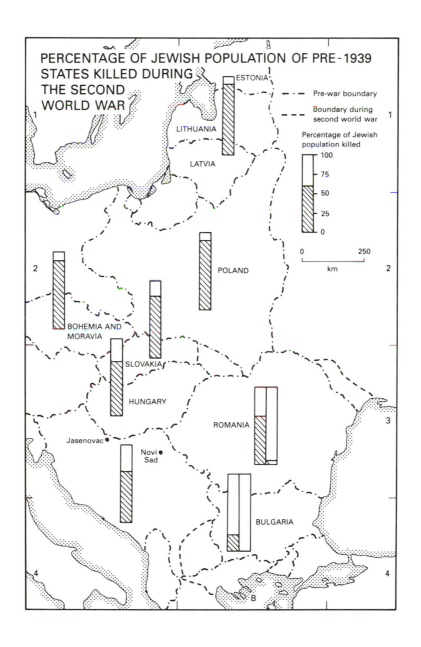

PERCENTAGE OF JEWISH POPULATION OF PRE-1939 STATES KILLED DURING THE SECOND WORLD WAR

Pre-war boundary

Boundary during second world war

Percentage of Jewish population killed

100

75

50

25

0

0   250
km

ESTONIA
LITHUANIA
LATVIA
POLAND
BOHEMIA AND MORAVIA
SLOVAKIA
HUNGARY
Jasenovac
Novi Sad
ROMANIA
BULGARIA

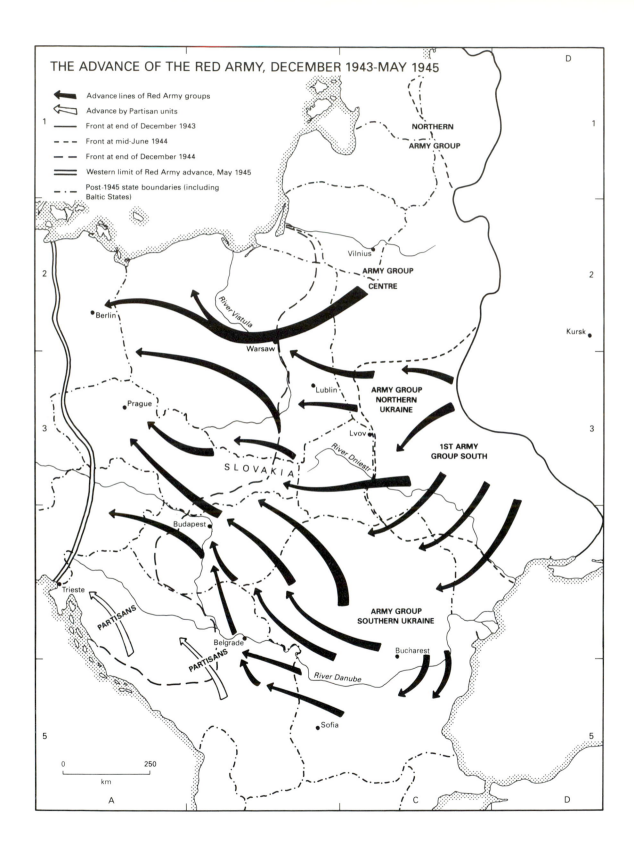

THE ADVANCE OF THE RED ARMY, DECEMBER 1943-MAY 1945

Advance lines of Red Army groups
Advance by Partisan units
Front at end of December 1943
Front at mid-June 1944
Front at end of December 1944
Western limit of Red Army advance, May 1945
Post-1945 state boundaries (including
Baltic States)

NORTHERN
ARMY GROUP

Vilnius

ARMY GROUP
CENTRE

Kursk

Berlin

River Vistula

Warsaw

Lublin

ARMY GROUP
NORTHERN
UKRAINE

Prague

Lvov

1ST ARMY
GROUP SOUTH

River Dniestr

S L O V A K I A

Budapest

ARMY GROUP
SOUTHERN UKRAINE

Trieste

PARTISANS

Belgrade

PARTISANS

Bucharest

River Danube

Sofia

0   250

km

140

contain the full apparatus of gas chambers and crematoria they nevertheless achieved much the same results. In some cases camps were used to indulge local ethnic rivalries as well as to implement German plans for the destruction of the Jewish population; at Jasenovac in Croatia Serbs as well as Jews were slaughtered.

In all these hideous places, large or small, thousands upon thousands of Jews, Gypsies and others whom the Nazis thought dangerous or undesirable were done to death. The inevitability of military defeat seemed to intensify the demonic urge to destroy, and German army commanders frequently found precious resources being diverted to transport victims to the death camps.

For Jews in areas under direct German rule there was little if any hope of escape but in states which were nominally independent the situation was slightly less bleak. In Slovakia three deported Jews escaped, one from Treblinka, one from Sobibór and one from Majdanek, and their reports of what was happening persuaded the Slovak government to suspend the transports in October 1942. They were resumed only after the Germans took full control of Slovakia in August 1944. Within the pre-1941 boundaries of Bulgaria the Jews were forced to wear the yellow star and they were exiled from the cities where most of them had always lived, but Bulgarian opinion was revolted by reports in 1943 that the Jews were to be sent to Poland. Fierce protests by politicians, the press and the churches strengthened King Boris in his determination to resist German demands for the deportation of Bulgarian Jews, though those in areas under Bulgarian occupation did not escape. A similar picture emerged in Romania where again the Jews in the pre-1941 kingdom survived but those in areas occupied after June 1941 were liquidated. (The columns on the map on p. 139 show the percentage of Jews who died in the areas covered by the Bulgarian and Romanian kingdoms during the war and then in the original kingdoms.) In Hungary Admiral Horthy's regime refused to hand over its Jews, who were discriminated against but were for the most part safe until after the German takeover of Hungary in October 1944, although there was a particularly brutal pogrom by extremist local Hungarian fascists against Jews in Novi Sad in January 1942.

The advance of the Red Army, 1943–5

After its defeat at Stalingrad at the beginning of 1943 the German cause in the east was doomed.

The Soviet drive to the west, however, began slowly. It was not until the early months of 1944 that Soviet forces crossed the border into the areas of pre-war Poland. In these territories, which were disputed between the Soviet authorities and the Polish government-in-exile in London, the Polish resistance forces cooperated with the Red Army but many Polish officers were then arrested and their units dissolved or forced to merge with those of General Berling, a Pole who had stayed in the USSR and had formed an army which fought under the command of the Red Army. Inside Poland there were large resistance forces, the Polish Home Army (AK) being the fourth largest fighting force on the allied side, ranking behind the Soviet, American and British but before the French. On 1 August 1944 the AK in Warsaw staged a rising on the assumption that they would have to hold out for only a few days before they could hand over the city to the Red Army which was only a few miles away. The Red Army remained at that distance for two months during which the Polish forces in Warsaw fought hopeless but unwavering war against the German army. It was a savage struggle during which the non-communist forces in Poland were destroyed.

Whilst the Poles waited in vain for Soviet assistance the Slovaks, who had also risen against the Germans, experienced a similar fate. It could be that one reason for the failure of the First Army Group South to cross the Carpathians into Slovakia was that it and the Third Army Group were unexpectedly pulled southwards as a result

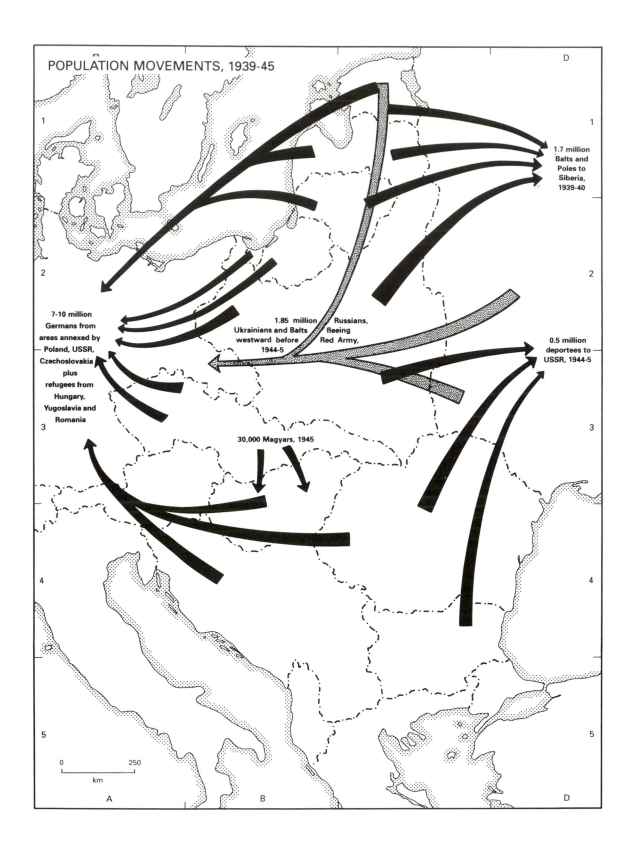

POPULATION MOVEMENTS, 1939-45

1.7 million
Balts and
Poles to
Siberia,
1939-40

7-10 million
Germans from
areas annexed by
Poland, USSR,
Czechoslovakia
plus
refugees from
Hungary,
Yugoslavia and
Romania

1.85 million Russians,
Ukrainians and Balts fleeing
westward before Red Army,
1944-5

0.5 million
deportees to
USSR, 1944-5

30,000 Magyars, 1945

0   250
km

142

of a *coup d'état* in Bucharest on 23 August 1944 when King Michael deposed General Antonescu. The Romanian coup brought the Red Army to the Danube which it crossed on 8 September to force Bulgaria to join the war on the allied side.

The Bulgarians had declared war on Britain and the USA but not on the Soviet Union. The Bulgarian army, however, had aided the Germans in anti-partisan operations in Yugoslavia. By the summer of 1944 the partisans under Marshal Tito were growing in strength, not least because of the supply of arms from Britain, and in October 1944 Tito's forces assisted the Red Army in taking Belgrade.

In the autumn of 1944 the Soviet forces, now joined by the Romanian and Bulgarian armies, fought their way into the central Danubian plain but Budapest was not to be taken until after a protracted siege in which much of the city was destroyed.

In the late months of 1944 the advance in the south was more rapid than in the north because in the latter the Germans were massing their forces for the defence of the heartland of the Reich. The westward drive resumed, however, early in 1945 with the remains of Warsaw being taken in January. Thereafter the enormous weight of the Army Group Centre and the Army Group Northern Ukraine ground inexorably westward into Prussia and towards Berlin. Meanwhile, further south, the First Army Group South and the Army Group Southern Ukraine crossed into Austria and joined in the race towards Prague. An American army under General Patten was the competitor in that race and it crossed into Bohemia only to be ordered to halt its advance to comply with previous political agreements concluded between the Soviets and the Western allies.

Population movements in Eastern Europe, 1939–50

The Second World War and its immediate aftermath brought about the largest movement of populations seen in Europe in recorded history. They profoundly altered the ethnic composition of the area and if they did not mean the end of national minorities they did greatly simplify the ethnic map.

In the first place the Jewish minorities had been reduced if not entirely eliminated in most states. Even in those countries where the Jews had been saved, Bulgaria and Romania, most of the survivors chose to leave their native lands for Israel or the New World; Europe seemed no longer safe. The Germans also decreased greatly in number. Some had already been moved during the war, though usually to colonise areas under German occupation. Many Germans from Bessarabia had been brought to settle in Zamość in Poland, for example, and others from the Bukovina, Bessarabia and the southern Dobrudja were planted in Slovenia. The Baltic Germans were moved westward under an agreement with the Soviets after the pact of 1939, only

to return to their erstwhile homes after 1941 and then flee again or be deported to Siberia after the restoration of Soviet power in 1945. In many other cases the Germans had fled before the oncoming Red Army and the retribution which they feared it would bring, and in this flight they were joined by those who had worked with them in the war against the Soviets; it was this movement which brought tens of thousands of Russians, Cossacks, Lithuanians, Latvians and Estonians to the displaced persons camps of the allied zones of occupation in western Germany. Some three million of these refugees were repatriated during the following decade.

After the war the huge German populations of the Sudeten areas and of the provinces acquired by Poland (see p. 135) were driven out, frequently at short notice and with considerable brutality. This process involved the forcible movement of perhaps ten million individuals.

A similar plan to remove the Hungarian minority from southern Slovakia was drawn up but was abandoned shortly after it was introduced; only about 30,000 Magyars were affected but they were numerous enough to demand compensation after the fall of the communist system in 1989.

Soviet occupation also brought ethnic change. In the period 1939–40 over one and a half million Poles and Balts were deported to Siberia where the majority of them perished. Further deportation of Lithuanians, Latvians and Estonians took place in the years immediately after the war. In addition, in the same years the Soviet forces shipped up to half a million people from their zones of occupation in Eastern Europe to the USSR.

Deportations carried out by both the Nazis and the Soviets had clear political intentions and results. In addition to the all-out war on the Jews the Nazis, and the Soviets, persecuted those amongst the occupied population most likely to oppose foreign rule. This meant primarily the intelligentsia and the middle classes. After the war, therefore, the communists had little to fear from these natural opponents.

The new frontiers which emerged after the war also strengthened the drift to ethnic homogeneity. Poland lost its Belorussian and Ukrainian minorities in the east, and Czechoslovakia no longer had its Ukrainians now that Ruthenia had become Soviet. Romania also lost its Ukrainians when Bessarabia was also handed to the USSR, though there were still minorities in the Banat and Transylvania.

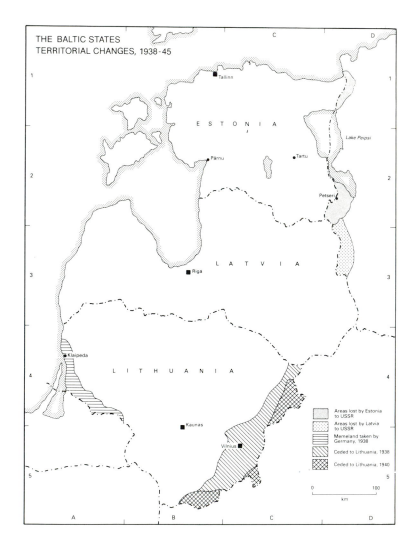

THE BALTIC STATES
TERRITORIAL CHANGES, 1938-45

Areas lost by Estonia to USSR
Areas lost by Latvia to USSR
Memeland taken by Germany, 1938
Ceded to Lithuania, 1938
Ceded to Lithuania, 1940

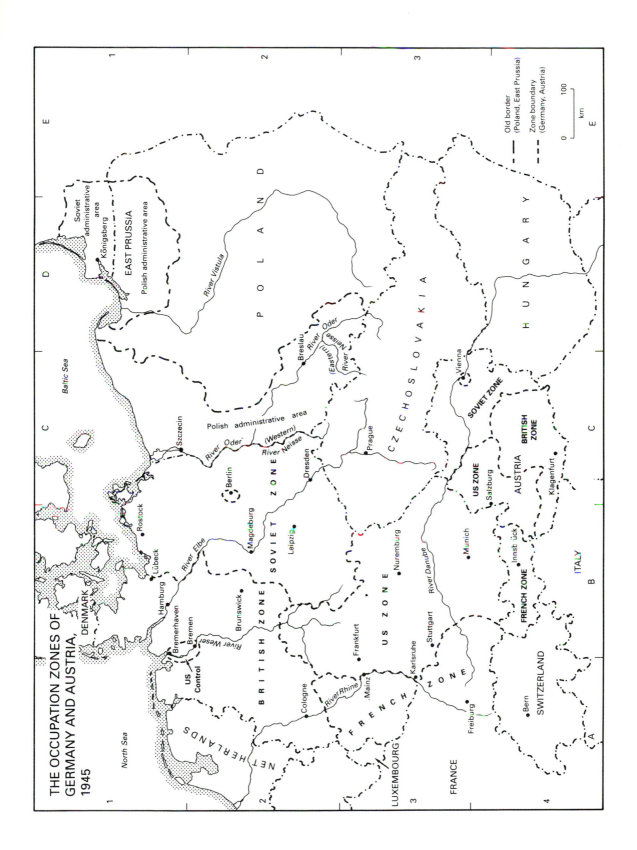

THE OCCUPATION ZONES OF
GERMANY AND AUSTRIA,
1945

Old border
(Poland, East Prussia)

Zone boundary
(Germany, Austria)

100

km

0

DENMARK

Baltic Sea

North Sea

NETHERLANDS

BELGIUM

LUXEMBOURG

FRANCE

SWITZERLAND

ITALY

AUSTRIA

HUNGARY

CZECHOSLOVAKIA

POLAND

EAST PRUSSIA

Soviet administrative area

Polish administrative area

Königsberg

River Vistula

Breslau

River Oder

River Neisse (Eastern)

Polish administrative area

River Oder (Western)

River Neisse

Szczecin

Rostock

Lübeck

Hamburg

Bremerhaven

Bremen

US Control

River Weser

River Elbe

Brunswick

Berlin

Magdeburg

Leipzig

Dresden

Prague

Vienna

SOVIET ZONE

BRITISH ZONE

US ZONE

FRENCH ZONE

Cologne

River Rhine

Mainz

Frankfurt

Karlsruhe

Stuttgart

Nuremburg

River Danube

Munich

Salzburg

Innsbruck

Klagenfurt

SOVIET ZONE

BRITISH ZONE

US ZONE

FRENCH ZONE

Freiburg

Bern

145

EASTERN EUROPE, 1900

A

SWEDEN

•Riga

LITHUANIA

Baltic Sea

•Königsberg

R U S S I A

1

•Hamburg

•Berlin

•Warsaw

•Brest-Litovsk

POLAND

GERMANY

•Kiev

2

SILESIA

G A L I C I A

•Prague

•Lvov

BOHEMIA

MORAVIA

•Vienna

•Budapest

A U S T R I A - H U N G A R Y

3

CROATIA-SLAVONIA

TRANSYLVANIA

•Cluj

•Milan

•Trieste

•Zagreb

•Bucharest

BOSNIA AND
HERCEGOVINA

ROMANIA

DALMATIA

•Belgrade

SERBIA

•Florence

•Niš

BULGARIA

ITALY

SANJAK

•Sofia

MONTENEGRO

MACEDONIA

•Constantinople

4

•Rome

ALBANIA

•Naples

•Salonika

OTTOMAN EMPIRE

GREECE

•Athens

5

0   250

km

Mediterranean Sea

C

EASTERN EUROPE, 1923

SWEDEN

DENMARK

• Copenhagen

Baltic Sea

Berlin •

GERMANY

• Danzig

ESTONIA

• Tallinn

• Riga

LATVIA

LITHUANIA

• Memel   • Kaunas

• Vilnius

SOVIET UNION

P O L A N D

• Warsaw

• Kiev

Prague •

CZECHOSLOVAKIA

• Teschen

• Lvov

River Danube

Vienna •   • Bratislava

AUSTRIA

• Budapest

HUNGARY

River Dniestr

BESSARABIA

River Prut

ROMANIA

TRANSYLVANIA

• Zagreb

Belgrade •

YUGOSLAVIA

• Bucharest

River Danube

Black Sea

ITALY

Adriatic
Sea

BULGARIA

• Sofia

ALBANIA

• Rome

Tirana •

GREECE

TURKEY

0   250
km

148

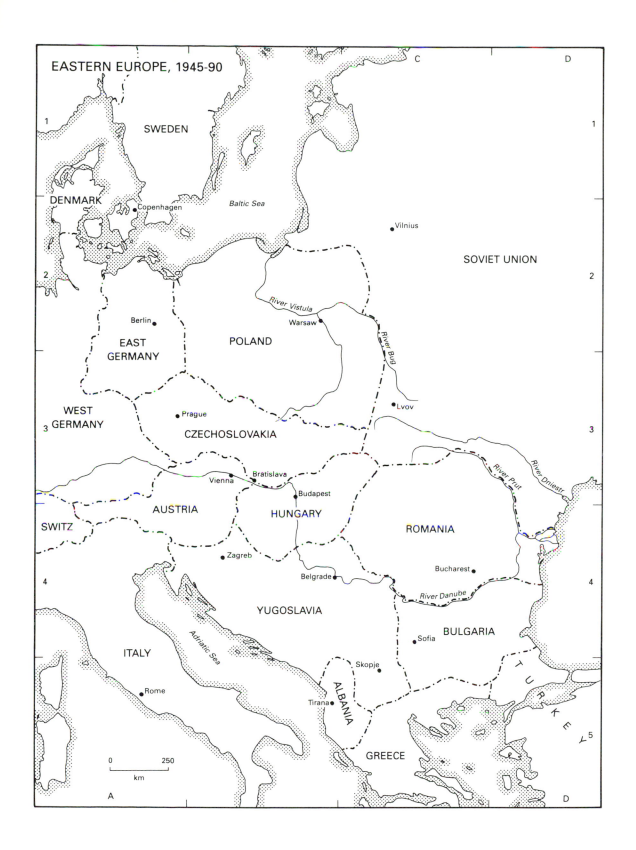

EASTERN EUROPE, 1945-90

149

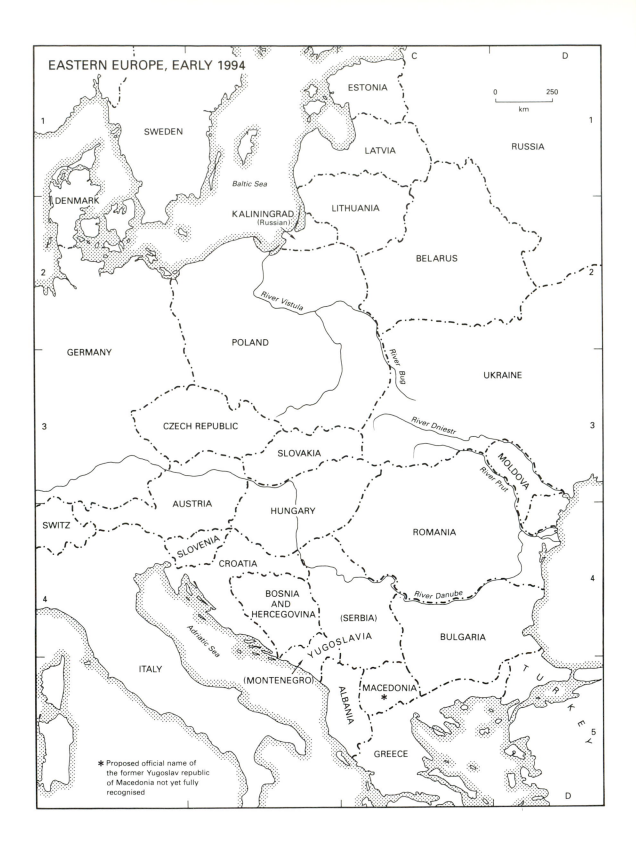

EASTERN EUROPE, EARLY 1994

* Proposed official name of
the former Yugoslav republic
of Macedonia not yet fully
recognised

150

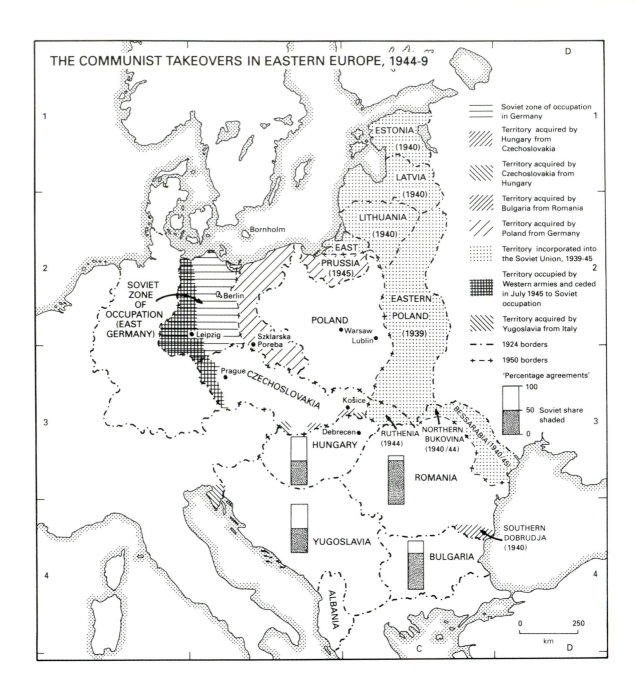

THE COMMUNIST TAKEOVERS IN EASTERN EUROPE, 1944-9

ESTONIA
(1940)

LATVIA
(1940)

LITHUANIA
(1940)

EAST
PRUSSIA
(1945)

EASTERN
POLAND
(1939)

POLAND
• Warsaw
Lublin •

Bornholm

SOVIET
ZONE
OF
OCCUPATION
(EAST
GERMANY)

Berlin

Leipzig •

Szklarska
• Poreba

Prague • CZECHOSLOVAKIA

Košice

BESSARABIA (1940/45)

Debrecen •
HUNGARY

RUTHENIA
(1944)

NORTHERN
BUKOVINA
(1940/44)

ROMANIA

YUGOSLAVIA

BULGARIA

SOUTHERN
DOBRUDJA
(1940)

ALBANIA

Soviet zone of occupation
in Germany

Territory acquired by
Hungary from
Czechoslovakia

Territory acquired by
Czechoslovakia from
Hungary

Territory acquired by
Bulgaria from Romania

Territory acquired by
Poland from Germany

Territory incorporated into
the Soviet Union, 1939-45

Territory occupied by
Western armies and ceded
in July 1945 to Soviet
occupation

Territory acquired by
Yugoslavia from Italy

— · — · — 1924 borders

+ — + — + 1950 borders

'Percentage agreements'
100

50 Soviet share
shaded
0

0   250
km

152

5 EASTERN EUROPE UNDER COMMUNIST DOMINATION

The communist takeovers in Eastern Europe, 1944–9

As the Red Army moved into Central Europe there were signs that it intended to establish communist regimes. In Lublin in July 1944 a pro-Moscow virtual provisional government was established and later in the year Hungarian communists secured domination within a provisional government formed at Debrecen.

Churchill seemed to abet Stalin's expansionist ambitions when he proposed in Moscow in October 1944 a 'percentage deal' which placed most of the Balkans in the Soviet sphere of influence, though leaving Greece to Western domination. Churchill had hoped to find a means of agreeing with Stalin on minor issues, the Balkans, to pave the way for a compromise on what was then the major problem, Poland. In territorial terms it had already been agreed, at Tehran in December 1943, that Poland would lose its eastern provinces and receive compensation in the west at the expense of Germany. At Yalta in February and at Potsdam near Berlin in July–August 1945 it was agreed that the Soviet Union would also retain its gains of 1940 whilst the question of its absorption of Ruthenia in 1944 was hardly raised. The Yalta conference in effect divided Europe, with the Soviets giving only vague promises to conduct democratic elections in the areas they had 'liberated'.

In fact liberation by the Red Army was not the automatic precursor to communist domination. Though the Soviets occupied Bornholm and part of Austria communist rule was not established there, whilst the Red Army had but a passing presence in Yugoslavia and did not set foot in Albania, both of which saw the communists in power by the end of 1945.

Communist domination for most countries came gradually and by stealth. The communists secured domination of vital ministries – the Interior, which controlled the police; and Justice. Secure in the domination of these institutions they proceeded to neutralise their enemies one by one, a process the Hungarian communist leader Mátyás Rákosi described as 'salami tactics'. But the process was not completed until 1948. Czechoslovakia had returned to parliamentary government after the Košice declaration of April 1945; Hungary, despite the Debrecen provisional government, saw the communists defeated in the general election of November 1945, though, thanks to Soviet pressure, they kept control of the Ministry of the Interior. In the Soviet zone of occupation in Germany similar pressures were exerted to force the local social democrats to fuse with the communists. Thereafter, communist influence in the Soviet zone increased inexorably; that zone excluded the western sector of Berlin which had been passed to allied control after US and British forces had withdrawn from those parts of Germany and Czechoslovakia assigned to Soviet occupation under an agreement of May 1945.

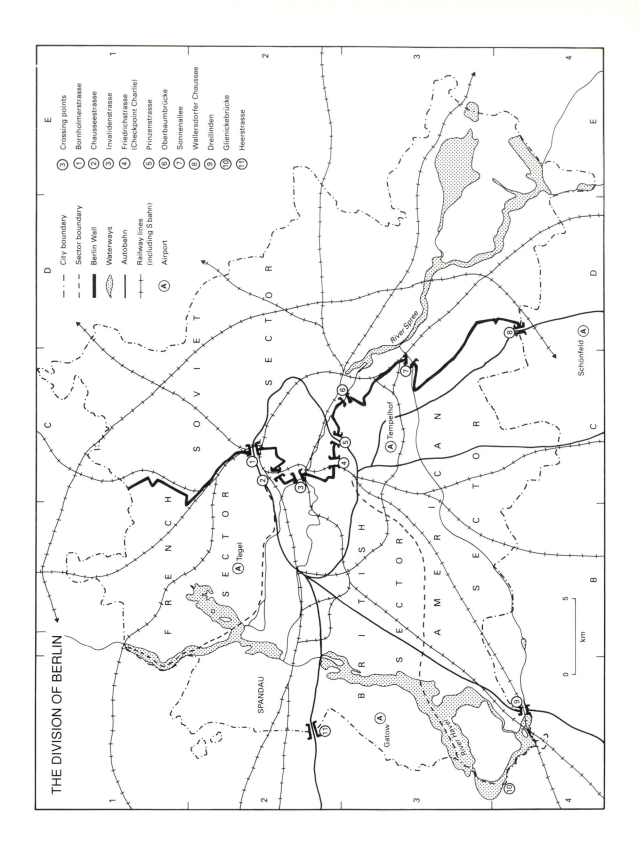

THE DIVISION OF BERLIN

Crossing points

① Bornholmerstrasse
② Chausseestrasse
③ Invalidenstrasse
④ Friedrichstrasse (Checkpoint Charlie)
⑤ Prinzenstrasse
⑥ Oberbaumbrücke
⑦ Sonnenallee
⑧ Wallersdorfer Chaussee
⑨ Dreilinden
⑩ Glienickebrücke
⑪ Heerstrasse

City boundary
Sector boundary
Berlin Wall
Waterways
Autobahn
Railway lines (including S bahn)
Airport

FRENCH SECTOR
SOVIET SECTOR
BRITISH SECTOR
AMERICAN SECTOR

Tegel
Tempelhof
Gatow
Schönfeld

SPANDAU

River Spree
River Havel

km
0   5

In those states which had fought with the Germans – Romania, Hungary, and Bulgaria – allied control commissions functioned until the signature of peace treaties in February 1947. At times Western officers offered encouragement, usually futile, to anti-communists such as the Bulgarian agrarian leader Nikola Petkov who resisted valiantly until subjected to judicial murder in September 1947.

By then divisions between East and West had hardened. The communists were ejected from coalition governments in France and Italy, the Truman doctrine in the spring announced there would be American resistance to any further communist expansion in Europe or the Middle East. Greece and Turkey were the prime candidates, and the Marshall Plan, announced shortly afterwards, promised economic assistance to states adopting the Western as opposed to the Soviet economic system. In retaliation the Soviets convened a meeting of European communist parties at Szklarska Poreba and founded Cominform to coordinate communist resistance to Western pressures. When the Prague coup of February 1948 placed Czechoslovakia under communist rule the takeover of Eastern Europe was completed.

The division of Berlin

When fighting ended in Europe in May 1945 the American armies were in possession of considerable territory to the east of the Elbe and to the east of the line previously drawn to demarcate Soviet and Western zones of occupation. In July Western troops were withdrawn from these areas in return for which the Western powers were given administrative responsibility for fourteen of the twenty districts of the city of Berlin.

The Western zones were soon to become an embarrassment to the Soviets and their East German dependants. In the Soviet Zone of Occupation a Socialist Unity Party (SED) had been formed from the communists and the historic German Social Democratic Party (SPD). When elections were held in the eastern part of Germany in August 1946 Greater Berlin was the only region where the old SPD had survived as a separate entity and could compete against the SED; the SPD took 48.7 per cent of the votes as against the SED's 19.8 per cent.

There were increasing friction between the Soviet authorities in eastern Germany and the Americans, British and French in the Western zones. The primary cause of tension was reparations and the Soviet willingness to take industrial production and machinery from the West without handing over the agreed quantities of food in return. When, in June 1948, a new currency was introduced into the Western zones in order to stimulate the local economy, the Soviets and their East German allies feared that the new currency and the revived economy in the West would act as an enormous magnet to the population of eastern Germany. Berlin was therefore sealed off and all land access from the West was denied. The city was saved by a massive airlift. By the end of June two hundred aircraft per day were landing at Gatow in the British sector and similar traffic was flying into the other available airfields with one aircraft landing every four minutes. The blockade ended on 12 May 1949 by which time over seventy allied airmen had died during the operation. Berlin had been transformed from the epitome of Prussian militarism into a symbol of embattled liberty.

During the 1950s East Germany strengthened its borders with the West, making it very difficult to cross at any point except in Berlin which was subject to four-power allied control. There was a constant stream of refugees escaping through the city. Mostly they were people the East German regime, which was trying to build a new and advanced industrial economy and society, could ill afford to lose. Between 1945 and 1961 an estimated 3.6 million East Germans left, a number roughly equivalent to the population of Norway; approximately half those leaving were under 25. In the summer of 1961 an agreement between the Soviet and East German govern-

EAST EUROPEAN STALINISM

- ▲ Mountain peak named 'Stalin'
- ⊙ Town named 'Stalin' or after Stalin
- ■ Labour camp
- ☐ Major prison
- ⊡ Prison camp

Fünfkirchen

Sachsenhausen

GDR

Torgau Eisenhüttenstadt POLAND

Buchenwald Bautzen

Karl Marx Stadt

Jachymov

Pribram Prague Mirov Katowice

CZECHOSLOVAKIA Gerlachovo

Leopoldov

Vac

Budapest
Dunapentele Aiud

HUNGARY ROMANIA Brașov

Dorog Pitești Bucharest

Jilava

Goli Otok Danube-Black Sea Canal

YUGOSLAVIA River Danube

Belene Varna

Pasard Dam Lovech

Sofia

BULGARIA

▲ Musala

Kucovë

0   250

km

ments gave the latter more freedom of action, though it in no way impaired Western rights in West Berlin. The agreement increased fears that the escape hatch might be closed and the flow of refugees became a flood. On 13 August the border was closed and a week later construction of a wall began. By the end of the month the city was totally divided.

Crossing points were opened but they were strictly controlled, the most famous of them being Friedrichstrasse and Glienickebrücke, the former famous because it was the access point for Westerners, the latter for the exchanges of spies it witnessed.

The Berlin Wall became the symbol of oppressive communism, and its breaching heralded the collapse of the system throughout Europe.

East European Stalinism

Between 1949 and 1953 Eastern Europe endured its variant of Stalinism. Collectivisation and industrialisation were part of this process but so too were the cult of Stalin's personality and the imposition of terror.

The cult of personality meant that most states named one of their cities after Stalin. 'Stalin' was the name given to Varna (Bulgaria), Braşov (Romania), and Kucovë (Albania), whilst in East Germany the newly founded town of Eisenhüttenstadt was first called 'Stalinstadt', in Hungary Dunapentele was named 'Sztalinváros', and in Poland Katowice was for a while 'Stalinogoród'. Czechoslovakia did not name a town after Stalin but its highest mountain, Gerlachovo, was known as 'Stalin Peak', as was Bulgaria's highest point, Musala. Bulgaria also renamed the Pasard Dam near Sofia, 'Stalin Dam'.

The processes of forced collectivisation, industrialisation and urbanisation created huge social tensions. These had to be contained. And at the same time discipline had to be re-enforced in the communist parties, most of which had expanded rapidly in the recent past – especially when new, communist-dominated left-wing coalitions were formed. To contain social discontent and to guarantee discipline within the party the local leaders, egged on by Moscow, unleashed savage purges both on their parties and on the societies over which they held sway. Between 1948 and 1953 far more communists were killed by their own party than had been killed by the Nazis and fascists. At the top level of the party it was alleged that the victims were supporters of the Titoist heresy; after the break between Moscow and Belgrade in 1948, Stalin was terrified lest heresy inside the camp might make it easy for the infidel to enter from outside. Show trials were therefore staged to 'prove' the guilt of figures such as László Rajk, a Hungarian communist hero of the resistance; Traicho Kostov, a Bulgarian graduate of monarchist prisons; and Rudolf Slánský, a long-standing member of the Czechoslovak communist leadership.

For the thousands of ordinary party members or non-party citizens who fell victim to the purges there was no need for such elaboration. They might be denounced by informers, condemned by 'administrative arrest', or simply deported. Hundreds of thousands languished in prisons such as that at Aiud in Transylvania, where leading political opponents were interned, including the aged National Peasant Party leader, Iuliu Maniu. In Germany former Nazi concentration camps, including Buchenwald, Sachsenhausen, and Torgau were reopened. Many victims were sent to forced labour in mines, such as those at Dorog in Hungary, or at Jachymov in Czechoslovakia where uranium was extracted. In Romania prison labour (that is, slave labour) was used to begin construction of the Danube–Black Sea Canal, a vast undertaking which was abandoned in the mid-1950s only to be completed by Ceauşescu three decades later.

Labour and prison camps were dotted all over Eastern Europe and many prisoners were used as conscript, cheap labour in ordinary factories and mines. Poland stood aloof from the worst excesses of the purges. Its potential Titoist, Władisław Gomułka, was interned but he was not subjected to a show trial. Arrests were fewer in Poland than elsewhere, although large numbers of former non-communist resistance fighters remained in prison.

Yugoslavia did not have Stalinist purges but there was little political freedom there either. Most opponents of Tito who had survived the blood-letting of the post-war period and who had not fled were still in prison, and a new prison camp was opened off the Croatian coast on the island of Goli Otok to house the 'cominformists' – that is, those who sided with Moscow against Tito.

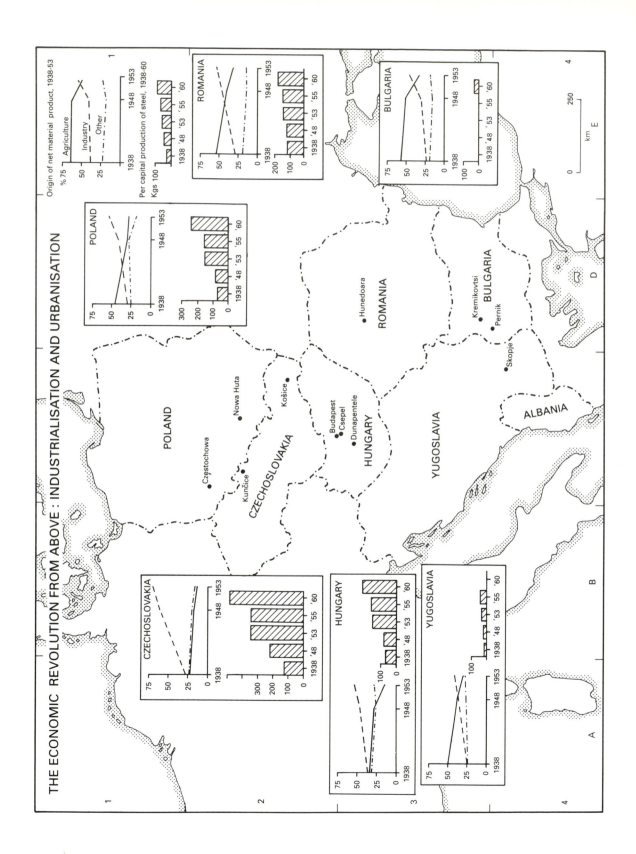

THE ECONOMIC REVOLUTION FROM ABOVE : INDUSTRIALISATION AND URBANISATION

Origin of net material product, 1938-53

Per capital production of steel, 1938-60

158

The economic revolution from above: industrialisation and urbanisation

Planning of the economy began soon after the war in most East European states with the introduction of reconstruction plans, usually of two to three years' duration. Thereafter came the five-year plans (fyp): in 1949 in Bulgaria and Czechoslovakia, in 1950 in Hungary and Poland, and in 1951 in Romania. Yugoslavia introduced a reconstruction plan in January 1947, and after the break with the USSR in 1948 incorporated that plan into the first fyp which ran until 1952.

The plans shifted investment and labour into the heavy industrial sector at the cost of agriculture and consumer goods. There were massive planned increases in production, however, in both the industrial and agrarian sectors (see Table 16).

The intention was to create an industrial infrastructure which would produce the proletariat for whom Communist Party rule was designed and which, according to Marxist theory, would inevitably inherit the earth. The plans set out to expand vastly the energy-producing and the metallurgical sectors of the economy (see Table 17).

Steel was accorded a special significance, not least because that had been the Soviet practice, and per capita production figures are shown on the map. (Figures for Albania are unavailable or unreliable.) Great propaganda effort was devoted to steel production, especially at newly founded plants. In Poland these were the Lenin Plant at Nowa Huta near Cracow, and the Bierut Complex, an extended version of the Rakow plant near Częstochowa. In both cases these plants were intended to inject a greater proletarian presence into liberal and/or Catholic areas. In Czechoslovakia the new Gottwald Steel Mills were erected at Kunčice in the Moravska–Ostrava industrial belt; in Hungary Dunapentele and Csepel were the main areas of expanded steel production; in Romania existing plants in and near Hunedoara in Transylvania were also

Table 16 Planned output according the first five-year plan (pre-war = 100)

	Industry	Agriculture
Bulgaria	403	135
Czechoslovakia	213	138
Hungary	434	140
Poland	417	115
Romania	306	160
Yugoslavia	494	151

Table 17 Scheduled annual increases in output in the first five-year plan

	Coal	Pig iron	Steel	Electricity
Bulgaria	11.3	–	–	29.2
Czechoslovakia	5.2	13.4	10.5	7.7
Hungary	8.8	24.5	20.9	13.8
Poland	3.8	17.9	12.6	15.4
Romania	21.5	19.0	17.5	17.4

greatly enlarged. Bulgaria entered the metallurgical stakes late with the small Lenin plant at Pernik opening in 1953 to be followed a decade later by the massive Kremikovtsi complex near Sofia. The rush for steel and other metals was not always successful. After the breach with the Soviet Union Yugoslavia abandoned plans for a huge steel production facility outside Skopje, and the Czechoslovaks did the same with a scheme for the massive Huko metallurgical plant near Košice.

The plans, even if implemented, were not always beneficial. Too many heavy metallurgical plants were built and it would have been far better to invest more in chemicals and plastics. Furthermore, the fyps, with their rigidly imposed production quotas, enforced concentration on the quantity rather than the quality of production.

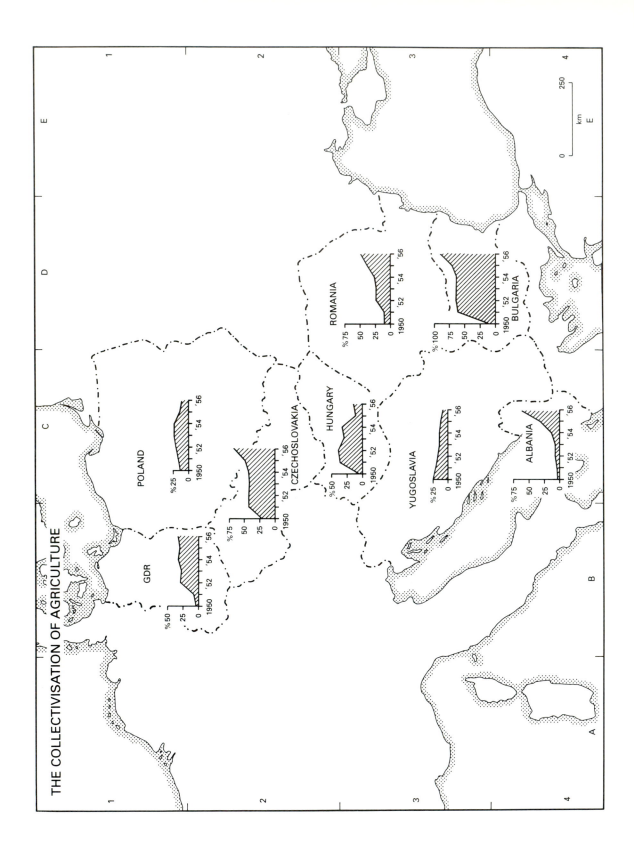

THE COLLECTIVISATION OF AGRICULTURE

The collectivisation of agriculture

The socialisation of agriculture was a vital step in building socialism. It would eliminate bourgeois elements in the countryside, it would allow party and state more easily to impose central plans, and it would release vast quantities of surplus labour for work in the rapidly expanding industrial centres.

Socialisation was essentially of two types: the setting-up of state farms whose staff were employed workers; and the formation of agricultural collectives in which those who contributed land became technical partners. In fact, both state and collective farms were immediately placed under firm Party control, and by the 1970s the differences between the two were minimal.

The percentages given on the map are for arable land. Mountain pastures and small farms were usually unsuitable for collectivisation and were generally left in private hands with a limitation on the amount of land any one family might own. Few peasants welcomed collectivisation and therefore were subjected to massive fiscal pressures and, failing this, physical intimidation.

The process was initiated in the heyday of East European Stalinism, the later 1940s and early 1950s. Between 1953 and 1956 there was a pause during which the 'New Course' advocated by Stalin's successors in Moscow was applied. This involved a relaxation of collectivising pressures, not least because of the generally appalling economic effects it had produced. After the suppression of the Hungarian revolution of 1956 most states saw a reassertion of ideological rigidity and in the more repressive of regimes, Albania, Romania, Bulgaria, Czechoslovakia and the GDR, there was a marked increase in the pace of collectivisation. In 1957 Bulgaria announced that it was the first of the East European states to complete the process.

Most other states soon followed Bulgaria's example, though after the events of 1956 pressures were more refined and the pace less hectic. In Hungary itself the revolution of 1956 had seen the dissolution of a number of collectives. After the reimposition of party control there was an intense debate as to whether this land should be taken again into social ownership and the collectivisation process continued. In January 1959 it was decided, under considerable pressure from the Soviets, to revert to socialisation, though this time it was to be collectivisation with kid gloves. By 1962 three-quarters of Hungary's arable land had been collectivised.

Poland too had seen national protest and revolt in 1956 but this had been contained by the party. Even at its peak, collectivisation in Poland had affected less than a quarter of the arable land and in 1956 the process was abandoned. Most collectives were dissolved and the few which remained, together with state farms, meant that no more than 10 per cent of Polish agriculture was socialised in the remaining three and a half decades of communist domination.

In the immediate post-war years the Yugoslav communists had been as radical as any other in their agrarian policies. Pressure for socialisation was intense and by the late 1940s almost a quarter of the land had ceased to be in private hands. The results were not encouraging and after the break with Stalin in 1948 a reassessment was possible. Somewhat reluctantly, the ideologues of the Yugoslav ruling party accepted that private ownership alone would revitalise a devastated agrarian sector. In March 1953 the agricultural collectives were dissolved, though a few state farms remained. Limits were, however, placed on the amount of land any individual might own and there were attempts, not entirely unsuccessful, to promote cooperation in marketing and in the provision of technical assistance. Thereafter almost all the land which remained in the socialised sector in Yugoslavia was state-owned rather than collectively owned.

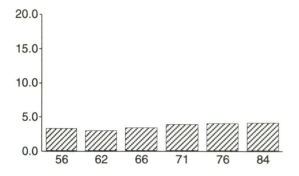

Figure 110 Albania (% population)

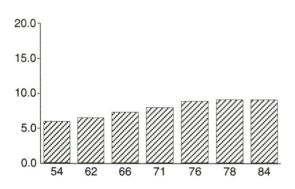

Figure 111 Bulgaria (% population)

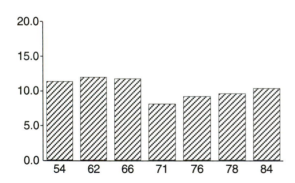

Figure 112 Czechoslovakia (% population)

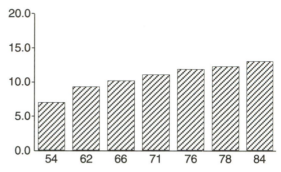

Figure 113 German Democratic Republic (% population)

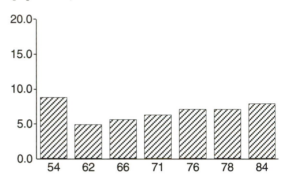

Figure 114 Hungary (% population)

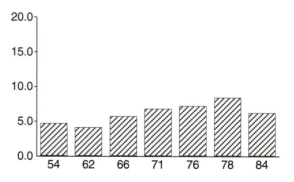

Figure 115 Poland (% population)

Communist Party membership

Party membership was the key to political, social and economic power in the communist system. No one who did not enjoy the party's approval could expect promotion or privileges such as the right to travel abroad. The local Party organisations kept lists of important local posts (the *nomenklatura*) and no one whose personal file included anything untoward could expect any of those posts. This guaranteed the party's social power as effectively as the secret police and the labour camps had guaranteed its political security in the early years.

Party membership, because of the power and influence it bought, was restricted to a relatively small proportion of the population. In terms of Marxist theory it should have been the developed industrial societies of the GDR, Czechoslovakia and Poland, with their more numerous working classes, which should have had the largest proportion of party members. It was true that in Albania the proportion never reached beyond 5 per cent but the rule does not hold good much beyond that. Party membership did rise to over 13 per cent in the GDR but it was also high by the 1980s in Yugoslavia, and in Romania one of the means Ceauşescu used to entrench his dictatorship was to extend party membership to increase the number of families with a stake in the regime.

Party membership generally rose as a percentage of the total population as the system became more entrenched; the party began to be less suspicious of the people and the people accepted the party as a fact of life to which they had to accommodate. There were exceptions to the rule of steadily rising party membership; in Czechoslovakia after 1968 purges and popular distaste stripped the pre-invasion party of one in three of its members. In Poland, too, the use of force, this time the imposition of martial law in 1981, led to a decline in Party membership; in Hungary in 1956 the existing party dissolved and a new one was formed after the Soviet invasion; this new party, too, had by the mid-1980s failed to achieve a proportion of popular membership equal to that which existed before the invasion. In Bulgaria the Party probably enjoyed more genuine popular support than in any other state except Czechoslovakia before 1968. Like the pre-1968 Czechoslovak party the Bulgarian had long historic roots and had enjoyed a great deal of electoral support whenever the electoral system had allowed a free vote.

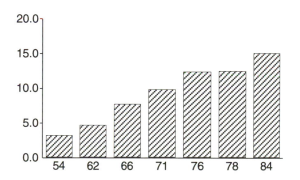

Figure 116 Romania (% population)

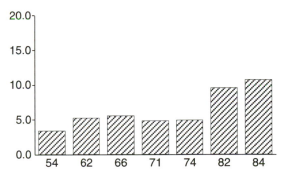

Figure 117 Yugoslavia (% population)

Soviet–East European trade, 1960, 1970, 1980

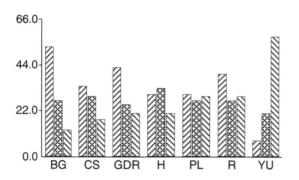

Figure 118 Distribution of trade, 1960 (% value)

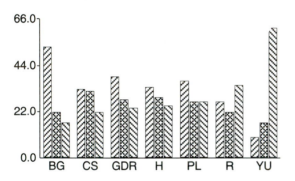

Figure 119 Distribution of trade, 1970 (% value)

Note: The columns in figures 118–120 represent the proportion of trade with, respectively, the USSR, the other East European states and the West.

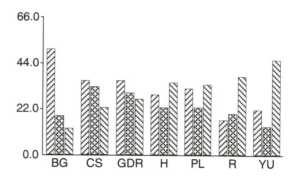

Figure 120 Distribution of trade, 1980 (% value)

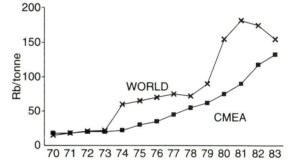

Figure 121 Soviet oil prices to CMEA and world

Soviet energy supplies to Eastern Europe (see map on page 165)

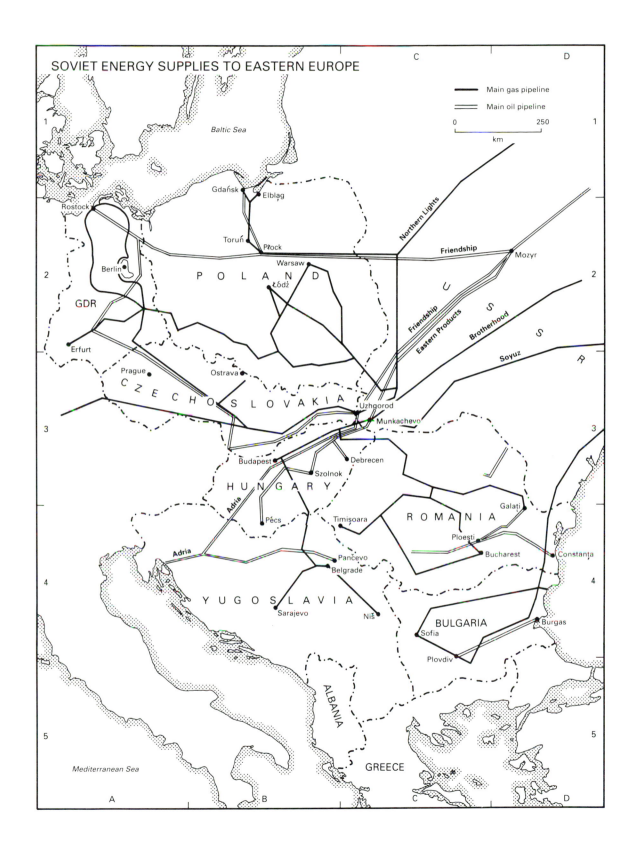

SOVIET ENERGY SUPPLIES TO EASTERN EUROPE

Main gas pipeline

Main oil pipeline

0   250

km

Baltic Sea

Gdańsk
Elbląg
Rostock
Toruń
Płock
Warsaw
Berlin
Łódź

GDR
P O L A N D

Erfurt

Prague
Ostrava

C Z E C H O S L O V A K I A

Uzhgorod
Munkachevo

Budapest
Szolnok
Debrecen

H U N G A R Y

Adria

Pécs
Timişoara

R O M A N I A

Galaţi

Ploesti

Adria
Pancevo
Belgrade
Bucharest
Constanţa

Y U G O S L A V I A

Sarajevo
Niš

BULGARIA
Burgas
Sofia

Plovdiv

ALBANIA

GREECE

Mediterranean Sea

Northern Lights
Friendship
Mozyr
Friendship
Eastern Products
Brotherhood
Soyuz
U S S R

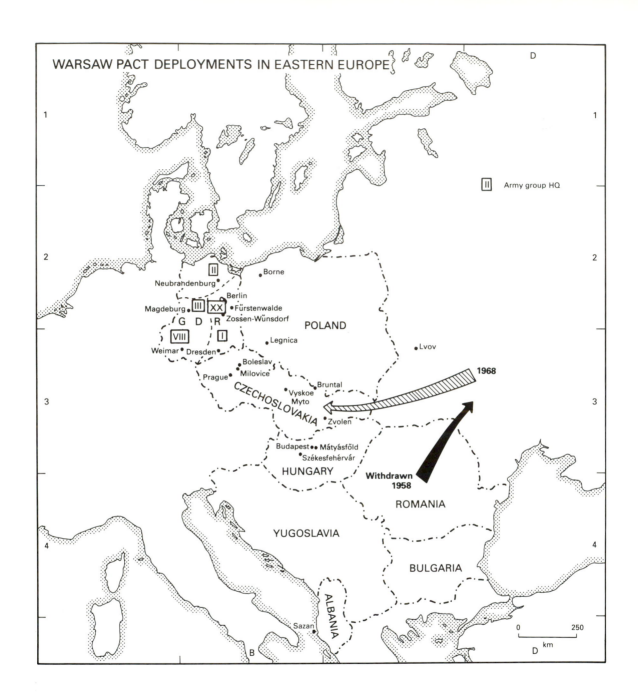

WARSAW PACT DEPLOYMENTS IN EASTERN EUROPE

‖ Army group HQ

POLAND

• Borne
Neubrandenburg •
‖‖

Magdeburg • ‖‖ XX • Fürstenwalde
Berlin
G D R Zossen-Wünsdorf
VIII ‖
Weimar • • Dresden • Legnica • Lvov
Boleslav •
Prague • Milovice •
CZECHOSLOVAKIA Vyskoe Bruntal • 1968
Myto
• Zvolen

Budapest • • Mátyásföld
• Székesfehérvár
HUNGARY Withdrawn
1958

ROMANIA

YUGOSLAVIA

BULGARIA

ALBANIA

• Sazan
0   250
km

166

Warsaw Pact deployments in Eastern Europe

After the consolidation of communist power in the region East European military machines were rapidly put under Soviet domination. All senior officers became party members, and all of them had to receive some of their training in Moscow or with the Soviet forces. At the same time, all East European forces were supplied with Soviet equipment, were dressed in Soviet-style uniforms, and trained according to Soviet methods.

In 1955, with West Germany being integrated into the Western defence system, the Warsaw Treaty Organisation (WTO), or Warsaw Pact, was created. Its headquarters were established in Lvov. The Pact had no formal structure, though its Political Consultative Committee was occasionally used to exchange views. The Pact was totally dominated by the Soviets; East European formations were slotted into the Soviet chain of command, and Soviet military representatives were attached to every non-Soviet division outside the USSR.

The original members were the Soviet Union, Albania, Bulgaria, Czechoslovakia, the German Democratic Republic, Hungary, Poland and Romania. Albania was to cease to be an effective member of the alliance in 1960 after an increasingly bitter dispute with Moscow, and in 1968 formally left the organisation; Albania's defection deprived the Soviets of their submarine bases at Sazan in the Adriatic. In 1968 Bulgaria, the GDR, Poland and Hungary joined the USSR in its military intervention in Czechoslovakia; the Romanians refused to participate and thereafter Romania's commitment to the Pact also declined.

In strategic terms the WTO's main preoccupation was always in the 'northern tier': the GDR and Poland. The Soviet Group of Northern Forces stationed in these two countries were concentrated overwhelmingly in the GDR which had garrisons of around 400,000 – ten times the number stationed in Poland. The Soviet forces in East Germany consisted of the Second Guards Tank Army (HQ, Neubrandenburg), the Third Shock Army (Magdeburg), the Twentieth Guards Army (Fürstenwalde), the Eighth Guards Army (Weimar), and the First Guards Tank Army (Dresden). In addition there were ten tank divisions, nine motorised rifle brigades, and one artillery and one air-assault brigade attached to the Group HQ in Zossen-Wünsdorf. The forces in Poland were commanded from Legnica but consisted of only two tank divisions with support from helicopters and combat aircraft, most of the latter being based at Borne in northern Poland.

The central tier was made up of Czechoslovakia and Hungary. There were no Soviet troops in Czechoslovakia until the invasion of 1968 after which some 85,000 in five divisions were garrisoned in the country, their bases being Boleslav (Eighteenth Guards Motor Rifle Division), Milovice (an air base and home of the Fifteenth Guards Tank Division), Vyskoe Myto near Olomouc (Forty-ninth Motor Rifle Division), Bruntal (Fifty-first Tank Division), and Zvolen (Thirtieth Guards Motor Rifle Division), the only major Soviet base in Slovakia. It seems unlikely to be coincidence that the Soviet divisions were stationed behind Czechoslovak units which would be required to meet any onslaught from the West.

Soviet forces in Hungary numbered in the region of 65,000 and were controlled from Group and Army HQ Budapest–Mátyásföld, where two tank and two motorised rifle divisions were stationed together with an air-assault brigade. There was also a large air base near Székesfehérvár.

After the Romanians had shown that they were determined to prevent the Hungarian revolution of 1956 spreading to their Hungarian minority, the Soviets felt confident that Romania could be relied upon to preserve Communist Party authority and Red Army units were withdrawn from Romania in 1958.

Bulgaria had not been home to Soviet forces since nine months after the signing of the peace treaty in February 1947.

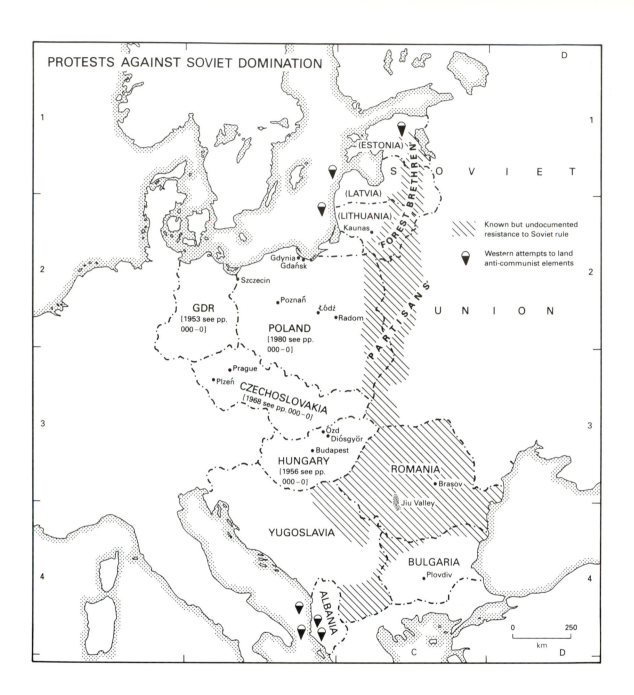

PROTESTS AGAINST SOVIET DOMINATION

(ESTONIA)

(LATVIA)

(LITHUANIA)

Kaunas

S O V I E T

FOREST BRETHREN

U N I O N

Gdynia
Gdańsk

Szczecin

GDR
[1953 see pp. 000−0]

Poznań

Łódź
Radom

POLAND
[1980 see pp. 000−0]

PARTISANS

Prague

Plzeň

CZECHOSLOVAKIA
[1968 see pp. 000−0]

Ózd
Diósgyör

Budapest

HUNGARY
[1956 see pp. 000−0]

ROMANIA

Brasov

Jiu Valley

YUGOSLAVIA

BULGARIA

Plovdiv

ALBANIA

Known but undocumented
resistance to Soviet rule

Western attempts to land
anti-communist elements

0   250

km

168

Protests against Soviet domination

The extent of outside attempts to destabilise the new regimes of Eastern Europe is still largely undocumented. Albanian émigrés were parachuted into their native land, only to be arrested by security forces forewarned by the treachery of Kim Philby. Little is as yet known of the so-called 'Forest Brethren', or those who took to the woods and marshes to resist the new or reinstated communist authorities in Poland, Belorussia, Ukraine, and the Baltic states. That outside assistance was given to them is beyond doubt.

Less was done to help the many peasants who staged spontaneous, uncoordinated resistance against the collectivisation of their land. Such resistance certainly took place in north-western Bulgaria as well as in the Vojvodina and other parts of Serbia; in Romania party leader Gheorghiu-Dej admitted to the arrest of over 80,000 disaffected peasants.

The workers, in whose name the communists exercised power, also periodically expressed discontent. In May 1953 there were strikes by the traditionally pro-communist tobacco workers of Plovdiv, and by 20,000 workers in the Skoda plant at Plzeň who were protesting at disguised wage cuts. In Hungary in the following months there were similar outbreaks by workers in the Mátyás Rákosi steelworks in Csepel outside Budapest and in factories in Ozd and Diósgyör as well as amongst the farmers of the great plain. Then came the great outbreak in the GDR in June (see p. 171). In Poland there was endemic unrest amongst the workers. At the end of June 1956 strikes at the Cegielski railway works in Poznań rocked the communist establishment and began the process which in October led to the reinstatement as party leader of Władisław Gomułka. In 1970 action by workers in the Baltic ports of Gdańsk, Gdynia and Szczecin and then amongst the textile workers in Łódź led to the replacement of Gomułka by Edvard Gierek, whilst in 1976 threatened food price increases brought a rash of strikes during which the party headquarters in Radom were ransacked. Four years later came Solidarity (see pp. 175–7). Spontaneous industrial action was one of the few methods of expressing anger at the increasingly dictatorial regime of Nicolae Ceaușescu in Romania. Such outbursts occurred in August 1977 when 30,000 miners in the Jiu valley struck, refusing to return to work until Ceaușescu himself had come to negotiate with them. Ten years later, in November 1987, there was a violent demonstration and strike by workers from the Red Star tractor plant in Brașov where, again, the party headquarters was attacked and its stores of food looted.

The opposite of spontaneous industrial action is the long-term conspiracy. There were a small number of these in Eastern Europe between 1945 and 1989. Bulgarian army officers attempted to depose their party leader Todor Zhivkov in 1965, and in 1983 there was a military plot against Ceaușescu.

Individual protest also occurred and no doubt many instances of this have gone unrecorded. That of Jan Palach in Prague in January 1969 is the most well known but his example of self-immolation was followed by Romas Kalanta on 14 May 1972 in Kaunas, Lithuania, and he was not the only Lithuanian to take this drastic step.

In Czechoslovakia over 1,000 people eventually signed the 'Charter '77' petition which asked their government to observe its own laws. And in the 1980s as the regimes lost the will to take draconian measures 'civil society', or organisations outside party control, multiplied. The first great example of this had been the Polish organisation, KOR, formed to protect workers arrested after the disturbances of 1976.

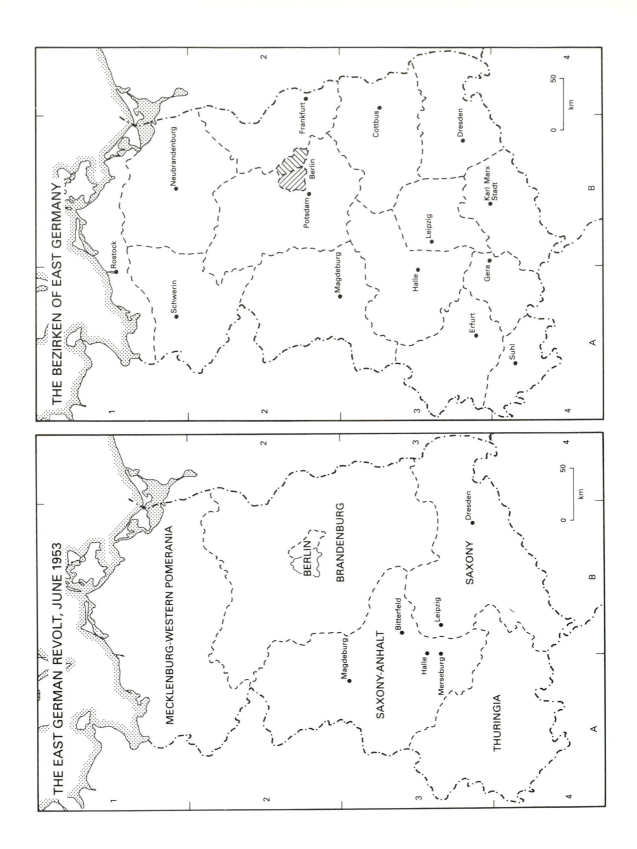

THE EAST GERMAN REVOLT, JUNE 1953

MECKLENBURG-WESTERN POMERANIA

BERLIN

BRANDENBURG

Magdeburg

SAXONY-ANHALT

Bitterfeld

Halle
Merseburg
Leipzig

SAXONY

Dresden

THURINGIA

50
km
0

A   B

1

2

3

4

THE BEZIRKEN OF EAST GERMANY

Rostock

Schwerin

Neubrandenburg

Frankfurt

Berlin
Potsdam

Cottbus

Magdeburg

Halle

Leipzig

Dresden

Karl Marx
Stadt

Gera

Erfurt

Suhl

50
km
0

A   B

1

2

3

4

The East German revolt, June 1953

In May 1952, in an effort to prevent the incorporation of western Germany into the Western defence system, Stalin proposed that the whole of Germany should be neutralised and then unified. When the West refused this offer the Soviets determined to bind the German Democratic Republic (GDR) fully into their system.

At its second congress in June 1952 the ruling Socialist Unity Party (SED) adopted a number of measures for the 'systematic construction of socialism' in the GDR. These included a switch of investment from consumer to capital goods, increases in expenditure on the security forces, more collectivisation of agriculture, and the abolition of the five historic provinces (Mecklenburg-Western Pomerania, Brandenburg, Saxony-Anhalt, Saxony, and Thuringia) which were to be replaced by fourteen districts (*Bezirken*) with greatly reduced powers.

These measures only increased the number of East Germans fleeing to the West. In April 1953, a month after Stalin's death, the East German leadership turned to Moscow for help only to be told that the GDR should adopt the 'New Course' followed by Stalin's successors. This was to involve a great relaxation of the class struggle, concessions to the churches, reduced pressure on farmers to join collectives, and a greater degree of political freedom. Stalin's plans for a unified but neutral Germany had not been lost sight of, and if socialism were to stand any chance in elections in a reunited Germany it had to be of a relaxed, non-Stalinist variety.

One prominent item of the old course, however, was not rescinded. Increases in work-norms of 10 per cent, promulgated in May, were to remain, the trade union newspaper announced on 16 June. To many workers it seemed that they were being required to make sacrifices in order that the country should be made safe for bourgeois democracy. Builders on the huge construction sites on Berlin's Stalinallee (formerly the Frankfurterallee and at the time of writing the Karl Marx Allee) downed tools and marched to trade union headquarters. After some confusion an official conceded that the increase in work-norms would be withdrawn but by then the strikers had added political items to their list of demands.

Although the strikers and demonstrators dispersed in the evening the country was soon aware of what had happened in its capital, not least because Western radio stations had given full coverage to the events in Berlin. On 17 June the GDR was in turmoil. Strikes were recorded in over three hundred locations and were especially strong in citadels of the pre-1933 German Social Democratic Party such as Magdeburg, Halle, Merseberg, and Bitterfeld. The red flag was torn from the Brandenburg Gate in Berlin and party leader Walter Ulbricht fled from the city.

There were some attacks on SED buildings but in general the strikers remained loyal to socialism; in Leipzig those who attacked the party headquarters burnt every portrait they found except that of Marx, and there was widespread opposition to the notion of a new, East German, army. There was also widespread denunciation of the West German political leader, Konrad Adenauer.

Soviet tanks appeared on the streets during the afternoon of 17 June and the revolt was easily contained with casualties numbering in the region of three thousand. Liberal elements within the party apparatus were purged and there was a return to full-blown Soviet-style socialism, though the increase in work-norms was dropped. In August 1961 the Berlin Wall was constructed to complete the division of the two Germanies.

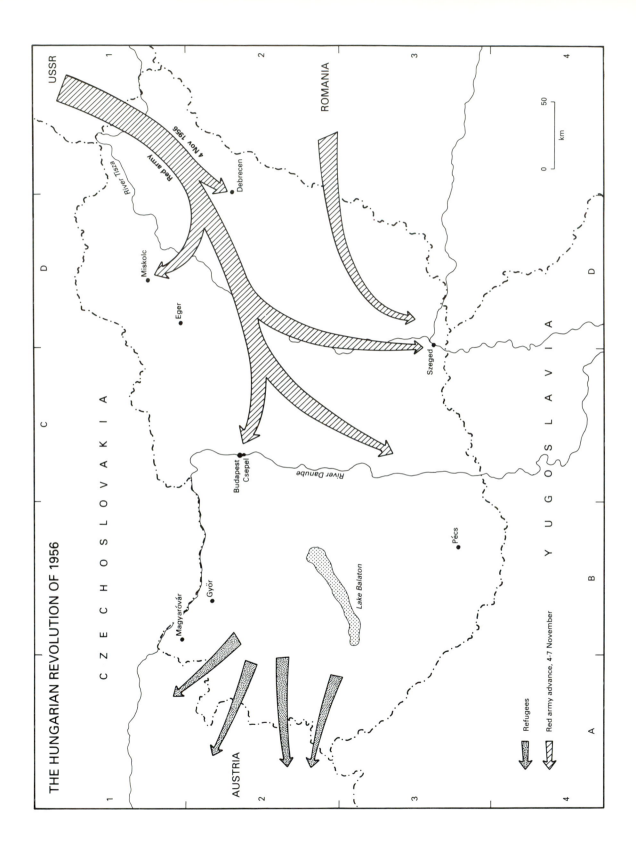

THE HUNGARIAN REVOLUTION OF 1956

CZECHOSLOVAKIA

USSR

ROMANIA

River Tisza

Red army
4 Nov 1956

Debrecen

Miskolc

Eger

Szeged

Budapest
Csepel

River Danube

Pécs

Lake Balaton

Magyaróvár

Győr

AUSTRIA

YUGOSLAVIA

50

0

km

Refugees

Red army advance, 4-7 November

The Hungarian revolution of 1956

The political purges in Hungary had been of a particularly widespread and vicious nature. When former prisoners were released following Stalin's death in 1953 their stories greatly depressed the morale of the party rank and file. At the same time the leadership was divided between the conservatives under Mátyás Rákosi and the reformists led by Imre Nagy who was prime minister from 1953 to 1955.

In March 1956 Rákosi attempted to achieve some credit by rehabilitating László Rajk, chief victim of the show-trials, but the concession was announced not in Budapest but in the provincial town of Eger. By the summer Rákosi's position had become untenable and the Soviets insisted he resign as party leader.

This did nothing to contain the growing unrest which had its origin in poor living conditions, frustration at constant official propaganda, and above all in deep resentment at Soviet domination of Hungary. The victory of Polish nationally-inclined communists in securing the appointment of Gomułka as party leader in October (see p. 169) brought matters to a head. On 23 October students from the Technological University in Budapest drew up a list of demands and then decided to march to the statue of General Bem, a Pole who had fought against the Russians in the Polish revolt of 1830 and in the Hungarian revolution of 1848 after which the tsarist forces had executed him.

After reaching the statue the marchers divided, one group going to Parliament Square where they demanded, successfully, to be addressed by Nagy, and the other to the headquarters of Hungarian Radio. Here they were fired upon by men from the secret police, the AVH. The Red Army then responded to a call for assistance. The Hungarian revolution, the bloodiest of all confrontations between Soviet communism and a satellite people, had begun.

The Hungarian army rapidly went over to the side of the revolutionaries but the AVH did not. In a number of centres, particularly Magyaróvár, they carried out indiscriminate massacres, in return for which the revolutionaries exacted a ruthless revenge. The Red Army could do relatively little to help; it was not trained to operate in urban centres and its tanks were ill-suited to street fighting. Youths and workers were soon in command of the cities; working-class strongholds such as Csepel on the outskirts of Budapest showed no loyalty to the communist regime.

By 27 October that regime had been replaced by a coalition under Nagy, and on the following day the Hungarian Socialist Party (the communists) dissolved itself and the Soviets agreed to withdraw their forces from the country. Much of the pressure to secure such radical objectives had come from provincial councils which emerged during the revolution. Based on cities such as Debrecen, Győr, Miskolc and Szeged, they exercised enormous influence.

That influence was to be short-lived. After consultations with other East European and Chinese leaders, Soviet party boss Khrushchev decided upon the liquidation of the Hungarian revolution. On 4 November Soviet tanks returned to Hungary. Nagy declared that Hungary would leave the Warsaw Pact and become a neutral state, but he was no longer in control of the country. Despite incredible resistance the weight of Soviet armour was too much for the Hungarians and within ten days fighting had ceased and a reconstituted Communist Party under János Kádár had been placed in office.

The cost was enormous. In addition to at least three thousand killed Hungary had lost over two hundred thousand of its most able and active citizens who fled across the border to Austria. In addition the Soviets deported an unknown number of young people to the USSR.

Czechoslovakia, 1968

By the 1960s Czechoslovakia had fallen behind other socialist countries. Its economy was not developing as rapidly as many others and above all its political system had undergone little de-stalinisation; not until 1961 was Prague's Stalin statue, the largest in Europe, removed.

When the thaw came it developed rapidly. Cultural freedoms expanded, economic reforms were drafted, and the Slovaks began to press for more power. At the end of 1967 the leader of the old guard, Antonín Novotný, was replaced as head of the Communist Party of Czechoslovakia by Alexander Dubček, the first Slovak ever to hold that post. Within a few months a complete sweep had been made of conservatives within the uppermost echelons of the party.

The reforms with which Dubček was to be associated came to be known as 'Socialism with a Human Face'. They were directed at, and mostly determined by, the intelligentsia in the large cities. The party set out to liberalise its own procedures and to withdraw from many of the non-political activities in which it had been involved since 1948. Personal freedoms were greatly expanded. Passports and exit visas were easily obtainable, restrictions on the formation of civil groups were removed, and censorship ceased to exist. The ending of the party's monopoly over social organisations meant the virtual disappearance of the old, centralised, Party-dominated institutions such as those for youth; they were replaced by ones which frequently stressed local affiliations – for example, that set up by the students of Bohemia and Moravia at Olomouc in May. At the same time, the new media freedoms enabled the intelligentsia, including that within the party, to launch a massive debate over the purges of the

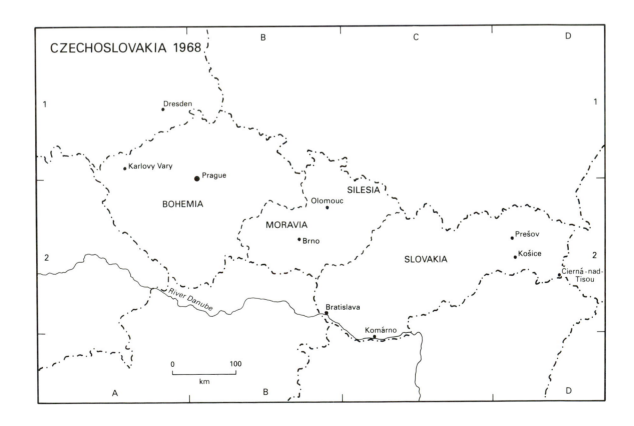

early 1950s. And there were serious discussions on how to give the Slovaks more equality, particularly in the party apparatus.

The relaxation of party controls in the economy meant decentralisation. Farms were now left to determine their own crop rotations and harvesting and sowing times; many factories were to seek out their own markets and find their own raw materials; in some sectors of the service industries a degree of private enterprise was to be allowed. At the same time enterprises were also required to be far less reliant on state subsidies, and a number of chronically inefficient plants closed, causing unemployment.

There were moves to extend religious freedom. Most striking of all was the relegalisation in June of the Uniate Church. It had been banned in 1950 but its underground leaders resurfaced and in April met in Košice. Even after the suppression of the 'Prague Spring' the Uniates retained a bishopric in Prešov.

The Soviets were anxious that these reforms might spread to Ukraine, where the Uniate Church remained under interdict. But above all the Soviets and their conservative allies in Eastern Europe feared the relaxation of party controls. A warning letter was sent from Dresden in March and pressure thereafter increased, either by the retention of Warsaw Pact troops in Czechoslovakia after their manoeuvres had ended or by visits from conservatives such as Ulbricht who arrived unannounced in Karlovy Vary (Karlsbad) on 12 August.

Hungarian Party leader János Kádár came to Komarnó a week later to warn Dubček, but it was too late. On the night of 21 August troops from the USSR, the GDR, Poland, Hungary and Bulgaria poured over the frontier to reimpose authoritarian rule.

What became known as 'normalisation' took two to three years and included some bloody confrontations; on the first anniversary of the invasion there were large demonstrations, four people being killed in that in Brno. Most famously, Jan Palach immolated himself in Wenceslas Square in the centre of Prague in January 1969. In March Soviet buildings were vandalised as delirious Czechs celebrated an ice-hockey victory over the USSR in Stockholm. The Soviets used this as an excuse for further clampdowns; in April Dubček was replaced by Gustav Husák and later in the year the Czechoslovak party began an extensive purge of reformers.

Poland, 1980–1

When a new pricing system was introduced in Poland on 1 July 1980 it was met with immediate strike action by workers in Warsaw, and this was followed by a strike in Lublin which cut the Soviet Union's rail links with its garrisons in the GDR; there were also major stoppages in Poznań and Łódź. The focal point of the unrest, however, was on the Baltic coast. On 14 August workers at the Lenin shipyard in Gdańsk struck over the dismissal of a crane driver. The strike spread rapidly along the coast to Gdynia and Szczecin. Communist Party boss Edvard Gierek flew back from holidays to try and talk the strikers back to work.

He failed. At the end of the month he was forced to sign a twenty-one point agreement with the strikers. Whilst negotiations on the agreement had been in progress the strikers had formed inter-factory strike committees which spread throughout the country. The national coordinating committee of these committees, established in September, was the ruling body of the new force which dominated Poland: Solidarity. It was led by an electrician from Gdańsk, Lech Wałesa.

Support for Solidarity was overwhelming, and in the autumn of 1980 the government was forced to allow it legal recognition. By the end of the year the Soviet Union was making threatening gestures and in secret had let the Polish communist leaders know that if they could not put their house in order the Red Army would have to do it for them. From that moment the war minister, General Jaruzelski, began prepara-

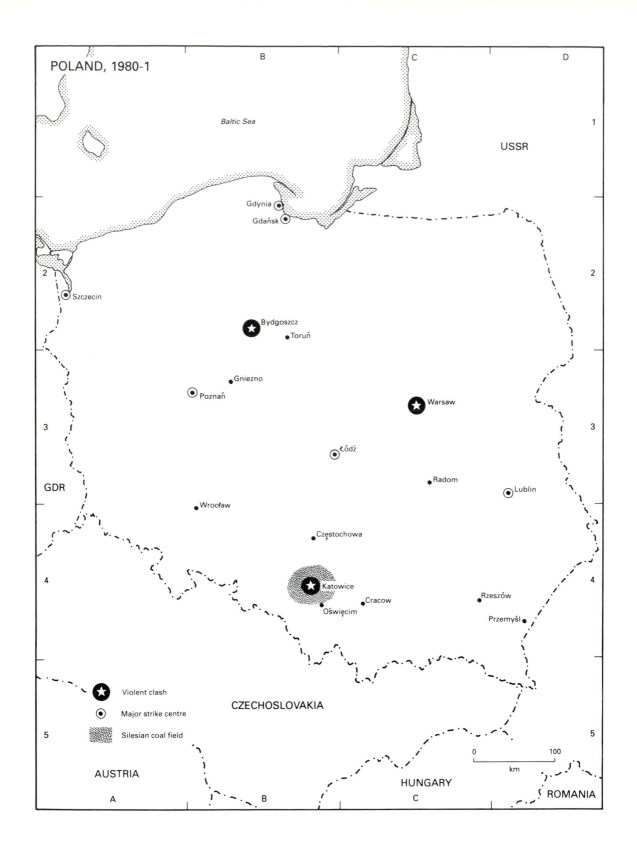

POLAND, 1980-1

Baltic Sea

USSR

GDR

CZECHOSLOVAKIA

AUSTRIA

HUNGARY

ROMANIA

Gdynia
Gdańsk
Szczecin
Bydgoszcz
Toruń
Gniezno
Poznań
Warsaw
Łódź
Radom
Lublin
Wrocław
Częstochowa
Katowice
Cracow
Oświęcim
Rzeszów
Przemyśl

Violent clash
Major strike centre
Silesian coal field

0   100
km

tions for a military coup.

In the spring of 1981 the major bone of contention was rural solidarity, which the authorities were reluctant to recognise because it consisted not of workers but of petty bourgeois peasant landowners; it was also strongly backed by the Roman Catholic Church. Its stronghold was in the south-east in centres such as Rzeszów and Przemyśl. In February a massive sit-in was organised in Rzeszów to press for recognition of rural solidarity, and on 19 March Solidarity activists raised the same question in a meeting of the municipal council of Bydgoszcz. The savage repression meted out to them was the worst confrontation before the imposition of martial law.

In April 'horizontalists', or those who wished to see the party, in response to Solidarity's successful regionalism, reorganised with a much stronger local basis, held a conference in Toruń; horizontalism was a challenge from within the party to one of its ruling principles, democratic centralism.

By the autumn relations between the party and Solidarity were deteriorating despite Wałesa's best efforts to find a compromise. The government and the party were also growing in confidence and took punitive action against extremists in Solidarity strongholds such as Katowice and Wrocław. On 2 December 1981 the police in Warsaw used helicopters to land on the roof of the Firemen's School where a strike was in progress. The Solidarity leadership went into immediate emergency session in Radom where police informers made tapes of compromising speeches.

The die was now cast. Despite frantic efforts by Solidarity and the Catholic Church to find an agreement with Jaruzelski, who by now was party leader and prime minister as well as minister of defence, the army and riot police moved into action on the night of 13–14 December. Political authority passed to a new Military Council of National Salvation.

There was strong resistance to the military coup, especially in the Silesian coalfield and in cities such as Warsaw and Cracow, but Solidarity was not an armed organisation and by Christmas resistance had been crushed – for the time being.

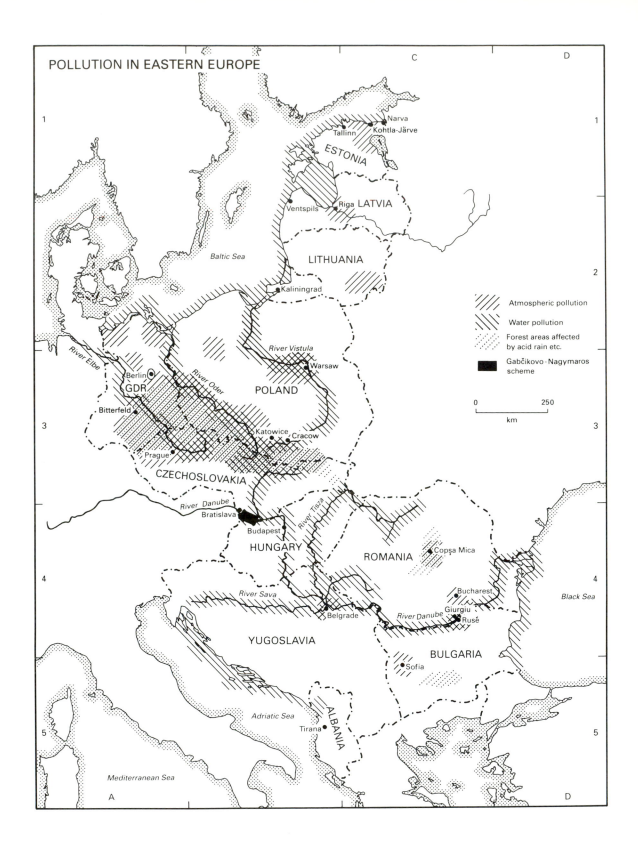

POLLUTION IN EASTERN EUROPE

Atmospheric pollution

Water pollution

Forest areas affected
by acid rain etc.

Gabčikovo · Nagymaros
scheme

0   250
km

Narva
Kohtla-Järve
Tallinn
ESTONIA
Riga LATVIA
Ventspils
LITHUANIA
Baltic Sea
Kaliningrad
River Vistula
Warsaw
River Elbe
Berlin
River Oder
GDR
POLAND
Bitterfeld
Katowice
Cracow
Prague
CZECHOSLOVAKIA
River Danube
Bratislava
Budapest
River Tisza
HUNGARY
ROMANIA
Copşa Mica
River Sava
Bucharest
Giurgiu
YUGOSLAVIA
Belgrade
River Danube
Ruse
Black Sea
BULGARIA
Sofia
ALBANIA
Adriatic Sea
Tirana
Mediterranean Sea

6 EASTERN EUROPE AT THE END OF THE COMMUNIST PERIOD

Pollution in Eastern Europe

The degradation of the environment in the years of communist rule far exceeds anything experienced in Western Europe, both in extent and intensity. The prime cause of this despoliation was the regimes' obsession with production and plan-fulfilment, no matter what the cost. The five-year plans concentrated overwhelmingly on production and made little or no provision for environmental protection, and thus no filters were fitted to factory chimneys and little if any restraint imposed on the disposal of even toxic waste.

Atmospheric pollution is widespread and covers a huge area of south-eastern Germany, southern Poland and northern Czechoslovakia. The Silesian basin, with concentrations of heavy industry in Katowice, is amongst the worst affected places in Poland, though Cracow, sandwiched between a huge chemical plant and the gargantuan steelworks at Nowa Huta, also suffers enormously, as the crumbling beauty of the old city centre attests. In Romania the citizens of Copşa Mica have to endure the fall-out from local metallurgical and extractive industries, and many other cities could report similar conditions. The Baltic Sea, being almost entirely enclosed, has become a matter of grave concern to the surrounding states, all of which on its southern shore have had to close some beaches because of the dangers to health. Albania, which because of the relatively limited extent of industrialisation had been affected less than most other states, had to endure a particular emergency in 1993 when it was discovered that peasants in the north had found drums of discarded toxic chemicals which they then emptied and used for storing water. In 1994 decaying drums of German pesticides presented another danger. The grandiose Gabčikovo-Nagymaros dam on the Danube, originally planned as a joint Czechoslovak–Hungarian hydro-electric scheme and then abandoned by the post-communist Hungarian authorities, threatens ecological destruction on a massive scale.

Environmental pollution played an important part in mobilising opposition to the communist regimes. The communists could not dismiss environmental concerns as class-based or derived from 'reactionary religious' beliefs, and concern for the environment frequently brought the intelligentsia into contact with the masses. In Bulgaria the city of Rusé suffered from periodic malfunctioning in a chemical plant in Girugiu on the Romanian bank of the Danube. In 1987 an exhibition in Rusé, approved by the local communist authorities, showed that the incidence of lung disease in the city had risen from 969 per 100,000 in 1975 to 17,386 per 100,000 in 1985. The publication of such information initiated a chain reaction which had profound political results. In January 1988 ecological groups in the GDR began to coalesce in the 'Ark-Green Movement' which was one of that country's first examples of civil society and which by November of that year had over 150 constituent groups; it also made an influential film about the appalling

ATOMIC POWER STATIONS

Area affected by fall-out from Chernobyl

▽ Nuclear waste facility

▲ Working nuclear power station

△ Nuclear power station projected or under construction

ESTONIA

Paldiski ▽ Kurchatov

LATVIA

LITHUANIA

Liepaja ▲

▲ Ignalina

Zarnowiec ▲

△ Kujawy

POLAND

Greifswald ▲

▲ Rheinberg

Stendal △   Berlin

GDR

Prague ●

CZECHOSLOVAKIA

Ceske Budějovice △

▲ Dukovaný

▲ Trnava

△ Levice

Budapest ●

HUNGARY

△ Paks

▲ Krško

ROMANIA

Pitesti △   Cernavoda △
Bucharest ●

Turnu Severin ●

YUGOSLAVIA

Kozlodui ▲   △ Belene

● Sofia

BULGARIA

ALBANIA

0   250
          km

pollution in and near Bitterfeld. In the Baltic states the first real protests were sparked by the incidence of disease in the Kohtla Järve oil-shale mining areas and around the uranium extraction works near Narva in Estonia; other causes of pollution were the fumes given off by the petrochemical complex in Ventspils in Latvia, and by the fact that in Riga a resident professor of medicine could liken the city to a disaster zone where as many as one in four babies were reported to be born defective.

After the fall of communism the successor governments were left with the problem of containing and trying to reverse the damage done to the environment. The cost of such operations will be greater than was ever imagined, east or west of the iron curtain. But it is a task which cannot be shirked.

The nuclear problem in Eastern Europe

Few issues are more contentious in Eastern Europe than nuclear energy. Some states, especially Bulgaria, have few fossil fuels and have come to rely heavily on nuclear power. The power stations concerned were constructed or planned under the communist regime and frequently do not measure up to Western safety standards.

After 1989 the Federal German authorities closed down one of the GDR's nuclear plants, that at Greifswald. In Bulgaria construction of the plant at Belene was abandoned in 1990, though three years later there was talk of recommencing work in an attempt to meet Bulgaria's growing energy needs. Bulgaria's problems centre to a considerable degree on the existing nuclear complex at Kozlodui on the Danube. Of its six reactors two are of the old Soviet pressurised (light) water (VVER) variety and give rise to constant concern; the EU has set aside $13m to help make the plant safe. The work is desperately urgent; in 1993 a government commission reported seepage of millions of litres of radioactive water from the plant, and there were even threats from extremists in Serbia that in certain circumstances they would make the plant the objective of a terrorist attack.

Romania under Ceauşescu had grandiose plans for building as many as fourteen reactors at Cernavoda. The first stage of the plant did not become operational until 1994, using nuclear fuels produced at Piteşti and heavy water manufactured at Turnu-Severin. Both the latter installations saw accidents in July 1993. In Turnu-Severin three people were killed when a container full of nitrogen exploded, and in Piteşti there was a fire in two of the plant's cooling towers.

Estonia was the site of one of the Soviet Union's nuclear waste facilities, at Kurchatov. The 93rd Soviet Navy Training Base at Paldiski, which specialised in training submariners, contained two nuclear reactors which, according to an agreement reached in the summer of 1993, were to be dismantled and taken to Russia.

The nuclear power station at Ignalina in eastern Lithuania is, say its opponents, built in a geologically unsuitable area. In March 1993 they took the temporary shutting down of the reactors due to abnormal vibrations as vindication of their view. In June 1993 radiation levels forty times above the official safety level were reported at a former Soviet military air-base near Siauliai; former employees reported that radioactive waste had been buried at the airport.

The Austrian government has for years been campaigning for the closure of all nuclear power plants in the former Czechoslovakia. There seems no prospect of this. The Slovak authorities will, they say, decommission the plant at Trnava when that under construction at Levice comes on stream; they also plan to privatise the latter. In the Czech republic workers at the Dukovaný plant in Moravia threatened to strike in June 1993 because of poor management practices; promises of a commission of enquiry and further consultation with technicians averted the strike. Hungary, meanwhile, found that nuclear waste storage facilities at Paks were rapidly filling up; Russia had no contractual obligation to take the waste which Ukraine was in any case reluctant to see transported through its territory. Negotia-

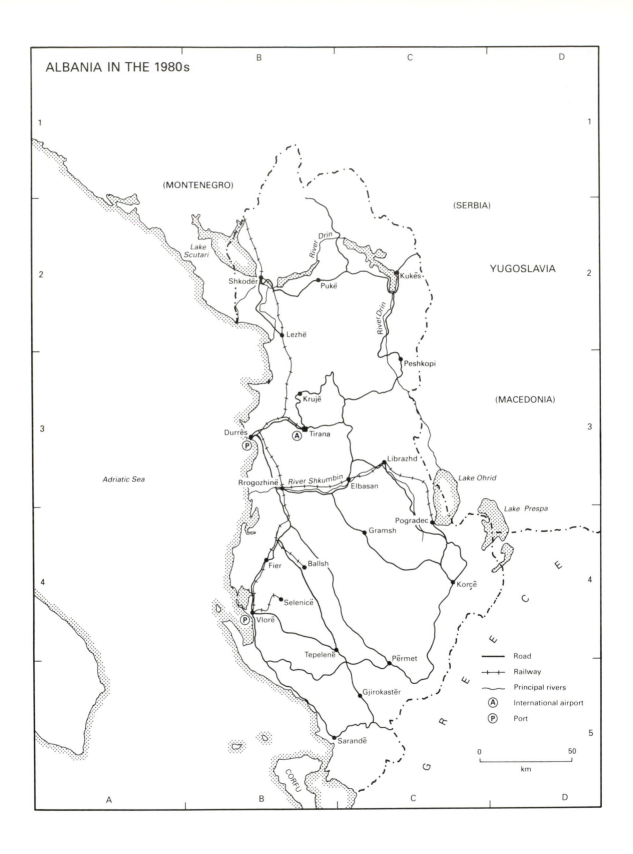

ALBANIA IN THE 1980s

(MONTENEGRO)

(SERBIA)

YUGOSLAVIA

Lake Scutari

River Drin

Shkodër

Pukë

Kukës

River Drin

Lezhë

Peshkopi

(MACEDONIA)

Krujë

Durrës

Tirana

Adriatic Sea

Librazhd

Lake Ohrid

Rrogozhinë

River Shkumbin

Elbasan

Lake Prespa

Pogradec

Gramsh

Fier

Ballsh

Korçë

Selenicë

Vlorë

Tepelenë

Përmet

Gjirokastër

G R E E C E

Sarandë

CORFU

	Road
	Railway
	Principal rivers
Ⓐ	International airport
Ⓟ	Port

0   50
km

tions with Western firms were begun.

Clouding all discussion of nuclear power in Eastern Europe is, of course, the Chernobyl disaster of April 1986. Large areas of Poland, Romania, Bulgaria and the Baltic states were affected, and the authorities in most states made the problem worse by keeping secret or falsifying the statistics of the fall-out. In Estonia labour was conscripted to take part in the clear-up operations and this contributed significantly to the growing anger of Estonians with the central, communist authorities in Moscow.

Albania in the 1980s (see facing page)

Albania in the 1980s: demographic

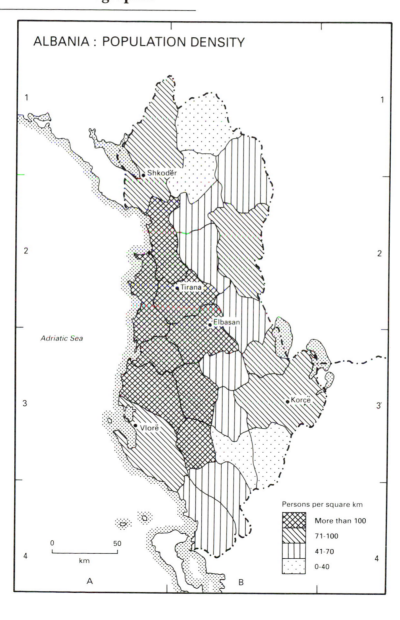

ALBANIA : POPULATION DENSITY

Shkodër

Adriatic Sea

Tirana

Elbasan

Korcë

Vlorë

0   50
km

A   B

Persons per square km

More than 100
71-100
41-70
0-40

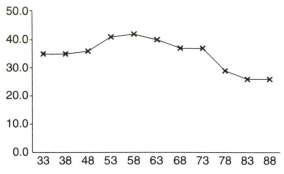

Figure 122 Births (per thousand population)

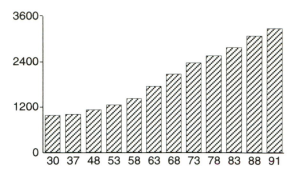

Figure 124 Population (000s)

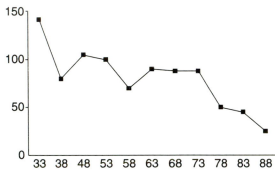

Figure 123 Infant mortality (per thousand live births)

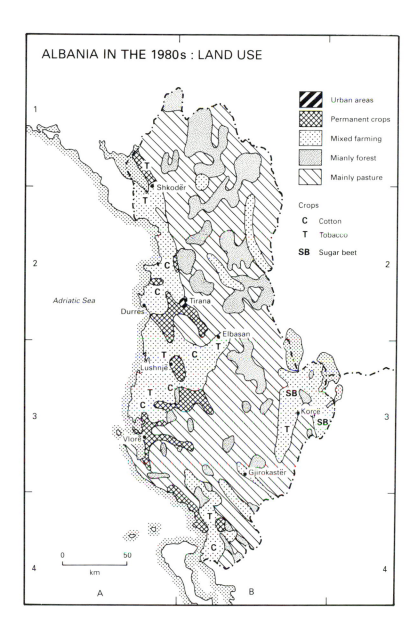

ALBANIA IN THE 1980s : LAND USE

Urban areas
Permanent crops
Mixed farming
Mianly forest
Mainly pasture

Crops

C Cotton
T Tobacco
SB Sugar beet

Adriatic Sea

Shkodër
Tirana
Durrës
Elbasan
Lushnjë
Korçë
Vlorë
Gjirokastër

0   50
km

A   B

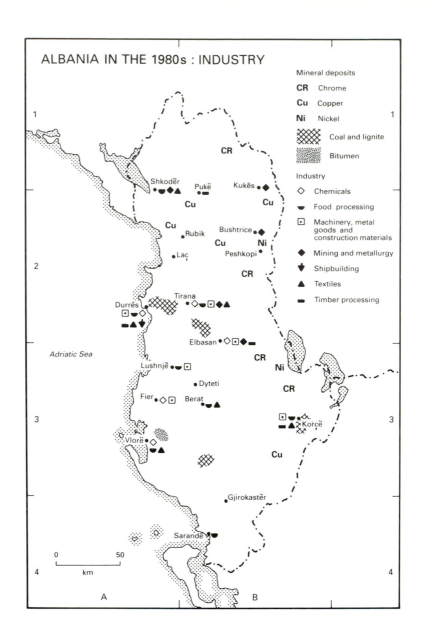

ALBANIA IN THE 1980s : INDUSTRY

Mineral deposits

CR Chrome
Cu Copper
Ni Nickel
⊠ Coal and lignite
▦ Bitumen

Industry

◇ Chemicals
◖ Food processing
⊡ Machinery, metal goods and construction materials
◆ Mining and metallurgy
▼ Shipbuilding
▲ Textiles
▬ Timber processing

Shkodër
Pukë
Kukës
CR
Cu
Cu
Cu
Cu
Rubik
Bushtrice
Ni
Cu
Laç
Peshkopi
CR
Tirana
Durrës
Elbasan
CR
Ni
Adriatic Sea
Lushnjë
Dyteti
CR
Fier
Berat
Korçë
Vlorë
Cu
Gjirokastër
Sarandë

0   50
km

A   B

186

Albania in the 1980s: social

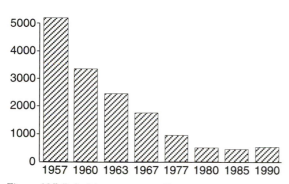

Figure 125 Inhabitants per medic

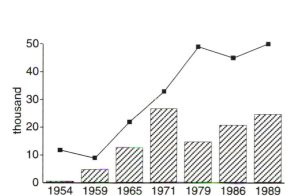

Figure 126 University students: total and % women (line)

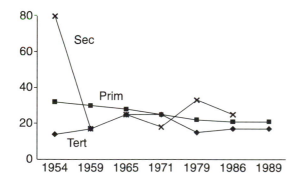

Figure 127 Teacher–pupil ratios

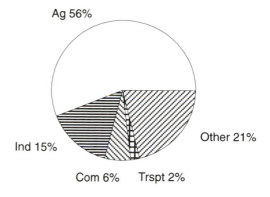

Figure 128 Labour force by economic sector, 1960

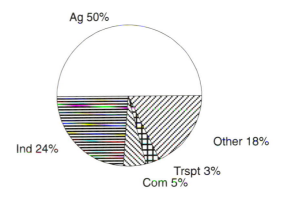

Figure 129 Labour force by economic sector, 1989

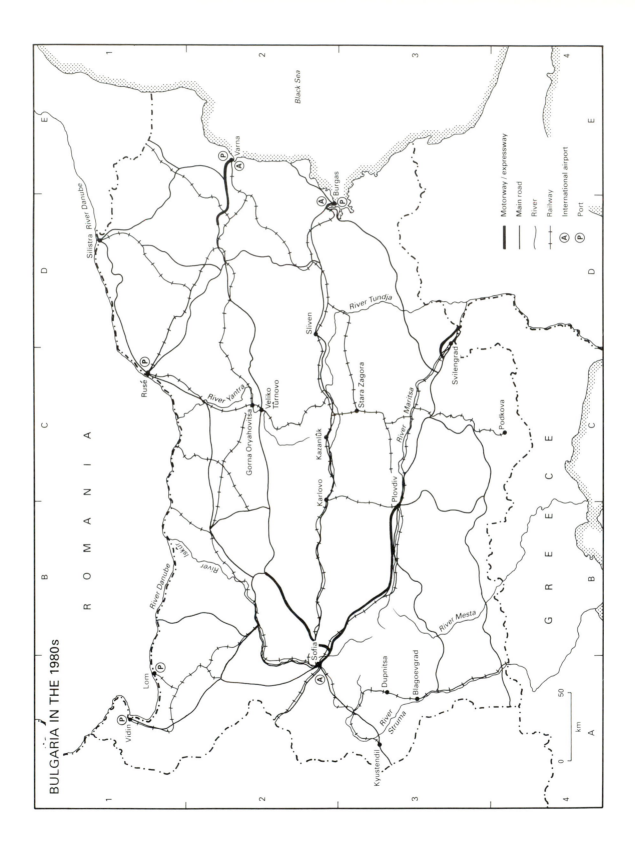

BULGARIA IN THE 1980s

Bulgaria in the 1980s (see facing page)

Bulgaria in the 1980s: demographic

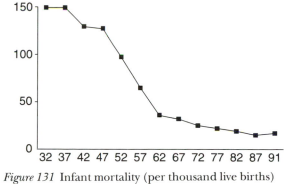

Figure 131 Infant mortality (per thousand live births)

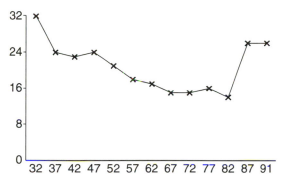

Figure 130 Births (per thousand population)

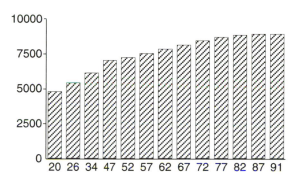

Figure 132 Population (000s)

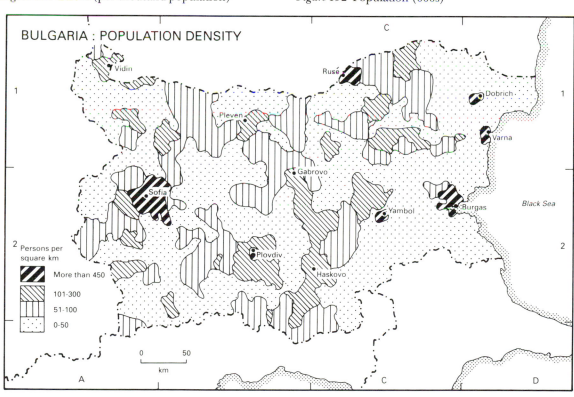

BULGARIA : POPULATION DENSITY

Vidin

Rusé

Dobrich

Pleven

Varna

Gabrovo

Sofia

Yambol

Burgas

Black Sea

Persons per square km

More than 450

101-300

51-100

0-50

Plovdiv

Haskovo

0   50

km

189

Bulgaria in the 1980s: economic

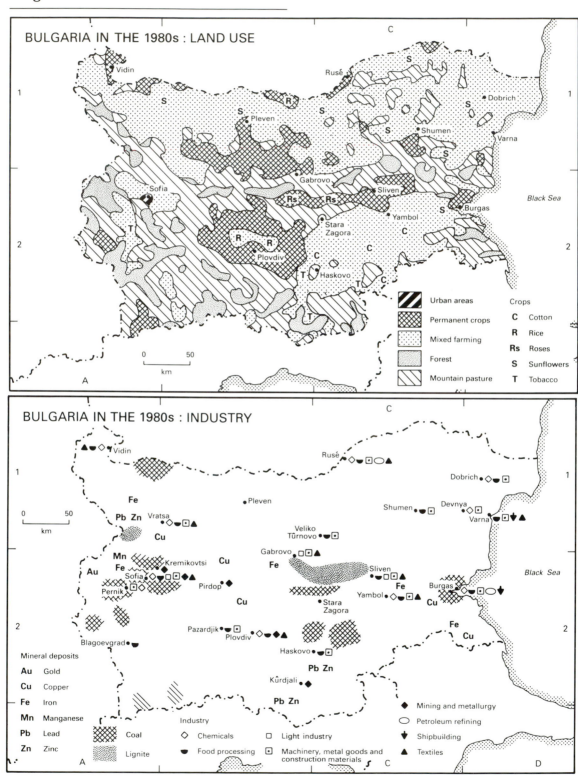

BULGARIA IN THE 1980s : LAND USE

Vidin

Rusé

S

S

R

Pleven

S

Dobrich

S

Shumen

Varna

Gabrovo

Black Sea

Sofia

Sliven

Rs

Rs

Burgas

S

T

R

R

Stara Zagora

Yambol

C

Plovdiv

C

C

T

Haskovo

C

T

C

T

	Urban areas		Crops
	Permanent crops	**C**	Cotton
	Mixed farming	**R**	Rice
	Forest	**Rs**	Roses
	Mountain pasture	**S**	Sunflowers
		T	Tobacco

0   50
km

A

BULGARIA IN THE 1980s : INDUSTRY

Vidin

Rusé

Dobrich

Fe

Pleven

Shumen

Devnya

Pb Zn   Vratsa

Varna

Cu

Veliko Tûrnovo

Mn

Gabrovo

Black Sea

Au

Fe

Kremikovtsi

Cu

Fe

Sliven

Sofia

Fe

Pernik

Pirdop

Cu

Yambol

Burgas

Stara Zagora

Cu

Pazardjik

Fe

Plovdiv

Cu

Blagoevgrad

Haskovo

Pb Zn

Kûrdjali

Pb Zn

Mineral deposits

Au   Gold
Cu   Copper
Fe   Iron
Mn   Manganese
Pb   Lead
Zn   Zinc

0   50
km

Coal	◇ Chemicals	□ Light industry
Lignite	◗ Food processing	⊡ Machinery, metal goods and construction materials

◆ Mining and metallurgy
◯ Petroleum refining
▼ Shipbuilding
▲ Textiles

Industry

A   C   D

Bulgaria in the 1980s: social

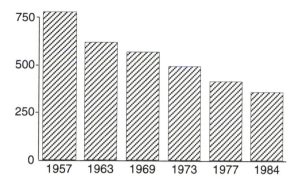

Figure 133 Inhabitants per medic

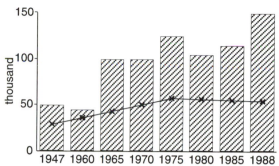

Figure 136 University students: total and % women (line)

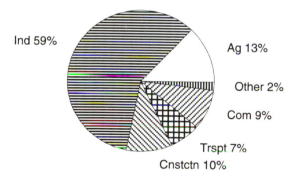

Figure 134 NMP by economic sector, 1987

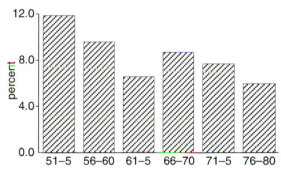

Figure 137 Average annual growth per 5-yr period, 1951–80

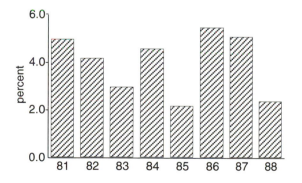

Figure 135 Growth per annum, 1981–8

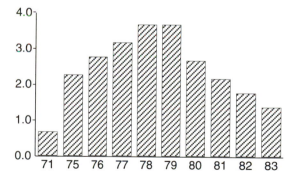

Figure 138 Net hard currency debt, 1971–83 ($bn)

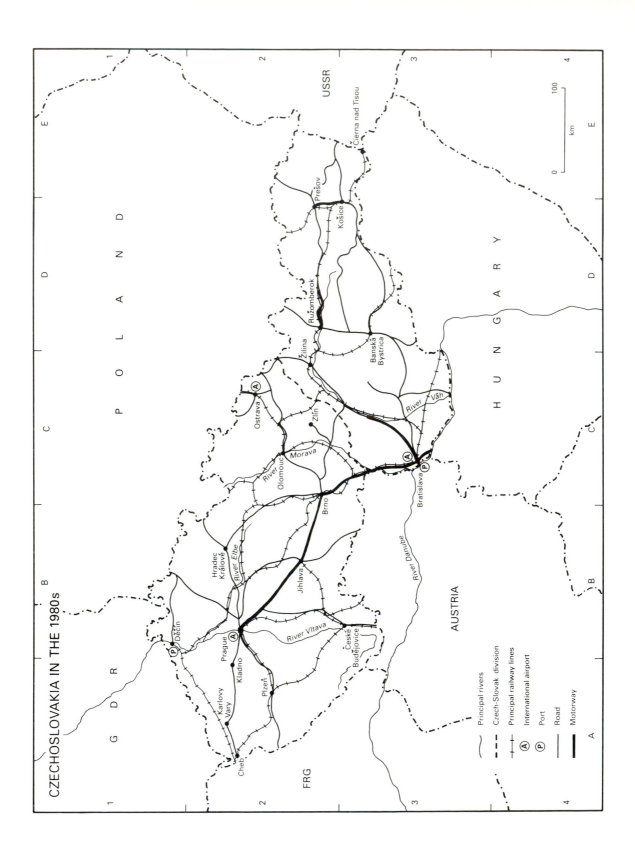

CZECHOSLOVAKIA IN THE 1980s

Principal rivers
Czech-Slovak division
Principal railway lines
Ⓐ International airport
Ⓟ Port
Road
Motorway

Czechoslovakia in the 1980s (see facing page)

Czechoslovakia in the 1980s: demographic

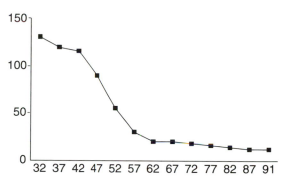

Figure 140 Infant mortality (per thousand live births)

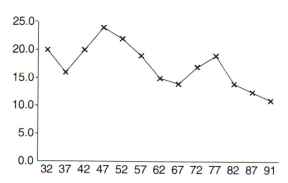

Figure 139 Births (per thousand population)

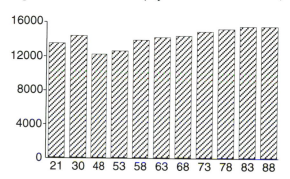

Figure 141 Population (000s)

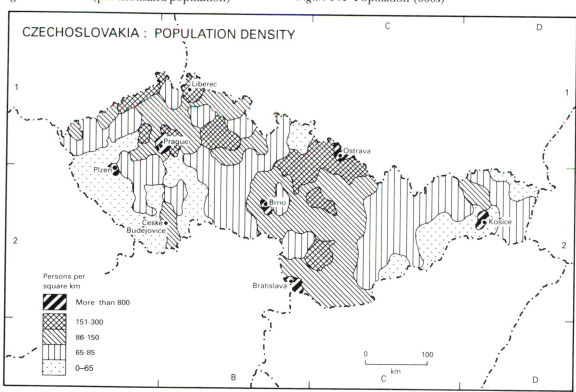

CZECHOSLOVAKIA : POPULATION DENSITY

Liberec

Prague

Ostrava

Plzeň

Brno

Košice

České Budějovice

Bratislava

Persons per square km

More than 800

151-300

86-150

65-85

0–65

0   100   km

193

Czechoslovakia in the 1980s: economic

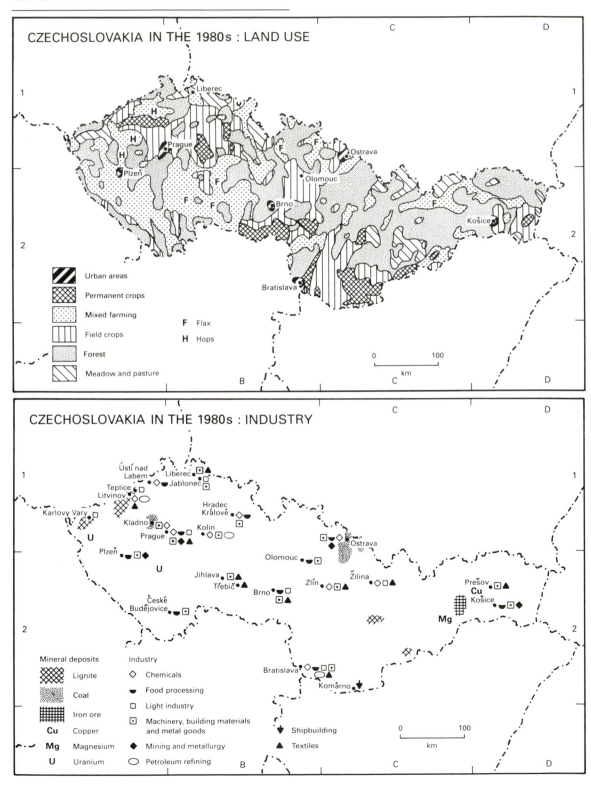

CZECHOSLOVAKIA IN THE 1980s : LAND USE

Liberec
H
H
H
Prague
Plzeň
F
F
F
F
Ostrava
Olomouc
Brno
F
Košice
Bratislava

	Urban areas
	Permanent crops
	Mixed farming
	Field crops
	Forest
	Meadow and pasture

F   Flax
H   Hops

0   100
km

CZECHOSLOVAKIA IN THE 1980s : INDUSTRY

Ústí nad Labem
Liberec
Jablonec
Teplice
Litvínov
Karlovy Vary
U
Kladno
Hradec Králové
Prague
Kolín
Plzeň
U
Jihlava
Třebíč
Brno
Olomouc
Ostrava
Zlín
Žilina
Prešov
Cu
Košice
Mg
České Budějovice
Bratislava
Komárno

Mineral deposits

	Lignite
	Coal
	Iron ore
Cu	Copper
Mg	Magnesium
U	Uranium

Industry

	Chemicals
	Food processing
	Light industry
	Machinery, building materials and metal goods
	Mining and metallurgy
	Petroleum refining
	Shipbuilding
	Textiles

0   100
km

194

Czechoslovakia in the 1980s: social

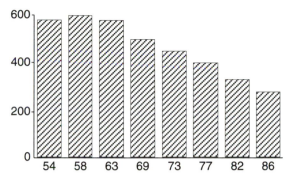

Figure 142 Inhabitants per medic

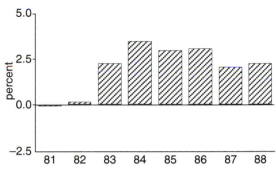

Figure 145 Growth per annum, 1981–8

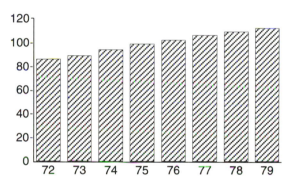

Figure 143 per capita NMP at constant prices, 1972–9 (1975 = 100)

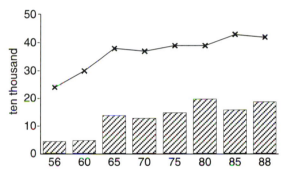

Figure 146 University students: total and % women (line)

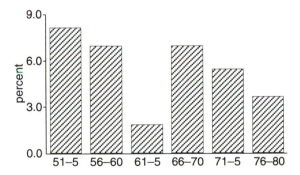

Figure 144 Average annual growth per 5-yr period, 1951–80

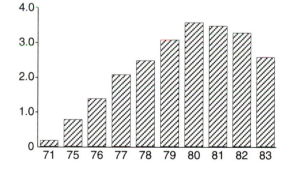

Figure 147 Net hard currency debt, 1971–83 ($bn)

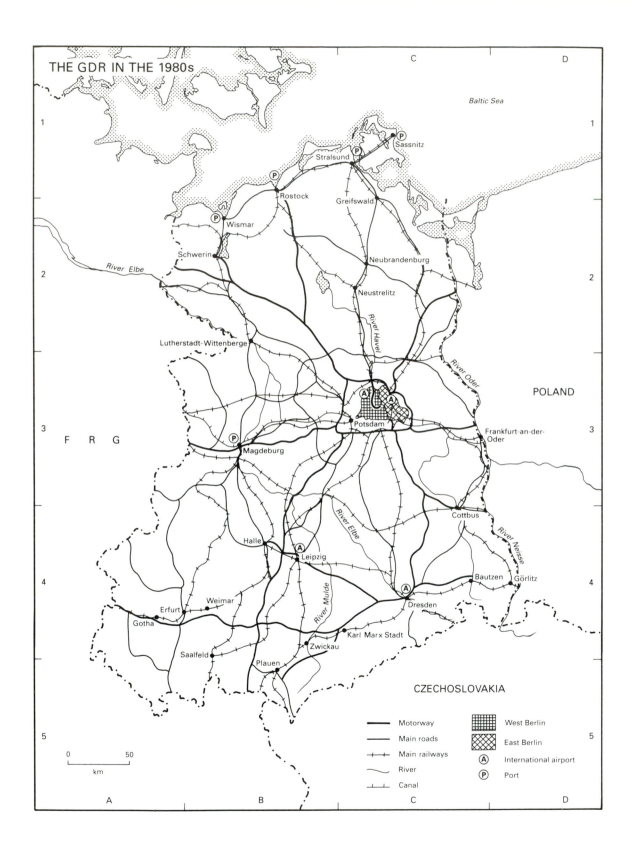

THE GDR IN THE 1980s

Baltic Sea

Sassnitz
Stralsund
Rostock
Greifswald
Wismar
Schwerin
Neubrandenburg
Neustrelitz

River Elbe

River Havel

River Oder

POLAND

Lutherstadt-Wittenberge

F R G

Potsdam

Frankfurt-an-der-Oder

Magdeburg

Cottbus

River Elbe

River Neisse

Halle
Leipzig
Bautzen
Görlitz

Weimar
River Mulde
Dresden

Erfurt
Gotha

Karl Marx Stadt
Saalfeld
Zwickau
Plauen

CZECHOSLOVAKIA

0   50
km

—— Motorway	▦ West Berlin
—— Main roads	▨ East Berlin
+—+ Main railways	Ⓐ International airport
River	Ⓟ Port
Canal	

The German Democratic Republic in the 1980s (see facing page)

The German Democratic Republic in the 1980s: demographic

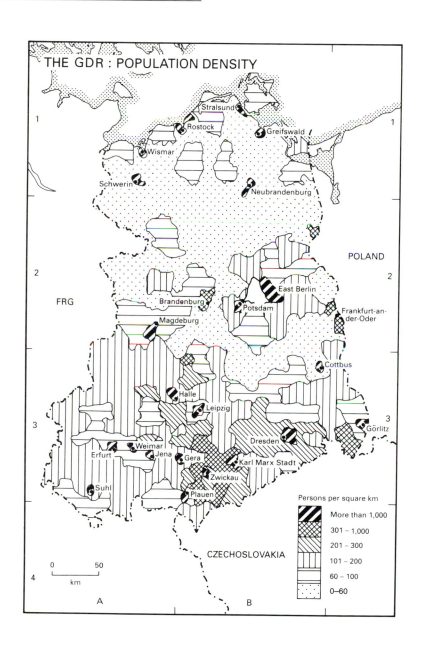

THE GDR : POPULATION DENSITY

Stralsund
Rostock
Greifswald
Wismar
Schwerin
Neubrandenburg
POLAND
FRG
Brandenburg
East Berlin
Potsdam
Frankfurt-an-der-Oder
Magdeburg
Cottbus
Halle
Leipzig
Görlitz
Dresden
Weimar
Erfurt Jena Gera
Karl Marx Stadt
Zwickau
Suhl
Plauen
CZECHOSLOVAKIA

Persons per square km
More than 1,000
301 – 1,000
201 – 300
101 – 200
60 – 100
0–60

0   50
km

197

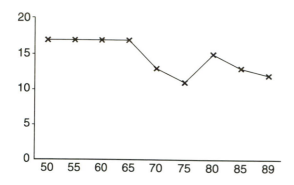

Figure 148 Births (per thousand population)

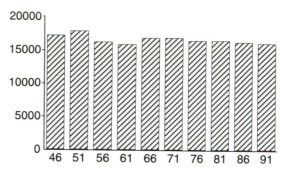

Figure 150 Population (000s)

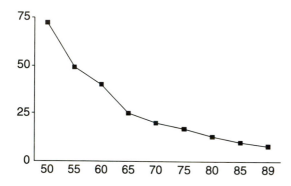

Figure 149 Infant mortality (per thousand live births)

198

The German Democratic Republic in the 1980s: economic

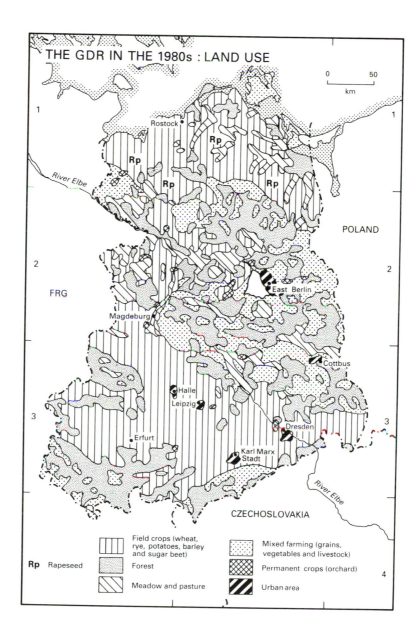

THE GDR IN THE 1980s : LAND USE

0   50

km

Rostock

Rp

Rp

Rp   Rp

River Elbe

POLAND

FRG

East Berlin

Magdeburg

Cottbus

Halle
Leipzig

Erfurt

Dresden

Karl Marx
Stadt

River Elbe

CZECHOSLOVAKIA

	Field crops (wheat, rye, potatoes, barley and sugar beet)		Mixed farming (grains, vegetables and livestock)
Rp	Rapeseed		Permanent crops (orchard)
	Forest		Urban area
	Meadow and pasture		

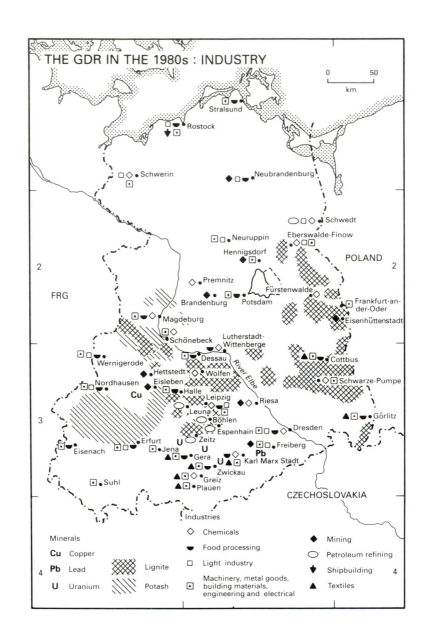

THE GDR IN THE 1980s : INDUSTRY

0   50
km

Stralsund

Rostock

Schwerin

Neubrandenburg

Schwedt

Neuruppin   Eberswalde-Finow

Hennigsdorf   POLAND

FRG   Premnitz

Brandenburg   Potsdam   Fürstenwalde

Magdeburg   Frankfurt-an-
                                  der-Oder
Schönebeck   Eisenhüttenstadt
              Lutherstadt-
              Wittenberge
Dessau   Cottbus
Wernigerode   Wolfen
       Hettstedt   Schwarze-Pumpe
Nordhausen   Eisleben
             Halle
       Cu   Leipzig
             Leuna   Riesa
             Böhlen
             Espenhain   Dresden   Görlitz
             Zeitz
Eisenach   Erfurt   U   Freiberg
       Jena   Gera   Pb
              U   Karl Marx Stadt
       Suhl   Zwickau
              Greiz
              Plauen   CZECHOSLOVAKIA

Industries

Minerals   ◇ Chemicals   ◆ Mining

Cu Copper   ◗ Food processing   ◯ Petroleum refining

Pb Lead   Lignite   □ Light industry   ▼ Shipbuilding

U   Uranium   Potash   ⊡ Machinery, metal goods,   ▲ Textiles
                           building materials,
                           engineering and electrical

200

The German Democratic Republic in the 1980s: social

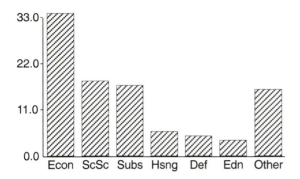

Figure 151 Budget expenditure, 1988 (%)

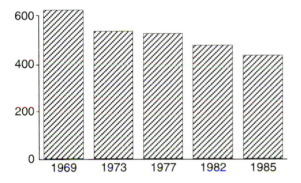

Figure 152 Inhabitants per medic

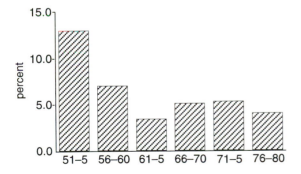

Figure 153 Average annual growth per 5-yr period, 1951–80

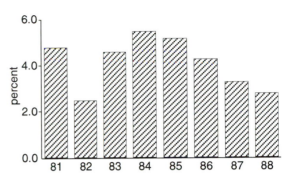

Figure 154 Growth per annum, 1981–8

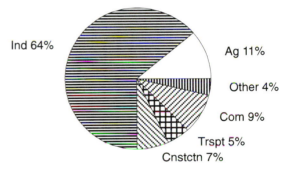

Figure 155 NMP by economic sector, 1987

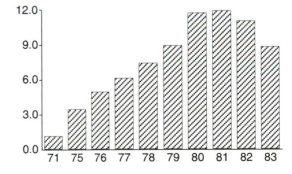

Figure 156 Net hard currency debt, 1971–83 ($bn)

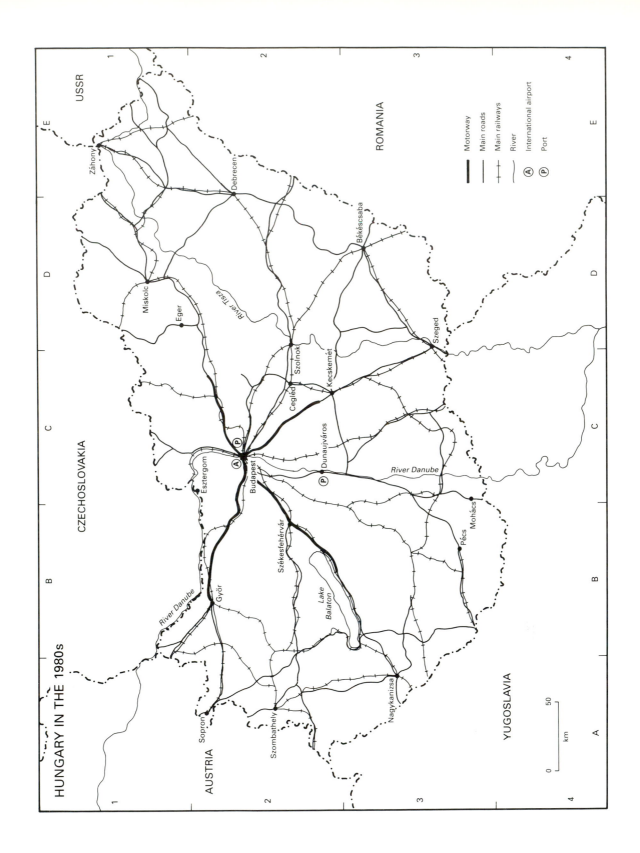

HUNGARY IN THE 1980s

Legend:
Motorway
Main roads
Main railways
River
Ⓐ International airport
Ⓟ Port

USSR

CZECHOSLOVAKIA

AUSTRIA

YUGOSLAVIA

ROMANIA

Záhony
Debrecen
Békéscsaba
Miskolc
Eger
River Tisza
Szolnok
Cegléd
Kecskemét
Szeged
Esztergom
Budapest
Dunaújváros
River Danube
Mohács
Pécs
Székesfehérvár
Győr
River Danube
Lake Balaton
Sopron
Szombathely
Nagykanizsa

km
0   50

Hungary in the 1980s (see facing page)

Hungary in the 1980s: demographic

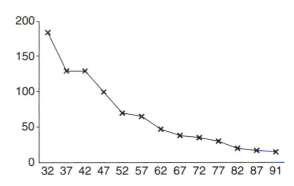

Figure 158 Infant mortality (per thousand live births)

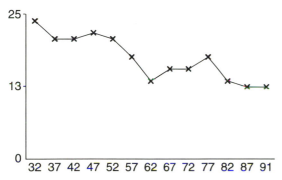

Figure 157 Births (per thousand population)

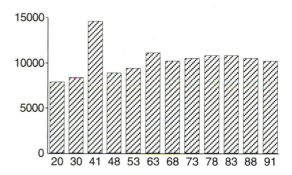

Figure 159 Population (000s)

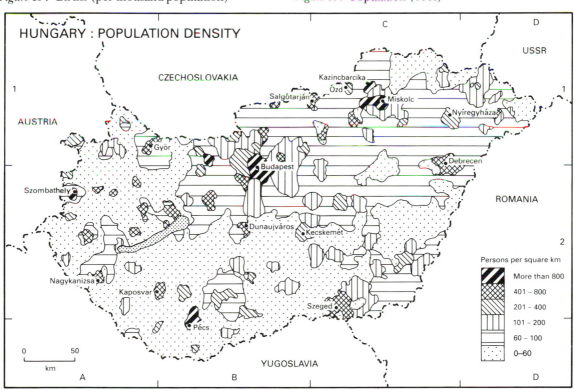

Hungary in the 1980s: economic

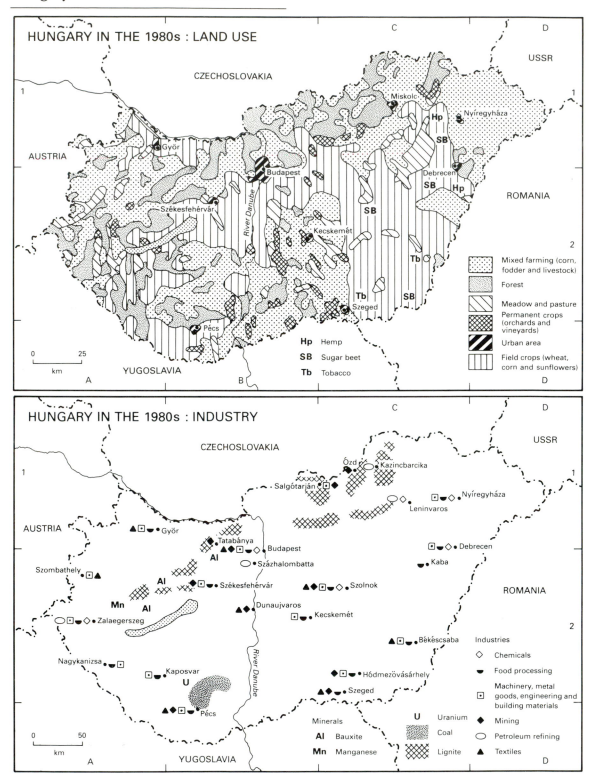

HUNGARY IN THE 1980s : LAND USE

CZECHOSLOVAKIA

USSR

AUSTRIA

Győr

Miskolc

Hp

Nyíregyháza

SB

Budapest

Debrecen

SB **Hp**

Székesfehérvár

ROMANIA

SB

Kecskemét

Tb

Tb **SB**

Szeged

Pécs

0 25
km

YUGOSLAVIA

	Mixed farming (corn, fodder and livestock)
	Forest
	Meadow and pasture
	Permanent crops (orchards and vineyards)
	Urban area
	Field crops (wheat, corn and sunflowers)

Hp Hemp
SB Sugar beet
Tb Tobacco

HUNGARY IN THE 1980s : INDUSTRY

CZECHOSLOVAKIA

USSR

Ózd Kazincbarcika

Salgótarján

Nyíregyháza

Leninvaros

AUSTRIA

Győr

Tatabánya

Al Budapest

Debrecen

Szombathely

Százhalombatta

Kaba

Al

Székesfehérvár

Szolnok

Mn **Al**

Dunaujvaros

ROMANIA

Zalaegerszeg

Kecskemét

Békéscsaba

Nagykanizsa

Kaposvar

U

Hódmezővásárhely

Szeged

Pécs

0 50
km

YUGOSLAVIA

Industries

◇ Chemicals
◗ Food processing
⊡ Machinery, metal goods, engineering and building materials
◆ Mining
○ Petroleum refining
▲ Textiles

Minerals

Al Bauxite
Mn Manganese

U Uranium
Coal
Lignite

204

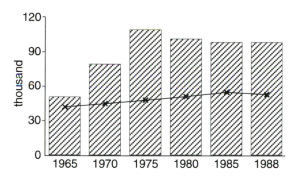

Figure 160 University students: total and % women (line)

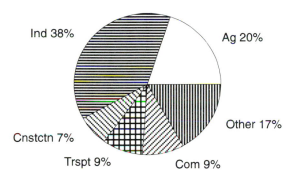

Figure 161 NMP by economic sector, 1987

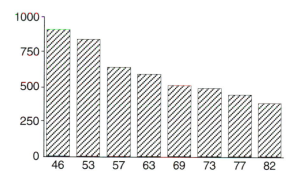

Figure 162 Inhabitants per medic

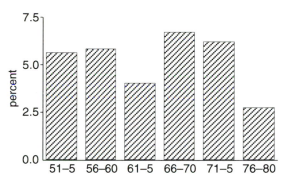

Figure 163 Average annual growth per 5-yr period, 1951–80

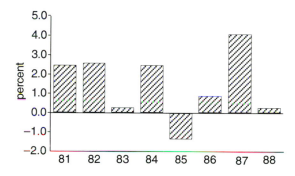

Figure 164 Growth per annum, 1981–8

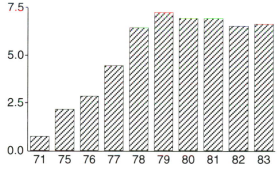

Figure 165 Net hard currency debt, 1971–83 ($bn)

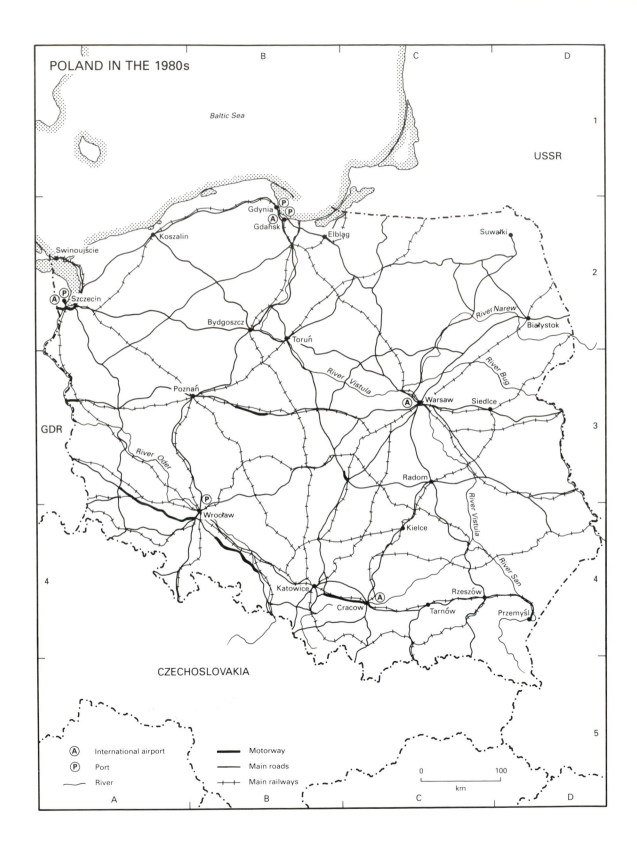

POLAND IN THE 1980s

Baltic Sea

USSR

Gdynia
Gdańsk
Elbląg
Suwałki
Koszalin
Świnoujście
Szczecin
Bydgoszcz
Toruń
River Narew
Białystok
GDR
Poznań
River Oder
River Vistula
River Bug
Warsaw
Siedlce
Wrocław
Radom
River Vistula
Kielce
Katowice
Cracow
Rzeszów
River San
Tarnów
Przemyśl

CZECHOSLOVAKIA

(A) International airport
(P) Port
River

Motorway
Main roads
Main railways

0   100
km

Poland in the 1980s (see facing page)

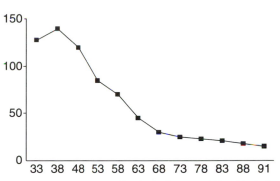

Figure 167 Infant mortality (per thousand live births)

Poland in the 1980s: demographic

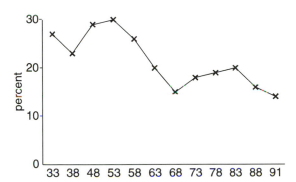

Figure 166 Births (per thousand population)

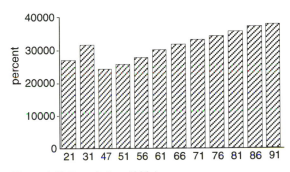

Figure 168 Population (000s)

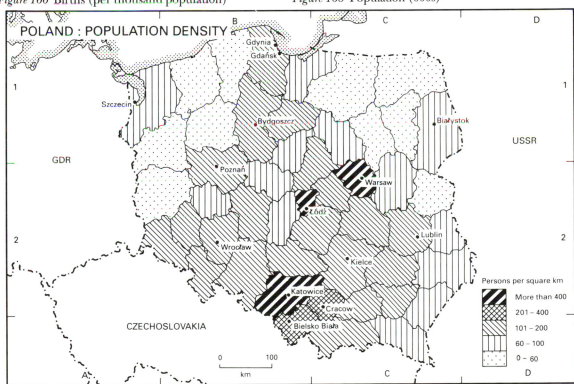

207

Poland in the 1980s: economic

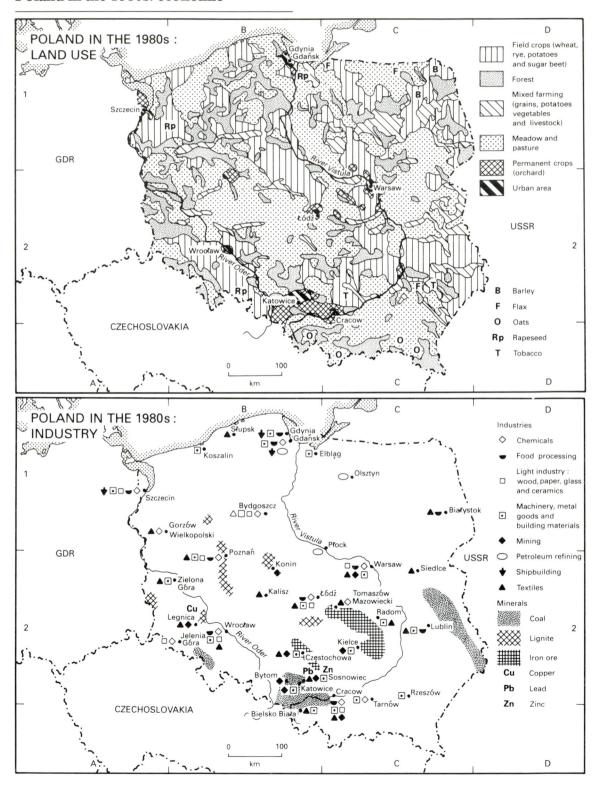

POLAND IN THE 1980s : LAND USE

Field crops (wheat, rye, potatoes and sugar beet)

Forest

Mixed farming (grains, potatoes vegetables and livestock)

Meadow and pasture

Permanent crops (orchard)

Urban area

GDR

USSR

Szczecin
Rp
Rp
Gdynia
Gdańsk
Rp
F
B
B
River Vistula
Warsaw
Łódź
Wrocław
River Oder
F
T
Rp
Katowice
T
Cracow
CZECHOSLOVAKIA
O
O
O
O

B Barley
F Flax
O Oats
Rp Rapeseed
T Tobacco

0   100
km

POLAND IN THE 1980s : INDUSTRY

Industries

◇ Chemicals

◗ Food processing

□ Light industry : wood, paper, glass and ceramics

▣ Machinery, metal goods and building materials

◆ Mining

◯ Petroleum refining

▼ Shipbuilding

▲ Textiles

Minerals

Coal

Lignite

Iron ore

Cu Copper
Pb Lead
Zn Zinc

GDR

USSR

Słupsk
Gdynia
Gdańsk
Koszalin
Elbląg
Olsztyn
Szczecin
Białystok
Bydgoszcz
Płock
Gorzów Wielkopolski
Poznań
Konin
Warsaw
Zielona Góra
Kalisz
Łódź
Siedlce
Tomaszów Mazowiecki
Cu
Legnica
Wrocław
Radom
Lublin
Jelenia Góra
Kielce
Czestochowa
Bytom
Pb Zn
Sosnowiec
Katowice
Cracow
Rzeszów
Tarnów
CZECHOSLOVAKIA
Bielsko Biała
River Vistula
River Oder

0   100
km

Poland in the 1980s: social

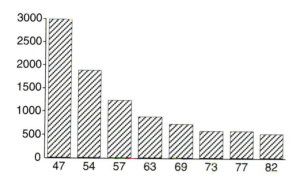

Figure 169 Inhabitants per medic

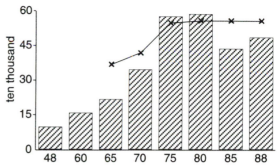

Figure 172 University students: total and % women (line)

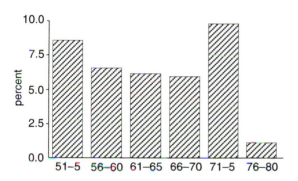

Figure 170 Average annual growth per 5-yr period, 1951–80

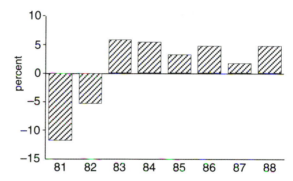

Figure 173 Growth per annum, 1981–8

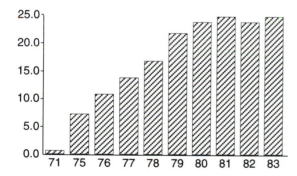

Figure 171 Net hard currency debt, 1971–83 ($bn)

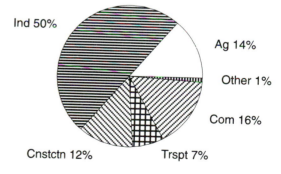

Figure 174 NMP by economic sector, 1987

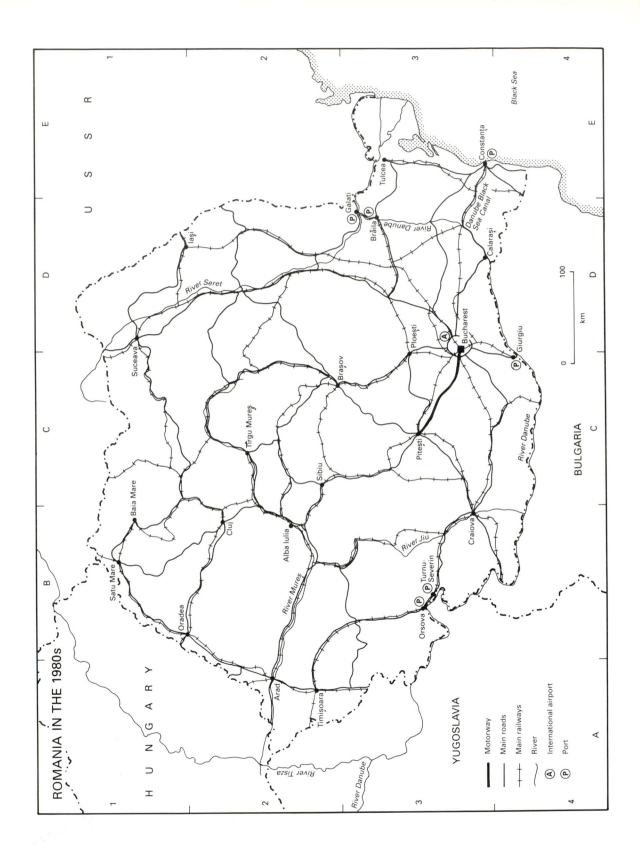

ROMANIA IN THE 1980s

U S S R

Black Sea

Constanţa

Tulcea

Galati
Brăila
River Danube

Iasi

Danube Black Sea Canal

Calarasi

River Seret

Suceava

Ploesti

Bucharest

Giurgiu

Brasov

Pitesti

Tirgu Mures

River Danube

Sibiu

Baia Mare

Cluj

Craiova

River Jiu

Alba Iulia

Satu Mare

Turnu-
Severin

River Mures

Oradea

Orsova

BULGARIA

Arad

Timisoara

River Tisza

River Danube

H U N G A R Y

YUGOSLAVIA

Motorway
Main roads
Main railways
River
Ⓐ International airport
Ⓟ Port

100

km

0

Romania in the 1980s (see facing page)

Romania in the 1980s: demographic

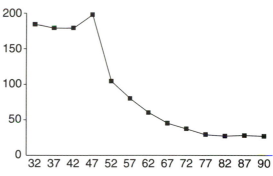

Figure 176 Infant mortality (per thousand live births)

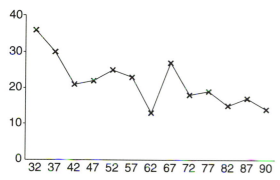

Figure 175 Births (per thousand population)

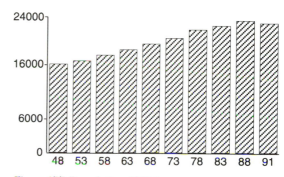

Figure 177 Population (000s)

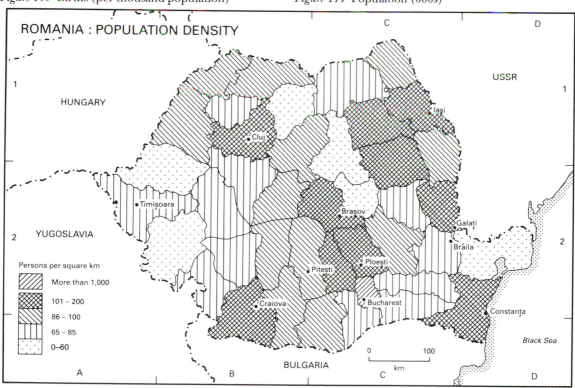

ROMANIA : POPULATION DENSITY

HUNGARY

YUGOSLAVIA

Persons per square km

	More than 1,000
	101 – 200
	86 – 100
	65 – 85
	0–60

Cluj
Timisoara
Brasov
Pitesti
Ploesti
Craiova
Bucharest
Iasi
Galati
Bráila
Constanta

USSR

BULGARIA

Black Sea

0   100
km

211

Romania in the 1980s: economic

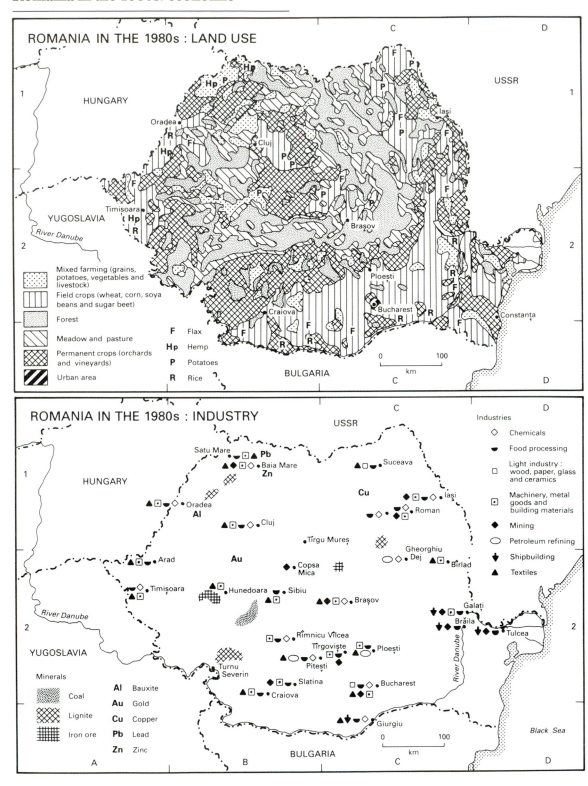

ROMANIA IN THE 1980s : LAND USE

HUNGARY

USSR

Oradea

Cluj

Iasi

YUGOSLAVIA

River Danube

Timisoara

Brasov

Ploesti

Craiova

Bucharest

Constanta

BULGARIA

F Flax
Hp Hemp
P Potatoes
R Rice

	Mixed farming (grains, potatoes, vegetables and livestock)
	Field crops (wheat, corn, soya beans and sugar beet)
	Forest
	Meadow and pasture
	Permanent crops (orchards and vineyards)
	Urban area

0   100
km

ROMANIA IN THE 1980s : INDUSTRY

USSR

Satu Mare
Pb
Baia Mare
Zn

Suceava

Cu

HUNGARY

Oradea
Al

Iasi
Roman

Cluj

Arad

Au

Tîrgu Mureș

Gheorghiu Dej
Bîrlad

Copsa Mica

Timisoara

Hunedoara

Sibiu

Brașov

Galați
Brăila
Tulcea

River Danube

Rîmnicu Vîlcea

Tîrgoviste
Ploești

YUGOSLAVIA

Turnu Severin

Pitești

Slatina

Bucharest

Craiova

River Danube

Giurgiu

Black Sea

BULGARIA

Industries

◇ Chemicals
◗ Food processing
□ Light industry : wood, paper, glass and ceramics
⊡ Machinery, metal goods and building materials
◆ Mining
○ Petroleum refining
⬇ Shipbuilding
▲ Textiles

Minerals

	Coal
	Lignite
	Iron ore

Al Bauxite
Au Gold
Cu Copper
Pb Lead
Zn Zinc

0   100
km

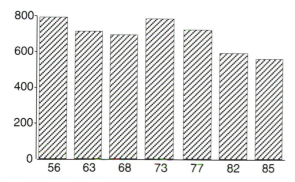

Figure 178 Inhabitants per medic

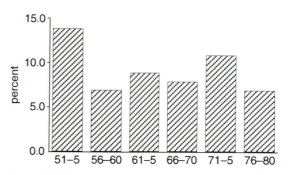

Figure 181 Average annual growth per 5-yr period, 1951–80

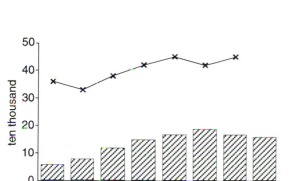

Figure 179 University students: total and % women (line)

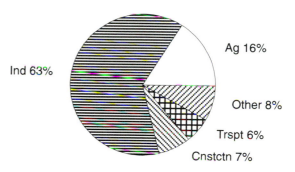

Figure 182 NMP by economic sector, 1987

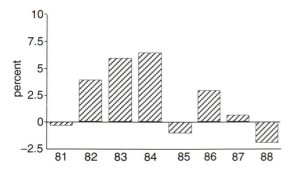

Figure 180 Growth per annum, 1981–8

213

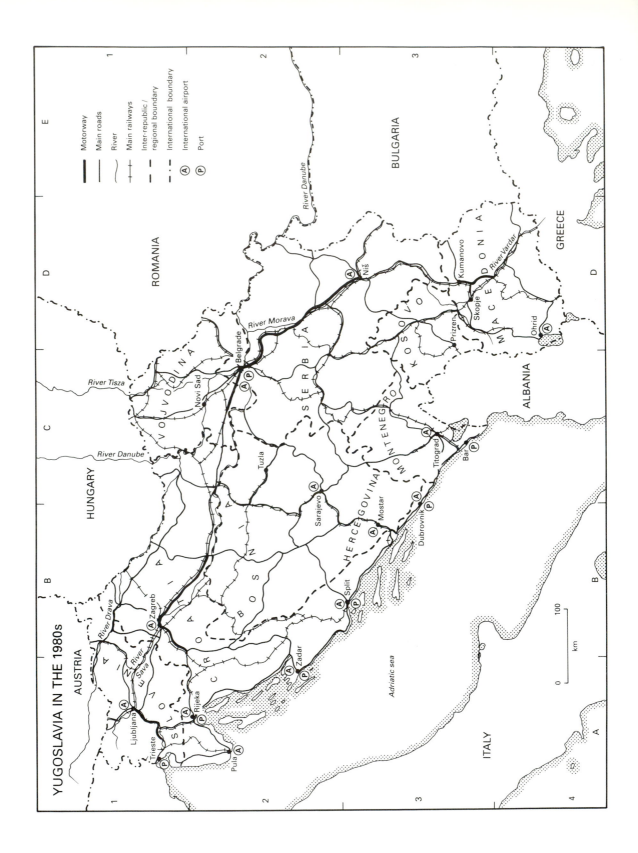

YUGOSLAVIA IN THE 1980s

Legend:
- Motorway
- Main roads
- River
- Main railways
- Inter-republic / regional boundary
- International boundary
- Ⓐ International airport
- Ⓟ Port

AUSTRIA

HUNGARY

ROMANIA

BULGARIA

GREECE

ALBANIA

ITALY

Adriatic sea

River Drava

River Sava

River Tisza

River Danube

River Danube

River Morava

River Vardar

SLOVENIA

CROATIA

VOJVODINA

SERBIA

BOSNIA

HERCEGOVINA

MONTENEGRO

KOSOVO

MACEDONIA

Ljubljana

Trieste

Pula

Rijeka

Zadar

Split

Zagreb

Novi Sad

Belgrade

Tuzla

Sarajevo

Mostar

Dubrovnik

Titograd

Bar

Niš

Prizren

Kumanovo

Skopje

Ohrid

0   100
km

Yugoslavia in the 1980s (see facing page)

Yugoslavia in the 1980s: demographic

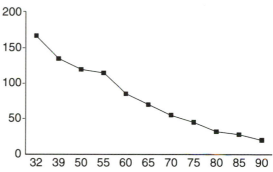

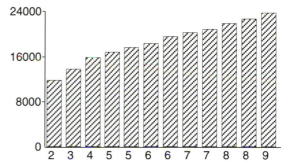

Figure 184 Infant mortality (per thousand population)

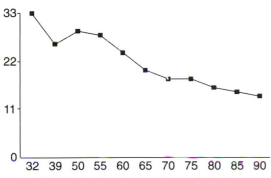

Figure 183 Births (per thousand population)

Figure 185 Population (000s)

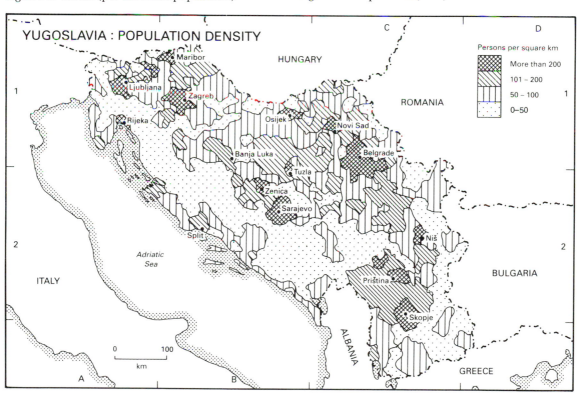

Yugoslavia in the 1980s: ethnicity and office-holding

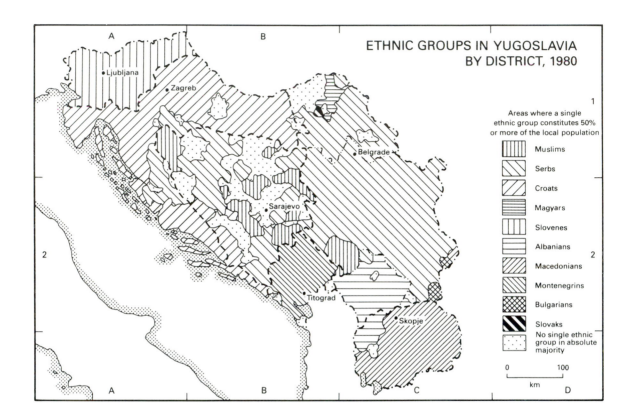

ETHNIC GROUPS IN YUGOSLAVIA
BY DISTRICT, 1980

Areas where a single
ethnic group constitutes 50%
or more of the local population

- Muslims
- Serbs
- Croats
- Magyars
- Slovenes
- Albanians
- Macedonians
- Montenegrins
- Bulgarians
- Slovaks
- No single ethnic group in absolute majority

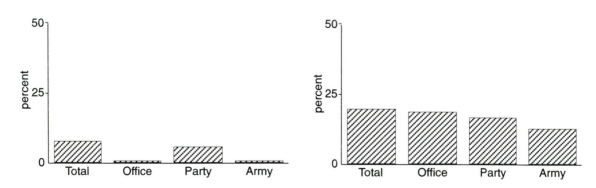

Figure 186 Albanians

Figure 187 Croats

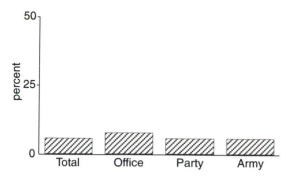

Figure 188 Macedonians

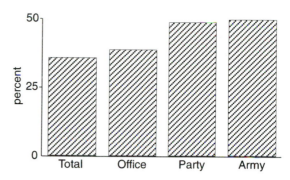

Figure 191 Serbs

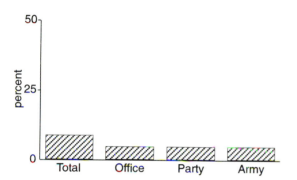

Figure 189 Muslims

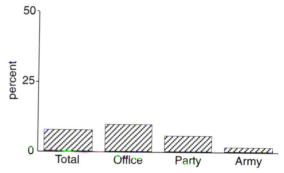

Figure 192 Slovenes

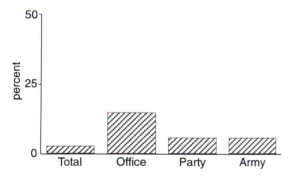

Figure 190 Montenegrins

It was a frequent accusation of the discontented in Yugoslavia that the federation was a construction to perpetuate Serbian domination; the non-communist Serbs, on the other hand, believed the federation was a device to suppress Serbian influence.

In Figures 187–93 column 1 shows the percentage of a particular group as a percentage of the total population, column 2 the percentage of state offices held by that group, column 3 the percentage of party members from that group, and the final column the percentage of army officers. The predominance of the Serbs amongst party and army officers is clear. The Slovenes were willing to become part of the state administrative apparatus but much less keen to join the party or the army, and much the same could be said of the Croats. The Albanians clearly had no wish to join, or were not encouraged to join any section of the state or party machine. The high profile of the Serbs in the state administration had much to do with the domination of Serbs, and especially Serbs from Croatia and Bosnia, in the partisan movement during the war. These young leaders of the war-time struggle then took jobs in the communist state, jobs which, because of their youth, they kept for up to forty years.

Yugoslavia in the 1980s: economic

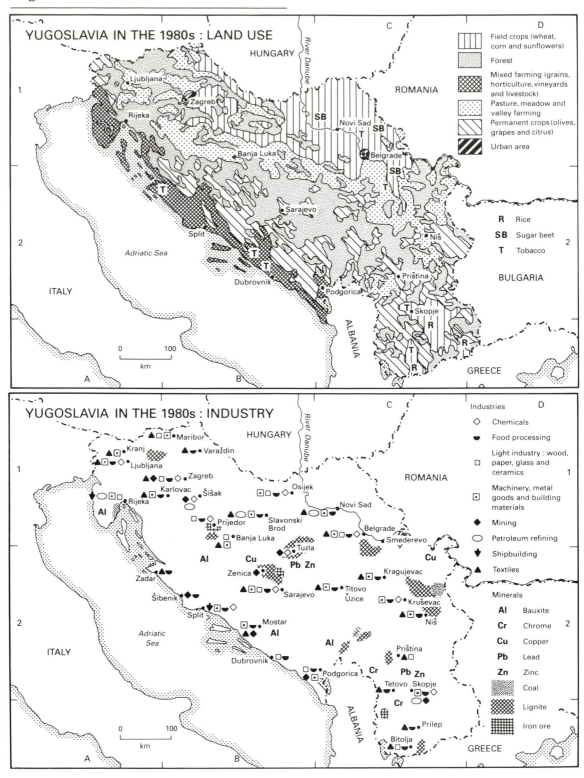

YUGOSLAVIA IN THE 1980s : LAND USE

HUNGARY

River Danube

ROMANIA

Ljubljana

Zagreb

Rijeka

SB

Novi Sad   SB

T   SB

Banja Luka   Belgrade

SB

T

Sarajevo

Niš   2

Adriatic Sea

Split   T

T   T

T   Priština   BULGARIA

Dubrovnik

Podgorica

ALBANIA

T   Skopje

R

0   100   T   R

km   R

GREECE

ITALY

Legend:
- Field crops (wheat, corn and sunflowers)
- Forest
- Mixed farming (grains, horticulture, vineyards and livestock)
- Pasture, meadow and valley farming
- Permanent crops (olives, grapes and citrus)
- Urban area

- R   Rice
- SB   Sugar beet
- T   Tobacco

YUGOSLAVIA IN THE 1980s : INDUSTRY

HUNGARY   River Danube

Maribor

Kranj   Varaždin

Ljubljana   ROMANIA

Zagreb

Karlovac   Šišak

Rijeka   Osijek

Al   Novi Sad

Prijedor   Slavonski Brod   Belgrade

Banja Luka   Smederevo   Cu

Al   Cu   Tuzla

Zenica   Pb Zn   Kragujevac

Zadar   Sarajevo   Titovo Užice

Šibenik   Kruševac

Split   Niš

Mostar

Al   Al   Priština

Dubrovnik   Cr   Pb Zn

Podgorica   Tetovo Skopje

Cr

ALBANIA   Prilep

Bitolja   GREECE

ITALY   Adriatic Sea

0   100
km

Industries:
- ◇ Chemicals
- ◖ Food processing
- ▫ Light industry : wood, paper, glass and ceramics
- ⊡ Machinery, metal goods and building materials
- ◆ Mining
- ◯ Petroleum refining
- ▼ Shipbuilding
- ▲ Textiles

Minerals:
- Al   Bauxite
- Cr   Chrome
- Cu   Copper
- Pb   Lead
- Zn   Zinc
- Coal
- Lignite
- Iron ore

218

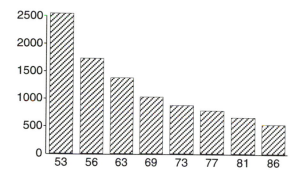

Figure 193 Inhabitants per medic

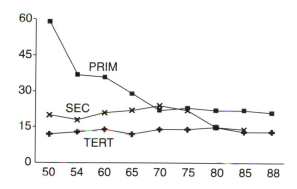

Figure 194 Teacher–pupil ratios

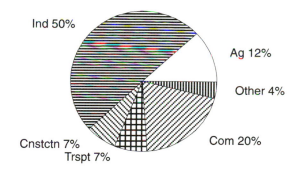

Figure 195 GMP by economic sector, 1987

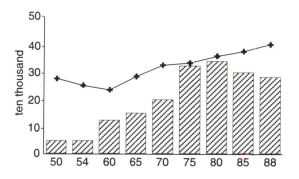

Figure 196 University students: total and % women (line)

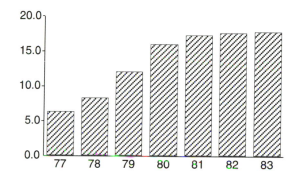

Figure 197 Net hard currency debt, 1977–83 ($bn)

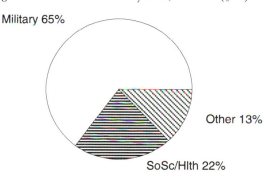

Figure 198 Budget expenditure, 1987

7 THE END OF COMMUNIST RULE AND POST-COMMUNIST EASTERN EUROPE

Albania: basic data

Official name:	Republic of Albania
Area:	28,748 sq km
Population:	3,422,300 (1993)
Population density:	119 per sq km (1993)
Ethnic composition:	Albanians 98 per cent; Greeks 1.8 per cent Macedonians 0.1 per cent; Others 0.1 per cent (1989)
Official language:	Albanian
Official religion:	None
Religious affiliation:	A large, but unspecified part of the population remained non-religious; of those who confessed to a religion 65 per cent were Muslim, 20 per cent Orthodox, 13 per cent Roman Catholic, and others 2 per cent (1992)
Capital:	Tiranë 243,000 (1990)
Major cities:	Durrës 85,400; Elbasan 83,300; Shkodër 81,800 (1990)

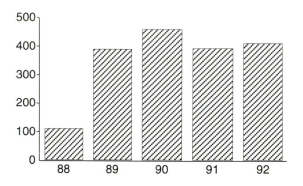

Figure 199 Hard currency debt, 1988–92 ($m)

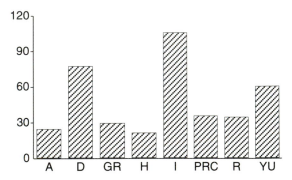

Figure 200 Main trading partners, 1990 ($m)

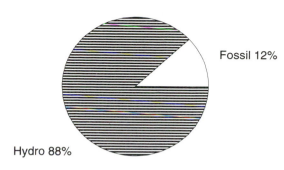

Fossil 12%

Hydro 88%

Figure 201 Source of generated power, 1990

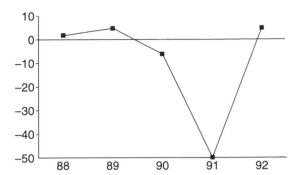

Figure 202 Change in industrial output, 1988–92 (%)

Albanian elections, 1991–2

The first round of Albania's first free elections since 1945 were held on 31 March 1991. The Party of Labour in Albania (PLA) (the communists), won over 60 per cent of the votes and 160 seats; the turnout was 98.9 per cent and the

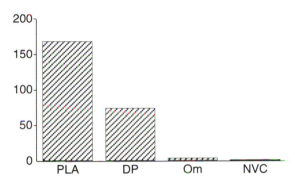

Figure 203 People's Assembly, April 1991 (seats won)

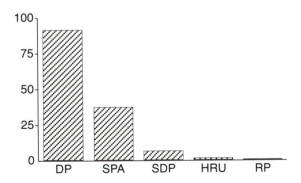

Figure 204 People's Assembly, March 1992 (seats won)

voting proceeded in an orderly and calm manner. Further rounds of voting on 7 and 14 April chose deputies in constituencies where, in the first round, no candidate had secured an overall majority.

The main strength of the PLA was in the rural constituencies, particularly in the south which had always been a communist stronghold. The Democratic Party (DP) advocated land privatisation and the depoliticisation of state institutions such as the army. Its supporters were predominantly urban and in one Tiranë constituency the DP candidate defeated the PLA leader, Ramiz Alia.

Omonia represented the Greek minority, whilst the National Veterans' Committee (NVC) was pro-communist. A number of other parties and social organisations, together with seventeen independents, failed to secure representation.

Legislation in February 1992 altered the electoral system so that in the second general election 100 seats were to be single-member constituencies determined on the majority principle, and forty were to be decided by PR, a party's performance being assessed by the number of first-choice votes it received in the single-member constituencies in the first round of voting. The law also banned parties supporting one ethnic group.

The first round of voting took place on 22 March 1992 with a turnout of just over 90 per cent of the electorate. The DP secured 62 per cent of the vote and ninety of the 100 single-member seats; it later received two further seats from the PR allocation. The Socialist Party of Albania (SPA), the reformed communists, received 25 per cent of the vote, and secured six victories in the single-member constituencies and thirty-two from the PR list. The Human Rights Union (HRU) represented the interests of the Greek minority, its previous political

organisation, Omonia, having been made illegal by the February 1922 electoral law.

The DP's victory was largely due to the increasing food shortages in Albania. The political process was now much less orderly, and four people, including the local DP leader, were killed in Shkodër during riots immediately after the results of the first round of voting were made known.

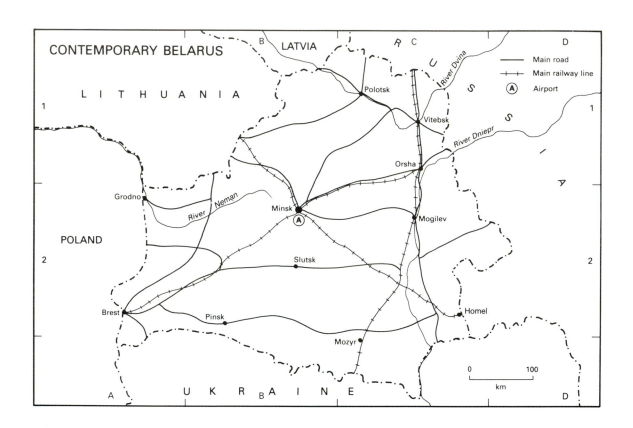

Belarus: basic data

Official name:	Republic of Belarus
Area:	207,600 sq km
Population:	10,260,400 (1991)
Population density:	49.4 per sq km (1991)
Ethnic composition:	Belorussian 77.9 per cent;
	Russian 13.2 per cent;

Polish 4.1 per cent;
Ukrainian 2.9 per cent;
Jewish 1.1 per cent;
Others 0.8 per cent
(1989)

Official language:	Belorussian
Official religion:	None

| Religious affiliation: | Most professing Christians are Belorussian Orthodox though the Polish minority and some others are Catholic (1991) | Capital: | Minsk 1,633,600 (1991) |
| | | Major cities: | Homel 503,300; Vitebsk 369,000; Mogilev 363,000; Grodno 284,800 (1991) |

Contemporary Belarus

Belarus faces formidable problems. It has little sense of nationhood and little experience in practical politics. National consciousness was slow to develop because there was no church with which the Belorussians could associate: the Roman Catholic Church was, and still is, controlled from Warsaw; the Uniates were suppressed in 1839; and Orthodoxy was always pro-Russian. Furthermore, the towns were Jewish- or Russian-dominated.

The area is devoid of any mineral resources of significance, its main asset being its arable land and forests. Dependence upon agriculture intensified the disaster of Chernobyl in April 1986. Nearly three-quarters of the area affected by fallout was in Belarus; inside the republic 20 per cent of arable land and 15 per cent of the forests were rendered unusable. The enormous costs of resettlement and repair could never be met by Belarus alone. There has been industrial development but it is of the heavy or highly technological variety which is firmly controlled from Moscow, where the profits also go.

Dependence on the Soviet Union was marked also in the political sphere. There was little in the way of an indigenous movement for independence, though a Popular Front was given legal recognition in the dying hours of the USSR, in June 1991. Multi-candidate but not multi-party elections were held to the Supreme Soviet in Minsk in March 1990. On 1 September of that year Belorussian was made the official language. But there have been no free elections and the old Communist Party *apparat* is largely unchanged and untouched.

Belarus set out in 1990 and 1991 with an ambitious scheme for privatisation of much of the economy, hoping to use its economic ties with the Baltic states to speed the road to economic modernisation. It did not work. Most of the important, viable concerns were still dominated by Moscow which continued to take the profits. There has been little change in agriculture, where there has been no response to the call for individual or family leasing of plots; the peasants do not regard the legal changes as permanent and there is a lurking fear that the Polish owners of the inter-war years might return

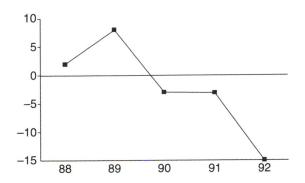

Figure 205 Change in NMP, 1988–92 (%)

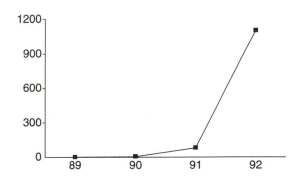

Figure 206 Consumer price inflation, 1989–92 (%)

to claim their former property if full-scale privatisation is introduced.

By the end of 1993 one in three of the population were living at or below the poverty line and the government in Minsk was seeking reintegration with the Russian economy.

In March 1994 a new constitution was adopted giving Belarus a presidential-style government. The first round of elections to the presidency took place on 23 June with five candidates competing. The two candidates with the most votes took part in the second round of elections on 10 July. Aleksandr Lukashenka, who had taken a surprising 44.8 per cent of the poll in June, emerged the victor with 80.1 per cent of the votes, as opposed to the 14.1 per cent of his rival, Vyacheslau Kebich. The remainder of the votes (5.8 per cent) were spoilt.

Bosnia and Hercegovina: basic data

Official name:	Republic of Bosnia and Hercegovina
Area:	51,129 sq km
Population:	4,422,000 (1993)
Population density:	86.3 per sq km (1993)
Ethnic composition:	Muslim 49.2 per cent; Serb 31.3 per cent; Croat 17.3 per cent; Others 2.2 per cent. (1991)
Official language:	Bosnian (which is very similar to and at times indistinguishable from Serbian and/or Croatian)

Official religion:	None
Religious affiliation:	Muslim 40 per cent; Serbian Orthodox 31 per cent; Roman Catholic 15 per cent; Protestant 4 per cent; Others 10 per cent. (1992)
Capital:	Sarajevo 415,631 (1991)
Major cities:	Banja Luka 142,634; Zenica 96,238. (1991)

Bosnia-Hercegovina since 1991

The concentration of Serbs in the north-west and south-west of Bosnia presents the Serbian state with the problem that if it wished to incorporate and have direct links with the Serbs of Bosnia it could do so only by conquering non-Serbian areas.

The Serbs of Bosnia had shown signs of discontent as early as April 1991 when those around Drvar north of Knin declared autonomy. With the secession of Slovenia and Croatia from Yugoslavia the situation became more complicated. In mid-August president Alija Izetbegović of Bosnia-Hercegovina announced that a referendum on the future of the republic would be held at a date to be decided by the republican assembly. Before this could be held the fighting in Croatia spread into Bosnia when Serb forces crossed the northern borders. Serbs living along the Montenegrin border declared themselves an autonomous province in September 1991 and many other Serb-dominated areas then followed suit; some of these so-called regions consisted of little more than a handful of villages. Bosnia-Hercegovina was in effect disintegrating.

Despite or perhaps because of the accelerating process of disintegration, Bosnia-Hercegovina on 15 October 1991 declared itself sovereign. In December it responded positively to the EC invitation to republics other than Croatia and Slovenia to apply for recognition. By this time frantic discussions at an international level had produced a peace conference under the auspices of the EC and a United Nations involvement which took the form on 15 December 1991 of an agreement to send a small UN group, 'including military personnel' to Yugoslavia.

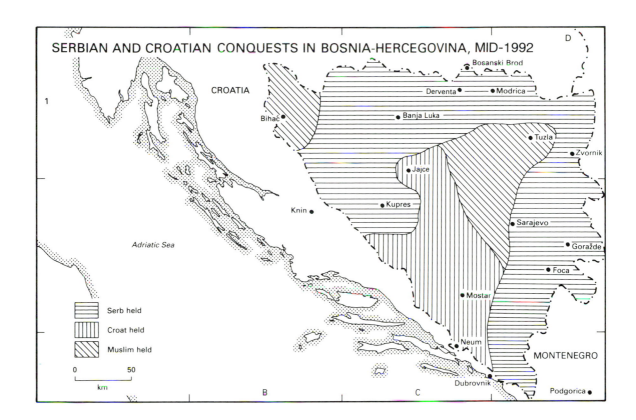

SERBIAN AND CROATIAN CONQUESTS IN BOSNIA-HERCEGOVINA, MID-1992

Serb held
Croat held
Muslim held

0   50
km

The EC peace conference on Yugoslavia reconvened in Brussels in January 1992 and recommended a delay in recognising Bosnia-Hercegovina until after a referendum. This was held at the end of February, but a Serb boycott meant the turnout was only 63 percent. An agreement negotiated under EC auspices produced a plan to divide Bosnia-Hercegovina into cantons which were to be autonomous. The Muslim Party of Democratic Action rejected the plan, and the Serbs announced they did not wish to leave Yugoslavia; on 27 March they proclaimed a Serbian Republic of Bosnia-Hercegovina.

On 6–7 April 1992 peace demonstrations in Sarajevo were fired on by snipers and Izetbegović declared a state of emergency. Serb forces in the north and east attempted to create a national corridor linking Serbia with the areas of Serbian settlement; the Bosnian war had begun and on 22 April Sarajevo itself came under artillery fire and was to remain under siege for two years. Operations by Serbian forces continued and there were strong suspicions that the Bosnian Serbs were being backed by the Yugoslav National Army (JNA) and Milošević's Republic of Serbia; by September the Serbs were in effective occupation of almost two-thirds of Bosnia-Hercegovina. In areas under their control they indulged in what became known as 'ethnic cleansing', a euphemism for the expulsion, or worse, of all non-Serb elements.

But the conflict was not merely one between Serbs and the others. By early autumn Croat forces had begun fighting with Muslims, whilst in July Croats in western Hercegovina had set up their own republic of 'Herceg-Bosna'; both sides to this conflict used much the same methods as the Serbs to 'cleanse' the areas they controlled.

Throughout 1992 and 1993 the war raged with major clashes or sieges at Maglaj, Gornji Vakuf, Tuzla and elsewhere. The casualties were enormous in numbers of killed and displaced; nor were they entirely human. The historic bridge at Mostar, the University library in Sarajevo, at least a dozen mosques in Banja Luka, and many other

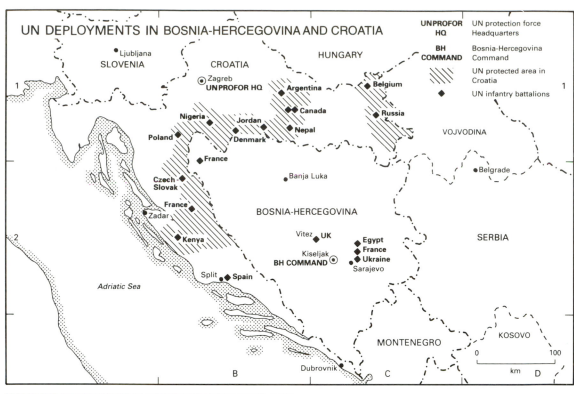

UN DEPLOYMENTS IN BOSNIA-HERCEGOVINA AND CROATIA

UNPROFOR HQ	UN protection force Headquarters
BH COMMAND	Bosnia-Hercegovina Command
	UN protected area in Croatia
◆	UN infantry battalions

SLOVENIA
• Ljubljana
CROATIA
HUNGARY
Zagreb
UN PROFOR HQ
◆ Argentina
◆ Belgium
◆ Canada
◆ Russia
Nigeria ◆
◆ Jordan
◆ Nepal
VOJVODINA
Poland ◆
◆ Denmark
◆ France
• Belgrade
Czech-Slovak ◆
• Banja Luka
France ◆
◆ Zadar
BOSNIA-HERCEGOVINA
Kenya ◆
SERBIA
Vitez ◆ UK
◆ Egypt
Kiseljak
◆ France
BH COMMAND ◎
◆ Ukraine
Split ◆ Spain
Sarajevo
Adriatic Sea
MONTENEGRO
KOSOVO
0 ____ 100
km
Dubrovnik

THE UN / EC (VANCE OWEN) PLAN

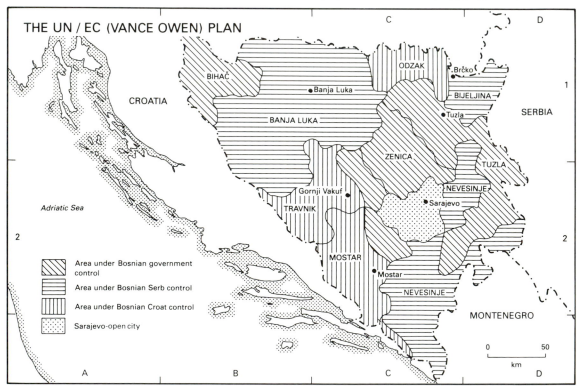

CROATIA
BIHAĆ
ODZAK
• Brčko
• Banja Luka
BIJELJINA
SERBIA
BANJA LUKA
• Tuzla
ZENICA
TUZLA
NEVESINJE
Gornji Vakuf
• Sarajevo
Adriatic Sea
TRAVNIK
MOSTAR
• Mostar
NEVESINJE
MONTENEGRO

Legend:
- Area under Bosnian government control
- Area under Bosnian Serb control
- Area under Bosnian Croat control
- Sarajevo-open city

0 ____ 50
km

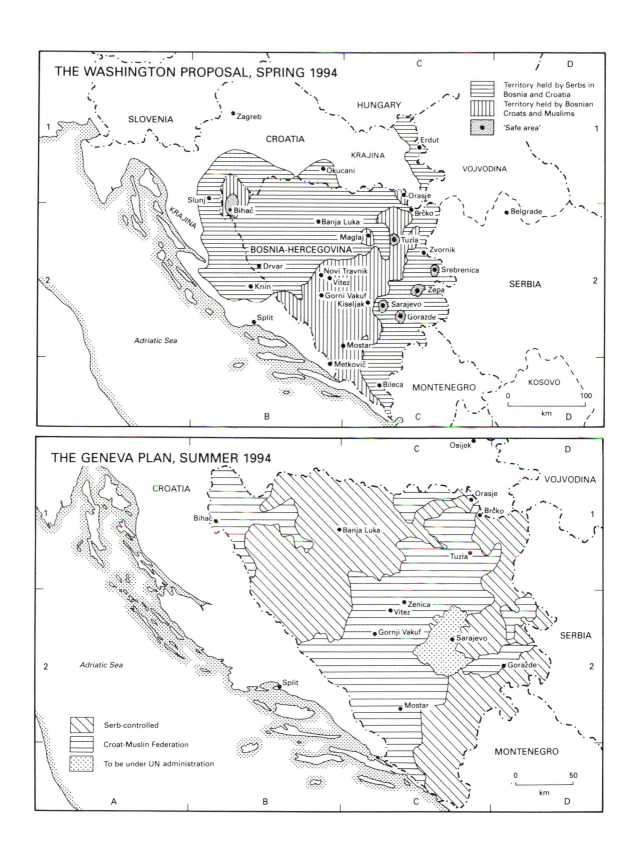

THE WASHINGTON PROPOSAL, SPRING 1994

SLOVENIA

• Zagreb

CROATIA

HUNGARY

KRAJINA

Territory held by Serbs in Bosnia and Croatia

Territory held by Bosnian Croats and Muslims

'Safe area'

• Erdut

VOJVODINA

• Okucani

KRAJINA

• Slunj

• Orasje

• Belgrade

• Bihać

• Brčko

• Banja Luka

Maglaj

• Tuzla

BOSNIA-HERCEGOVINA

• Zvornik

■ Drvar

• Novi Travnik

• Srebrenica

• Vitez

• Knin

• Gorni Vakuf

• Zepa

SERBIA

Kiseljak

• Sarajevo

Split

• Gorazde

Adriatic Sea

• Mostar

• Metković

MONTENEGRO

KOSOVO

• Bileca

0   100

km

THE GENEVA PLAN, SUMMER 1994

• Osijek

CROATIA

VOJVODINA

• Orasje

• Bihać

• Brčko

• Banja Luka

• Tuzla

• Zenica

• Vitez

Adriatic Sea

• Gornji Vakuf

• Sarajevo

SERBIA

• Gorazde

Split

• Mostar

Serb-controlled

MONTENEGRO

Croat-Muslin Federation

To be under UN administration

0   50

km

227

monuments, including both Orthodox and Catholic churches, had been destroyed by the end of 1993.

Efforts to secure a peace had initially been led by the EC but its conspicuous lack of success and its own internal disagreements meant that by the spring of 1992 the UN had become the chief external authority attempting to secure a settlement. By the summer of 1992 reports of detention camps and the severity of ethnic cleansing led the UN Security Council to pass resolution No. 770 (13 August) which was seen as empowering that body to send troops to the former Yugoslavia. Increased deployments began immediately and by the end of 1992 there were 7,500 soldiers in the Serbian-dominated areas of Bosnia-Hercegovina in addition to 11,000 in Croatia.

Diplomatic moves towards a settlement included a peace conference in London (26–27 August) after which Lord David Owen (EC) joined with Cyrus Vance (UN) to continue the search for a settlement. This produced a number of schemes but each one brought with it the problem of dividing the area in a manner satisfactory to all sides, a process which could not be completed without outside accusations that such a division would reward those who had practised ethnic cleansing. The Washington Agreement of February 1994 attempted to create a federation and though the Croats and the Muslims agreed, at the time of writing the Serbs have not. The siege of Sarajevo was, however, finally lifted in March 1994 thanks to the real threat of air strikes against the Serbs and the intervention, for the first time since the crisis began, of Russian diplomacy.

In the late summer of 1994 the Bosnian Serbs rejected a peace plan drawn up by the 'contact group' (Russia, the USA, Great Britain, France and Germany), as a result of which the Serbian state severed relations with the Bosnian Serb government.

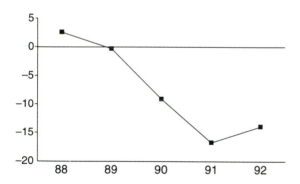

Figure 207 Change in GDP, 1988–92 (%)

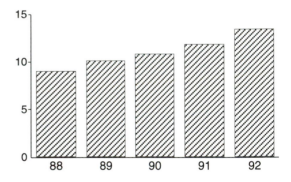

Figure 209 Hard currency debt, 1988–92 ($bn)

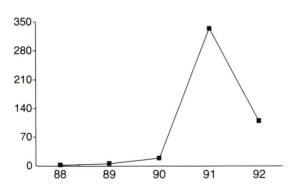

Figure 208 Consumer price inflation, 1988–92 (%)

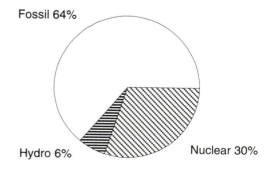

Figure 210 Source of generated power, 1990

Bulgaria: basic data

Official name:	Republic of Bulgaria
Area:	110,994 sq km
Population:	8,465,000 (1993)
Population density:	76.3 per sq km (1993)
Ethnic composition:	Bulgarian 85.8 per cent; Turkish 9.7 per cent; Gypsy 3.4 per cent; Other 1.1 per cent (1993)
Official language:	Bulgarian
Official religion:	None, though the constitution of 1991 refers to Orthodoxy as the country's 'traditional' religion.
Religious affiliation:	Orthodox 87.0 per cent; Muslim 12.7 per cent; Others 0.3 per cent. (1992) (The census of 1992 reflected traditional religious identity without recording non-believers who ten years previously had constituted 64.5 per cent of the population.)
Capital:	Sofia 1,140,795 (1991)
Major cities:	Plovdiv 379,112; Varna 316,231; Burgas 211,579; Rusé 190,229 (1991)

Bulgarian elections, 1990–2

Bulgarians went to the polls on 10 and 17 June 1990 to elect a Grand National Assembly of 400 deputies, half of whom were to be chosen by a majority vote in constituencies, and half of whom were to be selected by proportional representation. In the first round the turnout was 91 per cent; on 17 June there were contests in the eighty-one constituencies in which no candidate had secured an absolute majority in the first round of voting; the turnout was 84 per cent. Foreign observers reported some minor irregularities but did not consider these sufficiently serious to invalidate the result. Oppositionists in Bulgaria itself made the conduct of the elections the cause for a series of public demonstrations.

The great strength of the Bulgarian Socialist Party (BSP) lay in the countryside where incumbent party *apparatchiki* still wielded great influence. The BSP was also helped by some tactical errors on the part of its chief opponent, the Union of Democratic Forces (UDF), a coalition of sixteen anti-communist groups. The Bulgarian Agrarian National Union (BANU) had formerly been in technical coalition with the communists and for this it lost credibility; a number of anti-communist agrarians formed their own party which joined the UDF. The Movement for Rights and Freedom (MRF) did surprisingly well. Its main function was to represent the Turkish minority and the Pomaks, or Islamicised Bulgarians; it strongly denied being a party based on ethnic identity. Of the others, two were independents; two were from the Fatherland Union, the renamed version of the old communist umbrella organisation, the Fatherland Front; one was from the Bulgarian Social Democratic Party; and one was from the Fatherland Party of Labour which represented the more vociferous Bulgarian nationalists.

The Grand National Assembly enacted a new constitution in July 1991. Elections were held on 13 October of that year for a 240-member National Assembly or *Sûbranie*. Results were determined by PR with a 4 per cent threshold for representation in the *Sûbranie*. The latter regulation meant that a quarter of the total votes cast were given for parties which were not represented in the assembly. The turnout was 84 per cent.

The UDF secured a very slender victory, its

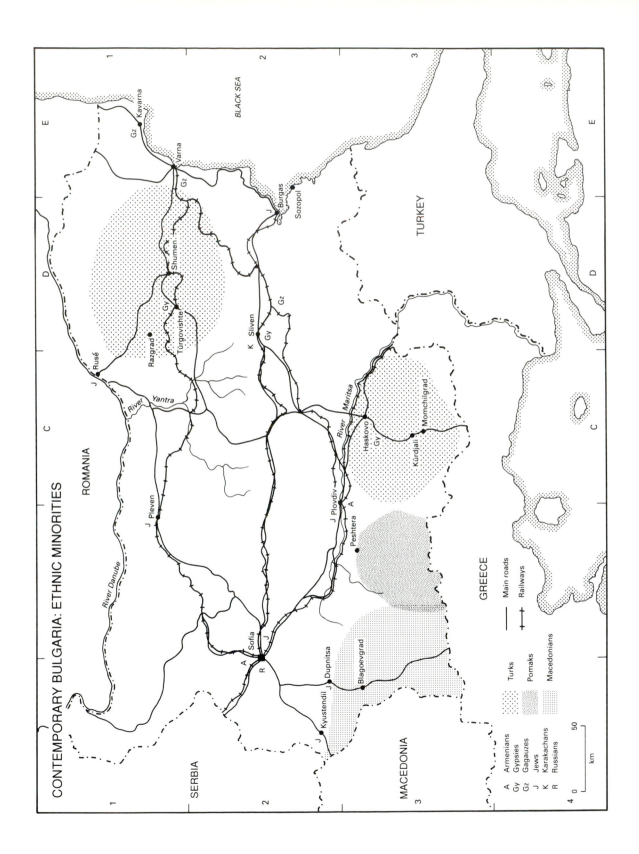

CONTEMPORARY BULGARIA: ETHNIC MINORITIES

SERBIA

ROMANIA

MACEDONIA

GREECE

TURKEY

BLACK SEA

River Danube

River Yantra

River Maritsa

Rusé
Razgrad
Türgovishte
Shumen
Varna
Kavarna
Pleven
Silven
Burgas
Sozopol
Sofia
Kyustendil
Dupnitsa
Blagoevgrad
Ploydiv
Peshtera
Haskovo
Kürdjali
Momchilgrad

Turks
Pomaks
Macedonians

A Armenians
Gy Gypsies
Gz Gagauzes
J Jews
K Karakachans
R Russians

Main roads
Railways

0   50
km

230

vote being less than 1 per cent greater than that of the BSP. The MRF was therefore left holding the balance in parliament. The UDF had been weakened before the poll by a number of splits and defections.

On 12 and 19 January 1992 presidential elections were held. In the first round there were twenty-two candidates, none of whom secured the absolute majority necessary for election. Of the three most prominent candidates Velko Vûlkanov was an independent backed by the BSP; Georgi Ganchev was a flamboyant character who had lived for many years in the West where he had taught at Eton and become a fencing champion; Zheliu Zhelev had been a dissident in communist Bulgaria, had become leader of the UDF, and had been elected interim president in August 1990. He had been widely expected to win outright in the first round. His vice-presidential running mate was Blaga Dimitrova, a poetess, who resigned in the summer of 1993.

Contemporary Bulgaria: economic

The post-totalitarian governments in Bulgaria have made clear their intentions to restructure the economy but progress has been disappointing. Privatisation was espoused at the beginning of the post-communist reform period but the full legal apparatus was not enacted until April 1992 by which time Bulgaria was the only former communist state except Albania not to have passed such a law. By the end of 1993 only 44 per cent of agricultural land had passed into private ownership, despite a stated objective of 100 per cent by that date, and only three major manufacturing enterprises had been privatised; on the other hand privatisation in trade and the service sector had progressed well and by the end of 1993 one estimate put the private sector as responsible for 18.5 per cent of GDP. Links with the Western economies had not strengthened greatly by the end of 1993. The European Community had concluded an interim trade agreement with Bulgaria in December 1992 but internal Community wranglings delayed full signature for a year. In the meantime Bulgaria has played a full part in developing the Black Sea Zone of Economic Cooperation but still sees the West, and in particular Europe, as the main focus for its economic orientation.

The problems faced by Bulgaria in its economic reforms are huge. The first is the social impact of major restructuring. Closing loss-making enterprises or slimming them down to staffing levels where private buyers and investors might be interested will deprive tens of thousands of their jobs. Unemployment had already risen from around 27,000 in January 1990 to 402,000 in January 1992 and has risen steadily since then. Inflation too is eating away at any state benefits given to the unemployed. Inflation is a social cost of modernisation which affects almost all wage-earners and though the rate of increase is falling, inflation is still a deadly threat to social stability.

Government inertia or weakness is cited as another reason for Bulgaria's slow rate of economic reform. In 1990 the opposition would not join a government of national responsibility, and since November 1990 far too much time has been wasted in squabbles over issues such as the files of the former secret police.

When the communists fell from power it became known that Bulgaria's foreign debt stood not at the officially stated figure of around $4 billion but at $11–12 billion. In March 1990 capital repayments, and in June interest payments, were suspended. This did not help Bulgaria in its search for Western loans. Long and arduous negotiations with Bulgaria's creditors finally produced an agreement in late 1993 that the debt should be cut by half. Bulgaria has had extreme ill-fortune since 1990 in that its strict and honourable adherence to UN sanctions, first against Iraq and then Yugoslavia, has inflicted enormous economic damage. Iraq was heavily in debt to Bulgaria and had agreed to repay its

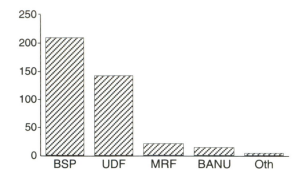

Figure 211 National Assembly, 1990 (seats won)

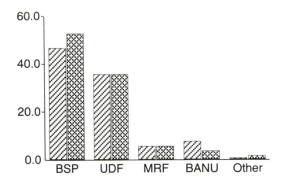

Figure 212 National Assembly, 1990 (% of votes and seats)

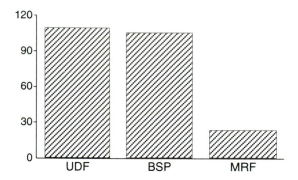

Figure 213 National Assembly, 1991 (seats won)

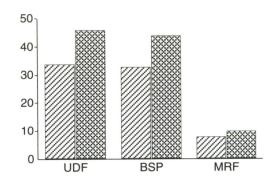

Figure 214 National Assembly, 1991 (% of votes and seats)

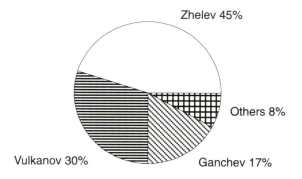

Figure 215 Presidential election, Jan. 1992, 1st round

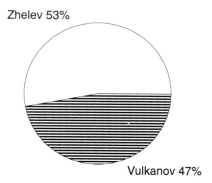

Figure 216 Presidential election, Jan. 1992, 2nd round

debts in oil; sanctions prevented this and Bulgaria therefore had to buy that quantity of oil on the world market. The ban of traffic through rump Yugoslavia meant that Bulgaria's chief export route to Europe was closed. The cost of this alone has been estimated at almost $3 billion.

Partly as a result of these difficulties the European Investment Bank agreed in July 1993 to lend $38.5 million for the improvement of Bulgaria's air transport systems and for the rebuilding of main roads to Greece, Romania, Turkey, and the Black Sea.

Early in 1994 Bulgaria's economic problems

were intensified by a sharp decline in the value of the leva, which fell from 35 to the US dollar in January to 50 in late March. Though this will help Bulgarian exports to the West it will make imports and debt payments much more difficult.

Bulgaria in the 1980s: ethnic composition

Ethnic tensions played a large part in bringing about the downfall of the old regime in Bulgaria but since 1989 they have been relatively well contained.

The largest minority is the Turkish. Exact figures are difficult to come by but it seems likely that the ethnic Turks are at least 10 per cent of the total population. Part of the difficulty in producing precise figures derives from the mass exodus staged in 1989 and the lesser second exodus in 1992. There had been large-scale departures of Turks, especially those of the north-east, in the late 1940s and early 1950s. This was because the land there is of high quality and the authorities were anxious to collectivise it quickly but were not as keen to absorb into the industrial sector the Turks who would be displaced by collectivisation. The exodus ended in the mid-1950s and was not resumed until a treaty signed in 1969 which allowed controlled emigration. The Bulgarians did not renew the agreement when it expired in 1979 and in the mid-1980s began a campaign aimed at the forcible assimilation of Bulgaria's Turks. In a number of areas the Turks resisted and the Bulgarians had to deploy their army, including its specialist 'red-beret' detachments. In the spring of 1989 Turkish leaders in Bulgaria began hunger strikes and within days much of the north-east of the country was in a state of virtual rebellion. In response communist leader Todor Zhivkov declared that any Bulgarian Turk who really preferred capitalist Turkey to socialist Bulgaria was free to leave. To his amazement 340,000 did so before the Turkish republic closed its borders in August. In December 1989 the new government, though still communist, restored all rights to the Turks; by the mid-spring of 1990 about a third of the émigrés of the previous summer had returned.

Since 1989 there has been no legal discrimination against the Turks, though the latter have complained that they have not been given a fair deal in the land privatisation process, and that government policy towards the tobacco industry, in which many Turks work, has been damaging. On the other hand, Turkish names have been restored, broadcasting and publication in Turkish is again legal, the Department of Turkish in Sofia University has been reopened, and Turkish children in some areas can receive some of their education in their mother tongue.

The Pomaks, or Bulgarian-speaking Muslims, were subjected to heavy assimilationist pressures in the 1970s. In the early 1990s there were allegations that Muslim pressure, much of it external, was forcing Pomaks to switch to Turkish and to register as Turkish in official returns.

The most contentious ethnic issue in Bulgaria could concern those who wish to be regarded as Macedonians. Until the early 1950s the communist rulers of Bulgaria recognised the Macedonians as a separate ethnic group, though this policy was never popular. At present the authorities, though they recognise the neighbouring Macedonian state, do not recognise a Macedonian nation, and have blocked all attempts to form political parties based on a concept of Macedonian nationhood.

The Gypsies do have separate political parties, however, and there are also some school textbooks in the Romany language. The Gypsies are difficult to enumerate but they have clearly survived the many attempts made in communist times to assimilate them.

Of the other groups the Jews number about five thousand, there having been massive emigration after the Second World War. The Karakachans were nomadic shepherds, known elsewhere as Vlachs, and are very few in number. The Gagauze are Turkish-speaking Christians.

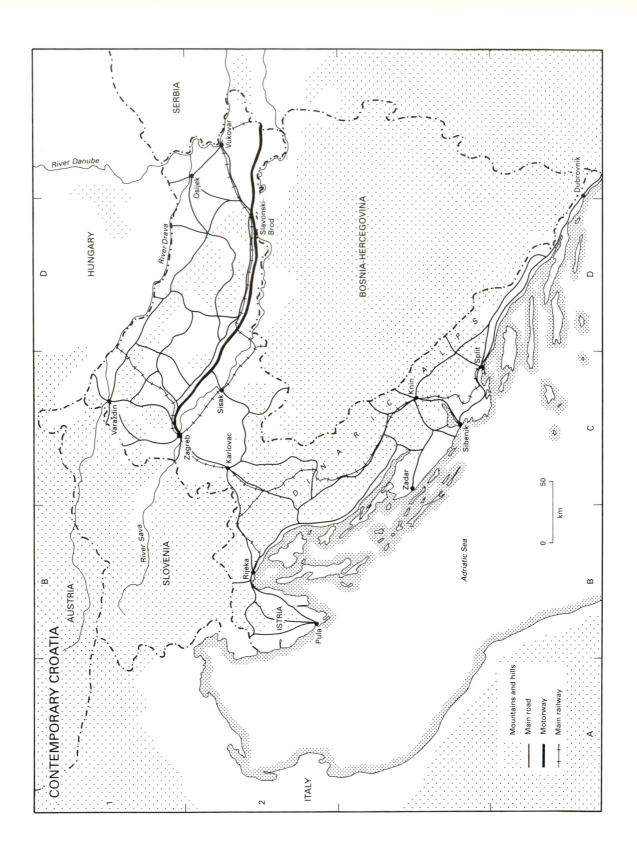

CONTEMPORARY CROATIA

Mountains and hills
Main road
Motorway
Main railway

SERBIA

River Danube

HUNGARY

River Drava

Vukovar

Osijek

Slavonski-
Brod

BOSNIA-HERCEGOVINA

Dubrovnik

Varaždin

Sisak

Zagreb

Karlovac

River Sava

SLOVENIA

AUSTRIA

Rijeka

ISTRIA

Pula

ITALY

Knin

Split

Šibenik

Zadar

DINARIC ALPS

Adriatic Sea

50

km

0

Croatia: basic data

Official name:	Republic of Croatia	Official religion:	None
Area:	56,538 sq km	Religious affiliation:	Roman Catholic 76.5 per cent; Orthodox 11.1 per cent; Muslim 1.2 per cent; Others 11.2 per cent (1991)
Population:	4,821,000 (1993)		
Population density:	85.3 per sq km (1993)		
Ethnic composition:	Croat 78.1 per cent; Serb 12.2 per cent; Bosnian 0.9 per cent; Magyar 0.5 per cent; Slovene 0.5 per cent; Others 7.8 per cent (1991)		
		Capital:	Zagreb 706,770 (1991)
		Major cities:	Split 189,388; Rijeka 167,964; Osijek 104,761; Zadar 76,343 (1991)
Official language:	Croatian		

Contemporary Croatia

Croatia's geographic shape does not give encouragement for an easy and successful economic life. Its natural line of communication is along the river Sava towards the Danube and Belgrade, though political considerations now make movement in that direction impossible. Connection can be made with the outside world to the north via the mountain passes into Austria; meanwhile links between the heartland of Croatia and the Croatian coast, which were never easy because of the terrain, are now immensely complicated because the Serbs of Croatia control the rail junction at Knin.

Before the break-up of Yugoslavia Croatia derived a healthy income from tourism along the Adriatic coast, an area of almost unbroken splendour from Dubrovnik northwards. That revenue has now all but disappeared. In fact, by early 1994 Croatia was financially dependent on the revenues brought in by the large UN presence in the country.

Despite these difficulties, however, there can be no doubting the determination of the Croats of all political denominations to make their country viable and successful.

Croatian elections since 1991

The new constitution adopted by Croatia on 22 December 1990 made the president more powerful than the parliament.

On 24 June 1992 incumbent president Franjo Tudjman announced that elections for both the presidency and the legislative assembly would be held on 2 August 1992. This met with immediate opposition from the leader of the Social Liberal Party (SLP), Dražen Budiša, who complained that the vote would exclude those thousands of Croatians who were now living under Serbian occupation or who were caught up in the chaotic situation in Bosnia. There was further dispute about the precise composition of the electorate when rumours circulated that the vote would be offered to anyone, anywhere in the world, who had one Croat parent and who intended to become a Croatian citizen. Such a wide franchise was not used, and on 2 August the votes cast in the elections were a little under 75 per cent of the total, indigenous electorate.

Of the individual candidates who won 4 per cent or more of the vote, only Silvije Degen was not the leader of an established political party.

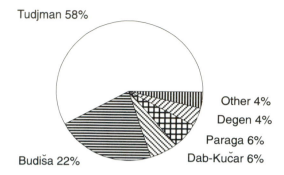

Figure 217 Presidential election, Aug. 1992

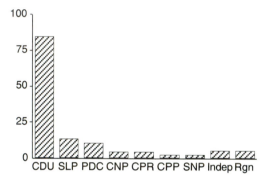

Figure 218 Chamber of Deputies (seats won)

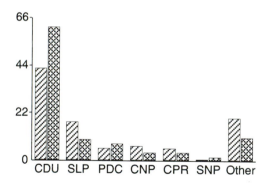

Figure 219 Chamber of Deputies (% votes and seats)

Budiša, as already noted, was chairman of the SLP; Tudjman led the Croatian Democratic Union (CDU); Savka Dabčević-Kučar headed the Croatian People's Party (CPP); and Dobroslav Paraga was leader of the extreme rightist Croatian Party of Rights (CPR).

In the elections for the Chamber of Deputies, the lower house of the legislative assembly, the CDU again dominated; the working of the constitution also gave it a considerable bonus in that its share of the seats was almost a third greater than its share of the votes.

Most of the Serbs in Croatia seem to have boycotted the poll; the Serbian National Party secured only 1.1 per cent of the votes, and few Serbs were thought to have voted for the Croat parties.

After the poll there were bitter complaints from the defeated parties of governmental interference with the voting.

Elections for the 63-member upper house, the Chamber of Districts, were held on 7 February 1993. Once again the CDU won an absolute majority.

Croatia: economic

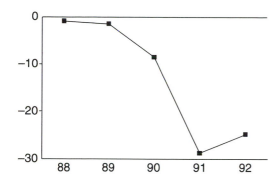

Figure 220 Change in social product, 1988–92 (%)

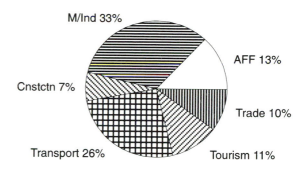

Figure 223 Origins of social production, 1991

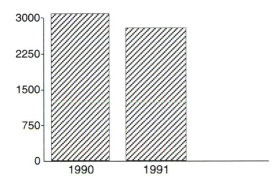

Figure 223 Hard currency debt, 1990–1 ($m)

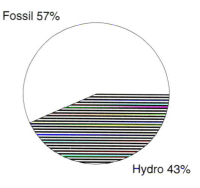

Figure 224 Source of generated power, 1990

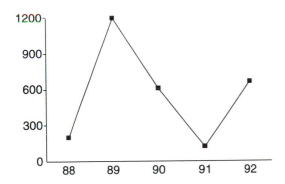

Figure 222 Consumer price inflation, 1988–92 (%)

The Czech Republic: basic data

Official name: Czech Republic
Area: 78,864 sq km
Population: 10,339,000 (1993)
Population density: 131.1 per sq km (1993)
Ethnic composition: Czech 81.3 per cent; Moravian 13.2 per cent; Slovak 3 per cent; Polish 0.6 per cent; German 0.5 per cent; Silesian 0.4 per cent; Gypsy 0.3 per cent; Hungarian 0.1 per cent; Ukrainian 0.1 per cent; Others 0.5 per cent (1991)
Official language: Czech
Official religion: None
Religious affiliation: Non-religious and Atheists 39.7 per cent; Roman Catholic 39.2 per cent; Czechoslovak Brethren Reformed 1.9 per cent; Hussite 1.7 per cent; Silesian Evangelical 0.5 per cent; Orthodox 0.2 per cent; Greek Catholic (Uniate) 0.1 per cent; Other 16.7 per cent (1991)
Capital: Prague 1,212,010 (1991)
Major cities: Brno 387,986; Ostrava 327,553; Plzen 173,129; Olomouc 105,690 (1991)

The Czech Lands, 1989–93: political

Voting for the Czechoslovak Federal Assembly and for the Czech and Slovak National Councils took place on 8 and 9 June 1990.

The Federal Assembly of the Czechoslovak Republic consisted of the House of the People and the House of Nationalities. The House of the People had 101 delegates from the Czech lands and forty-nine from Slovakia. The House of Nationalities consisted of seventy-five members from the Czech lands and an equal number from Slovakia.

The assembly was elected by proportional representation, but, unusually with PR, the system allowed electors to exercise a degree of personal preference amongst candidates from the same party. The minimum requirement for representation in the assembly was that a party should receive 5 per cent of the total vote in either the Czech lands or in Slovakia. The turnout was high, 97 per cent, and twenty-four parties or political groupings took part in the election. Representation in the Czech National Council, which had 200 members, also required a 5 per cent threshold.

Civic Forum (CF) was a wide-ranging alliance of parties from the moderate conservative right to the far left; all those parties committed themselves to a pluralist political system and a market economy. The CPCS (Communist Party of Czechoslovakia) conducted a restrained campaign, emphasising its acceptance of political pluralism and the market economy, but stressing that the state must continue to play a role in that economy. Devolutionist aspirations were voiced by MSD–SMS (Movement for Self-Governing Democracy – Society for Moravia and Silesia).

The strong performance of the CF candidates was due in the main to their strong stand for human rights, and was encouraged by the open support given by President Vaclav Havel who campaigned for CF. There was general surprise at the strong showing of the CPCS, which became the second strongest party in the Federal Assembly and in the Czech National Council. Despite a flood of resignations since November 1989 it has remained, with 900,000 members, the largest party in the country.

(For elections in Slovakia, see pp. 270–2.)

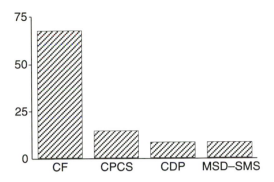

Figure 225 House of People, 1990 (seats won)

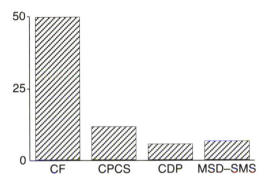

Figure 226 House of Nationalities, 1990 (seats won)

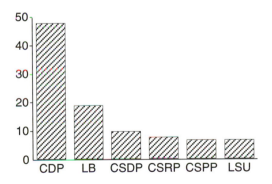

Figure 227 House of People, 1992 (seats won)

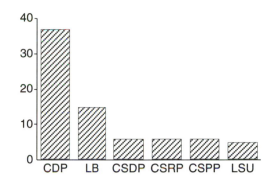

Figure 228 House of Nationalities, 1992 (seats won)

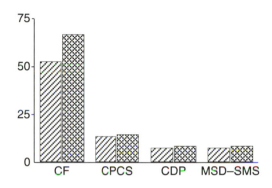

Figure 229 House of People, 1990 (% votes and seats)

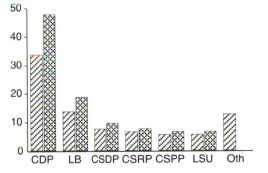

Figure 230 House of People, 1992 (% votes and seats)

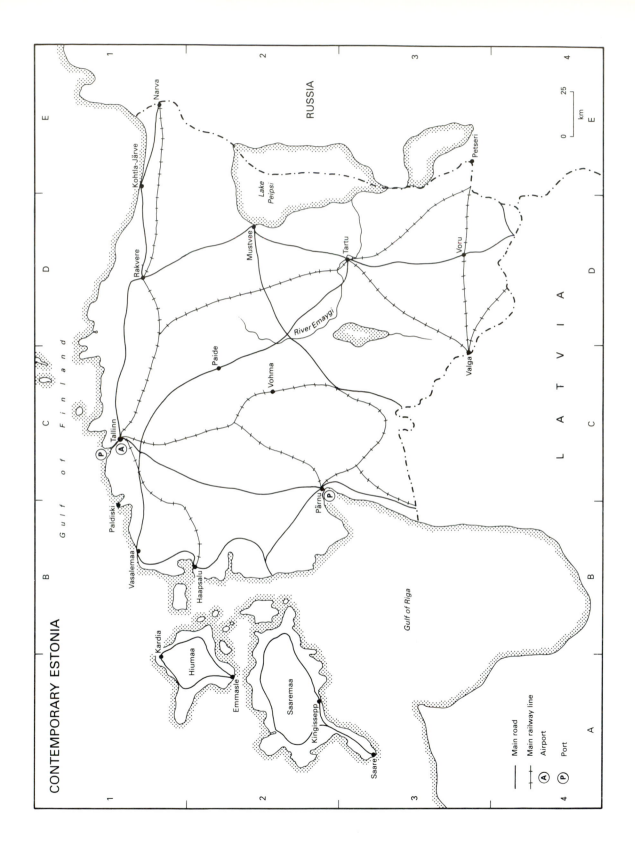

CONTEMPORARY ESTONIA

Narva
Kohtla-Järve
Rakvere
Mustvee
Lake Peipsi
RUSSIA
Tartu
Petseri
Voru
River Emaygi
Valga
Paide
Vohma
Tallinn
Paldiski
Vasalemaa
Haapsalu
Pärnu
Kardla
Hiumaa
Emmaste
Saaremaa
Kingissepp
Saare
Gulf of Finland
Gulf of Riga
LATVIA

Main road
Main railway line
Airport
Port

km
0   25

Estonia: basic data

Official name:	Republic of Estonia
Area:	45,215 sq km
Population:	1,592,000 (1992)
Population density:	35.2 per sq km (1992)
Ethnic composition:	Estonian 61.5 per cent; Russian 30.3 per cent; Ukrainian 3.1 per cent; Belorussian 1.8 per cent; Finnish 1.1 per cent; Others 2.2 per cent
Official language:	Estonian
Official religion:	None
Religious affiliation:	Figures not available, but most believers are Christians of the Lutheran Church with Orthodox and Baptist minorities
Capital:	Tallinn 499,800 (1991)
Major cities:	Tartu 115,400; Narva 82,300; Kohtla-Järve 76,800; Pärnu 54,200 (1991)

Contemporary Estonia

The first successful assertion of Estonian interests against the central power of Moscow was in the autumn of 1987 when protests against plans for the extension of phosphorite mining in northern Estonia produced widespread protests at the inevitable ecological damage.

In December 1987 the Estonian Heritage Society was set up and encouraged the study of Estonian history, the singing of Estonian songs and the display of still-forbidden national symbols. In October 1988 the Popular Front, founded in April, was formally constituted and in the following month the Estonian Supreme Soviet adopted a declaration on, but not of, sovereignty. Thereafter, the registration of citizens began but the definition used made it very difficult for any Russian to be enrolled.

Further nationalist gains were registered in 1989 and in October of that year the Popular Front joined with local Citizens' Committees to demand the calling of a Congress of Estonia which met in March 1990. It created a Council of Estonia, ten of whose seventy-one members came from Estonian communities abroad. The Council created an eleven-strong executive committee. In May the Council restored many national emblems but it did not issue a declaration of independence because this, it said, had been done in 1918.

Estonian citizens had in effect set up a political authority parallel to that of the Supreme Soviet in Tallinn, which was increasingly enfeebled and could do nothing to hinder the achievement of full independence in August 1991.

Even proportions of the Russian minority were in favour of Estonian independence, partly because Estonia offered a higher standard of living than Russia. Some Russians, however, did resist. In Kohtla-Järve in May 1990 two hundred representatives of the Interregional Soviet of People's Deputies and Workers of the Estonian Soviet Socialist Republic met to assert the interests of the Russian minority.

After independence there were attempts by the Russian population of Narva and Sillamäa near Kohtla-Järve to establish autonomous regions in Estonia. They were declared illegal.

The question of the Russian minority inevitably influenced Estonia's relations with its mighty neighbour and complicated discussions on the withdrawal of remaining Russian army units from the country. There were particularly intense debates over the Russian submarine training base at Paldiski which contained two nuclear reactors. In the summer of 1993 the Russians agreed to dismantle and remove the reactors. By September 1994 all Russian troops had left Estonia. There was no agreement, however, on the question of the area around Petseri annexed by Russia in 1945 (see pp. 141–3); the Russians regard the 1945 border as definitive whilst the Estonians insist that the legal line is that agreed by the Treaty of Tartu in 1920 which determined the inter-war boundary. The Estonians also raised questions concerning Estonians in Russia, many of whom had acquired Estonian citizenship.

Estonia: election results, 1992

The first elections since the confirmation of Estonian independence in September 1991 took place on 20 September 1992. Voting was held simultaneously for the presidency and for the 101-seat *Riigikogu*, or parliament; representation in the latter was determined by a complicated system of proportional representation. Considerable controversy was caused by a law which enfranchised only Estonian citizens, and citizenship was only granted to pre-war citizens of Estonia and their descendants. This effectively barred one-third of the population from voting. The turn-out for the poll of 20 September was 67 per cent.

In the presidential campaign Arnold Rüütel, the effective head of state since the elections to the Supreme Soviet of March 1990, presented himself as a moderate, as did Rein Taagepera. Both were supported by the Popular Front. Taagepera was a historian and a Canadian citizen; Rüütel, on the other hand, was a former leader of the Estonian Communist Party. Lennart Meri was the principal nationalist candidate; he had served as foreign minister until March 1992 when he had been made ambassador to Finland. Lagle Parek, the only female amongst the four presidential candidates, was a former political prisoner who was also the leader of the NIP.

The constitution required a presidential candidate to secure an absolute majority to ensure election. As this did not happen the new parliament was required to make the decision; it did so in favour of Meri.

Meri was selected primarily because he was the candidate of the Fatherland Group, *Isamaa*, which had emerged as the strongest party in the parliamentary elections. All parties which did well in the elections were from the right of the political spectrum, which meant that the question of the large Russian minority and its rights is bound to be prominent in future *Riigikogu* debates. Inevitably, the Russians linked the question of the Russian minority to that of the withdrawal of Russian troops from Estonia.

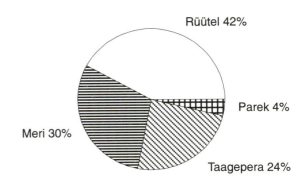

Figure 231 Presidential elections, Sept. 1992

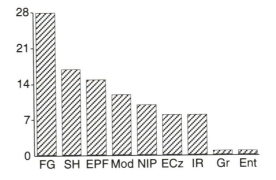

Figure 232 Parliamentary election, Sept. 1992 (seats won)

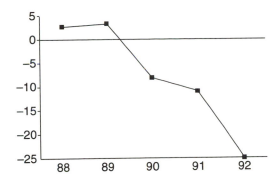

Figure 233 Changes in GDP, 1988–92 (%)

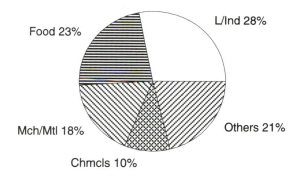

Figure 236 Principal exports, 1990

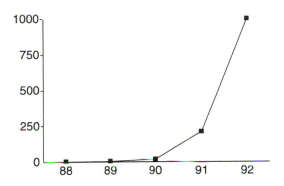

Figure 234 Consumer price inflation, 1988–92 (%)

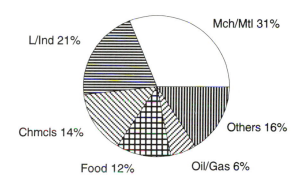

Figure 237 Principle imports, 1991

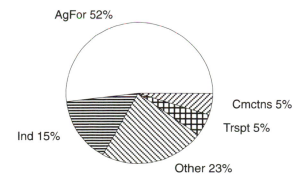

Figure 235 Origins of GDP, 1991 (%)

243

Hungary: basic data

Official name:	Republic of Hungary	Religious affiliation:	Roman Catholic 64.1 per cent; Protestant 23.3 per cent; Orthodox 0.5 per cent; Jewish 0.9 per cent; Atheist and Non-Religious 11.2 per cent (1989)
Area:	93,033 sq km		
Population:	10,296,000 (1993)		
Population density:	110.6 per sq km (1993)		
Ethnic composition:	Magyar 97.3 per cent; Gypsy 1.4 per cent; German 0.3 per cent; Croatian 0.1 per cent; Romanian 0.1 per cent; Slovak 0.1 per cent; Others 0.7 per cent (1990)	Capital:	Budapest 1,992,343 (1992)
		Major cities:	Debrecen 214,712; Miskolc 191,623; Szeged 177,506; Pécs 169,486 (1992)
Official language:	Hungarian		
Official religion:	None		

Hungarian elections since 1989

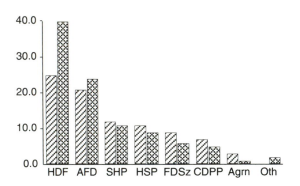

Figure 238 Parliamentary election, 1990 (% votes and seats)

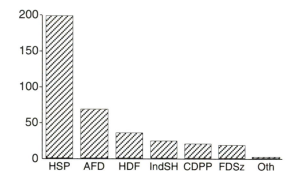

Figure 240 Parliamentary election, 1994 (seats won)

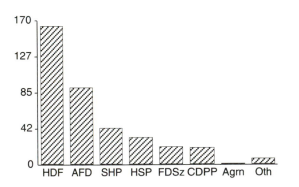

Figure 239 Parliamentary election, 1990 (seats won)

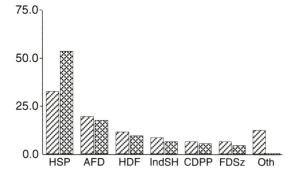

Figure 241 Parliamentary election, 1994 (% votes and seats)

Elections for the Hungarian parliament, the *Országgyülés*, were held on 25 March and 8 April 1990. The parliament consisted of 386 members who were elected in one of three different ways. The largest number, 176, were elected in single-member constituencies; where no candidate received an absolute majority a second round was held in which a simple majority secured election. The second bloc, consisting of 152 deputies, was to be chosen from regional lists according to a form of proportional representation, with a provision that a party had to secure at least 4 per cent of the vote to qualify for representation. The remaining fifty-eight seats were also determined by PR, but this time there was a single national list and the calculations were made on the basis of the votes 'unused' in determining the results in the other two blocs of seats. Each elector cast two votes, one for the local constituency and one for the county list. The turnout was 66 per cent. Only five of the 176 majority seats were decided in the first round of voting. Before the second round the Hungarian Democratic Forum (HDF), the Christian Democratic People's Party (CDPP) and the Smallholders' Party (SHP) formed an electoral pact.

The electoral law called for eight seats to be reserved for ethnic minorities – the Serbs, Croats, Germans and Gypsies – but this ruling was never implemented.

Of the main parties in the new assembly AFD (Alliance of Free Democrats) was originally an association primarily of elements of the intelligentsia and was founded in November 1988. It went into opposition after the elections. The CDPP had been founded in October 1944 and was reconstituted in April 1989. It is to the right of centre, advocates private ownership and is strong in its defence of national sovereignty. After the elections it became part of the governing coalition. The League of Young Democrats (FIDESz or FDSz) was founded in 1988 by radical students and thereafter became prominent in criticism of the ailing communist regime. It is strong in defence of minority rights, but lukewarm in its commitment to the introduction of a market economy. It refused to enter the government coalition and assumed an oppositionist stance similar to those adopted by liberal or moderate social democratic parties in the West. The HDF, established in 1987, had a proven record as an effective but pragmatic critic of the communists; a centre-right party, it advocates market reform but argues for the retention of a social safety net, and urges close association with and then membership of the European Union. It formed the core of the governing coalition after the elections. The Hungarian Socialist Party (HSP) was formed from a splinter group of the former Communist Party and by 1990 had adopted a centre-left position. The SHP was reconstitued in 1988, the original party having been established in 1930. The main plank of its platform was the need for land privatisation. After the election it joined the government coalition but by 1991 had become badly split.

The elections of 8 and 29 May 1994 saw a large swing to the HSP which was returned with an absolute majority. Voters were frustrated by Hungary's intensifying economic difficulties and by the apparent ineffectiveness of the 1990–4 government.

Hungary: economic

Until the elections of March–April 1990 had produced an administration which could have some claim to legitimacy amongst the nation, the Hungarian government was reluctant to embark on any radical economic reform. Even after the elections there was little advance. The composition of the ruling coalition did not help because the Smallholders insisted that all land confiscated by the communists after 1947 must be returned to the families of the original owners; this the other parties in the coalition could not accept. Also the prime minister, József Antall, was a historian and showed little taste for economic affairs, and certainly no boldness in tackling

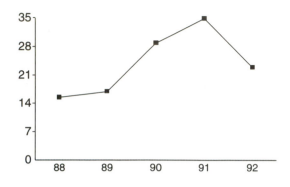

Figure 242 Consumer price inflation, 1988–92 (%)

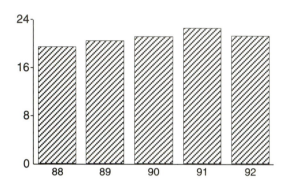

Figure 243 Hard currency debt, 1988–92 ($bn)

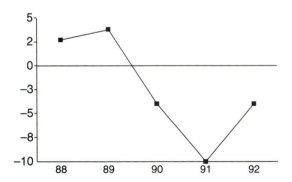

Figure 244 Change in GDP, 1988–92 (%)

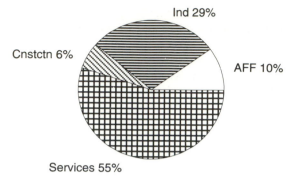

Figure 245 Origins of GDP, 1992

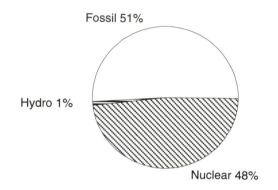

Figure 246 Source of generated power, 1990

them. Those ministers responsible for such affairs would have had an easy passage to reform if only they had agreed amongst themselves, but they did not. When, at the end of October, the government went back on a recent promise not to increase petrol prices and put them up by 75 per cent irate taxi drivers blockaded the bridges across the Danube in Budapest. The blockade spread across the country in a matter of hours. At the end of the year, the prime minister admitted that not enough had been done to reconstruct the economy and that a crisis was now being faced with a budget deficit three times higher than a year before and inflation at 30 per cent and rising.

In February 1991 the Kupa Plan, named after the minister of finance who introduced it, promised thoroughgoing economic reform. But again the pace was slow with privatisation being much less rapid than in Czechoslovakia or Poland. Nevertheless, Hungary attracted half of the Western funds invested in post-communist Eastern Europe. There were indications that by the end of 1991 inflation would rise no higher than 35 per cent and was expected to fall thereafter, and a reasonably healthy trade balance would be achieved. Further economic reform was enacted in November when the National Bank was given extensive freedoms. Unemployment was at the same time becoming more apparent and had topped 7 per cent by the end of the year, not a particularly high figure in Eastern Europe at the time. On the other hand, an estimated 40 per cent of Hungarians were living on or below the poverty line.

This state of basic economic equilibrium was maintained throughout 1992 when again Hungary succeeded in attracting around half the Western money going into Eastern Europe, and inflation seemed to be more or less contained at around the 20 per cent level. If industrial production fell this was in part because some shift away from the old subsidised concerns had taken place, and by September some upturn was noticeable.

This did not prevent pressure on the Hungarian currency which underwent five minor devaluations in 1993, the most important cause of this being a fall of 27 per cent in exports during the first seven months of 1993 compared to the same months in 1992. In October the minister of finance, announcing the 1994 budget, warned that some austerity measures were necessary to restrict increases in the deficit as a percentage of GDP, though a proposed law on minimum salaries for public employees was to be introduced in 1994 rather than 1995. There were also measures to encourage investment, particularly in agriculture which had been hard hit by drought in 1993.

Hungary's economy faces the difficulties of rising budget deficits and trade imbalances, but it remains one of the most successful in Eastern Europe. For that reason Hungary, early in 1994, became the first state in the region to announce that it was to apply for full membership of the European Union.

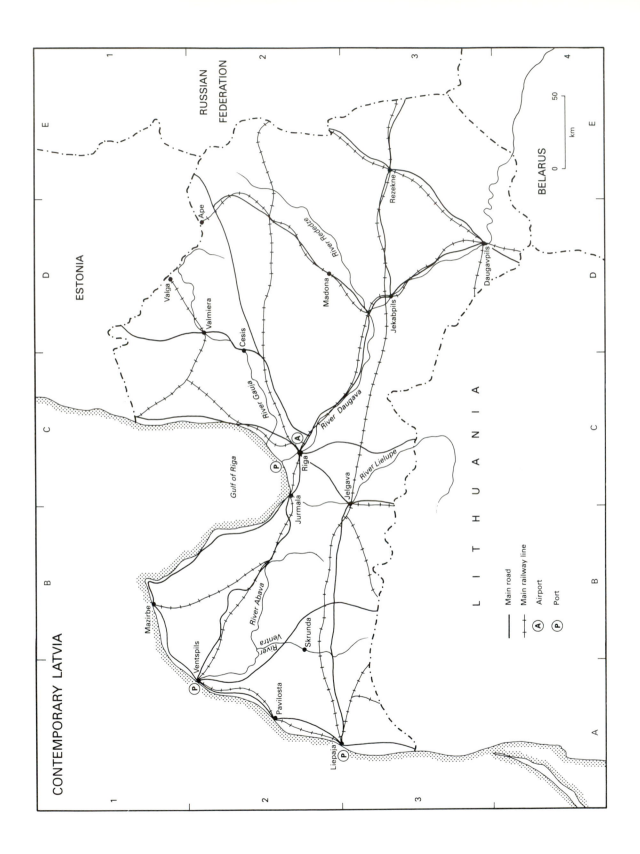

CONTEMPORARY LATVIA

Main road
Main railway line
Ⓐ Airport
Ⓟ Port

Latvia: basic data

Official name:	Republic of Latvia
Area:	64,610 sq km
Population:	2,596,000 (1993)
Population density:	40.2 per sq km (1993)
Ethnic composition:	Latvian 52.5 per cent; Russian 34 per cent; Belorussian 4.4 per cent; Ukrainian 3.4 per cent; Polish 2.2 per cent; Lithuanian 1.3 per cent; Jewish 1.6 per cent; Others 1.6 per cent (1992)
Official language:	Latvian
Official religion:	None
Religious affiliation:	No figures available but most professing Christians are Lutherans with Russian Orthodox and Roman Catholic minorities
Capital:	Riga 897,078 (1992)
Major cities:	Daugavpils 127,279; Liepaja 113,815 (1992)

Contemporary Latvia

The spearhead of the Latvian movement towards greater local autonomy was the Environmental Protection Club (EPC) established in the spring of 1986. In October 1986 it staged a protest against plans, drawn up in Moscow, to construct a hydro-electric station at Daugavpils on the river Daugava. When Moscow abandoned the project in November it was the first time in fifty years that local Latvian pressure had reversed a major decision taken in the Soviet capital. Other victories were to follow when a scheme to construct a metro system in Riga was jettisoned because of the damage it would cause to the foundations of historic buildings.

The EPC was not the only organisation defending Latvian rights. 'Helsinki 86' had been set up in the same year and in October 1988 a Popular Front was established to coordinate the movement for greater political decentralisation. Sovereignty and economic independence were declared in July 1989, and when elections were held to the Latvian Supreme Soviet in March 1990 a multi-party system was functioning. Full independence came with the collapse of the Soviet Union in August 1991.

Because its national minorities, particularly the Russian, were larger than in other Baltic states, Latvia had to tread with caution. The Russian Interfront, established in January 1989, was strong, and in January 1991 'Black Beret' troops of the Soviet Ministry of the Interior attacked that ministry's building in Riga. Nevertheless, ethnic tensions have been contained with some success in Latvia.

This is also in part due to the large number of Russian troops in Latvia, estimated at the end of 1990 to be one in ten of the population. The Russian and Latvian governments negotiated strenuously for many months at Jurmala on the withdrawal of Russian troops; the main points at issue were the Russians' insistence that they maintain their naval dockyard at Liepaja, their satellite monitoring station at Ventspils, and, most importantly, their radar tracking facilities at Skrunda. Agreement on the latter point was finally reached early in the summer of 1994 after which the Russians promised to evacuate all their forces from Latvia by the end of September of that year. By and large this seems to have been achieved, though the status of retired Soviet and Russian military personnel still in Latvia remains a cause of some dispute.

Latvia: election results, 1993

The elections to the Latvian parliament, *Saeima*, were held on 5 and 6 June 1993. The seats were distributed according to a form of proportional representation under which the votes cast for a party list were calculated as a percentage of the total votes cast. There was a 4 per cent threshold for representation in the *Saeima*; those votes cast for parties which did not pass the 4 per cent threshold were redistributed proportionally amongst those parties which did pass the threshold. This accounts for the fact that all parties represented had a slightly higher share of the seats than they did of the votes cast. Eleven per cent of the total votes went to parties which did not secure 4 per cent of the total; fifteen parties failed to pass the 4 per cent threshold. The turnout was 89.4 per cent.

Victory in the elections went to the right of centre parties, their combined representation in the 100-member assembly being 75: The Latvian Way – 36; The National Independence Movement for Latvia – 15; Latvian Farmers' Union – 12; For the Fatherland and Freedom – 6; and the Latvian Christian Democratic Union – 6. The Latvian Popular Front, which had emerged as the largest party in the elections to the Latvian Supreme Soviet in March 1990, was one of the parties which did not pass the 4 per cent threshold. The other parties represented regarded themselves as left of centre, but all parties, whatever side of the central divide, were relatively moderate in attitude and action.

Foreign observers confirmed that the elections had been carried out fairly, but there had been controversy before the poll over a citizenship law which allowed the vote only to citizens of pre-war Latvia and their descendants.

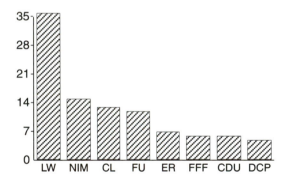

Figure 247 Parliamentary election, 1993 (seats won)

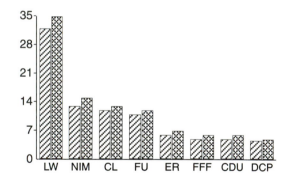

Figure 248 Parliamentary election, 1993 (% votes and seats)

Latvia: economic

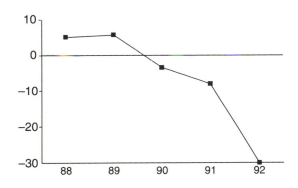

Figure 249 Changes in GDP, 1988–92 (%)

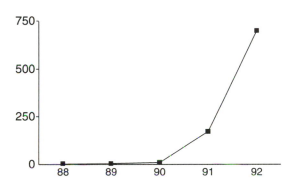

Figure 250 Consumer price inflation, 1988–92 (%)

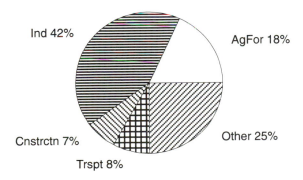

Figure 251 Origins of GDP, 1990

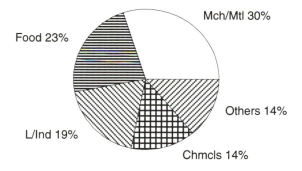

Figure 252 Principal exports, 1990

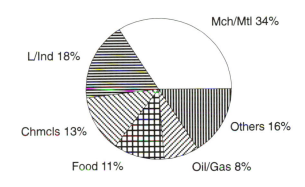

Figure 253 Principal imports, 1990

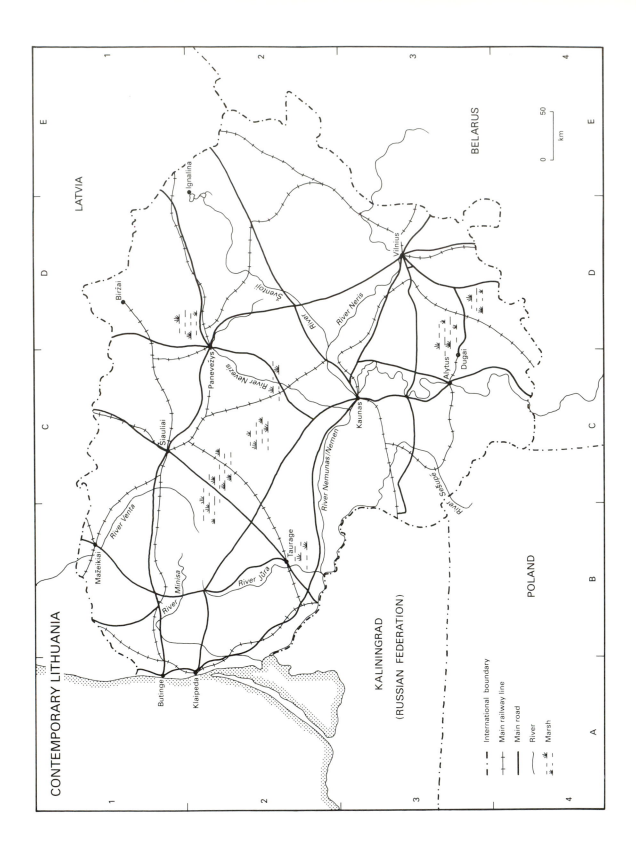

CONTEMPORARY LITHUANIA

LATVIA

BELARUS

Ignalina

Biržai

Vilnius

River Šventoji

River Neris

River Neris

Panevėžys

River Nevėžis

Alytus

Dugai

Šiauliai

Kaunas

River Nemunas/Nemen

Mažeikiai

River Venta

River Minisa

Taurage

River Jūra

River Šešupė

River

KALININGRAD
(RUSSIAN FEDERATION)

Butinge

Klaipeda

POLAND

International boundary
Main railway line
Main road
River
Marsh

50

km

0

Lithuania: basic data

Official name:	Republic of Lithuania
Area:	65,301 sq km
Population:	3,798,000 (1993)
Population density:	58.2 per sq km (1993)
Ethnic composition:	Lithuanian 79.6 per cent; Russian 9.4 per cent; Polish 7.0 per cent; Belorussian 1.7 per cent; Other 2.3 per cent (1992)
Official language:	Lithuanian
Official religion:	None
Religious affiliation:	No definite figures available in 1990; about 80 per cent of professing Christians were said to be Roman Catholic
Capital:	Vilnius 590,100 (1993)
Major cities:	Kaunas 429,600; Klaipeda 206,400 (1992)

Contemporary Lithuania

In their confrontation with Moscow, decentralisers and nationalists in Lithuania enjoyed two great advantages over their fellow aspirants in the other Baltic states. First, the proportion of Russians resident in the country was only 20 per cent, compared to 39 per cent in Estonia and 48 per cent in Latvia. Second, Lithuanians remained firmly attached to the Roman Catholic Church which gave them a strong supporter outside the USSR as well as a strong unifying element within Lithuania.

It was not the Catholic Church alone, however, which encouraged the movement to lessen Moscow's control in Lithuania. As in the other Baltic republics the environmental issue was also a powerful factor. Lithuania's green activists had appeared in 1986, and in August 1988, in an unprecedented act of defiance against the central authorities in Moscow, the council of ministers in Vilnius suspended financial support for the Ignalina reactor until completion of an inquiry into its safety.

Significant moves towards a loosening of ties with Moscow came in November 1988 with a law making Lithuanian the official language of the republic and restoring the pre-war flag and national anthem. By now the increasingly emboldened decentralisers had channelled their support into quasi-political bodies, the most vocal of which was *Sajudis* (Movement). Equally importantly, by the end of 1988, reformists had taken over most if not all posts in the state and party leaderships.

In 1989 Lithuania edged towards a break with Moscow. On 18 May the Supreme Soviet in Vilnius adopted a declaration of economic and political sovereignty for Lithuania; six months later, on 6 December, the same body abolished the authority of the Communist Party of the Soviet Union (CPSU) in Lithuania and allowed the formation of non-communist political parties; Lithuania had become the first Soviet republic to establish a multi-party system. On 19 December the Lithuanian Communist Party detached itself from the CPSU.

On 11 March 1990 Lithuania declared itself an independent state. The Kremlin now felt it had been pushed too far. It imposed a fuel embargo on Lithuania, which was forced in the summer of 1990 to 'suspend' its independence. In January 1991 outright violence was used, thirteen people being killed when Soviet troops stormed the television station in Vilnius. At the end of July eight more Lithuanians were killed when Soviet Ministry of the Interior forces attacked a Lithuanian border post. The collapse of the 19 August 1991 *putsch* in Moscow, however, removed all obstacles to full independence which Moscow recognised on 4 September 1991.

Since independence Lithuania has had to negotiate carefully with Russia concerning the latter's land access to Kaliningrad. There were also difficulties with Latvia over the construction of an oil terminal. Lithuania wished to place this on a floating platform off Butinge near the Latvian border. Latvia feared this might endanger its coastline.

The Lithuanian elections of 1992

The elections for the 141-member Lithuanian *Seimas* (parliament) were held on 25 October and 15 November 1992. The seats were divided into two categories. Seventy deputies were to be elected from a list of parties, the votes being tallied nation-wide and the seats distributed in proportion to votes cast; there was a 4 per cent threshold to qualify for representation in this category. Seventy-one deputies were to be chosen on the majority principle from territorial constituencies; if no candidate secured more than half of the votes a second round had to be held in which electors were required to choose between the top two candidates from the first round. On 25 October only thirteen constituencies produced a clear winner. The percentage of votes cast in Figure 256 is taken from the vote for the party lists.

In the first round of voting the Democratic Labour Party (DLP) won 35 seats, *Sajudis* 18, and the Christian Democratic Party (XtDP) 10; after the second round of voting on 15 November the DLP had 73 seats, *Sajudis* 30, the XtDP 18, the Social Democratic Party 8, and other groups 12. To ensure the presence of some deputies from the ethnic minorities the 4 per cent threshold did not apply to two parties representing their interests: the Lithuanian Union of Poles and the Concord of Lithuania.

The DLP was the former Communist Party of Lithuania which had declared itself independent of the Communist Party of the Soviet Union in December 1989. *Sajudis* was a coalition of the leading force in the struggle for independence. Its defeat was generally ascribed to public frustration at the economic privation which had followed the break with the Soviet Union.

On the day of the first round of the parliamentary elections there was also a referendum on a new constitution. The system presented to the electors on 25 October was a compromise between supporters of a strong presidency and those in favour of a dominant parliament; 75.42 per cent of the votes were for the new constitution, 21.06 per cent were against, and the remainder were spoiled ballots. Those in favour constituted 57.76 per cent of the electorate and the new constitution was adopted. It provided for a directly elected president who would have the power to appoint the prime minister. The latter, in turn, would nominate the cabinet.

The first direct presidential elections were

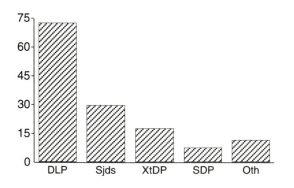

Figure 254 Parliamentary election, 1992 (seats won)

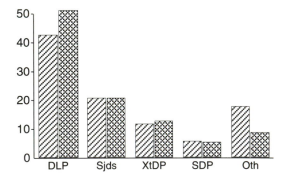

Figure 255 Parliamentary election, 1992 (% votes and seats)

held according to the provisions of the new constitution on 14 February 1993. Pro-DLP feeling was still running high; DLP leader Algirdas Brazauskas took 60.1 per cent of the votes as opposed to 38.3 per cent for *Sajudis* leader Vytautas Lansbergis.

Lithuania: economic

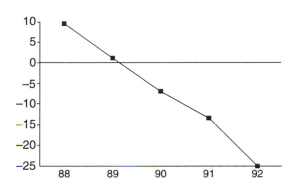

Figure 256 Change in GDP, 1988–92 (%)

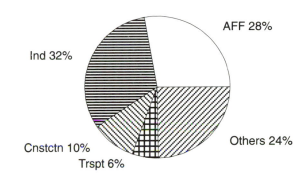

Figure 258 Origins of GDP, 1990

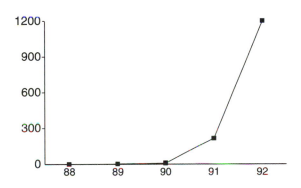

Figure 257 Consumer price inflation, 1988–92 (%)

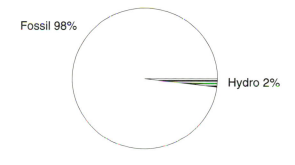

Figure 259 Source of generated power, 1990

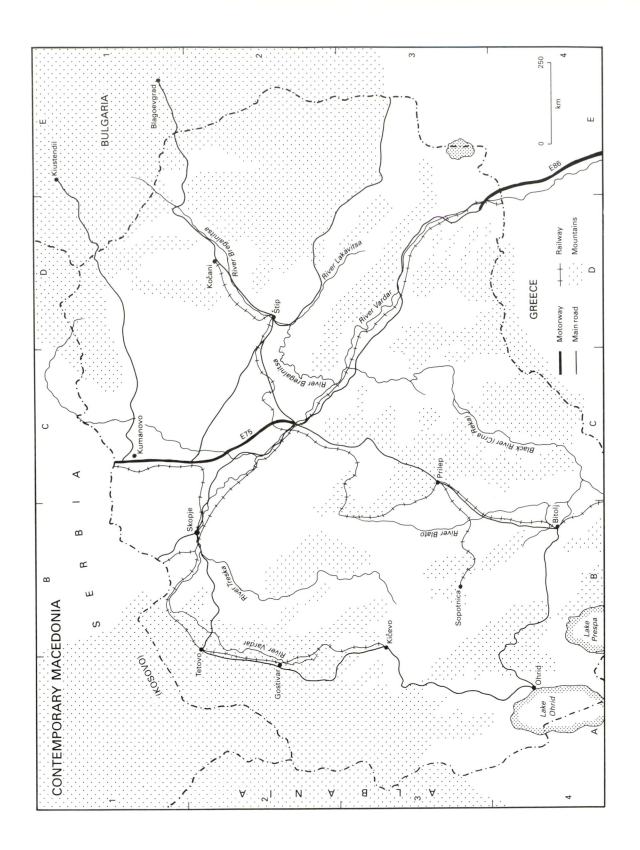

CONTEMPORARY MACEDONIA

Macedonia: basic data

Official name:	Republic of Macedonia, though Greece refuses to recognise this name; also used: the Former Yugoslav Republic of Macedonia (FYROM)
Area:	25,713 sq km
Population:	2,063,000 (1993)
Population density:	80.2 per sq km (1993)
Ethnic composition:	Macedonian 64.6 per cent; Albanian 21.0 per cent; Turkish 4.8 per cent; Romanian (Vlach) 2.7 per cent; Serb 2.2 per cent; Others 4.7 per cent (1991)
Official language:	Macedonian
Official religion:	None
Religious affiliation:	No figures available but most believers are Christians, the majority of them Orthodox. The Macedonian Orthodox Church is not recognised by other Churches of the Orthodox community. There are also substantial Muslim and Jewish communities
Capital:	Skopje 563,301 (1991)
Major cities:	Tetovo 181,654; Kumanovo 135,529; Bitolj 122,173 (1991)

Contemporary Macedonia

Early in 1990 there were clear signs of a burgeoning independence movement in Macedonia. It was not until 1991, however, that the separatist movement gathered real strength. On 25 January the Macedonian assembly passed a unanimous resolution calling for federal restructuring and declaring the assembly itself the sovereign power in Macedonia. In June the assembly renamed the republic, dropping the word 'socialist' from the title and abrogated to itself more of Belgrade's powers, including that of regulating the Macedonian balance of payments. On 4 August, when the Yugoslav National Army was used against the breakaway republic of Slovenia, Macedonia declared a state of emergency and on 23 August a draft new constitution was introduced which increased local rights almost to the point of independence. On 8 September 95 per cent of those who voted in a referendum held that day were in favour of a sovereign Macedonia with a right to *enter* a union of sovereign Yugoslav states. The constitution was adopted after a stormy debate on 17 November.

By then Croatia and Slovenia had been widely recognised as independent states and on 24 December Macedonia approached the European Union with a request for similar status. On 26 December the new constitution was amended to conform with the EU's guidelines for recognition.

Recognition by the EU was not granted because Greece objected to the use of the name 'Macedonia' which is also the name of a northern Greek province. This, the Greeks insisted, implied a claim upon Greek territory. The Macedonians amended their constitution yet again this time to emphasise that they had no territorial claims upon nor would they interfere in the internal affairs of any other state. The Greeks were not mollified and they were soon objecting to the use on the Macedonian flag of the sixteen-point star of Vergina which they saw as a Greek national symbol.

Macedonia did not remain entirely unrecognised. The first to accept it, in January 1992, had been Bulgaria which recognised the Macedonian state but not the Macedonian nation. Turkey granted recognition without conditions in Feb-

257

ruary, the other successor states of Yugoslavia did so in the spring, as did Russia in August. Greece was becoming increasingly isolated, the more so in November when the United Nations admitted Macedonia under the name of the Former Yugoslav Republic of Macedonia (FYROM). The UN sponsored talks to find a solution and in December the Security Council agreed to send a force of 700 troops to Macedonia to prevent incursions across the new state's borders.

In the first half of 1993 there seemed hope that relaxation of the tension would come about. A Greek blockade imposed in August 1992 was lifted and prime minister Mitsotakis said he would accept the title FYROM under certain conditions. After the October 1993 elections in Greece his successor as prime minister, PASOK leader Andreas Papandreou, was much less accommodating. He suspended the UN-sponsored talks and on 17 February 1994 reimposed the blockade. A few days earlier, on 9 February, the United States had recognised Macedonia.

Macedonia's difficulties are compounded by the fact that it does not enjoy great internal cohesion. The major division is between the Macedonian Slavs and the Albanians. The exact number of the latter is not known but is at least 30 per cent of the total population and some estimates say more. The areas centred on Tetovo in the north-west of the country are predominantly Albanian, but Albanians are to be found in large numbers in all cities, including Skopje. They have consistently demanded territorial and political autonomy and have boycotted referenda such as that of 6 September 1991.

Macedonia: political

Elections were held in Macedonia in November–December 1990 under a multi-party vote for a 120-member unicameral legislature. The results are shown in Table 18.

Table 18 Election results, November–December 1990

Internal Macedonian Revolutionary Organisation/Democratic Party for Macedonian National Unity	37
Macedonian League of Communists	31
Party for Democratic Prosperity and National Democratic Party	25
Alliance of Reform Forces	18
Socialist Party	4
Party of Yugoslavs	1
Independents	3
Seats vacant	1

The campaign was characterised by considerable tension between the Macedonians and the Albanians and after the results had been declared the Macedonians accused the Albanians of multiple voting on a massive scale. Evidence of fraud was discovered in over a quarter of the constituencies (33) but not all of these were in predominantly Albanian areas.

The Party for Democratic Prosperity (PDP) and the National Democratic Party (NDP) were separate parties but both represented Albanian interests and cooperated in the campaign.

After the elections the League of Communists reorganised itself and with a number of other small leftist groups formed the Social Democratic Alliance of Macedonia.

The Albanian question dominated much of internal political life after the secession from Yugoslavia. On 6 November 1992 three Albanians, and one Macedonian, were killed when police in Skopje fired on rioters who were complaining of increased food prices. Almost a year later the Macedonian authorities claimed that they had discovered a plot to overthrow the government by an 'All Albanian Army'; a former leader of the Party of Democratic Prosperity was arrested. There seemed little real danger of such an eventuality. The Albanians were not well-organised and their strongest political body, the PDP, split in February 1994.

The real danger for the weak government in Skopje lay in the contiguity of the compact areas of Albanian population along the borders with Kosovo. Albanian leaders in Macedonia have been open in their statements that they would assist their co-nationals in Kosovo if the Serbs took further strong measures against them. To prevent such an outcome is one of the responsi-bilities of the 700-strong force which the United Nations agreed in December 1993 to dispatch to guard Macedonia's borders.

Macedonia: economic

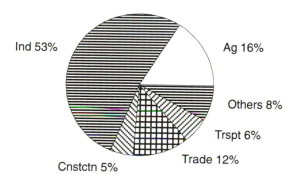

Figure 260 Population by economic sector, 1990

Figure 261 Source of generated power, 1990

Moldova: basic data

Official name:	Republic of Moldova
Area:	33,700 sq km
Population:	4,362,000 (1993)
Population density:	129.4 per sq km (1993)
Ethnic composition:	Moldovan 64.5 per cent; Ukrainian 13.8 per cent; Russian 13.0 per cent; Gagauze 3.5 per cent; Jewish 2 per cent; Bulgarian 1.5 per cent; Others 1.7 per cent (1989)

Official language:	Romanian
Official religion:	None
Religious affiliation:	No figures available but most of those claiming a religious affiliation are Orthodox Christians who belong to the Moldovan Orthodox Church (1989)
Capital:	Chişinău 753,500 (1991)
Major cities:	Tiraspol 186,000; Balţi 164,900; Tighina 141,500 (1991)

Contemporary Moldova

With the failure of the August 1991 coup in Moscow the Romanians of the Soviet Republic of Moldavia declared their independence (27 August), banned the Moldavian Communist Party, and adopted the Romanian name, Moldova, for their country. A referendum in December 1991 approved the declaration of independence. At the same time Mircea Snegur,

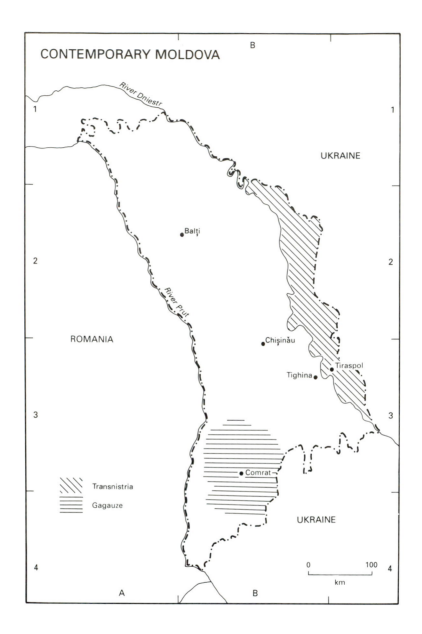

CONTEMPORARY MOLDOVA

Transnistria

Gagauze

a former communist leader, was elected president. The president is the most powerful figure in the country. The assembly, elected in March 1994, is dominated by the Agrarian Democratic Party which won 43.2 per cent of the votes and, after the redistribution of votes, fifty-six (53.85 per cent) of the 104 seats. The pro-Russian Socialist Party and Unity Movement Bloc received 22 per cent of the vote and twenty-eight (26.92 per cent) of the seats.

From the beginning Moldova was dominated by minority problems. The Russians who formed a majority in the 'Transnistria' region held their own referendum in December 1991 which the authorities in Chişinău declared illegal. Violence flared, which in the summer of 1992 reached substantial proportions and resulted in the Russian 14th Army under General Aleksandr Lebed occupying Transnistria. The area has in effect operated as an independent entity ever since and has stressed its strong affiliation with Russia and with the Soviet past. It has resisted, for example, the introduction of the Latin script and any education in Romanian, and it retains many of the symbols and the practices of the pre-1991 system.

In the Gagauze (Turkish-speaking Christian) areas there has been little conflict and the Moldovan government, unable to afford any further minority disputes, has granted the Gagauze considerable freedom of operation. A plan introduced in the summer of 1994 to allow the area autonomy was in fact criticised by the Council of Europe for going too far.

The majority of the population of Moldova is ethnically Romanian, but although some political groupings advocate union with Romania their strength has declined rather than increased. In the summer of 1994 Moldova abolished the Romanian national anthem which until then it had also used, and there were sharp exchanges of words between the Moldovan and Romanian capitals. Chişinău would prefer a closer relationship with Russia, not least to contain the dangers from Transnistria, but even if President Yeltsin agrees he has so far shown no sign of being able to control General Lebed.

Moldova: economic

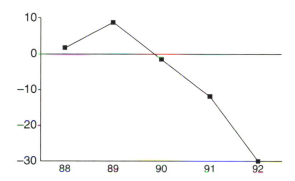

Figure 262 Change in NMP, 1988–92 (%)

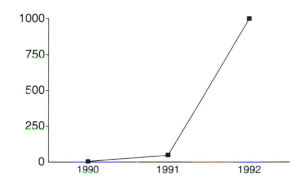

Figure 264 Consumer price inflation (%)

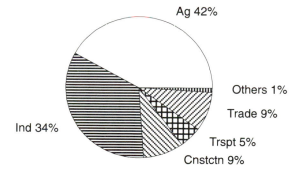

Figure 263 Origins of GDP, 1990

Poland: basic data

Official name:	Republic of Poland	Official religion:	None
Area:	312,683 sq km	Religious affiliation:	Roman Catholic 93.5 per cent; Others 6.5 per cent (1992)
Population:	38,521,000 (1993)		
Population density:	123.2 per sq km (1993)		
Ethnic composition:	Polish 98.7 per cent; Ukrainian 0.6 per cent; Others 0.7 per cent (1990)	Capital:	Warsaw 1,644,500 (1992)
		Major cities:	Łódź 838,400; Cracow 744,000; Wrocław 640,700; Poznań 582,900; Gdańsk 461,700 (1992)
Official language:	Polish		

Polish election results, 1991 and 1993

Poland's first fully free and open national elections were held on 27 October 1991 when voters elected a new 460-strong lower house (*Sejm*) and a Senate of 100 members.

In what seemed reminiscent of the early 1920s the voting system was complex and the parties numerous. In the *Sejm* 391 seats were to be decided by proportional representation in thirty-seven large electoral districts; candidates on the same party list were to be ranked according to the votes cast for them individually. The remaining sixty-nine seats were allocated according to the votes cast for national party lists. Parties could qualify to contest the election if they collected a set number of signatures of support; twenty-seven did so. Seats for the Senate were taken from forty-seven two-member constituencies, plus three from the Warsaw and three from the Katowice areas. The turnout was low, only 43 per cent, and no single party gained more than 13 per cent of the vote. The result was a large number of parties in parliament, none of which had anywhere near enough deputies to form an administration.

There was little surprise in the relatively strong showing of the Democratic Union (DU), the successor political organisation to Solidarity. That the Democratic Left Alliance (DLA), an association of former communists, won almost as many seats was not, however, expected. There

was considerable support for extreme parties such as the nationalist Confederation for an Independent Poland (CIP) or the bizarre such as the Beer Lovers' Party (BLP) which was led by a comedian. The Catholic Church exercised considerable influence by endorsing candidates who espoused what it saw as 'Christian' values.

The fragmented legislature inevitably produced political instability and after the defeat of Hanna Suchocka's government in May 1993 new elections were called. They took place on 19 September. Alterations to the electoral law now required all parties, except those representing national minorities, to secure 5 per cent of the vote if they were to be represented in the *Sejm*; for electoral alliances or blocs the threshold was 8 per cent. Any party receiving more than 7 per cent of the vote was awarded extra seats. Only six parties and alliances were represented in the new assembly compared to twenty-nine in the previous one; many parties, particularly on the right, failed to pass the threshold and no fewer than 35 per cent of the votes vast in the election went to parties which did not gain representation in parliament. The turnout was 52 per cent.

The election showed a distinct shift to the former political establishment, the two leading parties – the DLA and the Polish Peasant Party-Programmatic Alliance (PPP) – both having been part of the previous communist-dominated

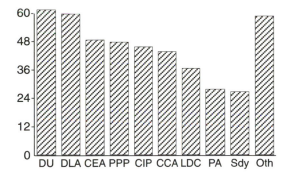

Figure 265 Sejm, Oct. 1991 (seats won)

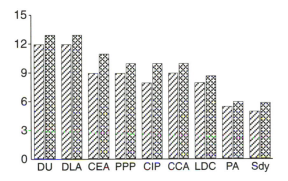

Figure 266 Sejm, Oct. 1991 (% votes and seats)

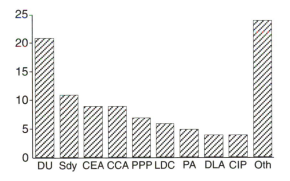

Figure 267 Senate, Oct. 1991 (seats won)

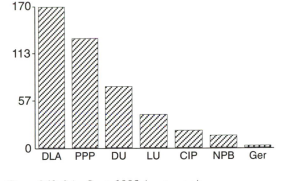

Figure 268 Sejm, Sept. 1993 (seats won)

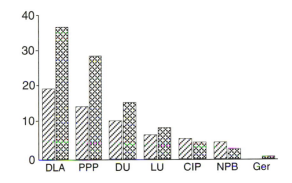

Figure 269 Sejm, Sept. 1993 (% votes and seats)

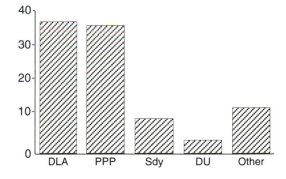

Figure 270 Senate, Sept. 1993 (seats won)

Polish United Workers' Party. The strong performance of the left and the weakness of the right had two main causes: the strains of the economic transformation, even though Poland had done better in this respect than any other East European state; and the close association of the right with the Catholic Church and with legislation such as the anti-abortion law adopted in January 1993.

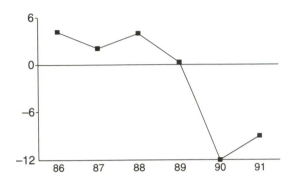

Figure 271 Change in GDP, 1986–91 (%)

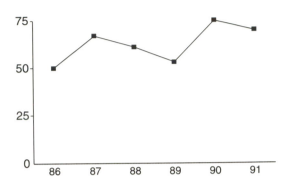

Figure 274 External debt as percentage of GDP, 1986–91

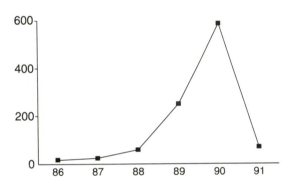

Figure 272 Consumer price inflation, 1986–91 (%)

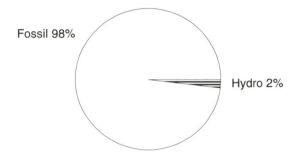

Figure 275 Source of generated power, 1990

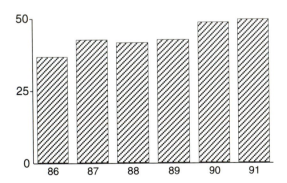

Figure 273 Total external debt, 1986–91 ($bn)

Romania: basic data

Official name:	Romania
Area:	237,500 sq km
Population:	22,789,000 (1993)
Population density:	95.6 per sq km (1993)
Ethnic composition:	Romanians 89.4 per cent; Magyars 7.1 per cent; Gypsy 1.8 per cent; German 0.5 per cent; Ukrainian 0.3 per cent; Jews 0.1 per cent; Other 0.8 per cent (1992)
Official language:	Romanian
Official religion:	None
Religious affiliation:	Romanian Orthodox Church 86.8 per cent; Roman Catholic 5.0 per cent; Greek Orthodox 3.5 per cent; Pentacostal 1.0 per cent; Muslim 0.2 per cent; Other 3.5 per cent (1992)
Capital:	Bucharest 2,064,474 (1992)
Major cities:	Constanţa 350,476; Iaşi 342,994; Timişoara 334,278; Cluj 328,008 (1992)

Romanian election results, 1990 and 1992

The first post-revolutionary Romanian presidential and parliamentary elections were held on 22 May 1990. The turnout was 86 per cent.

The three presidential candidates stood on party tickets. Ion Iliescu was leader of the NSF (National Salvation Front), which had taken power after the overthrow of Ceauşescu in December 1989. The other two candidates represented historic parties, (that is, ones which had participated in Romanian politics before the advent of the communists): Radu Campeanu was leader of the NLP (National Liberal Party), and Ion Raţiu of the NPP (National Peasant Party), an alliance of the Christian Democratic and National Peasant Parties.

Regulation of the elections for the Assembly, or Chamber of Deputies, and the Senate had been set out in a decree of March 1990 by which the country was divided into forty-two electoral districts. Proportional representation was to be used with seats being allocated according to the votes cast for party lists in each constituency. The NLP and the NPP attacked the NSF and argued for more rapid and more extensive economic reform and closer ties with the west.

The massive victory of the NSF in all three polls owed something to electoral management and government interference, but the result, in general, was held to be a reflection of popular opinion. The opposition parties were weakened by their very number – seventy-three had entered the party lists – and by inexperienced and often divided leaderships. The only exception to this was the DUR (Hungarian Democratic Union for Romania) for which nearly all Magyars voted.

For the second triple elections, held on 27 September 1992, the number of presidential candidates had increased but the number of parties contesting seats in parliament had declined. Iliescu had retained a commanding position, although the NSF had split earlier in the year, the majority forming the Democratic National Salvation Front (DNSF). Of the other candidates Emil Constantinescu was a respected academic but a political naive; Gheorghe Funar had made his reputation as the hard-hitting nationalist mayor of Cluj; Caius Dragomir had been chosen to represent the NSF because its most prominent figure, former prime minister Petre Roman, declined to stand; Ion Manzatu had previous associations with the Ceauşescu

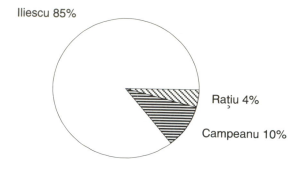

Figure 276 Presidential election, 1990

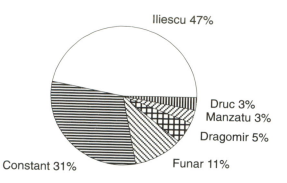

Figure 279 Presidential election, 1992

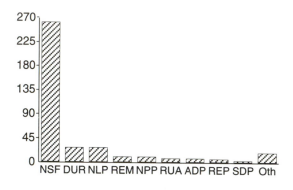

Figure 277 Assembly, 1990 (seats won)

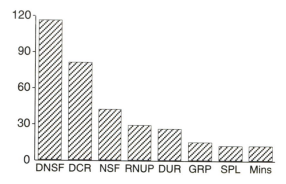

Figure 280 Assembly, 1992 (seats won)

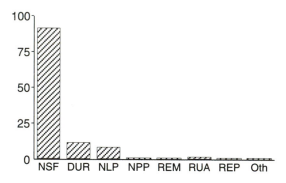

Figure 278 Senate, 1990 (seats won)

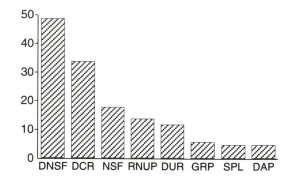

Figure 281 Senate, 1992 (seats won)

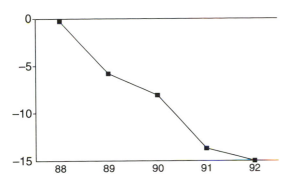

Figure 282 Change in GDP, 1988–92 (%)

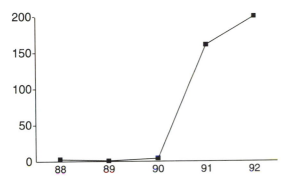

Figure 283 Retail price inflation, 1988–92 (%)

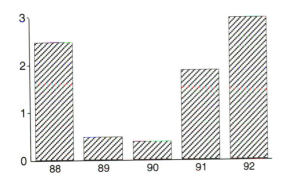

Figure 284 Gross external debt, 1988–92 ($bn)

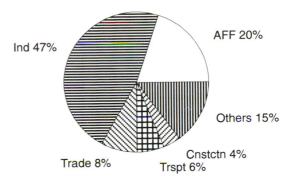

Figure 285 Origins of GDP, 1991

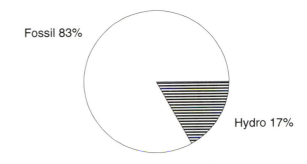

Figure 286 Source of generated power, 1990

267

regime and was in favour of slow and restricted reform; whilst the independent Mircea Druc, who hailed from Moldavia, advocated only one policy item: the unification of Moldova with Romania.

For the elections to the Chamber of Deputies and the Senate there had been some changes in the number of seats allocated to each constituency with the result that the assembly now had 328 rather than 387 members and the Senate 143 rather than 119. The lower house was also to have thirteen nominated deputies, one each for thirteen non-Magyar minority groups.

Proportional representation was again to be used but this time there was a threshold for the Chamber of Deputies of 3 per cent for an individual party; for blocs or alliances of parties the threshold was to increase by 1 per cent for each constituent party up to a maximum of 8 per cent.

Iliescu's DNSF again dominated the elections but its victory was not as sweeping as that of the NSF two years previously. The 1992 elections showed a decline in the 'green' vote and a substantial increase in the strength of the Romanian nationalist parties.

Romania: economic

Romania's post-communist leaders trod cautiously into the field of economic restructuring. They were determined not to unleash a flood of social problems, not least because in extreme circumstances those leaders chose to rely, literally, on the muscle of the traditional working class for the preservation of their authority.

Nevertheless, changes in the political order produced tension because they were not accompanied by concurrent restructuring of the economy. By the end of 1992 the foreign debt, reduced with brutal consequences by the Ceauşescu regime, stood at $3.2 billion, double its 1991 level. The government claimed that this borrowing consisted of loans from international lenders to finance market economy reforms. Others, however, argued that nearly 66 per cent of this new debt had been contracted by the state to finance the country's negative balance of trade.

Early in 1993 prime minister Nicolae Vacariou promised to introduce a new packet of economic reforms. Those who believed that at long last Romania was to undertake serious and fundamental economic restructuring were to be disappointed. The programme, published in March, was cautious, and although it pointed to the introduction of VAT in July it also talked of combining liberalism with significant social protection. This was in some part because the Romanian leadership was still wedded to interventionist, socialist ideology, and also because Vacariou and his associates feared social unrest if overly radical measures were undertaken; they had every reason to fear such unrest given the frequency of strikes which afflicted the country in March, August and especially December.

Initial indications suggest that the reforms had a mixed effect. The decline in GDP was halted but inflation still remained above the 200 per cent level, three times higher than official forecasts for December 1993. If unemployment was lower than in some East European states this was in part because subsidies to loss-making enterprises were still being handed out with considerable liberality. The IMF expressed its concern and withheld a loan.

The private sector did expand, and according to some sources accounted for 25 per cent of GDP in 1993, but it was not helped by growing concerns over the viability of the private pyramid banking concern, Caritas. In 1994 the worst fears of many investors were realised when Caritas collapsed, depriving thousands of their savings.

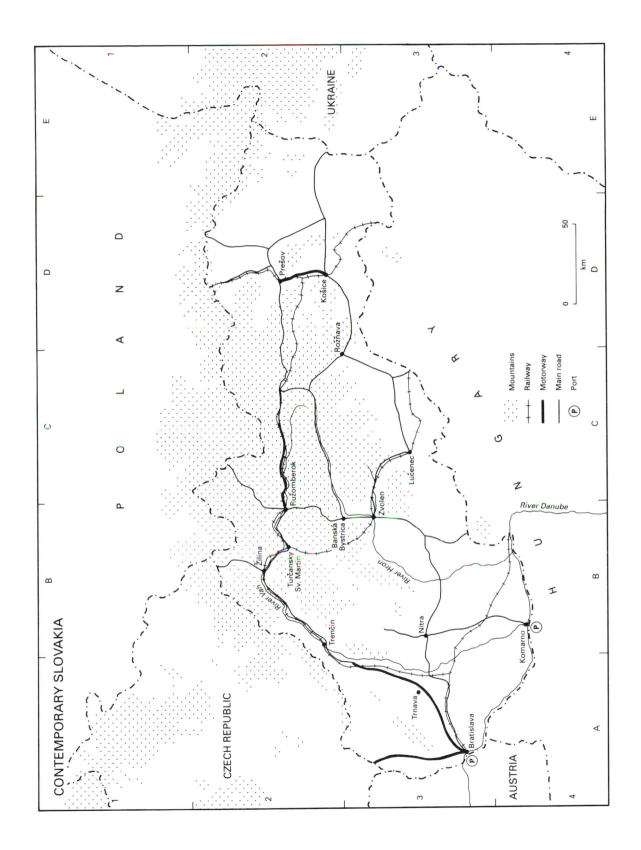

CONTEMPORARY SLOVAKIA

Slovakia: basic data

Official name:	The Slovak Republic
Area:	49,035 sq km
Population:	5,329,000 (1993)
Population density:	107.6 per sq km (1993)
Ethnic composition:	Slovaks 85.7 per cent; Magyars 10.8 per cent; Gypsy 1.4 per cent; Czechs 1.0 per cent; Ruthenian 0.3 per cent; Ukrainian 0.3 per cent; German 0.1 per cent; Moravian 0.1 per cent; Others 0.3 per cent (1991)
Official language:	Slovak
Official religion:	None
Religious affiliation:	Roman Catholic 60.3 per cent; non-religious and atheist 9.7 per cent; Slovak Evangelical Church 6.2 per cent; Reformed Christian (Protestant) 1.7 per cent; Greek Catholic (Uniate) 3.4 per cent; Eastern Orthodox 0.7 per cent; Others 18.0 per cent (1991)
Capital:	Bratislava 441,453 (1991)
Major cities:	Košice 234,840; Nitra 89,888; Prešov 87,788; Banská Bystrica 85,007 (1991)

Contemporary Slovakia (see page 269)

Slovak election results, 1990–4

Voting for the Slovak National Council took place simultaneously with that for the Czechoslovak Federal Assembly and for the Czech National Council on 8 and 9 June 1990. The Federal Assembly of the Czechoslovak Republic consisted of the House of the People and the House of Nationalities. The House of the People had forty-nine delegates from Slovakia; the House of Nationalities had seventy-five.

The electoral system was designed to ensure representation for all groups, ethnic and social. The minimum requirement for representation in the assembly was that a party should receive 5 per cent of the total vote in either the Czech lands or in Slovakia.

PAV (Public Against Violence) was the Slovak equivalent of the Czech Civic Forum (see p. 238). PAV worked in alliance with the Independent Hungarian Initiative, which naturally sought greater rights for the Hungarian minor-ity. Minority rights were also very much at the centre of the programme of the Hungarian Minority Coalition (HMC) or 'Coexistence', a grouping of Hungarian, Polish and other minority parties. The more extreme Slovaks supported the SkNP (Slovak National Party).

As in the Czech lands the CF–PAV alliance benefited from its recent record of opposition to totalitarianism and from the open support of president Vaclav Havel. Havel, however, was less popular in Slovakia where many were surprised that PAV polled more votes than the Christian Democratic Movement (CDM).

In the 1992 elections Slovak discontent with the consequences of the Czechoslovak federal government's free-market economic policies brought strong support of the Movement for a Democratic Slovakia (MDS). The Party of the Democratic Left (PDL) was the renamed Communist Party of Slovakia, although former com-

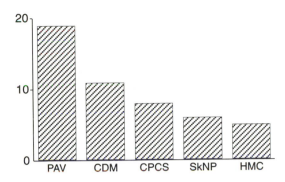

Figure 287 House of People, 1990 (seats won)

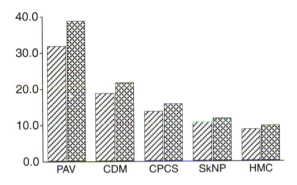

Figure 288 House of People, 1990 (% votes and seats)

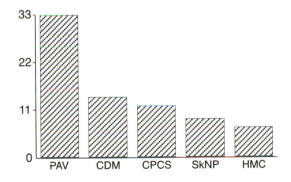

Figure 289 House of Nationalities, 1990 (seats won)

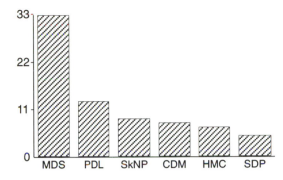

Figure 290 House of People, 1992 (seats won)

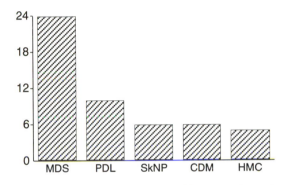

Figure 291 House of People, 1992 (% votes and seats)

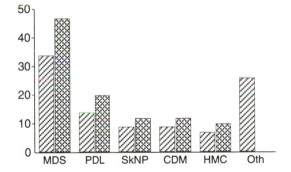

Figure 292 House of Nationalities, 1992 (seats won)

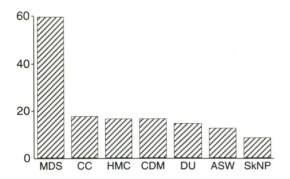

Figure 293 Parliament, 1994 (seats won)

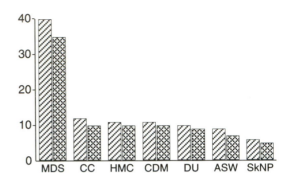

Figure 294 Parliament, 1994 (% votes and seats)

munist leader Alexander Dubček stood for the Social Democratic Party in Slovakia (SDP). The elections revealed a strong current of Slovak separatism which led to the 'velvet divorce' of Slovakia from the Czech Republic at the beginning of 1993.

On 30 September and 1 October 1994 Slovakia held its first separate elections. To secure representation in the 150-member assembly parties had to secure 5 per cent of the vote, or 7 per cent for coalitions of two or three parties and 10 per cent for those with four or more. Votes cast for parties which did not pass these hurdles were divided among the victors. The turnout was 75.65 per cent.

The elections brought about the expected victory of Vladimir Meciar's Movement for a Democratic Slovakia which was in coalition with the tiny Peasant Party. Its nearest rival was Common Choice (CC), a four-party left-wing coalition. But Meciar's support was not sufficient to secure an overall majority.

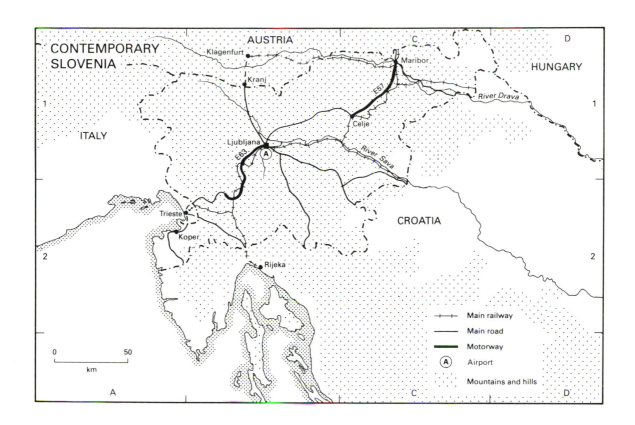

CONTEMPORARY SLOVENIA

Slovenia: basic data

Official name:	Republic of Slovenia
Area:	20,256 sq km
Population:	1,997,000 (1993)
Population density:	98.6 per sq km
Ethnic composition:	Slovene 87.8 per cent; Croat 2.8 per cent; Serb 2.4 per cent; Bosnian 1.4 per cent; Magyar 0.4 per cent; Others 5.2 per cent (1991)
Official language:	Slovene
Official religion:	None
Religious affiliation:	Precise figures are unavailable, but the great majority of the believers are Roman Catholics. There are small communities of the Slovene Old Catholic Church, some Protestant Churches, some Orthodox Christians and small Jewish and Muslim communities
Capital:	Ljubljana 276,133 (1991)
Major cities:	Maribor 108,122 (1991)

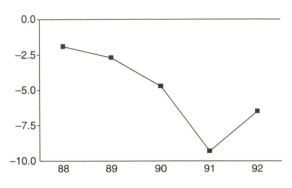

Figure 295 Change in GDP, 1988–92 (%)

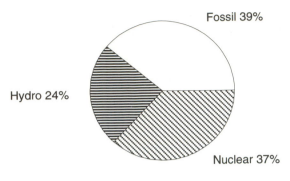

Figure 297 Source of generated power, 1990

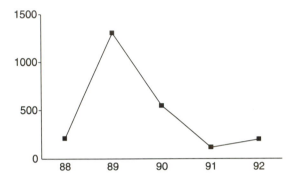

Figure 296 Retail price inflation, 1988–92 (%)

Contemporary Slovenia

Slovenia is one of the very few of the new states in Eastern Europe which has virtually no previous experience of independent or separate statehood. Nevertheless, it seems to have established itself at least as well as any of the successor states of Yugoslavia.

It is overwhelmingly a mountainous or hilly region with few natural lines of communication beyond the rivers Sava and Drava. In fact, Slovenia has for long relied more on man-made means of communication and these, in stark contrast to the rivers, run to the north towards Austria or east–west across the country. Its main

natural ports, Trieste and Rijeka, are both beyond its borders, a fact which intensifies its links with Austria to the north and, to a lesser degree, with Hungary to the east.

The first years of independence involved considerable economic upheaval. In 1990 the 17 million inhabitants of the rest of Yugoslavia had bought 35 per cent of Slovenia's exports. That market was lost. By mid-1993 half of Slovenia's 23,300 companies, which employed more than 486,000 workers, were on the brink of collapse. Unemployment had risen from 2 per cent (1988) to 14 per cent.

Slovene election results, 1992

Slovenia's first presidential and parliamentary elections after independence in 1991 were held on 6 December 1992. The turnout was 76 per cent.

In the vote for the presidency the clear favourite was the incumbent, Milan Kučan, a former communist who was now running as an independent. The other main candidates all had party affiliations. Ivo Bizjak stood on the ticket of the Christian Democratic Party (SKD), and Jelko Kacin on that of the Democratic Party (DS). There were four other candidates, although the constitution of December 1991 invested the president with little beyond symbolic powers.

The same constitutional reform abolished the Chamber of Associated Labour, thus making the Slovene legislature bicameral rather than tri-cameral. The lower house, the Chamber of Deputies, consisted of ninety members serving a four-year term of office. Two of the deputies were reserved for one representative each of the Italian and Magyar minorities, these deputies being appointed rather than elected. Of the remainder forty were chosen on the direct majority principle, the others being elected by a system of proportional representation which redistributed unused votes to those parties – and there were eight of them – which gained more than the 3 per cent of the total vote necessary to secure a seat in the assembly. The State Council consisted of forty members. Of these twenty-two were directly elected on 6 December. The remaining eighteen were appointed on 10 December to represent professional and other interest groups, an electoral college of the partic-ular interest group being made responsible for the selection.

In all some twenty-five parties contested the election. The Liberal Democratic Party (LDS) had its roots in the former socialist youth organi-sation and was led by the prime minister, Janez Drnovšek. Of the other parties the SKD and the Slovene People's Party (SLS) represented a con-tinuation of the historic influence of the Roman Catholic Church in Slovene politics, whilst the Associated List (AL) harboured some former communists. Very much at the opposite end of the political spectrum was the Slovene National Party (SNS) which espoused a xenophobic form of extreme nationalism; it was led by Zmago Jelinčić.

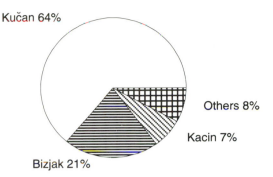

Figure 298 Presidential election, Dec. 1992

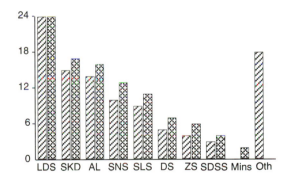

Figure 299 Parliamentary election 1992 (seats won)

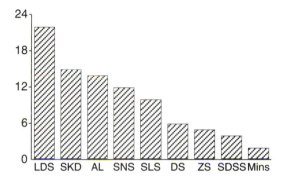

Figure 300 Parliamentary election, 1992 (% votes and seats)

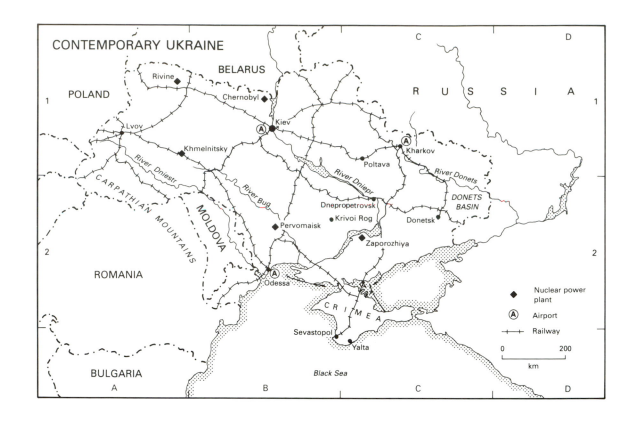

CONTEMPORARY UKRAINE

Ukraine: basic data

Official name: Ukraine
Area: 603,700 sq km
Population: 52,344,000 (1993)
Population density: 86.7 per sq km (1993)
Ethnic composition: Ukrainian 72.7 per cent;
Russian 22.1 per cent;
Jewish 0.9 per cent;
Belorussian 0.9 per cent;
Moldovan 0.6 per cent;
Bulgarian 0.5 per cent;
Polish 0.4 per cent;
Others 1.9 per cent
(1989)
Official language: The Ukrainian language
has state status. This
differs from official in that
it applies to the entire
country, while official
status refers only to
regions which are in
favour of second language
functioning alongside
Ukrainian

Official religion: None
Religious affiliation: Most professing
Christians are Ukrainian
Orthodox though there is
a Catholic minority. In the
western Ukraine there are
large numbers of Uniates,
or Greek-rite Catholics
Capital: Kiev 2,651,300 (1992)
Major cities: Kharkov 1,622,000;
Dnepropetrovsk
1,190,000; Donetsk
1,121,000; Odessa
1,096,000 (1992)

Contemporary Ukraine

Ukraine entered upon its renewed independence with as little prospect of healthy statehood as in 1918 (see p. 35). There were deep divisions between the west and the east. The former is more rural, has a high proportion of Uniates, and is nationalist; the centre and east are more industrialised, Orthodox, and show, especially in the east and south, more enthusiasm for renewed association with Russia. But even in the east there are divisions within the Orthodox community, who have no less than three separate churches.

The Crimea, made a part of Ukraine in 1954, has a predominantly Russian population and in a referendum in late 1993 elected a secessionist president.

Economic reform has been given only low priority by the Ukrainian government. There has been little if any progress towards privatisation and the market economy. Inflation rages almost unchecked and in late 1993 there were rumours that a state of emergency was to be declared with the object of re-introducing price regulation, nationalising commercial banks, and reimposing state control over production; one reformer confessed to fearing not 'south Americanisation' but 'Africanisation'.

There are continuing problems over nuclear issues. In the spring and summer of 1993 there were a series of incidents at the Zaporozhiya atomic power station, the largest in Europe. Chernobyl, too, continued to pose problems. Despite public sensitivity to nuclear dangers after the Chernobyl incident of April 1986, a strong pro-nuclear lobby has emerged in Ukraine, its main argument being that nuclear energy alone can release the country from dependence on increasingly expensive Russian oil and gas. Meanwhile, the Ukrainian government refused to return nuclear warheads to Russia until agreement over other issues, despite Russian complaints that SS-24 warheads stored in Pervomaisk were in a dangerous condition.

Ukraine: election results, 1994

The first round of the Ukrainian parliamentary elections on 27 March 1994 produced a turnout of 74.7 per cent, but only 49 of the 450 seats were decided. The remainder, fought between the two top candidates in the first round, were settled by voting on 2–3 and 9–10 April. Only about a quarter of the 5,833 candidates declared which party they were standing for, but the final results showed the most popular groups were the communists and the independents. The communists dominated the left, holding 86 of the total of 118 seats; the others were taken by the Peasants' Party (18 seats) and the Socialist Party (14 seats). The independents numbered 112. The centre groups were strong in their advocacy of economic reform and suffered accordingly, winning only 17 places in parliament. The moderate nationalists, who won 35 seats, included *Rukh* (20 seats), the Ukrainian Republican Party (8 seats), the Congress of Ukrainian Nationalists (5 seats) and the Democratic Party of Ukraine (2 seats).

On 27 March there were also virtual referenda in Donetsk, Lugansk and the Crimea. In all three

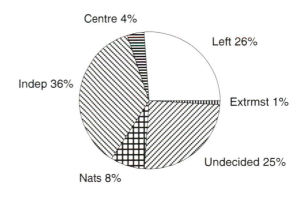

Figure 301 Ukrainian elections, 1994 (share of vote)

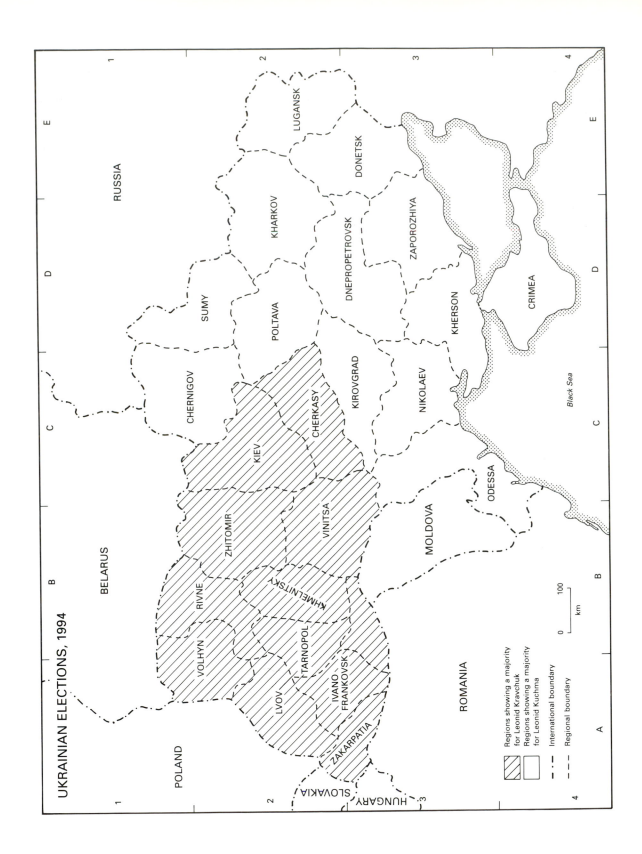

UKRAINIAN ELECTIONS, 1994

Regions showing a majority for Leonid Kravchuk

Regions showing a majority for Leonid Kuchma

International boundary

Regional boundary

POLAND

BELARUS

RUSSIA

VOLHYN

RIVNE

ZHITOMIR

KIEV

CHERNIGOV

SUMY

KHARKOV

LUGANSK

DONETSK

DNEPROPETROVSK

ZAPOROZHIYA

POLTAVA

CHERKASY

KIROVGRAD

VINITSA

KHMELNITSKY

TARNOPOL

LVOV

IVANO-FRANKOVSK

ZAKARPATIA

SLOVAKIA

HUNGARY

ROMANIA

MOLDOVA

ODESSA

NIKOLAEV

KHERSON

CRIMEA

Black Sea

100

km

0

a substantial majority expressed themselves in favour of closer ties with Russia, and in the Crimea there was also massive support for more autonomy from Kiev.

Observers from the UN and the CSCE criticised the elections as being inefficiently organised and unfair, especially in rural constituencies.

There were also two rounds of voting in the Ukrainian presidential elections of 1994. In the first, held on 26 June, five candidates were eliminated, leaving Leonid Kravchuk and Leonid Kuchma to fight the second round on 10 July. In the first round Kravchuk won 37.7 per cent of the vote and Kuchma 31.3 per cent. Even more so than in the parliamentary elections, regional factors were powerful. In the eastern regions, with their large Russian populations, particularly in the cities, there was strong support for Kuchma who was believed to be more pro-Russian than his rival. In the western areas Ukrainian nationalist sentiments were stronger, especially in areas where the Uniate Church was dominant; in Lvov, for example, only 3.9 per cent of those who voted preferred Kuchma to Kravchuk.

Ukraine: economic

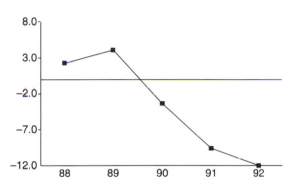

Figure 302 Change in NMP, 1988–92 (%)

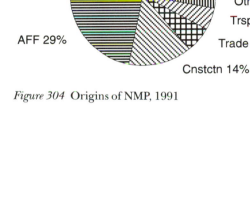

Figure 304 Origins of NMP, 1991

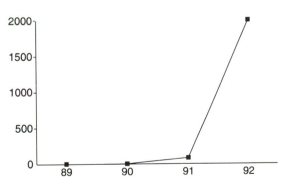

Figure 303 Consumer price inflation, 1989–92 (%)

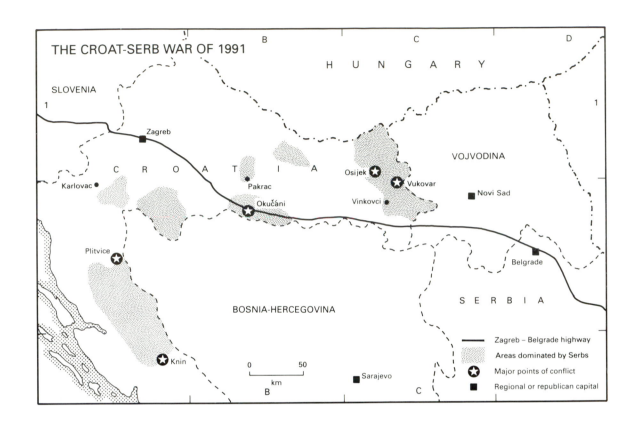

THE CROAT-SERB WAR OF 1991

The wars of Yugoslav succession

On 21 February 1991 the Croatian parliament adopted a law giving its legislation priority over that passed in the Federal Yugoslav assembly. The Serbs in Croatia took alarm and in March fighting began in Pakrac which continued until May. At that stage the Yugoslav National Army (JNA) intervened, ostensibly to separate the two sides, but Croats feared its intervention as being pro-Serb. On 12 May Serbs in the Krajina region between Knin and Plitvica held a referendum after which they declared an autonomous region of the Serbian Krajina. Another referendum, on 19 May, organised this time by the Croats, showed 93 per cent of those who voted were in favour of a 'sovereign and independent' Croatia.

On 25 and 26 June, respectively, Slovenia and Croatia declared full independence. The JNA moved into Slovenia to secure, it said, Yugoslavia's international borders, but its action was seen as an attempt to suppress secessionism. The Slovenes resisted and the JNA, after suffering embarrassing losses through desertion and capture, withdrew from Slovenia but then moved into Croatia which was less well prepared to defend itself. JNA garrisons in Zagreb were besieged, as was the eastern Croatian town of Vukovar which, when it fell to the Serb/JNA forces in November, had been almost completely destroyed. Further heavy fighting occurred in and around Osijek and on the edges of the Krajina. In the villages the local extremists indulged in what was to become known as 'ethnic cleansing'.

'Rump' Yugoslavia since 1991

The secession of Slovenia, Croatia, Bosnia-Hercegovina and Macedonia in the summer of 1991 left only Serbia and Montenegro within the Federal Republic of Yugoslavia.

The first elections for the truncated federal institutions were held on 31 May 1992. The federal assembly consisted of two houses. The Chamber of Citizens had 108 deputies from Serbia and thirty from Montenegro. Half of the Serbian deputies were elected by a majority system within constituencies, the remainder being chosen by proportional representation based on party lists. In Montenegro only six deputies were selected on the majority system and twenty-four by proportional representation. The Chamber of the Republics consisted of forty deputies, coming equally from Serbia and Montenegro. They were chosen by the individual republican assemblies in Serbia and Montenegro in proportion to the parties represented therein. Elections to these assemblies were held on the same day as the general election. In the predominantly Albanian region of Kosovo a constituent Republican Assembly was elected which the Serbian authorities then declared illegal.

The dominance of the Socialist Party of Serbia (SPS), the former Serbian League of Communists led by Slobodan Milošević, was in part the result of the main opposition groups' decision to boycott the poll.

The assemblies had been elected for a four-year term but fresh elections were held on 20 December 1992. The SPS lost ground but the advance of the more extreme Serbian Radical Party (SRP) under Vojislav Šešelj indicated that the fires of Serbian nationalism were by no means burnt out. The main opposition force was Depos, a coalition of fourteen parties formed in late May, which had now decided to contest the election. In Montenegro the former communists, now the Democratic Party of Socialists in Montenegro (DPSM), remained the dominant force although they lost almost a quarter of their seats.

In terms of power the most important vote held on 20 December was that for the presidency of the Serb Republic. The main opponent of Milošević was Milan Panić, a businessman who had spent much of his life in exile in North America. The SPS attempted to have his candidature declared illegal on the grounds that he did not meet the necessary residency qualifications, but in this they were overruled by the Supreme Court. There were five other candidates. After securing only 34 per cent of the vote Panić claimed that there had been widespread fraud and that new elections must be held. His claim was supported by foreign observers who reported that 5 per cent of the electorate had been prevented from casting their votes. The turnout was 67 per cent.

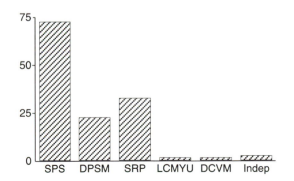

Figure 305 Federal Assembly, May 1992 (seats won)

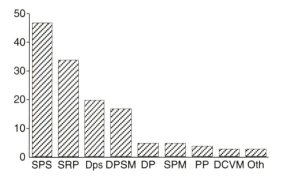

Figure 306 Federal Assembly, Dec. 1992 (seats won)

GLOSSARY OF TOPOGRAPHICAL NAMES

Key to glossary

Alb	Albanian	Lat	Latvian
Bul	Bulgarian	Lith	Lithuanian
Cmst	Communist	Mcd	Macedonian
Ct	Croatian	Pol	Polish
Cz	Czech	Rom	Romanian
Eng	English	Rus	Russian
Est	Estonian	Sb	Serbian
Fr	French	Slvn	Slovene
Ger	German	Svk	Slovak
Gk	Greek	Ts	Turkish
Hun	Hungarian	Ukn	Ukrainian
It	Italian		

Aa (Ger) Gauja (Lat)

Abrehenen (Ger) Abrene (Lat) Pytalovo (Rus)

Abrene (Lat) Pytalovo (Rus) Abrehenen (Ger)

Adrianople (Eng) Edirne (Ts) Odrin (Bul)

Agram (Ger) Zagreb (Sb,Ct) Zágráb (Hun)

Agyrokastron (Gk) Gyrokastër (Alb)

Alba Iulia (Rom) Gyulafehévár (Hun) Weissenburg (Ger)

Alexandroupolis (Gk) Dedeagach (Ts)

Allenstein (Ger) Olsztyn (Pol)

Altenburg (Ger) Mosonmagyaróvár (Hun)

Angerburg (Ger) Węgorzewo (Pol)

Antivari (It) Bar (Sb, Ct)

Ardeal (Rom) Transylvania (Eng) Siebenbürgen (Ger) Erdély (Hun)

Arensburg (Ger) Kuressaare (Est) Kingissepa (Est/Cmst – name given by Soviets) Yamburg (Rus)

Arnau (Ger) Hostinné (Cz)

Arnswalde (Ger) Choszczno (Pol)

Árva (Hun) Orawa (Pol) Orava (Cz) Oravsko (Svk)

Aš (Cz) Asch (Ger)

Asch (Ger) Aš (Cz)

Asmjany (Lith) Oszmiany (Pol)

Auschwitz (Ger) Oświęcim (Pol)

Babimost (Pol) Bomst (Ger)

Bad Polzin (Ger) Polczyń Zdrój (Pol)

Balázsfalva (Hun) Blasendorf (Ger) Blaj (Rom)

Banská Bystrica (Svk) Besztercze Bánya (Hun) Bistritz (Ger) Bistriţe (Rom)

Bar (Sb, Ct) Antivari (It)

Bartenstein (Ger) Bartoszyce (Pol)

Bartoszyce (Pol) Bartenstein (Ger)

Belgard (Ger) Białogard (Pol)

Bélovár-Körös (Hun) Kreutz (Ger) Bjelovar (Ct)

Benderey (Rus,Ts) Tighina (Rom)

Besztercze Bánya (Hun) Bistritz (Ger) Bistriţe (Rom) Banská Bystrica (Svk)

Beuthen (Ger) Bytom (Pol)

Białogard (Pol) Belgard (Ger)

Bílý Kostel (Cz) Weisskirchen (Ger)

Bischofsburg (Ger) Biskupiec (Pol)

Biskupiec (Pol) Bischofsburg (Ger)

Bistriţe (Rom) Banská Bystrica (Svk) Besztercze Bánya (Hun) Bistritz (Ger)

Bistritz (Ger) Bistriţe (Rom) Banská Bystrica (Svk) Besztercze Bánya (Hun)

Bitolya (Bul) Bitolj (Mcd/Sb) Monastir (Ts)

Bitolj (Mcd/Sb) Monastir (Ts) Bitolya (Bul)

Bjelovar (Ct) Bélovár-Körös (Hun) Kreutz (Ger)

Blagoevgrad (Bul/Cmst) Gorna Djumaya (Ts)

Blaj (Rom) Balázsfalva (Hun) Blasendorf (Ger)

Blasendorf (Ger) Blaj (Rom) Balázsfalva (Hun)

Bodenbach (Ger) Podmokly (Cz)

Bogatynia (Pol) Reichenau (Ger)

Böhmisch Leipa (Ger) Česká Lípa (Cz)

Bolesławiec (Pol) Bunzlau (Ger)

Bomst (Ger) Babimost (Pol)

Braniewo (Pol) Braunsberg (Ger)

Braşov (Rom) Brassó (Hun) Kronstadt (Ger)

Brassó (Hun) Kronstadt (Ger) Braşov (Rom)

Bratislava (Svk) Pressburg (Ger) Pozsony (Hun)

Braunau (Ger) Braunov (Cz)

Braunov (Cz) Braunau (Ger)

Braunsberg (Ger) Braniewo (Pol)

Breslau (Ger) Wrocław (Pol) Ventislav (Cz)

Brest-Litovsk (Rus) Brześć (Pol)

Brieg (Ger) Brzeg (Pol)

Brno (Cz) Brünn (Ger)

Bromberg (Ger) Bydgoszcz (Pol)

Brünn (Ger) Brno (Cz)

Bruntál (Cz) Freudenthal (Ger)

Brüx (Ger) Most (Cz)

Brzeg (Pol) Brieg (Ger)

Brześć (Pol) Brest-Litovsk (Rus)

Buda (Hun) Ofen (Ger)

Budweiss (Ger) České Budějovice (Cz)

Bunzlau (Ger) Bolesławiec (Pol)

Bütow (Ger) Bytów (Pol)

Bydgoszcz (Pol) Bromberg (Ger)

Bystrzyca Kłodzka (Pol) Habelschwert (Ger)

Bytom (Pol) Beuthen (Ger)

Bytów (Pol) Bütow (Ger)

Cammin (Ger) Kamień Pomorski (Pol)

Cattaro (It) Kotor (Sb, Ct)

Cerna (Cz) Schwarzbach (Ger)

Cernauţi (Rom) Czernowitz (Ger) Chernovtsy (Rus)

Cēsis (Lat) Wenden (Ger)

Česká Lípa (Cz) Böhmisch Leipa (Ger)

České Budějovice (Cz) Budweiss (Ger)

Český Krumlov (Cz) Krumau (Ger)

Cheb (Cz) Eger (Ger)

Chełm (Pol) Kholm (Rus) Khilm (Ukn)

Chemnitz (Ger) Karl-Marx-Stadt (Cmst)

Chernovtsy (Rus) Cernauţi (Rom) Czernowitz (Ger)

Chişinău (Rom) Kishinev (Rus)

Chojna (Pol) Königsberg (Ger)

Chorzów (Pol) Königshütte (Ger)

Choszczno (Pol) Arnswalde (Ger)

Chrastava (Cz) Kratzau (Ger)

Ciechanów (Pol) Zischenau (Ger)

Cieszyn (Pol) Teschen (Ger) Těšin (Cz)

Cilje (Slvn) Cilli (It)

Cilli (It) Cilje (Slvn)

Cluj (Rom) Kolozsvár (Hun) Klausenburg (Ger)

Constantinople (Eng) Istanbul (Ts) Tsarigrad (Slav)

Cosel (Ger) Koźle (Pol)

Cracovie (Fr) Krakau (Ger) Kraków (Pol) Cracow (Eng)

Cracow (Eng) Cracovie (Fr) Krakau (Ger) Kraków (Pol)

Crossen (Ger) Kosno Ordrzańskie (Pol)

Curzola (It) Korčula (Sb, Ct)

Czernowitz (Ger) Chernovtsy (Rus) Cernauţi (Rom)

Czluchów (Pol) Schlochau (Ger)

Danube (Eng) Donau (Ger) Dunava (Slav) Duna (Hun)

Danzig (Ger) Gdańsk (Pol)

Daugava (Lat) Dvina (Rus) Düna (Ger)

Daugavpils (Lat) Dünaburg (Ger) Dvinsk (Rus)

Děčín (Cz) Tetschen (Ger)

Dedeagach (Ts) Alexandroupolis (Gk)

Deutsch-Eylau (Ger) Iława (Pol)

Deutsche Krone (Ger) Walcz (Pol)

Dimitrovgrad (Cmst) Tsaribrod (Bul, Sb, Ct)

Dniestr (Rus) Nistru (Rom) [river]

Dobrich (Bul) Tolbukhin (Bul/Cmst)

Domžlice (Cz) Taus (Ger)

Donau (Ger) Dunava (Slav) Danube (Eng) Duna (Hun)

Dorpat (Ger) Tartu (Est)

Dramburg (Ger) Drawsko (Pol)

Drawsko (Pol) Dramburg (Ger)

Drohobych (Ukn) Drohobycz (Pol)

Drohobycz (Pol) Drohobych (Ukn)

Dubrovnik (Sb, Ct) Ragusa (It)

Duchcov (Cz) Dux (Ger)

Duna (Hun) Danube (Eng) Donau (Ger) Dunava (Slav)

Düna (Ger) Daugava (Lat) Dvina (Rus)

Dünaburg (Ger) Daugavpils (Lat) Dvinsk (Rus)

Dunava (Slav) Danube (Eng) Donau (Ger) Duna (Hun)

Dupnitsa (Bul) Stanke Dimitrov (Bul/Cmst)

Durazzo (It) Durrës (Alb)

Durrës (Alb) Durazzo (It)

Dux (Ger) Duchcov (Cz)

Dvina (Rus) Düna (Ger) Daugava (Lat)

Dvinsk (Rus) Daugavpils (Lat) Dünaberg (Ger)

Dvůr Králové (Cz) Königinhof (Ger)

Dyteti (Alb) Qyteti Stalin (Alb/Cmst)

Dzierzoniów (Pol) Reichenbach (Ger)

Edirne (Ts) Odrin (Bul) Adrianople (Eng)

Eger (Ger) Cheb (Cz)

Eisenbrod (Ger) Železný Brod (Cz)

Elbe (Ger) Laba (Pol)

Elbing (Ger) Elbląg (Pol)

Elbląg (Pol) Elbing (Ger)

Elbogen (Ger) Loket (Cz)

Ełk (Pol) Lyck (Ger)

Erdély (Hun) Ardeal (Rom) Transylvania (Eng) Siebenbürgen (Ger)

Eski Djumaya (Ts) Tûrgovishte (Bul)

Falkenau (Ger) Falknov (Cz)

Falkenberg (Ger) Niemodlin (Pol)

Falknov (Cz) Falkenau (Ger)

Fellinn (Ger) Viljandi (Est)

Fertö (Hun) Neusiedl (Ger)

Filibe (Ts) Plovdiv (Bul) Philipopolis (Gk)

Fischern (Ger) Rybáře (Cz)

Fiume (It) Rijeka (Sb, Ct)

Flatow (Ger) Złotów (Pol)

Frankenstein (Ger) Ząbkowice Śląskie (Pol)

Frankfurt-Ost (Ger) Słubice (Pol)

Františkovy Lázně (Cz) Franzensbad (Ger)

Franzensbad (Ger) Františkovy Lázně (Cz)

Fraustadt (Ger) Wschowa (Pol)

Freistadt (Ger) Frýdek (Cz)

Freiwaldau (Ger) Frývaldov (Cz)

Freudenthal (Ger) Bruntál (Cz)

Freystadt (Ger) Kozuchow (Pol)

Friedeberg (Ger) Frýdberk (Cz)

Friedeburg (Ger) Strzelce Krajenskie (Pol)

Friedland (Ger) Frýdlant (Cz)

Frýdberk (Cz) Friedeberg (Ger)

Frýdek (Cz) Freistadt (Ger)

Frýdlant (Cz) Friedland (Ger)

Frývaldov (Cz) Freiwaldau (Ger)

Fünfkirchen (Ger) Pécs (Hun)

Gablonz (Ger) Jablonec (Cz)

Gauja (Lat) Aa (Ger)

Gdańsk (Pol) Danzig (Ger)

Giżyoko (Pol) Lötzen (Ger)

Glatz (Ger) Kłodzko (Pol)

Gleiwitz (Ger) Gliwice (Pol)

Gliwice (Pol) Gleiwitz (Ger)

Glogau (Ger) Głogów (Pol)

Głogów (Pol) Glogau (Ger)

Głubczyce (Pol) Leobschütz (Ger)

Goldberg (Ger) Złotoryja (Pol)

Goleniów (Pol) Gollnow (Ger)

Gollnow (Ger) Goleniów (Pol)

Góra (Pol) Guhrau (Ger)

Goriska (Sb, Ct) Gorizia (It) Görz (Ger)

Gorizia (It) Görz (Ger) Goriska (Sb, Ct)

Görlitz (Ger) Zgorzelec (Pol)

Gorna Djumaya (Ts) Blagoevgrad (Bul/Cmst)

Görz (Ger) Goriska (Sb, Ct) Gorizia (It)

Gorzów Wielkopolski (Pol) Landsberg (Ger)

Gottschee (Ger) Kochevje (Ct, Sb)

Gottwaldow (Cmst) Zlin (Svk)

Graslitz (Ger) Kraslice (Cz)

Gratzen (Ger) Nové Hrady (Cz)

Greifenberg (Ger) Gryfice (Pol)

Greiffenhagen (Ger) Gryfino (Pol)

Grodków (Pol) Grottkau (Ger)

Gross-Strehlitz (Ger) Strzelce (Pol)

Gross-Wartenberg (Ger) Syców (Pol)

Grosswardein (Ger) Oradea Mare (Rom) Nagyvárad (Hun)

Grottkau (Ger) Grodków (Pol)

Grünberg (Ger) Zielona Góra (Pol)

Gryfice (Pol) Greifenberg (Ger)

Gryfino (Pol) Greiffenhagen (Ger)

Guben (Ger) Gubin (Pol)

Gubin (Pol) Guben (Ger)

Guhrau (Ger) Góra (Pol)

Györ (Hun) Raab (Ger)

Gyrokastër (Alb) Agyrokastron (Gk)

Gyulafehévár (Hun) Weissenburg (Ger) Alba Iulia (Rom)

Haapsalu (Est) Hapsal (Ger)

Habelschwert (Ger) Bystrzyca Kłodzka (Pol)

Haindorf (Ger) Hejnice (Cz)

Hapsal (Ger) Haapsalu (Est)

Heilsberg (Ger) Lidzbark (Pol)

Hejnice (Cz) Haindorf (Ger)

Hermannstadt (Ger) Sibiu (Rom) Nagyszeben (Hun)

Herrnskretchen (Ger) Hřensko (Cz)

Hindenburg (Ger) Zabrze (Pol)

Hirschberg (Ger) Jelenia Góra (Pol)

Hlučin (Cz) Hultschin (Ger)

Hohenelbe (Ger) Vrchlabí (Cz)

Hohenfurth (Ger) Vyšší Brod (Cz)

Hohensalza (Ger) Inowrocław (Pol)

Hořice (Cz) Höritz (Ger)

Höritz (Ger) Hořice (Cz)

Hostinné (Cz) Arnau (Ger)

Hradec Králové (Cz) Könniggrätz (Ger)

Hranice (Cz) Mährisch Weisskirchen (Ger)

Hřensko (Cz) Herrnskretchen (Ger)

Hultschin (Ger) Hlučin (Cz)

Iglau (Ger) Jihlava (Cz)

Iława (Pol) Deutsch-Eylau (Ger)

Inowrocław (Pol) Hohensalza (Ger)

Irzcianka (Pol) Schönlanke (Ger)

Istanbul (Ts) Tsarigrad (Slav) Constantinople (Eng)

Ivano-Frankovsk (Ukn/Cmst) Stanislaviv (Ukn) Stanisławów (Pol)

Jablonec (Cz) Gablonz (Ger)

Jáchymov (Cz) Joachimstal (Ger)

Jägerndorf (Ger) Krnov (Cz)

Jakobstadt (Ger) Jekabpils (Lat)

Jauer (Ger) Jawór (Pol)

Jawór (Pol) Jauer (Ger)

Jekabpils (Lat) Jakobstadt (Ger)

Jelenia Góra (Pol) Hirschberg (Ger)

Jelgava (Lat) Mitau (Ger)

Jewe (Ger) Jõhvi (Est)

Jihlava (Cz) Iglau (Ger)

Joachimstal (Ger) Jáchymov (Cz)

Johannisburg (Ger) Pisz (Pol)

Jõhvi (Est) Jewe (Ger)

Kaaden (Ger) Kadaň (Cz)

Kadaň (Cz) Kaaden (Ger)

Kaliningrad (Rus/Cmst) Königsberg (Ger)

Kamenets (Rus) Kamieniec Podolski (Pol) Kamjanec Podilskyj (Ukn)

Kamień Pomorski (Pol) Cammin (Ger)

Kamieniec Podolski (Pol) Kamjanec Podilskyj (Ukn) Kamenets (Rus)

Kamienna Góra (Pol) Landeshut (Ger)

Kamjanec Podilskyj (Ukn) Kamenets (Rus) Kamieniec Podolski (Pol)

Kaplice (Cz) Kaplitz (Ger)

Kaplitz (Ger) Kaplice (Cz)

Karl-Marx-Stadt (Cmst) Chemnitz (Ger)

Karlóca (Hun) Karlowitz (Ger) Karlovci Sremski (Sb, Ct)

Karlovac (Sb, Ct) Karlstadt (Ger) Károlyváros (Hun)

Karlovci Sremski (Sb, Ct) Karlóca (Hun) Karlowitz (Ger)

Karlovy Vary (Cz) Karlsbad (Ger)

Karlowitz (Ger) Karlovci Sremski (Sb, Ct) Karlóca (Hun)

Karlsbad (Ger) Karlovy Vary (Cz)

Karlstadt (Ger) Károlyváros (Hun) Karlovac (Sb, Ct)

Károlyváros (Hun) Karlovac (Sb, Ct) Karlstadt (Ger)

Kaschau (Ger) Košice (Svk) Kassa (Hun)

Kassa (Hun) Kaschau (Ger) Košice (Svk)

Katowice (Pol) Kattowitz (Ger)

Kattowitz (Ger) Katowice (Pol)

Kaunas (Lith) Kovno (Rus) Kowno (Pol)

Kętrzyn (Pol) Rastenburg (Ger)

Khilm (Ukn) Chełm (Pol) Kholm (Rus)

Kholm (Rus) Khilm (Ukn) Chełm (Pol)

Kienberg (Ger) Loučovice (Cz)

Kiev (Rus) Kjiv (Ukn)

Kingissepa (Est/Cmst – name given by Soviets) Yamburg (Rus) Arensburg (Ger) Kuressaare (Est)

Kishinev (Rus) Chişinău (Rom)

Kjiv (Ukn) Kiev (Rus)

Klaipeda (Lith) Memel (Ger)

Klausenburg (Ger) Cluj (Rom) Kolozsvár (Hun)

Kłodzko (Pol) Glatz (Ger)

Kluczbork (Pol) Kreuzberg (Ger)

Kochevje (Ct, Sb) Gottschee (Ger)

Kolberg (Ger) Kołobrzeg (Pol)

Kołobrzeg (Pol) Kolberg (Ger)

Kolozsvár (Hun) Klausenburg (Ger) Cluj (Rom)

Komarnó (Svk) Komárom (Hun) Komorn (Ger)

Komárom (Hun) Komorn (Ger) Komarnó (Svk)

Komorn (Ger) Komarnó (Svk) Komárom (Hun)

Komotau Aussig (Ger) Ústí Chomutov (Cz)

Königgrätz (Ger) Sadowa (Cz)

Königinhof (Ger) Dvůr Králové (Cz)

Königsberg (Ger) Kaliningrad (Rus/Cmst); also Chojna (Pol)

Königshütte (Ger) Chorzów (Pol)

Könniggrätz (Ger) Hradec Králové (Cz)

Korčula (Sb, Ct) Curzola (It)

Košice (Svk) Kassa (Hun) Kaschau (Ger)

Köslin (Ger) Koszalin (Pol)

Kosno Ordrzańskie (Pol) Crossen (Ger)
Košt'any (Cz) Kosten (Ger)
Kosten (Ger) Košt'any (Cz)
Kostrzyń (Pol) Küstrin (Ger)
Koszalin (Pol) Köslin (Ger)
Kotor (Sb, Ct) Cattaro (It)
Kovno (Rus) Kowno (Pol) Kaunas (Lith)
Kowno (Pol) Kaunas (Lith) Kovno (Rus)
Koźle (Pol) Cosel (Ger)
Kozuchow (Pol) Freystadt (Ger)
Krakau (Ger) Kraków (Pol) Cracow (Eng)
    Cracovie (Fr)
Kraków (Pol) Cracow (Eng) Cracovie (Fr)
    Krakau (Ger)
Krapkowice (Pol) Krappitz (Ger)
Krappitz (Ger) Krapkowice (Pol)
Kraslice (Cz) Graslitz (Ger)
Kratzau (Ger) Chrastava (Cz)
Kremsier (Ger) Kroměříž (Cz)
Kreutz (Ger) Bjelovar (Ct) Bélovár-Körös
    (Hun); also Krzyż (Pol)
Kreuzberg (Ger) Kluczbork (Pol)
Krk (Sb, Ct) Veglia (It)
Krnov (Cz) Jägerndorf (Ger)
Kroměříž (Cz) Kremsier (Ger)
Kronstadt (Ger) Braşov (Rom) Brassó (Hun)
Krumau (Ger) Český Krumlov (Cz)
Krzyż (Pol) Kreutz (Ger)
Kuressaare (Est) Kingissepa (Est/Cmst – name
    given by Soviets) Yamburg (Rus) Arensburg
    (Ger)
Küstrin (Ger) Kostrzyń (Pol)
Kwidzyń (Pol) Marienwerder (Ger)
Laba (Pol) Elbe (Ger)
Labez (Ger) Łobez (Pol)
Laibach (Ger) Ljubljana (Slvn)
Landeshut (Ger) Kamienna Góra (Pol)
Landsberg (Ger) Gorzów Wielkopolski (Pol)
Lauenberg (Ger) Lębork (Pol)
Lębork (Pol) Lauenberg (Ger)
Legnica (Pol) Leignitz (Ger)
Leignitz (Ger) Legnica (Pol)
Leitmeritz (Ger) Litoměřice (Cz)
Lemberg (Ger) Lvov (Eng, Rus) Lviv (Ukn)
    Léopol (Fr) Lwów (Pol)
Leobschütz (Ger) Głubczyce (Pol)
Léopol (Fr) Lwów (Pol) Lemberg (Ger) Lvov
    (Eng, Rus) Lviv (Ukn)
Libau (Ger) Liepaja (Lat)

Liberec (Cz) Reichenberg (Ger)
Lidzbark (Pol) Heilsberg (Ger)
Liepaja (Lat) Libau (Ger)
Litoměřice (Cz) Leitmeritz (Ger)
Ljubljana (Slvn) Laibach (Ger)
Łobez (Pol) Labez (Ger)
Lobositz (Ger) Lovosice (Cz)
Loket (Cz) Elbogen (Ger)
Lötzen (Ger) Giżyoko (Pol)
Loučovice (Cz) Kienberg (Ger)
Lovosice (Cz) Lobositz (Ger)
Löwenberg (Ger) Lwówek Śląski (Pol)
Lübben (Ger) Lubin (Pol)
Lubin (Pol) Lübben (Ger)
Lugansk (Ukn) Voroshilovgrad (Cmst)
Lviv (Ukn) Lwów (Pol) Lemberg (Ger) Lvov
    (Eng, Rus) Léopol (Fr)
Lvov (Eng, Rus) Lviv (Ukn) Lwów (Pol)
    Lemberg (Ger) Léopol (Fr)
Lwów (Pol) Lemberg (Ger) Lvov (Eng, Rus)
    Lviv (Ukn) Léopol (Fr)
Lwówek Śląski (Pol) Löwenberg (Ger)
Lyck (Ger) Ełk (Pol)
Mährisch Weisskirchen (Ger) Hranice (Cz)
Malbork (Pol) Marienburg (Ger)
Máramaros (Hun) Maramureş (Rom)
Maramureş (Rom) Máramaros (Hun)
Marburg (Ger) Maribor (Sb, Ct)
Mariánské Lázně (Cz) Marienbad (Ger)
Mariatheresiopol (Ger) Subotica (Sb, Ct)
    Szabadka (Hun)
Maribor (Sb, Ct) Marburg (Ger)
Marienbad (Ger) Mariánské Lázně (Cz)
Marienburg (Ger) Malbork (Pol)
Marienwerder (Ger) Kwidzyń (Pol)
Maros (Hun) Mureş (Rom) [river]
Medjumurje (Sb, Ct) Muraköz (Hun)
Memel (Ger) Klaipeda (Lith)
Memel (Ger) Nemunas (Lith) [river]
Meseritz (Ger) Międzyrzecz (Pol)
Miastko (Pol) Rummelsberg (Ger)
Międzyrzecz (Pol) Meseritz (Ger)
Mies (Ger) Stříbro (Cz)
Mikulov (Cz) Nikolsburg (Ger)
Milicz (Pol) Militsch (Ger)
Militsch (Ger) Milicz (Pol)
Mitau (Ger) Jelgava (Lat)
Mohrungen (Ger) Morąg (Pol)
Moldau (Ger) Vltava (Cz)

Monastir (Ts) Bitolya (Bul) Bitolj (Mcd/Sb)

Morąg (Pol) Mohrungen (Ger)

Mosonmagyaróvár (Hun) Altenburg (Ger)

Most (Cz) Brüx (Ger)

Mrągowo (Pol) Sensburg (Ger)

Munkačevo (Svk) Munkatsch (Ger) Munkács (Hun) Munkachevo (Ukn)

Munkachevo (Ukn) Munkačevo (Svk) Munkatsch (Ger) Munkács (Hun)

Munkács (Hun) Munkachevo (Ukn) Munkačevo (Svk) Munkatsch (Ger)

Munkatsch (Ger) Munkács (Hun) Munkachevo (Ukn) Munkačevo (Svk)

Muraköz (Hun) Medjumurje (Sb, Ct)

Mureş (Rom) Maros (Hun) [river]

Myśliborz (Pol) Soldin (Ger)

Nagyszeben (Hun) Hermannstadt (Ger) Sibiu (Rom)

Nagyszombat (Hun) Tyrnau (Ger) Trnava (Svk)

Nagyvárad (Hun) Grosswardein (Ger) Oradea Mare (Rom)

Namslau (Ger) Namysłów (Pol)

Namysłów (Pol) Namslau (Ger)

Neidenburg (Ger) Nidzica (Pol)

Nejdek (Cz) Neudek (Ger)

Nemunas (Lith) Memel (Ger) [river]

Neudek (Ger) Nejdek (Cz)

Neugard (Ger) Nowogard (Pol)

Neumarkt (Ger) Środa Śląska (Pol)

Neurode (Ger) Nowa Ruda (Pol)

Neusalz (Ger) Nowa Sól (Pol)

Neusatz (Ger) Novi Sad (Sb, Ct) Ujvidék (Hun)

Neusiedl (Ger) Fertö (Hun)

Neustadt (Ger) Pruknik (Pol)

Neustettin (Ger) Szczecinek (Pol)

Nidzica (Pol) Neidenburg (Ger)

Niemodlin (Pol) Falkenberg (Ger)

Nikolsburg (Ger) Mikulov (Cz)

Nistru (Rom) Dniestr (Rus) [river]

Nové Hrady (Cz) Gratzen (Ger)

Novi Sad (Sb, Ct) Ujvidék (Hun) Neusatz (Ger)

Nowa Ruda (Pol) Neurode (Ger)

Nowa Sól (Pol) Neusalz (Ger)

Nowogard (Pol) Neugard (Ger)

Nysa (Pol) Neisse (Ger)

Oder (Ger) Odra (Pol)

Odra (Pol) Oder (Ger)

Odrin (Bul) Adrianople (Eng) Edirne (Ts)

Oedenburg (Ger) Sopron (Hun)

Oels (Ger) Oleśnica (Pol)

Oesel (Ger) Saaremaa (Est)

Ofen (Ger) Buda (Hun)

Ohlau (Ger) Oława (Pol)

Oława (Pol) Ohlau (Ger)

Olecko (Pol) Treuburg (Ger)

Oleśnica (Pol) Oels (Ger)

Oleśno (Pol) Rosenberg (Ger)

Olmütz (Ger) Olomouc (Cz)

Olomouc (Cz) Olmütz (Ger)

Olsztyn (Pol) Allenstein (Ger)

Opava (Cz) Troppau (Ger)

Opole (Pol) Oppeln (Ger)

Oppeln (Ger) Opole (Pol)

Oradea Mare (Rom) Nagyvárad (Hun) Grosswardein (Ger)

Orany (Pol) Varéna (Lith)

Orava (Cz) Oravsko (Svk) Árva (Hun) Orawa (Pol)

Oravsko (Svk) Árva (Hun) Orawa (Pol) Orava (Cz)

Orawa (Pol) Orava (Cz) Oravsko (Svk) Árva (Hun)

Orneta (Pol) Wormidt (Ger)

Ortelsburg (Ger) Szczytin (Pol)

Osterode (Ger) Ostroda (Pol)

Ostroda (Pol) Osterode (Ger)

Oświęcim (Pol) Auschwitz (Ger)

Oszmiany (Pol) Asmjany (Lith)

Paide (Est) Weissenstein (Ger)

Pärnu (Est) Pernau (Ger)

Pasłęk (Pol) Preussisch-Holland (Ger)

Passarovic (Svk) Passarowitz (Ger)

Passarowitz (Ger) Passarovic (Svk)

Pécs (Hun) Fünfkirchen (Ger)

Peipsi (Est) Peipus (Ger)

Peipus (Ger) Peipsi (Est)

Pernau (Ger) Pärnu (Est)

Petschur (Ger) Petseri (Est) Petsory (Rus)

Petseri (Est) Petsory (Rus) Petschur (Ger)

Petsory (Rus) Petschur (Ger) Petseri (Est)

Philipopolis (Gk) Filibe (Ts) Plovdiv (Bul)

Piła (Pol) Schneidemühl (Ger)

Pilsen (Ger) Plzeň (Cz)

Pisz (Pol) Johannisburg (Ger)

Pleskau (Ger) Pskov (Rus)

Pless (Ger) Pszczyna (Pol)

Plovdiv (Bul) Philipopolis (Gk) Filibe (Ts)

Plzeň (Cz) Pilsen (Ger)

Podmokly (Cz) Bodenbach (Ger)
Polanga (Lith) Polangen (Ger)
Polangen (Ger) Polanga (Lith)
Polczyń Zdrój (Pol) Bad Polzin (Ger)
Posen (Ger) Poznań (Pol)
Poznań (Pol) Posen (Ger)
Pozsony (Hun) Bratislava (Svk) Pressburg
  (Ger)
Prachatice (Cz) Prachatitz (Ger)
Prachatitz (Ger) Prachatice (Cz)
Prag (Ger) Praha (Cz) Prague (Eng)
Prague (Eng) Prag (Ger) Praha (Cz)
Praha (Cz) Prague (Eng) Prag (Ger)
Pressburg (Ger) Pozsony (Hun) Bratislava (Svk)
Pressnitz (Ger) Prisecnice (Cz)
Preussisch-Holland (Ger) Pasłęk (Pol)
Prisecnice (Cz) Pressnitz (Ger)
Prossnitz (Ger) Prostějov (Cz)
Prostějov (Cz) Prossnitz (Ger)
Pruknik (Pol) Neustadt (Ger)
Pskov (Rus) Pleskau (Ger)
Pszczyna (Pol) Pless (Ger)
Puck (Pol) Putzig (Ger)
Putzig (Ger) Puck (Pol)
Pyritz (Ger) Pyrzyce (Pol)
Pyrzyce (Pol) Pyritz (Ger)
Pytalovo (Rus) Abrehenen (Ger) Abrene (Lat)
Qyteti Stalin (Alb/Cmst) Dyteti (Alb)
Raab (Ger) Györ (Hun)
Racibórz (Pol) Ratibor (Ger)
Radošov (Cz) Rodisfort (Ger)
Ragusa (It) Dubrovnik (Sb, Ct)
Rakvere (Est) Wesenberg (Ger)
Rastenburg (Ger) Kętrzyn (Pol)
Ratibor (Ger) Racibórz (Pol)
Raudnig (Ger) Roudníky (Cz)
Regenwalde (Ger) Resko (Pol)
Reichenau (Ger) Bogatynia (Pol)
Reichenbach (Ger) Dzierzoniów (Pol)
Reichenberg (Ger) Liberec (Cz)
Reppen (Ger) Rzepin (Pol)
Resko (Pol) Regenwalde (Ger)
Reszel (Pol) Rössel (Ger)
Reval (Ger, Rus) Tallinn (Est)
Rēzekne (Lat) Rezhitsa (Rus) Rositten (Ger)
Rezhitsa (Rus) Rositten (Ger) Rēzekne (Lat)
Rijeka (Sb, Ct) Fiume (It)
Rivne (Ukn) Równo (Pol) Rovno (Rus)
Rodisfort (Ger) Radošov (Cz)

Römerstadt (Ger) Rymarov (Cz)
Rosenberg (Ger) Susz (Pol) or Oleśno (Pol)
Rositten (Ger) Rēzekne (Lat) Rezhitsa (Rus)
Rössel (Ger) Reszel (Pol)
Rotava (Cz) Rothau (Ger)
Rothau (Ger) Rotava (Cz)
Roudníky (Cz) Raudnig (Ger)
Rovno (Rus) Rivne (Ukn) Równo (Pol)
Równo (Pol) Rovno (Rus) Rivne (Ukn)
Rummelsberg (Ger) Miastko (Pol)
Rybáře (Cz) Fischern (Ger)
Rymarov (Cz) Römerstadt (Ger)
Rzepin (Pol) Reppen (Ger)
Saaremaa (Est) Oesel (Ger)
Saatig (Ger) Stargard (Pol)
Saaz (Ger) Žatec (Cz)
Sadowa (Cz) Königgrätz (Ger)
Sagan (Ger) Zagan (Pol)
Salonika (Eng) Thessaloniki (Gk) Solun (Slav)
  Selânik (Ts)
Satu Mare (Rom) Szatmár (Hun)
Schivelbein (Ger) Swidwin (Pol)
Schlauen (Ger) Šiauliai (Lith)
Schlawe (Ger) Sławno (Pol)
Schlochau (Ger) Czluchów (Pol)
Schluckenau (Ger) Sluknov (Cz)
Schneidemühl (Ger) Piła (Pol)
Schönlanke (Ger) Irzcianka (Pol)
Schüttenhofen (Ger) Sušice (Cz)
Schwarzbach (Ger) Černa (Cz)
Schweidnitz (Ger) Świdnica (Pol)
Schwerin (Ger) Skwierzyna (Pol)
Scutari (It, Eng) Shkodër (Alb)
Seinai (Lith) Seiny (Rus) Sejny (Pol)
Seiny (Rus) Sejny (Pol) Seinai (Lith)
Sejny (Pol) Seinai (Lith) Seiny (Rus)
Selânik (Ts) Thessaloniki (Gk) Solun (Slav)
  Salonika (Eng)
Semlin (Ger) Zemun (Sb)
Senj (Sb, Ct) Zengg (Ger)
Sensburg (Ger) Mrągowo (Pol)
Shkodër (Alb) Scutari (It, Eng)
Šiauliai (Lith) Schlauen (Ger)
Sibiu (Rom) Nagyszeben (Hun) Hermannstadt
  (Ger)
Siebenbürgen (Ger) Erdély (Hun) Ardeal
  (Rom) Transylvania (Eng)
Skopje (Slav) Usküb (Ts)
Skwierzyna (Pol) Schwerin (Ger)

Sławno (Pol) Schlawe (Ger)

Słubice (Pol) Frankfurt-Ost (Ger)

Sluknov (Cz) Schluckenau (Ger)

Słupsk (Pol) Stolp (Ger)

Soldin (Ger) Myśliborz (Pol)

Solun (Slav) Salonika (Eng) Thessaloniki (Gk)
 Selânik (Ts)

Sopron (Hun) Oedenburg (Ger)

Sorau (Ger) Żary (Pol)

Spiš (Cz) Zips (Ger) Spišsko (Svk) Szepes (Hun)
 Spisz (Pol)

Spišsko (Svk) Szepes (Hun) Spisz (Pol) Spiš
 (Cz) Zips (Ger)

Spisz (Pol) Spiš (Cz) Zips (Ger) Spišsko (Svk)
 Szepes (Hun)

Split (Sb, Ct) Spolato (It)

Spolato (It) Split (Sb, Ct)

Sprottau (Ger) Szprotawa (Pol)

Srem (Sb, Ct) Syrmien (Ger) Szrem (Hun)

Sroda Śląska (Pol) Neumarkt (Ger)

Stanisławów (Pol) Stanislaviv (Ukn)
 Ivano-Frankovsk (Ukn/Cmst)

Stanislaviv (Ukn) Stanisławów (Pol)
 Ivano-Frankovsk (Ukn/Cmst)

Stanke Dimitrov (Bul/Cmst) Dupnitsa (Bul)

Stargard (Pol) Saatig (Ger)

Steinamanger (Ger) Szombathely (Hun)

Stettin (Ger) Szczecin (Pol)

Stolp (Ger) Słupsk (Pol)

Strehlen (Ger) Strzelin (Pol)

Stříbro (Cz) Mies (Ger)

Strzelce (Pol) Gross-Strehlitz (Ger)

Strzelce Krajenskie (Pol) Friedeburg (Ger)

Strzelin (Pol) Strehlen (Ger)

Stubm (Ger) Sztym (Pol)

Stuhlweissenburg (Ger) Székesfehérvár
 (Hun)

Subotica (Sb, Ct) Szabadka (Hun)
 Mariatheresiopol (Ger)

Sudauen (Ger) Suvalkai (Lith) Suvalki (Rus)
 Suwałki (Pol)

Sulechów (Pol) Zullichau Schweibus (Ger)

Sulęcin (Pol) Zielinzig (Ger)

Sušice (Cz) Schüttenhofen (Ger)

Susz (Pol) Rosenberg (Ger)

Suvalkai (Lith) Suvalki (Rus) Suwałki (Pol)
 Sudauen (Ger)

Suvalki (Rus) Suwałki (Pol) Sudauen (Ger)
 Suvalkai (Lith)

Suwałki (Pol) Sudauen (Ger) Suvalkai (Lith)
 Suvalki (Rus)

Svitavy (Cz) Zwittau (Ger)

Świdnica (Pol) Schweidnitz (Ger)

Swidwin (Pol) Schivelbein (Ger)

Swinemünde (Ger) Świnoujście (Pol)

Świnoujście (Pol) Swinemünde (Ger)

Syców (Pol) Gross-Wartenberg (Ger)

Syrmien (Ger) Szrem (Hun) Srem (Sb, Ct)

Szabadka (Hun) Mariatheresiopol (Ger)
 Subotica (Sb, Ct)

Szatmár (Hun) Satu Mare (Rom)

Szczecin (Pol) Stettin (Ger)

Szczecinek (Pol) Neustettin (Ger)

Szczytin (Pol) Ortelsburg (Ger)

Szeged (Hun) Szegedin (Ger)

Szegedin (Ger) Szeged (Hun)

Székesfehérvár (Hun) Stuhlweissenburg (Ger)

Szepes (Hun) Spisz (Pol) Spiš (Cz) Zips (Ger)
 Spišsko (Svk)

Szombathely (Hun) Steinamanger (Ger)

Szprotawa (Pol) Sprottau (Ger)

Szrem (Hun) Srem (Sb, Ct) Syrmien (Ger)

Sztym (Pol) Stubm (Ger)

Tachau (Ger) Tachov (Cz)

Tachov (Cz) Tachau (Ger)

Tallinn (Est) Reval (Ger, Rus)

Tarnopol (Pol) Ternopil' (Ukn)

Tartu (Est) Dorpat (Ger)

Taurage (Lith) Tauroggen (Ger)

Tauroggen (Ger) Taurage (Lith)

Taus (Ger) Domžlice (Cz)

Temesvár (Hun) Timişoara (Rom)

Teplice Šanov (Cz) Teplitz Schönau (Ger)

Teplitz Schönau (Ger) Teplice Šanov (Cz)

Terezin (Cz) Theresienstadt (Ger)

Ternopil' (Ukn) Tarnopol (Pol)

Teschen (Ger) Těšin (Cz) Cieszyn (Pol)

Těšin (Cz) Cieszyn (Pol) Teschen (Ger)

Tetschen (Ger) Děčín (Cz)

Theiss (Ger) Tisza (Hun)

Theresienstadt (Ger) Terezin (Cz)

Thessaloniki (Gk) Solun (Slav) Salonika (Eng)
 Selânik (Ts)

Thorn (Ger) Toruń (Pol)

Tighina (Rom) Benderey (Rus, Ts)

Timişoara (Rom) Temesvár (Hun)

Tisza (Hun) Theiss (Ger)

Tolbukhin (Bul/Cmst) Dobrich (Bul)

Toruń (Pol) Thorn (Ger)

Transylvania (Eng) Siebenbürgen (Ger) Erdély (Hun) Ardeal (Rom)

Trautenau (Ger) Trutnov (Cz)

Třbenice (Cz) Trebnitz (Ger) Trzebnica (Pol)

Trebnitz (Ger) Trzebnica (Pol) Třbenice (Cz)

Treuburg (Ger) Olecko (Pol)

Trnava (Svk) Nagyszombat (Hun) Tyrnau (Ger)

Troppau (Ger) Opava (Cz)

Trutnov (Cz) Trautenau (Ger)

Trzebnica (Pol) Trebnitz (Ger) Třbenice (Cz)

Tsaribrod (Bul, Sb, Ct) Dimitrovgrad (Cmst)

Tsarigrad (Slav) Constantinople (Eng) Istanbul (Ts)

Tuckum (Ger) Tukums (Lat)

Tukums (Lat) Tuckum (Ger)

Turčanský Světí Martin (Svk) Turóczszentmartón (Hun)

Tûrgovishte (Bul) Eski Djumaya (Ts)

Turmezö (Hun) Turopolje (Sb, Ct)

Turóczszentmartón (Hun) Turčanský Světí Martin (Svk)

Turopolje (Sb, Ct) Turmezö (Hun)

Tyrnau (Ger) Trnava (Svk) Nagyszombat (Hun)

Ujvidék (Hun) Neusatz (Ger) Novi Sad (Sb, Ct)

Ungvár (Hun) Uzhgorod (Ukn) Užhorod (Cz, Svk)

Usküb (Ts) Skopje (Slav)

Ústí Chomutov (Cz) Komotau Aussig (Ger)

Uzhgorod (Ukn) Užhorod (Cz, Svk) Ungvár (Hun)

Užhorod (Cz, Svk) Ungvár (Hun) Uzhgorod (Ukn)

Valga (Est) Walk (Ger) Valka (Lat)

Valka (Lat) Valga (Est) Walk (Ger)

Valmiera (Lat) Wolmar (Ger)

Valona (It) Vlorë (Alb)

Várasd (Hun) Warasdin (Ger) Varašdin (Sb, Ct)

Varašdin (Sb,Ct) Várasd (Hun) Warasdin (Ger)

Varéna (Lith) Orany (Pol)

Varsovie (Fr) Warsaw (Eng) Warszawa (Pol) Warschau (Ger)

Veglia (It) Krk (Sb, Ct)

Venta (Lat) Windau (Ger) [river]

Ventislav (Cz) Breslau (Ger) Wrocław (Pol)

Ventspils (Lat) Windau (Ger)

Veröcze (Hun) Virovica (Sb, Ct)

Viljandi (Est) Fellinn (Ger)

Vilnius (Lith) Wilno (Pol) Wilna (Ger)

Vimperk (Cz) Winterberg (Ger)

Vinnitsa (Rus) Winnica (Pol) Winnycja (Ukn)

Virovica (Sb, Ct) Veröcze (Hun)

Vlorë (Alb) Valona (It)

Vltava (Cz) Moldau (Ger)

Volary (Cz) Wallern (Ger)

Vormsi (Est) Worms (Ger)

Voroshilovgrad (Cmst) Lugansk (Ukn)

Võrts (Est) Wirz See (Ger)

Võru (Est) Werro (Ger)

Vrchlabí (Cz) Hohenelbe (Ger)

Vyšší Brod (Cz) Hohenfurth (Ger)

Wałbrzych (Pol) Waldenburg (Ger)

Walcz (Pol) Deutsche Krone (Ger)

Waldenburg (Ger) Wałbrzych (Pol)

Walk (Ger) Valka (Lat) Valga (Est)

Wallern (Ger) Volary (Cz)

Warasdin (Ger) Varašdin (Sb, Ct) Várasd (Hun)

Warsaw (Eng) Warszawa (Pol) Warschau (Ger) Varsovie (Fr)

Warschau (Ger) Varsovie (Fr) Warsaw (Eng) Warszawa (Pol)

Warszawa (Pol) Warschau (Ger) Varsovie (Fr) Warsaw (Eng)

Węgorzewo (Pol) Angerburg (Ger)

Weissenburg (Ger) Alba Iulia (Rom) Gyulafehévár (Hun)

Weissenstein (Ger) Paide (Est)

Weisskirchen (Ger) Bílý Kostel (Cz)

Wenden (Ger) Cēsis (Lat)

Werro (Ger) Võru (Est)

Wesenberg (Ger) Rakvere (Est)

Wilna (Ger) Vilnius (Lith) Wilno (Pol)

Wilno (Pol) Wilna (Ger) Vilnius (Lith)

Windau (Ger) Venta (Lat) [river]

Windau (Ger) Ventspils (Lat)

Winnica (Pol) Winnycja (Ukn) Vinnitsa (Rus)

Winnycja (Ukn) Vinnitsa (Rus) Winnica (Pol)

Winterberg (Ger) Vimperk (Cz)

Wirz See (Ger) Vorts (Est)

Wohlau (Ger) Wołów (Pol)

Wolmar (Ger) Valmiera (Lat)

Wołów (Pol) Wohlau (Ger)

Wormidt (Ger) Orneta (Pol)

Worms (Ger) Vormsi (Est)

Wrocław (Pol) Ventislav (Cz) Breslau (Ger)

Wschowa (Pol) Fraustadt (Ger)

Yamburg (Rus) Arensburg (Ger) Kuressaare

(Est) Kingissepa (Est/Cmst – name given by Soviets)

Ząbkowice Śląskie (Pol) Frankenstein (Ger)

Zabrze (Pol) Hindenburg (Ger)

Zadar (Ct, Sb) Zara (It)

Zagan (Pol) Sagan (Ger)

Zágráb (Hun) Agram (Ger) Zagreb (Sb, Ct)

Zagreb (Sb, Ct) Zágráb (Hun) Agram (Ger)

Zara (It) Zadar (Ct, Sb)

Żary (Pol) Sorau (Ger)

Žatec (Cz) Saaz (Ger)

Železný Brod (Cz) Eisenbrod (Ger)

Zemun (Sb) Semlin (Ger)

Zengg (Ger) Senj (Sb, Ct)

Zgorzelec (Pol) Görlitz (Ger)

Zielinzig (Ger) Sulęcin (Pol)

Zielona Góra (Pol) Grünberg (Ger)

Zips (Ger) Spišsko (Svk) Szepes (Hun) Spisz (Pol) Spiš (Cz)

Zischenau (Ger) Ciechanów (Pol)

Zlin (Svk) Gottwaldow (Cmst)

Złotoryja (Pol) Goldberg (Ger)

Złotów (Pol) Flatow (Ger)

Znaim (Ger) Znojmo (Cz)

Znojmo (Cz) Znaim (Ger)

Zullichau Schweibus (Ger) Sulechów (Pol)

Zwittau (Ger) Svitavy (Cz)

INDEX